An Introduction to Interaction

Also available from Bloomsbury

An Introduction to Conversation Analysis: Second Edition, Anthony J. Liddicoat
An Introduction to Sociolinguistics, Sharon K. Deckert and Caroline H. Vickers
An Introduction to the Nature and Function of Language, Howard Jackson and Peter Stockwell
Bloomsbury Companion to Discourse, edited by Ken Hyland and Brian Paltridge
Discourse Analysis, Brian Paltridge
Linguistics: An Introduction, William McGregor

An Introduction to Interaction

Understanding Talk in Formal and Informal Settings

Angela Cora Garcia

B L O O M S B U R Y

LONDON • NEW DELHI • NEW YORK • SYDNEY

Bloomsbury Academic

An imprint of Bloomsbury Publishing Plc

50 Bedford Square	1385 Broadway
London	New York
WC1B 3DP	NY 10018
UK	USA

www.bloomsbury.com

First published 2013

British Library Cataloguing-in-Publication Data
A catalogue record for this book is available from the British Library.

ISBN: HB: 978-1-4411-2768-6
PB: 978-1-4411-5761-4
ePub: 978-1-6235-6152-9
PDF: 978-1-6235-6934-1

Library of Congress Cataloging-in-Publication Data
Garcia, Angela Cora.
An introduction to interaction : understanding talk in formal and informal settings / Angela Cora Garcia.
pages cm
Includes bibliographical references and index.
ISBN 978-1-4411-2768-6 (hardcover) -- ISBN 978-1-4411-5761-4 (pbk.) --
ISBN 978-1-62356-934-1 (ebook (pdf)) -- ISBN 978-1-62356-152-9 (ebook (epub))
1. Conversation analysis--Social aspects. 2. Social interaction. 3. Oral communication--Psychological aspects. 4. Business communication--Discourse analysis. 5. Communication in organizations. I. Title.
P95.45.G275 2013
302.34'6--dc23
2013018689

Typeset by Fakenham Prepress Solutions, Fakenham, Norfolk NR21 8NN
Printed and bound in India

Contents

List of Figures and Tables

A Companion Website, including a comprehensive Instructor's Manual
to accompany this book, can be found online at:
www.bloomsbury.com/uk/introduction-to-interaction-9781441157614

Acknowledgments

I would like to thank all the students I have taught in conversation analysis classes over the last twenty years, especially the students in the first class in conversation analysis I taught at the University of Wisconsin, Eau Claire, in 1992, and also those in many subsequent classes at the University of Cincinnati and at Bentley University. I would particularly like to thank the students in So 265 "Talk at Work" at Bentley University during Spring semester, 2012 who read and provided helpful feedback on draft chapters of this book—I am indebted to you for your ideas about how to improve the book.

The people who taught me conversation analysis were wonderful teachers and inspired me to study and teach this topic: Janet Tallman at Hampshire College, Candace West at the University of California, Santa Cruz, and Don H. Zimmerman at the University of California, Santa Barbara. They set me on a path of researching and teaching conversation analysis which prepared me for the task of writing this book.

I would like to thank Bentley University for a Rauch grant which provided the seed money for this project. My editor at Bloomsbury Academic, Gurdeep Mattu, has been so helpful with suggestions and advice as I put this book together; I can't thank him enough. Thanks also to Jennifer Laing for an excellent job of copyediting the manuscript, and to Karolin Thomas for constructing the index.

Thanks so much to Gail Fairhurst and the anonymous reviewers for their suggestions for the improvement of this manuscript; they have made a huge difference.

I would like to dedicate this book to my daughter Martha who is a joy and an inspiration always, and to my new son Zachary; we are so glad you have come into our lives.

Part I
Theory, Method and Data for Conversation Analysis

Introduction to the Study of Conversation Analysis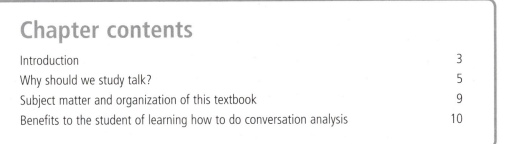

Chapter contents

Introduction

Consider the excerpt below from an interaction between four people. What do you notice as you read the excerpt? Who do you think these people are, and why are they having this conversation? What was it in the conversation that led you to these conclusions?

Excerpt 1: (Garcia Midwest Data Site A, Tape 8, p. 19; simplified transcript)

1	Ken:	I normally pick her up, I guess at after I get off work. Just
2		anywhere between five thirty and six. And I usually keep her until
3		nine, ten o'clock.
4	MA:	Okay, so what is it that you would like, Ken?
5	Ken:	That I'd like?
6	MA:	Yes. In terms of parenting time with Tina.
7	Ken:	I would like to see her every day.
8	MA:	That's what most parents tell us. That that's the hardest thing
9		about divorce, is not seeing your child every day. Do you think
10		that it's possible to see her every day?
11	Ken:	I don't know.
12	MB:	Do you live pretty near one another? How's your residential set-
13		up?
14	Ken:	We live about five, it's about five minutes of each other.
15	MB:	And what does Tina's schedule look like. Is she in child care
16		or?

17 Cindy: No, I work at home. She lives with me.
18 MB: Okay, so she's home with you all day.

You have probably discerned from your examination of the excerpt that this is not an ordinary conversation between friends or relatives. The people in this conversation are participating in a divorce mediation session. Ken and Cindy are the parents of Tina, a four year old girl. The two mediators ("MA" and "MB") are working to help the couple create a parenting plan for the care of their daughter after their divorce. There are clues in the excerpt as to the identity of the participants and the nature of the interaction. For example, the information that Ken is going through a divorce could be discerned from Mediator A's question about "parenting time with Tina" (line 6), and her statement about divorce (lines 8–10). However, not all of the "clues" come from the subject matter of the talk. There are also clues based on the roles the participants play in the interaction. For example, Mediator A and Mediator B ask a lot of questions, while Ken and Cindy answer questions instead of asking them. The mediators guide the discussion and control the direction of the topic through their questions. For example, at one point Mediator B redirects the topic to how far away the spouses live from each other (lines 12 and 13). While in an ordinary conversation, any participant can choose to speak or introduce a new topic, in mediation sessions topics are more focused and are often directed by the mediators who facilitate the session.

You may also notice that no one interrupts anyone in this excerpt. Each person waits for their turn to speak. If these people were four friends having a casual conversation, it is likely there would be some overlapping talk. The interaction in Excerpt 1 is well organized and should enable the participants to achieve the goals of the mediation session. Let's compare this interaction with an excerpt from a different mediation session which did not go as smoothly. How is the interaction in Excerpt 2 different from Excerpt 1? Why do you think these two mediation sessions are so different?

Excerpt 2: (Garcia, West Coast Data, Tape 4, simplified transcript)
1   Liz: The same woman that organized that parked so that I could
2   not get out of my complex.
3   Nancy: You were parked…
4   Liz: one morning.
5   Nancy: She was parked, in her space and she…
6   MB: Yeah, but I was just saying I remember you saying, you
7   know?
8   Nancy: parked next to you.
9   MB: that you felt you were overwhelmed with people.
10 Liz: There was nowhere else to park.
11 Nancy: You still can not park in someone else's parking place.
12 MB: So I thought,
13 Liz: It happens all the time, Nancy,
14 MB: Yes,

15 Liz: why doesn't she do it with other people, and that's not…
16 MA: I don't want any cross talk, thank you.

Excerpt 2 is from a mediation session involving a dispute is between two neighbors, Nancy and Liz. In this excerpt Mediators A and B are trying to help them discuss a problem that occurred in the parking lot of the apartment complex the two women live in.

This excerpt differed from Excerpt 1 in several ways. The conversation did not unfold smoothly. Instead of waiting until a speaker was finished before beginning, Liz and Nancy frequently interrupted each other and Mediator B. Instead of speaking in a polite and calm manner, they argued with each other and complained about each other. While Mediator B makes several attempts to redirect the conversation to end the arguing, these attempts are not successful. In the last line of the excerpt, Mediator A finally ends the argument by saying (in a very loud voice!), "I don't want any cross talk, thank you." This sanction is finally successful in ending the argument.

The contrast between these two excerpts illustrates some of the ways conversation analysis can be useful for helping us understand how interaction works. The participants created a successful mediation session (or not) by their actions—by their choices about what to say, and when and how to say it. How were they able to do this? In other words, how did each person know when it was time for them to talk or to be silent? How did they know what to say and how to say it? Why do the mediators in these excerpts behave differently than the mediation clients? It is the business of conversation analysis to study and attempt to understand how participants create interactions of different types, and how they conduct themselves in these interactions. Our study of conversation analysis will enable us to discover why some interactions are successful, and why others are not. We will learn what types of problems can emerge in interactions, and how can they be resolved or avoided. We will learn how participants organize their talk in different types of interactional contexts and social settings, including informal interactions between family and friends and workplace interactions in a wide range of organizational settings.

Why should we study talk?

The ability to use language has long been considered one of the defining characteristics of what it means to be human. Linguists and anthropologists have viewed language as a fundamental part of the culture of human societies. The interest of linguists is often focused on understanding the rules of the language—rules for constructing and pronouncing words and for organizing words into grammatical sentences. However, these approaches to the study of language typically did not include the study of interaction. The development of conversation analysis and other related research approaches (such as the pragmatics of communication, discursive psychology and critical discourse analysis) has enabled us to explore how people communicate through talk. These approaches focus not on the construction of language per se, but on how people structure and coordinate their actions to produce a coherent interaction. This research addresses not just verbal communication, but also embodied action—the nonverbal realm of body orientation, facial expression, gestures, and the like).

Conversation analysis has also proved useful for the study of technologically mediated interactions. While in today's society interaction with others is increasingly technologically mediated (e.g. via cell phone, text message, or social media website), face to face oral communication is still a fundamental part of our social world. Our social interactions throughout the day, with friends, colleagues, fellow students and family members form a major part of our lives. Understanding how these interactions work is thus essential.

The Importance of Studying Everyday ("Ordinary") Conversation. Conversation analysts use the term "**ordinary conversation**" to refer to everyday interactions between friends, relatives, colleagues, or others which are not specifically work or task oriented. These ordinary conversations can nevertheless communicate much of interest to the participants and to researchers as well. For example, Hopper and LeBaron (1998) analyze an excerpt from an ordinary conversation in which the participants' ideas and stereotypes about gender become relevant. In Excerpt 3, Pip's response to Jill's announcement about signing up for a car maintenance and repair class appears to be problematic for Jill (note the silence in line 5). Pip seems to interpret Jill's lack of response as a silent commentary on his assumption that only women would benefit from those classes. He repairs this problem in lines 6 and 7. This excerpt shows how participants can convey their ideas and beliefs about gender, interpret the actions of others, and work to repair any problems that emerge in the interaction between them.

Excerpt 3: (Hopper and LeBaron, 1998, p. 69)
1   Jill: I've signed up for one of those informal classes about
2   car maintenance and repair.
3   Pip: That's a good idea. A lot of women can really learn a
4   lot from these classes
5   ((short pause))
6   Pip: Well, I guess there's a lot of guys who can learn from
7   'em too.

Conversation analysts find that how participants construct everyday, ordinary conversations provides a basis for the organization of talk in all other types of interactional contexts, institutional and social settings. Drew and Heritage (1992) discuss the importance of understanding ordinary conversation, and what knowledge about ordinary talk can contribute to our understanding of talk in institutional settings:

[Conversation analytic] research has, in part, been inspired by the realization that ordinary conversation is the predominant medium of interaction in the social world. It is also the primary form of interaction to which, with whatever simplifications, the child is initially exposed and through which socialization proceeds. Thus the basic forms of mundane talk constitute a kind of benchmark against which other more formal or "institutional" types of interaction are recognized and experienced. Explicit within this perspective is the view that other "institutional" forms of interaction will show systematic variations and restrictions on activities and their design relative to ordinary conversation (Sacks, Schegloff, and Jefferson 1974: 629; Atkinson and Drew 1979; Atkinson 1982; Heritage 1984). The study of ordinary conversation, preferably casual conversation between peers, may thus offer a principled approach to determining what is distinctive about interactions involving, for example, the specialisms of the school or the hospital or the asymmetries of status, gender, ethnicity, etc. A clear implication is that comparative analysis that treats institutional interaction in contrast to normal and/or normative procedures of interaction in ordinary conversation will present at least one important avenue of theoretical and empirical advance. (Drew and Heritage, 1992, p. 19)

Thus studying ordinary conversations in everyday contexts is important for two reasons. One, it enables us to understand the most prevalent mode of interaction between people of all ages as they live their lives. Two, it is the basis for interaction in organizations and institutional settings, through which we live our work lives, receive services, and conduct other business.

Interaction in Organizations and Workplace Settings. Interaction is a major part of most types of work in today's society. Drew and Heritage (1992) discuss the nature of talk in workplace and other institutional settings:

[T]alk-in-interaction is the principal means through which lay persons pursue various practical goals and the central medium through which the daily working activities of many professionals and organizational representatives are conducted. (Drew and Heritage, 1992, p. 3)

For some types of jobs, the worker may be engaged in interaction with others constantly. For example, a telephone sales representative may spend their entire workday talking on the phone while entering information into the computer. Gronn (1983) observed and recorded a school principal at work, and found that he spent more time talking to his employees than doing any other type of work; the work of running the school was done primarily through talk. For other types of jobs, talk may be a minor or incidental part of the work. However, even for jobs which may seem to involve little need for interaction, the ability to interact with others may be far more central than we might think.

For example, one job that is considered to be largely manual labor is the job of "bellhop"— the person who stands in front of a hotel and takes guests' bags out of their cars and into the hotel. A friend once told me that when he arrived at a hotel the bellhop took his bags out of his car and welcomed him by name. At first puzzled as to how the bellhop knew his name, he then realized that his name was on the tag on his luggage. The bellhop had taken the extra step of reading the label so that he could personally welcome the arriving guest by name. This example illustrates that even a job which is largely manual labor is often done better when an employee effectively uses interaction. This bellhop not only understood his role as an employee representing his organization, but understood society's conventions about how greetings are conducted. The formality or informality of a social context and the status levels of the interactants is related to whether first names or last names with titles should be used. The bellhop correctly addressed the guest with the more formal title and last name.

A major line of research incorporates the use of conversation analysis to understand how people do their work. Heath and Luff (2000) give an example which illustrates how important talk can be for the effective accomplishment of work, and how interactionally skilled employees can perform tasks more efficiently than those who are not so skilled. Garcia et al. (2006) summarize their description of how work is done by editors in a Reuters newsroom:

> [J]ournalists assigned to particular subject areas are expected to "identify relevant stories for their particular customers and to tailor the news with regard to the practical interests of the members of the respective financial institutions working in particular areas" (Heath & Luff, 2000, p. 63). Technology assists in this effort as news stories are delivered to each journalist via a computer monitor. The journalists can then edit the stories at their keyboard and transmit them to the appropriate destination. However, the task of determining what information is useful to whom is left to the discretion of each individual journalist. The journalists must determine if any information that comes across their desks would be helpful to another desk, and, if so, find the best way to communicate that information.
>
> The journalists shared a large room furnished with rows of computer terminals. They sat only a few feet from each other, being close enough to lean over and read their neighbors' computer screens. Heath and Luff (2000) found that the journalists took advantage of this proximity to communicate with each other about articles of potential interest to one or more journalists in the room. The journalists at Reuters worked at a very fast pace, and sometimes had to "turn around" stories within as little as a minute of receiving them (Heath & Luff, 2000, p. 64). Because they were all working at such an intense pace, the journalists rarely explicitly interrupted each other to share information on a story. Rather, when they had a story they thought might be of use to someone else, they would "throw out" a comment about the article to no one in particular. If other journalists did not feel the story being "advertised" was of use to them, they did not have to stop working in order to respond. Alternatively, they could respond and elicit more information about the story or ask to have a copy sent to them. In this study, Heath and Luff (2000) make the case that neither talk nor technology can stand alone, but are in fact deeply interdependent and interrelated. (Garcia et al. 2006, p. 409)

This example also illustrates the importance of the setting the interaction occurs within, for how workers enact their institutional roles and the tasks associated with their jobs. The Reuters employees described above took advantage of their proximity to their colleagues to share information (Heath and Luff, 2000). Similarly, a study by Gronn (1983) shows how a school administrator's job is shaped by the geography of his workplace. He spent much of his day talking to people in various parts of the school building. Gronn notes:

> The first point to note is the significance of architecture and territory in these exchanges. Corridors are crucial territories in most schools. Classrooms and offices open off them, so that a good deal of organizational work is done in corridors. There is constant movement between classes and at

breaks, messages are transmitted from offices to teachers, and people always mingle and gather informally. It is common for a principal to put his or her head around a teacher's door to have a chat. The teacher leaves the class and comes over, and both individuals straddle the door way between a bit of the school and the school as a whole. This may be the principal's respite from the telephone, but it is crucial to administering a school. Teachers and principals both know that what might appear as "prowling" (Darling, 1967: 64) is also a way of the principal showing the staff that he or she is around and keeping in touch with the pulse of the school. In using the corridor in this way, the principal gets caught up in the staff's concerns. Being narrow and long, corridors seem to force individuals to gaze, smile at or greet one another as they go past. Such encounters afford the staff access to a principal that they might not have if he or she were ensconced in an office with the door shut. (Gronn, 1983, p. 7)

Boden (1994) studied talk in business and organizational settings, and explained why understanding talk in such organizations is critical for understanding how their work is done:

In most organizations, most of the time, people mix work tasks with sociable interaction and they do so largely through talk. Since the organizing and structuring of organizations is also a primarily talk-based process, talk and task tend to intertwine in finely tuned ways. The casual talk that fills the air at the beginning of a meeting, or in a colleague's doorway, or around the high-tech work stations of the modern office deftly weaves sociable personal news and stories with organizational maxims, practical advice, direct queries about work in progress, tales of distant divisions, gossip about new accounting procedures, rumors of reorganization, and outright myths about organizational battles of old. In the process, talk at work is merged with talk *as* work. The meetings, telephone calls, and "quick" consults that make up the organizational day are all talk and (mostly) work. Moreover, they build the relationships, alliances, and coalitions that blend individual into collective, discrete actions into collective efforts, people into collectivities... [I]t is the concerted and coordinated actions of individuals that *dominate* organizations, rather than the self-interested, self-optimizing objects proposed by rational choice theory (and related versions thereof). People, as we shall see, *talk* their way to solutions, talk themselves into working agreements, talk their coalitions into existence, talk their organizational agendas, and, occasionally, talk through or past each other. Moreover, through their talk they not only reproduce the institutionalized arrangements of the organization and its environment, but significantly create and recreate fine distinctions that actually make the organization come alive. (Boden, 1994, pp. 51–2)

Fairhurst (2011), Gronn (1983) and others study how talk in interaction is central to leadership roles in organizations. Understanding talk in business and other organizational settings is therefore critical for the success of individuals working for or receiving services from these organizations, as well as for the success of the organizations themselves.

Subject matter and organization of this textbook

This textbook will provide you with a comprehensive introduction to the major research findings of conversation analysis. The book covers both informal everyday interactions between friends, family members, and acquaintances, and the interactions (formal or otherwise) that occur in organizational settings and in a broad range of workplace contexts. The book focuses on understanding the procedures used to organize talk in interaction, and aims to teach students both how talk is typically organized and what types of problems in interaction tend to emerge.

This book will be useful to students in courses on communication and interaction in sociology, linguistics, communication, and business departments. The book also teaches the theory and methodology of conversation analysis, and the chapters are designed to help students learn how to use the research method of conversation analysis to analyze interactions themselves. While the original conversation analytic studies were conducted on English language interactions, the field has since spread to dozens of countries around the world. Throughout the text you will see examples of research done on a wide range of languages, including Spanish, Japanese, Chinese, German, French, and Danish, among others.

The book begins with a basic introduction to the theoretical perspective underlying conversation analysis (Chapter 2 on the "ethnomethodological" perspective). Chapter 3 provides a general introduction to conversation analysis and its method of research. Chapter 4 explains the methods of recording and transcribing interactions for close, detailed analysis.

The next nine chapters of the book address the fundamental organizing principles of everyday interaction, including how participants exchange speaking turns, begin or end an interaction, change topics of talk, or perform such actions as telling stories or making invitations or requests.

The thirteen chapters following explore interactions in a wide range of institutional settings. The book covers talk in business settings (including customer service calls, business meetings and interviews), interactions on broadcast media (including television news interviews and radio talk shows), interactions in medical settings, interactions in legal settings (including trials, hearings, interrogations, and mediation sessions), and technologically mediated interactions (such as air traffic communications and mobile phone interactions).

Benefits to the student of learning how to do conversation analysis

There are personal, practical and academic benefits to students who learn how to do conversation analysis.

Strengthening Listening Skills and Communicative Competence. Studying conversation analysis will benefit students personally by teaching them to understand human communication better. They will learn to listen well and to pay close attention to what people say and how they say it. In addition, they will learn how to diagnose problems that occur in interactions and to come up with ideas for how to avoid them. These skills will benefit students both in their personal and work lives.

Relevance of Conversation Analysis to Business Students. Those students studying business will benefit from the intensive exploration of interactions in a wide range of workplace and organizational settings. Students will find that many of the issues analyzed in one type of institutional interaction may be useful in other workplace contexts. For example, understanding how mediators help clients discuss areas of conflict without degenerating into argument can help managers solve problems between employees in the workplace or effectively run meetings. Understanding the techniques attorneys use to handle evasive witnesses in trials could be useful for employers conducting job interviews. Understanding the best methods doctors use to deliver good and bad diagnostic news to patients could be useful to a wide range of businesses in communicating with clients or employees.

Relevance of Conversation Analysis for Students Majoring in Communication. Students majoring in communication will benefit from learning the most important qualitative approach to research in communication today. In addition to the chapters on talk in broadcast media, the chapters on talk in organizational and workplace settings will help communication students familiarize themselves with a wide range of genres of communication.

Relevance of Conversation Analysis for Students Majoring in the Social Sciences. Sociologists and other students in the social sciences will benefit from learning a method of analysis that provides direct access to human action and social interaction. The ethnomethodological approach to conversation analysis taught in this book fills a major gap in social science approaches to understanding social life and work in organizational settings.

Learning How to Do Qualitative Research. Academically, students will benefit by learning a powerful theoretical/methodological approach to doing research in sociological and related social science disciplines. Students in a range of disciplines will also benefit from learning how to use a specific method of qualitative research. Their expanded knowledge of language and social interaction will be relevant to their progress in communication, anthropology, sociology, linguistics, or other programs.

Developing Critical Thinking and Analytical Skills. All students using this textbook will benefit from its emphasis on critical thinking skills. This book is not a "how to" manual, it is a course which teaches students how to analyze interaction. Students in all disciplines will benefit from developing these analytical skills.

2 Understanding Ethnomethodology

Chapter contents

Introduction

Conversation analysis initially emerged from the work of sociologists who were developing a theoretical perspective called ethnomethodology. Today conversation analysis is also used by some scholars in communication, anthropology, psychology, linguistics and other fields. In this chapter we will briefly explain ethnomethodology and its sociological roots, and demonstrate how it can be a useful perspective for the study of talk in a wide range of settings.

For those of you who have taken an introduction to sociology course, you may have seen sociology defined as the study of human society. Sociologists tend to study social groups, social organizations, and social structures, as well as the social factors that affect life experiences and outcomes for individuals and groups. A common focus of study for sociologists is the root causes of social facts or social problems (e.g. gender inequality, poverty or crime). In addition to focusing attention on the causes and explanations for social behavior and social facts, sociologists tend to use a model of social structure which treats it as a "container" within which people's lives are lived rather than as a product of human action. **Ethnomethodology** is an approach to sociological inquiry that challenges the way sociologists typically conceptualize and study the social world:

> Ethnomethodology offers a distinctive perspective on the nature and origins of social order. It rejects "top-down" theories that impute the organization of everyday life to cultural or social structural phenomena conceived as standing outside of the flow of ordinary events. Adopting a thoroughly "bottom-up" approach, ethnomethodology seeks to recover social organization as an emergent achievement that results from the concerted efforts of societal members acting within local situations. Central to this achievement are the various methods that members use to produce and recognize courses of social activity and the circumstances in which they are embedded. The mundane intelligibility and accountability of social actions, situations, and structures is understood to be the outcome of these constitutive methods or procedures. (Maynard and Clayman, 2003, p. 174)

From an ethnomethodological perspective, social structure is viewed as a cultural artifact much like any other cultural artifact, whether it be a physical object such as a vase or a cell phone, or a cultural practice such as music or science. Social structure and social organization exist because of the actions of humans. Ethnomethodologists investigate how this is done, by studying the procedures and methods people use to create social facts, social structure and social order.

Ethnomethodology is both a <u>theory</u> of social action and social order, and a <u>method</u> of studying human action. As a theory, ethnomethodologists note that when people act, they do so in ways that display their understanding of the social context they are acting within and reflexively constructing through their actions. By using commonly shared procedures and relying on shared assumptions about how interaction should work, people are able to coordinate their actions with others. Group members share an understanding of the procedures and assumptions of their cultural or societal subgroup. For example, consider the following excerpt from Matthew Polly's (2007) book about his experiences in China during the early 1990s:

> Whereas in America most conversation between strangers getting to know each other begins with a recitation of their resumes—occupation, education background, accomplishments—in China, conversations began with you complimenting the person you've just met as extravagantly as possible and your new acquaintance deflecting those compliments as self-effacingly as possible. There were several options for false modesty: straight denial like "No, no, no, my Chinese is terrible," a general rejection of flattery such as "No need to be polite," or the classic, "Where? Where? Where?"—as if the flattery must have been aimed in a direction other than yours. When Mao Zedong's attractive wife first visited America, the American translator said to her in Chinese, "You are very beautiful." She replied, "Where? Where? Where?" Not understanding this was a generic response, he answered, "Your face is beautiful, your eyes, your body, um your hands." (Polly, 2007, pp. 225–6)

This example shows that social structures and social relationships (in this case, a professional acquaintance) are created through a series of procedures that people in a culture use to accomplish that purpose. Although in America, a series of questions about one's position in life may be seen as normal and necessary to "get to know" someone, Polly (2007) found that in China it would be considered immodest to begin an interaction by talking about one's accomplishments. The giving and rejecting of compliments is a way people display their worthiness for friendship by displaying their modesty, an important social value. As long as both interactants share an understanding of the conventions in their society for how meeting someone is done, the interaction is likely to go off smoothly. However, if the participants do not share the same procedures and background assumptions about how the interaction should go, there are likely to be misunderstandings and problems, as in the example Polly (2007) provides. In order to discover what procedures and background assumptions are relevant in a particular interaction, it is necessary to study human behavior in that context directly and closely.

There are a number of social science perspectives which study culture (e.g., some areas in sociology, the field of anthropology, and some areas of communication scholarship). Ethnomethodology differs from these perspectives in its observation that participants display the procedures they use for each other as they interact. Because participants' actions display their understanding of <u>others</u>' actions, how people create social organization and social order can be studied via direct observation. Ethnomethodology thus facilitates and requires a research approach which enables us to understand social organization by directly observing how people accomplish it. Ethnomethodology fills a large gap in sociology by focusing on what people actually do, and how they do it.

Ethnomethodology was developed by Harold Garfinkel in the late 1960's. He created the term ethnomethodology because he was trying to study people's methods for creating social order and social organization ("ethno" means people or culture, the suffix "ology" means "the study of"). He designed studies (called "**breaching experiments**") to reveal the proce-dures underlying social processes in a wide range of situations (e.g., within the family, in ordinary conversation, in the process of doing research, or in the process of doing therapy; see Garfinkel, 1967). His approach in these breaching experiments was to learn about social norms by breaking rules, then observing what happened and how people reacted. He found that when expectations were violated and routine procedures not followed, people reacted emotionally, thus revealing how they normally expected things to go.

The goal of ethnomethodology is to discover the methods, procedures, and background assumptions people use to accomplish almost any aspect of social life. For example, ethnomethodology can be used to show how people do work (Luff et al., 2000; Rouncefield and Tolmie, 2011), argue (Goodwin, 1983; Maynard, 1985), conduct a telephone survey (Lavin and Maynard, 2001; Maynard et al., 2010), present oneself as male or female (West and Zimmerman, 1987), do scientific research (Garfinkel et al., 1981; Lynch, 1991), or tell a story (Goodwin, 1984).

Ethnomethodology complements traditional sociology by providing a way of studying people's methods of creating social structure, social order and social action. Most aspects of society are organized or accomplished through talk. Talk is therefore the central locus of the creation of the social world as we know it, and should be studied by sociologists. People do work through talk; the work of communicating, the work of constructing and conveying our social roles, and the work of creating social structure. Talk is central to most human activity, whether it be a classroom interaction, going out with a friend, conducting a TV news interview, taking a medical history, or communicating with others in the workplace. Ethnomethodology enables us to study this work as it is being done and to accurately and precisely discover how it is done, why things go wrong when they do go wrong, and how problems can be avoided.

Garfinkel's development of ethnomethodology

Garfinkel (1967) demonstrated that our experience of the world is such that when social action is accomplished in a routine way, we fail to notice the work that is done to accomplish it. Actions as simple as walking from one part of the room to another are typically done without self-consciousness or without thought as to how to do them. It is only when circumstances bring something to our attention (such as when we accidentally bump into someone or trip while walking) that we become conscious of that activity and actively try to control how we are doing it. Another quote from Polly (2007), in which he describes the experience of trying to "act natural" for a film crew that was taping a story about his martial arts studies in China, illustrates this well. It shows how the routine, taken-for-granted actions that we participate in on a daily basis can become challenging and problematic when circumstances are not typical:

> The producer, the cameraman, and I went up to the hotel where I was staying after lunch. They wanted to film me walking down the hall, opening the unlocked door, and entering my room. I was confident I knew how to walk, open doors, and enter rooms. Apparently I did not. It took me five takes to get it right. Next they wanted a shot of me reading in my room. Despite many years of practice, I wasn't very good at this, either. It took eight takes before I was able to turn the pages properly. I had seen countless of these background segments on TV shows without ever realizing that they were so elaborately staged. There are few things more nerve-racking than trying to act normal with a camera in your face and someone shouting at you to "act normal." By the time we arrived in the training hall I was already a wreck. (Polly, 2007, p. 58)

This example serves to illustrate the work done to produce ordinary everyday activities. We are typically not aware of the procedures we are following for doing so, unless something out of the ordinary brings them into focus.

Harold Garfinkel's "breaching experiments" and what they demonstrate

Ethnomethodology was first developed by Harold Garfinkel (1963; 1967). He designed a series of studies to reveal the procedures underlying social processes in a wide range of different realms of social life (including family life, scientific research and psychotherapy).

The goal of these studies was to discover the "common sense understandings" and "background assumptions" that members of society base their actions on (and rely on to interpret each other's actions). An effective method for exploring and demonstrating the nature of human action was to deliberately breach the norms of everyday reality. Garfinkel reasoned that if a specific understanding or procedure was in fact a social norm, then when it was violated people would respond to that violation. His method was therefore to "breach" routine behavior, observe what happened, and then learn about social norms by observing participants' reactions when routine patterns are disrupted. He found that confusion, anger or other negative responses occurred when procedures were systematically breached. Maynard and Clayman (2003) characterize the **breaching experiments** as follows:

> Garfinkel (1967) instructed his confederates to demand that subjects explain and clarify the meaning of their most casual remarks, to act as boarders in their own homes, to act on the assumption that subjects had some hidden motive, and so forth. Although he was hesitant to use the term "experiment" in reference to such studies, preferring to characterize them more modestly as "demonstrations" (Garfinkel 1967: 38), nevertheless the approach is reminiscent of the earlier incongruity experiments of Ash (1946, 1951) and Bruner and his associates (Bruner 1961; Bruner and Postman 1949). Garfinkel's demonstrations, however, were designed to be not merely incongruous with subjects' expectations but also massively senseless. (Maynard and Clayman, 2003, p. 178)

One set of breaching experiments involved instructing his undergraduate students to ask their co-interactants to clarify commonsense remarks (Garfinkel, 1967). This experiment was designed to demonstrate the **indexicality** of human action. Indexicality refers to the observation that the meaning of utterances comes not from the words alone, but from their use in a specific context (see Potter, 1996, p. 43). We normally make assumptions about what is meant by an utterance by interpreting it in the light of the context it occurs within. Garfinkel's students were asked to take nothing for granted and to ask for definitions and explanations of anything remotely ambiguous. In other words, they were asked to pretend that language is *not* indexical. The three quotes below from Garfinkel's analysis of the students' conversations illustrate the charged reactions of the research subjects to this "breaching experiment":

> The subject was telling the experimenter, a member of the subject's car pool, about having had a flat tire while going to work the previous day.
>> (S) I had a flat tire.
>> (E) What do you mean, you had a flat tire?

> She appeared momentarily stunned. Then she answered in a hostile way: "What do you mean, 'What do you mean?' A flat tire is a flat tire. That is what I meant. Nothing special. What a crazy question!" (Garfinkel, 1967, p. 42)

> (S) Hi, Ray. How is your girlfriend feeling?
> (E) What do you mean, "How is she feeling?" Do you mean physical or mental?

(S) I mean how is she feeling? What's the matter with you? (He looked peeved.)

(E) Nothing. Just explain a little clearer what do you mean?

(S) Skip it. How are your Med School applications coming?

(E) What do you mean, "How are they?"

(S) You know what I mean.

(E) I really don't.

(S) What's the matter with you? Are you sick? (Garfinkel, 1967, p. 42)

The victim waved his hand cheerily.

(S) How are you?

(E) How am I in regard to what? My health, my finances, my school work, my peace of mind, my…?

(S) (Red in the face and suddenly out of control.) Look! I was just trying to be polite. Frankly, I don't give a damn how you are. (Garfinkel, 1967, p. 44)

Garfinkel argued that this "breaching experiment" illustrated several facts about human action and social order. Although language is by nature indexical, people have ways of dealing with this ambiguity and rendering it non-problematic. People do not normally have trouble understanding each other. They know what a flat tire is, even if it is not explained to them. Participants interpret other's actions (including their verbal utterances) in terms of the context they occur within. For example, they may observe who is talking, when are they talking, and in what type of social situation are they talking.

Finally, when the experimenters violated (breached) basic norms of interaction the subjects reacted with surprise, consternation and even annoyance. When commonsense understandings are ignored and shared norms of behavior are violated, people will react emotionally. Garfinkel (1967) argues that this type of reaction demonstrates the moral accountability of action—that it is not just the *communication* that suffers, it is our perceptions about the *person* who breaches the norm.

People typically make great efforts to normalize situations, to act as if they are routine, if at all possible. For example, Garfinkel asked two graduate students to knock on the doors of houses in Beverly Hills, California, and ask them if they could inspect their closets. The graduate students had to carry a portable tape recorder with them. In those days (the 1960s) tape recorders were quite large and bulky; too big to be hidden in a pocket. So they wore trench coats and held the tape recorder hidden under the trench coat. Garfinkel expected that when they showed up at resident's doors with this strange request, they would be turned away. However, a surprising number of people actually let them in. Since they had not expected to be let in, they did not know what to do next. They quickly improvised a routine of banging and pounding on the inside of the closets, and then announcing that the closets were in good condition (personal communication, Don Zimmerman). This experience illustrates the extent to which people will go to "normalize" their experiences—to assume that other's behavior is accountable and treat it as that way.

The documentary method of interpretation

One of the concepts Garfinkel (1967) uses in his description of ethnomethodology is Karl Mannheim's "**documentary method of interpretation.**" Human actions are treated as if they were "documents" that were produced by an underlying process whose nature can be inferred by the nature of the document (the action). In terms of speech, Potter (1996, p. 49) argues that "a particular utterance is seen as evidence of an underlying pattern and, in turn, the fact that the utterance is part of this underlying pattern is used to make sense of it." The concept of the documentary method of interpretation describes how we interpret each other's actions. We do not just read the "document" of their actions, we infer what underlying procedures were used to produce that document, and use that knowledge to understand the action.

Garfinkel's (1967) constructed a breaching experiment to demonstrate the documentary method of interpretation. He constructed a deliberately fake experimental situation in which undergraduate research subjects believed they were talking to a therapist in order to get advice for personal problems. The students were asked to communicate with the therapist via a computer terminal, and were instructed to ask only yes or no questions. They were informed that the therapist would answer either yes or no, and would not elaborate their answers. Unbeknownst to the students, there was no therapist. Instead, students were fed a random series of yes or no answers in response to their questions. Garfinkel discovered that instead of rejecting the validity of the advice offered (on the basis that it was random, irrational or unhelpful), the subjects were actually able to make sense of the random responses. They created accounts or explanations for them, and inferred the therapist's opinions or points of view underlying the yes or no answers. Subjects created the "therapist's" reasons for their answers. When inconsistencies arose between the answer to one question and the next (because of the random nature of the replies), subjects worked to resolve inconsistencies. Subjects did not doubt the meaning of the answers. They assumed that explanations lay behind the answers. In short, the yes or no answers were treated as *documents underlying a pattern*—in this case, "the underlying pattern" was the therapist's reasoning as they decided how to respond to the student's question. Garfinkel (1967) uses this quote to illustrate one student's response:

> Subject: I would like to know whether or not I should change my major at the present time. I have a physics major with quite a deficit in grade points to bring up to get my C average in physics. I would like to switch over to mathematics. I have a little difficulty in it, but I think maybe I could handle it. I have failed several math courses here at U.C.L.A., but I have always repeated them and had C's. I have come close to getting a B in math in one specific course because I studied a little more than in others but my question is still should I change my major?
> Experimenter: My answer is no.
> Subject: Well he says no. And if I don't then I will have to make up my deficit in grade points which will be awfully difficult because I am not doing too well this semester. If I pull through this semester with seven units of A then I can count on possibly going on to get my degree in physics in February, but then I have this stigma of nuclear physics facing me. I thoroughly dislike the study of nuclear physics. Nuclear Physics 124 will be one of my required courses to get a degree in physics.

> Do you think I could get a degree in physics on the basis of this knowledge that I must take Physics 124?
> Experimenter: My answer is yes.
> Subject: He says yes. I don't see how I can. I am not that good of a theorist. My study habits are horrible. My reading speed is bad, and I don't spend enough time studying.
>   Do you think that I could successfully improve my study habits?
> Experimenter: My answer is yes. (Garfinkel, 1967, pp. 85–6)

Another set of breaching experiments, in which Garfinkel (1967) asked students to pretend to be boarders in their own homes, illustrates the documentary method of interpretation in action and other commonsense understandings. The experiment revealed how the students' behavior was interpreted by their parents when they acted as if they were renting a room in their parents' house instead of being a member of the family. The students' actions were not taken at face value. It was assumed that they stood for or represented something problematic underlying the action itself. For example, the student's silence would be seen as a symptom of an underlying pattern such as illness, rudeness, a misguided attempt at humor, etc.

> Family members demanded explanations: What's the matter? What's gotten in to you? Did you get fired? Are you sick? What are you being so superior about? Why are you mad? Are you out of your mind or are you just stupid? One student acutely embarrassed his mother in front of her friends by asking if she minded if he had a snack from the refrigerator. "Mind if you have a little snack? You've been eating little snacks around here for years without asking me. What's gotten into you?" One mother, infuriated when her daughter spoke to her only when she was spoken to, began to shriek in angry denunciation of the daughter for her disrespect and insubordination and refused to be calmed by the student's sister. A father berated his daughter for being insufficiently concerned for the welfare of others and of acting like a spoiled child. (Garfinkel, 1967, pp. 47–8)

In addition to illustrating the documentary method of interpretation, this breaching experiment also shows us something about how ordinary family life is organized—the "background assumptions" and "commonsense knowledge" underlying family life. Here is a potential list of rules of procedures for acting as if one is a member of a family that could be abstracted from Garfinkel's findings:

1. Know who the people in the family are.
2. Treat yourself as part of the family, not an outsider.
3. Participate in family life, do not just observe.
4. Avoid being too polite (informality is the norm).
5. Expect few boundaries between family members (intrusion in other's affairs is the norm).

Garfinkel's breaching experiments were thus useful for improving our understanding of social action on several levels. They were useful as a method of inquiry, to test guesses about what the rules and procedures were in a given social situation. They were also useful to investigate specific areas of social life, such as how to conduct a conversation, how patients understand their psychotherapists, or how family relationships are ordinarily conducted.

Ethnomethodological perspectives on talk and interaction

Sacks' (1984a) article, "On Doing Being Ordinary," highlights some of the issues involved in conveying normalcy in everyday life. Sacks was an ethnomethodologist, and was particularly interested in studying how people talk. Talk is not only central to the organization of human activity, it is easily recorded so that a precise record of the interaction can be preserved and studied in detail (Sacks, 1984b). This is necessary because it is through the details that people coordinate their actions with each other.

First, Sacks (1984a) notes that what makes us "ordinary" is not who we are (e.g. an ordinary citizen as opposed to a celebrity). What makes us "ordinary" is how we construct our actions. Ordinariness is therefore something we *do* rather than something we *are*. Our presentation of self to others as normal is an "accomplishment" that we achieve through following the shared procedures and background assumptions our culture relies on.

Sacks (1984a) notes several of the ways in which people do "being ordinary"—how they behave in a way that is accountably normal in our society. One example has to do with the level of detail that people typically provide. While you might think that it would be seen as desirable to be accurate and precise, what Sacks shows is just the opposite. In everyday life, when interacting with friends and acquaintances, speaking precisely and describing things in detail could be seen as odd or abnormal. Sacks illustrates this with an excerpt from a conversation in which a woman is describing a man she met to a friend of hers:

> He's just a real, dear, nice guy. Just a real, real nice guy. So we were really talking up a storm, and having a real good time, had a few drinks and so forth, and he's real easygoing. He's intelligent, and he's uh, not handsome, but he's nice looking, and uh, just real real nice, personable, very personable, very sweet. (Sacks, 1984a, p. 416)

This quote is almost maddeningly vague. What do we know about this person after hearing her description? Not much. However this type of description is seen as normal and received as normal by her co-interactant. What would have been weird is if she had included such details as he keeps his nails trimmed to 1/16 of an inch, he double knots his shoelaces, and he said the word "the" 46 times during the evening.

In order to demonstrate what failing to "do being ordinary" might look like, Sacks (1984a) ask us to consider a hypothetical interaction in which someone reports on a car trip to a friend:

> [I]f you come home and report what the grass looked like along the freeway; that there were four noticeable shades of green, some of which just appeared yesterday because of the rain, then there may well be some tightening up on the part of your recipient. And if you were to do it routinely, then people might figure that there is something odd about you... you might lose friends. (Sacks, 1984a, pp. 418–19)

In short, it is normal ("ordinary") to be vague and repetitious when giving descriptions; it is not normal to be precise. There are ordinary, typical ways of doing things, which the members of a culture know. If you do things in a nonordinary way, people will notice and make assumptions about you; your failure to conform will be "accountable."

Sacks analyzes how people tell stories in order to show how people conduct themselves as normal, ordinary people. He observes and collects a wide range of stories that people tell each other, and then analyzes the underlying procedures that people use to shape how the stories were structured and interpreted. Sacks' (1984a) analysis revealed four common aspects of "ordinary" stories that enable them to be perceived and interpreted by others as accountable.

1. Use an appropriate level of detail

If someone asked you what you did last weekend, you would probably say something like, "I went to a movie with a friend," or "I had to work this weekend." You probably would not say, "On Saturday morning I woke up at 8:45 and got dressed in my blue shirt and my black pants, I brushed my teeth for two minutes, combed my hair, cleaned up the dishes I had left in the sink from last night, made a cup of coffee..." That level of detail, while completely accurate, would also be seen as strange. You would be seen as someone who is definitely *not* ordinary. You clearly do not share your culture's assumptions about what it means to ask "What did you do last weekend?" This question does not ask for a laundry list of tasks or events, but instead provides you the opportunity to tell about something newsworthy (e.g., "I went to the movies with a friend."), or to report that nothing particularly newsworthy happened (e.g., "Not much."). It does not give you license to take the question literally and provide a report of exactly everything you did in numbing detail.

2. Construct an "accountable" story

Sacks (1984a) describes a story told by a woman who drove by a store that sold expensive items and saw police cars out front. Although no one told her what was happening, she created an explanation (an account) for the presence of the police cars. She apparently assumed that a burglary was committed, because that was the type of store a burglar might target. The details in her story display her underlying assumptions about what happened.

3. Construct a story that reflects the teller's relationship to the events

While it may be the case that anybody can tell a story about anything they want to, the way they tell that story should be carefully matched to who they are and what their relationship to the story is. For example, consider the telling of "ethnic jokes." Today, ethnic jokes are typically considered only marginally acceptable, or even outright "politically incorrect." But notice that whether an ethnic joke can be told at all, or how it is likely to be received if it is told, has something to do with who is doing the telling. If the person telling the ethnic joke is a member of the ethnic group that is the target of the joke, the impact of the joke is different than if the teller of the joke is from a different ethnic group. The teller's relationship to the story they are telling will affect how it is interpreted by its recipients. The meaning of an ethnic joke, and its likely reception by the audience, will differ depending on who is doing the telling—a member of the group that is the punch line of the joke, or a member of a different group.

Sacks (1984a) notes that people have different "entitlement to experiences" depending on their relationship to the event they are describing. Someone who merely witnessed a bad car accident, and was perhaps inconvenienced by the traffic delays that ensued, certainly has a "right" to tell that story, and to express concern about what has happened. However, they do not have the "entitlement" to have a major nervous breakdown because of observing a wreck at the side of the road. The witness to the accident does have a greater entitlement to feel bad about the accident than someone who was not there, who perhaps only read about it in the paper. On the other hand, a *participant* in the accident has the entitlement to feel emotionally distraught. How these individuals then tell their story of the accident should reflect their relationship to the event—their entitlement to experiences.

Sacks (1984a, p. 424) illustrates this point with an excerpt from a conversation between two friends in which one reports having seen the site of a serious traffic accident on the side of the freeway. She characterizes the wreck as serious ("the most gosh awful wreck"; "I've never seen a car smashed into such a small space"; "there were people laid out and covered over on the pavement"). However, she then reports that although she had intended to listen to the news report about the accident on the television after she got home, she did not do so, and instead watched another show. She thus shows that although the accident was serious, she is not very emotionally engaged in it. This level of engagement with the events described is appropriate ("ordinary") for someone who was a witness but not a participant in the accident.

4. Tell the story at an appropriate time

The timing of the telling of a story is a delicate matter. If it is an ordinary, mundane event that is being described, the teller should wait for an appropriate place in the conversation to tell that story. However, if it is something urgent or shocking, the news can be told earlier in the conversation. Knowing when to tell stories is as important for successfully telling them in an "ordinary" way as is the nature of the story itself. For example, one day years ago, I was walking on a college campus with a friend when we noticed a car on fire near some tennis courts. We immediately knocked on the door of a faculty member who lived on campus (this was in the days before cell phones!). He opened the door, smiled and greeted us. Instead of returning the greeting, however, we said "there's a car on fire by the tennis courts!" This utterance, although woefully out of place in terms of the ordinary development of a conversation (we would have been expected to return the professor's greeting, at the very least), was appropriately placed for a "story" of that nature—an urgent matter that had to be taken care of immediately. The nature of the story provided an account for its placement within the greeting sequence of the encounter. Conversely, try to imagine what would have happened if we had *not* interrupted to provide the urgent information, and instead had waited until after the greetings, the exchange of "how are you"s, and other preliminary "chit chat" had been completed. Most importantly, the car might have burnt up before help could have been sent. In addition, when we did finally produce the information, the faculty member would have been shocked and dismayed at our delay in telling the urgent information. We would definitely *not* have been seen as "ordinary."

In short, something as mundane as the details through which we tell stories to others reflects a number of underlying assumptions about how we see our world and how we organize our activities. The ethnomethodological perspective is an essential foundation for the conversation analytic approach to the study of talk and interaction.

Summary

In this chapter we have gained a basic understanding of what ethnomethodology is and what one might learn from using its approach to studying the social world. Ethnomethodology is a *method* of studying people's methods of creating social order, social structure and situated action. It is also a *theory* of social action, of the nature of social order and how it is created. The ethnomethodological perspective fills a gap in sociology by focusing on what people actually do, and how they do it. This refusal to ignore the proverbial "black box" of situated action (the workings or machinery that lead to social outcomes) is one of ethnomethodology's key contributions to social science.

Ethnomethodological studies are wide ranging. They may focus on everyday life and ordinary conversation, on talk in institutional settings or on interactions in the workplace. Whatever social setting you choose to apply this method to, you will learn about people's methods for creating and orienting to social structure and social order, and will understand human action in a more precise and grounded way than provided by many other sociological approaches.

As Boden (1994) and Drew and Heritage (1992) noted, most aspects of society are organized or accomplished through talk. Hence, talk is the central locus of the creation of the social world as we know it, and therefore should be a focal point of studies by sociologists as well as by linguists, communication scholars and others. The work of communicating, constructing and conveying one's social role, creating social organization or social structure are all largely accomplished through talk. Ethnomethodology enables us to study this work as it is being done and to accurately and precisely discover how it is done, why things go wrong when they do, and how problems can be avoided.

The practical applications of ethnomethodological conversation analytic research are many and direct. As we will see in the chapters that follow, we can learn how to save lives by doing emergency phone calls better (Whalen et al., 1988; Whalen and Zimmerman, 1998;

Whalen, M. and Zimmerman, 1990; Zimmerman, 1984, 1992a), how to improve business performance by conducting better customer service calls (Baker et al., 2001; Reiter, 2006; Whalen and Whalen, 2011), how to design technology that fits realistically with how people interact and use it (Harper, 2010; Heath and Luff, 2000), how to fly planes more safely (e.g. Nevile, 2001; 2004; 2007); and how to conduct doctor/patient consultations so that patients accept their diagnoses and comply with treatment recommendations (Frankel and Beckman, 1989; Gill, 2005; Heritage and Maynard, 2006a; 2006b; Heritage and Sefi, 1992; Lutfey, 2004; Stivers, 2005). In the second half of this book we will study the research findings for many of these applications of the study of talk at work.

The ethnomethodological perspective is unique theoretically and methodologically. It asks the analyst to discover the procedures used by participants in interactions by closely observing their actions in their sequential context. By using this perspective to study "talk at work"—how participants conduct interaction in a variety of every day and workplace settings—we will be able to gain a deeper understanding of how interaction works. Participants do work through talk, and construct the social context through their actions, whether it is an informal conversation with a friend or a task-oriented business meeting. The application of ethnomethodology to the study of talk is called "conversation analysis." We now turn to an explanation of the conversation analytic method and its application to understanding talk in everyday settings.

Student activities

1. Indexicality: It is not recommended that one try to reproduce Garfinkel's breaching experiments with one's friends or family members, because people may be quite disturbed by your behavior. However, comedy often involves breaching the indexicality of human action. In the movie "Airplane" (Paramount Pictures, 1980) the characters often fail to treat actions or utterances as indexical. Watch the film and see how many instances of the breach of indexicality you can find.
2. On "Doing Being Ordinary". Sacks (1984a) identifies four ways people can tell stories in "ordinary" ways. Write a short dialogue in which you find a way to violate each of these procedures.

Recommended readings

Garfinkel, Harold. 1963, "A Conception of, and Experiments with 'Trust' as a Condition of Stable Concerted Actions", pp. 187–238, in *Motivation and Social Interaction*, O. J. Harvey (ed.). New York: Ronald Press.

Garfinkel, Harold. 1967, *Studies in Ethnomethodology*. Cambridge: Polity Press.

Heritage, John. 1984, *Garfinkel and Ethnomethodology*. Cambridge: Cambridge University Press.

Sacks, Harvey. 1984a, "On Doing Being Ordinary", pp. 413–29, in *Structures of Social Action*, J. M. Atkinson and J. Heritage (eds). Cambridge: Cambridge University Press.

Sacks, Harvey. 1984b, "Notes on Methodology", pp. 21–7, in *Structures of Social Action*, J. M. Atkinson and J. Heritage (eds). Cambridge: Cambridge University Press.

Understanding and Doing Conversation Analysis: Methodological Approach

3

Introduction

As we learned in Chapter 2, conversation analysis is an approach to the study of talk in interaction which developed out of the sociological perspective called ethnomethodology. Ethnomethodology is the study of people's methods for accomplishing just about any aspect of social life. The goal of ethnomethodology is to discover how people accomplish social action, social order and social structure via their actions. Since talk is the primary means of accomplishing social action it is necessary to understand how it works.

Many of the classic studies in ethnomethodology illustrate how this perspective can help us understand human action in a wide range of social contexts and institutional settings. For example, ethnomethodological studies have shown how scientists work together to make scientific discoveries (Garfinkel et al., 1981), how case workers in a welfare agency do the work of deciding who should receive aid (Zimmerman, 1969), how police officers collect and record evidence to be used to handle juvenile crime (Meehan, 1986), and how the way residents and staff at a halfway house for ex-convicts construct their social world works against their rehabilitation (Wieder, 1974). Each of these studies illustrates how a close examination of participants' actions in a given social setting can lead to theoretical insights as well as practical solutions to social problems such as the rehabilitation of ex-convicts or improving how police work is done.

While Garfinkel was developing the ethnomethodological perspective at the University of California in the 1960s he worked with a graduate student named Harvey Sacks. Sacks realized that spoken interaction was an ideal data source for ethnomethodological research because talk could be tape recorded and therefore studied repeatedly in its intricate detail (Sacks, 1984b). The field that became conversation analysis thus developed out of the ethnomethodological concern to understand social organization and human action by observing people's methods directly. Because talk is central to the aspects of social life studied by a variety of disciplinary approaches, conversation analysis has spread beyond sociology departments, and is now used by researchers in some communication, anthropology, linguistic and psychology departments. Conversation analytic methods have been found to be useful for studying the informal conversation we have with friends, relatives, and others as we go through our daily life (e.g. Sacks et al., 1974). They have also been used to study talk in a wide range of organizational and institutional contexts (Drew and Heritage, 1992). Conversation analytic research is perhaps best known for its work in medical settings (e.g., Heritage and Maynard, 2006a), legal settings (e.g. Atkinson and Drew, 1979; Greatbatch and Dingwall, 1997; Watson, 1990; Lynch and Bogen, 1996), and broadcast media (e.g. Clayman and Heritage, 2002; Greatbatch, 1988). However the types of institutional settings conversation analysis has been used to study is extremely broad, including for example, such wide-ranging topics as educational testing (Maynard and Marlaire, 1992); survey research (Hootkoop-Steenstra, 2000; Schaeffer and Maynard, 1996), and business (Boden, 1994).

In Harvey Sacks' early work he described the methodological approach of conversation analysis. Conversation analysts rely on tape recorded or videotaped records of interaction which are transcribed using a detailed system of symbols and conventions developed by Gail Jefferson (Jefferson, 1984a; 2004a). The analyst then studies individual interactions or collections of related excerpts from a range of interactions. This analysis involves a search for patterns by closely examining participants' actions and how others respond to them.

Early conversation analysts investigated how conversations had the orderly properties they display. They were interested in discovering, for example, how participants performed such actions as taking turns at talk, resolving instances of interruptions or simultaneous speech, or performing common actions such as asking questions (e.g. Sacks et al., 1974; Sacks, 1992a).

Sacks suggested that an effective guide for conversation analysts as they studied these tapes and transcripts was to ask the question "why that now?" In other words, each action should be examined with an eye to explaining why the participant performed that action at that place in the conversation. As will become clear as we proceed with our study of conversation analysis, the sequential position of an utterance in the interaction is critical for understanding human action. The position of an utterance is one of the resources participants use to determine the meaning of the utterance (recall the definition of indexicality from Chapter 2).

Sacks argued that the goal of conversation analysis should be discovering the "grammar" or "machinery" of conversation (Sacks, 1985). Just as linguists worked to understand the grammar of language, conversation analysts were to discover the procedures people use to organize talk. Sacks studied talk in ordinary conversation between friends and acquaintances, but also investigated talk in institutional settings such as calls to a suicide prevention hotline (Sacks, 1987b). Our goal in this text is to learn how conversation analysts study talk, and to understand the major conversation analytic research findings. We will apply this knowledge to the analysis of talk in a wide variety of everyday and institutional settings, including a wide variety of workplace settings.

How to study interaction from a conversation analytic perspective

In your introductory classes, whether in sociology, communication, anthropology or linguistics, your instructor probably spent quite a bit of time talking about theories. The goal of most traditional disciplinary research in the social sciences is proposing and testing theories of how the social world works. The generation of new theories is seen as one of the most prestigious roles a scientist can play. The theories conversation analysts develop are based on the close analysis of actual interactions, rather than hypotheses which are developed prior to the examination of data (as is the case in traditional, "positivist" science). In order to understand why this is not only a valid but a necessary approach to the study of interactional data, consider Harvey Sack's (1984b) chapter on "Notes on Methodology." In this chapter, Sacks notes that ethnomethodology is a "natural observational science." Like the early science of botany, conversation analysts collect examples of, observe closely, and attempt to categorize or describe conversational events in a way that makes their social organization (the procedures used to create them) visible.

While the social world may seem incredibly complex (just as the biological world of plants is very complex), when examined closely and systematically it reveals a great degree of order. In fact, even the chaos that is occasionally observed in interaction (as when a conversation deteriorates into an argument, or six people begin speaking at once), is found to be orderly when examined in detail, as it unfolds. For example, Clayman and Whalen (1988/9) analyzed a television news interview that happened a number of years ago between journalist Dan Rather and the then Vice President, George Bush. The interview degenerated into an argument, with both parties at times speaking simultaneously and vehemently (and sometimes loudly!) disagreeing with each other. Steven E. Clayman and Jack Whalen show that even when the parties were speaking at the same time, they were also listening to each other—as evidenced by their subsequent responses to things the other said during simultaneous talk. Their argument was conducted in an "orderly" fashion.

Sacks argues that in interaction there is "order at all points" (Sacks, 1992a). Order is everywhere, because people use shared methods for constructing their actions. If we study the methods and procedures people use to construct interactions, we can develop a "grammar" of social action with as much accuracy as a linguist can explain how a language's grammatical rules are constructed. The "grammar" of social action is the procedures participants use to construct and coordinate their actions with others so that they can mutually understand each other.

There are several reasons why conversation analysts believe that these discoveries can be best made by direct observation of social action rather than through a more traditional positivist approach. In part, it is because of the complex nature of the phenomena conversation analysts study. Sacks (1984b) argues that because the social world is so complex, and because the procedures used to organize it are types of things we would not typically notice, we cannot rely on our imaginations to figure out what reasonable hypotheses about how interactions work would be.

Sacks' insight is that as scientists we are limited in terms of what we can hypothesize by what we can imagine. Social life is much more complex than we could imagine, so a deductive hypothesis-generation approach will not effectively lead us to an understanding of how participants construct their actions in everyday life. Instead, we use direct observation as a basis for theorizing (Heritage, 1987).

As Heritage (1987) argues, we should assume that data are orderly for analysts because they are orderly for participants. Human action is accomplished through specific actions performed in real time. By observing human behavior directly we can develop accurate theories about how people coordinate their activities and create intersubjective understanding.

Heritage (1987) gives an ethnomethodological perspective on why talk is orderly rather than chaotic. First, there are procedures by which participants structure their talk. Since these procedures are shared among members of a culture, co-interactants know how to use them and interpret them. Second, social action works not *in spite of*, but *because* of its details. Schegloff and Sacks (1973) explain the basis of the conversation analytic approach as follows:

> We have proceeded under the assumption (an assumption borne out by our research) that insofar as the materials we worked with exhibited orderliness, they did so not only for us, indeed not in the first place for us, but for the coparticipants who had produced them. If the materials (records of natural conversations) were orderly, they were so because they had been methodically produced by members of the society for one another, and it was a feature of the conversations that we treated as data that they were produced so as to allow the display by the coparticipants to each other of their orderliness, and to allow the participants to display to each other their analysis, appreciation, and use of that orderliness. (Schegloff and Sacks, 1973, p. 290)

For example, even a very brief pause may be used by a participant to interpret another person's actions (Heritage, 1987). Imagine that you have just gotten a new hair style, and you walk up to a good friend and say "Do you like my hair style?". If your friend pauses for a second or two before responding with "Yes," you are likely to interpret their response differently than if they produced the same response immediately.

Some research approaches treat the content of talk as something that can be extracted from the interaction. For example, a sociologist using the method of "content analysis" might record an interview with a subject and then make a list of the facts stated in the interview which relate to the researcher's subject of interest. If the researcher was interested in how early experiences in school affected one's later desire to go to college, for example, they might ask subjects about their experiences in grade school and record events such as whether they enjoyed reading, had many friends, or were bullied. For this type of research question it may make sense to extract the content of talk from the interaction through which it was produced. However, from an ethnomethodological perspective the content of talk is inextricable from the stream of human action unfolding on a moment by moment basis. While what people are talking about, the "content" of talk, is typically of interest to both to participants and researchers, conversation analysts are not primarily interested in the subject matter of the talk. They are interested in how people are able to create the organization of the talk itself. The subject matter of interaction cannot be separated from an understanding of the procedures used to create the interaction.

Similarly, while participants' thoughts and feelings can often be inferred from their behavior, the goal of conversation analysis is not to discover or decipher these underlying feelings. When participants are interacting with each other, the only access they have to each other's emotions, thoughts or intentions is through observing each other's actions. Their actions, including the words spoken, their facial expressions, gestures, and the timing of their actions, display their orientation to the interaction. As we learned in the discussion of ethnomethodology in Chapter 2, actions are accountable. Participants therefore make assumptions about their co-interactants as to what is going on inside the other person's head, based on their interpretation of the other's actions. However, participants do not *know* what is going on in each other's heads, and they do not really need to know, in order to competently interact with each other. But if their inferences are incorrect, and they display this incorrect inference in their response, their misunderstanding may be corrected by another. Participants are thereby able to create and maintain intersubjective understanding through the interactional procedures they use to construct their talk. This means, of course, that people can trick or mislead each other. If you are a good actor you can successfully convey an intention or emotion that you do not actually have. This skill can be used in every day interaction (e.g. when telling "white lies"), or when trying to con or swindle someone (Goffman, 1959; 1967).

Sacks (1992a) advised conversation analysts to ask "Why that now?" when trying to understand a particular segment of talk. Human action occurs in real time, in specific instances and occasions, rather than in the abstract or in general. This requires that we look at the context of the interaction in order to understand it. The context can consist of such things as the immediately prior actions, the time and place of the conversation, and the nature of the participants. "Why that now?" then becomes a very specific question. Why does someone say "hm mm" at a specific point in the conversation rather than 0.2 seconds earlier or later? Each action in an interaction can only be understood by co-interactants (or analysts) by examining it in its sequential context.

In short, action is **situated action**, not decontextualized action. Thus when we examine human action we discover that it is impossible to speak about "cause and effect" relationships between actions, because the relationship between one action and another is not mechanistic. The occurrence of the first action does not determine the second. Participants decide how to respond to actions based on their interpretation of that action in the context it occurs within.

Furthermore, as noted in Chapter 2 on "Ethnomethodology," there is a reflexive relationship between human action and context. For example, an action such as asking a question creates a situation in which another is expected to produce an answer. Asking questions may also be a way that a person holding a specific social role (e.g. that of teacher), enacts that role and creates the interaction we know of as "classroom interaction." The context (classroom interaction), is therefore constructed by the talk, while at the same time how participants produce and interpret the talk is shaped by the context. Fairhurst (2009) notes:

> Conversation analysis, in particular, rejects a 'bucket' view of context (Heritage, 1987) in which a priori institutional conditions 'enclose' interaction instead casting context as a product of actors' talk-in-interaction (Heritage, 1997). Similarly, the organization is not some reified object whose properties enclose interaction, but a form that takes shape in and through what actors orient to in talk-in-interaction (Boden, 1994). For example, Gronn (1983) used conversation analysis to demonstrate 'talk as the work', or how administrative work is achieved, in part, by the ways in which conversational sequences both tighten and loosen the reins between a school principal and his teachers. Hierarchy takes shape in conversation analyses of supervisor turn-taking that suggests interactional dominance over subordinates (Tannen, 1994), while male supervisors have been shown to talk longer and interrupt more than female supervisors in committee meetings (Woods, 1988; Zimmerman & West, 1975). In Boden's (1994) ethnomethodologically informed conversation analysis of an academic dean's interactions (and others), we see the organizing potential of leadership actors' turn-taking, agenda-setting, report-giving, decision-making, and the like. For Boden, organizational action coheres as a sequence, and the sequential pacing of talk is 'deeply implicative of organizations themselves' (Boden, 1994: 206). (Fairhurst, 2009, p. 1611)

Data collection for conversation analytic research

Due to the complexity of interaction (and the limits of our memories), conversation analysts rely on technology to create records of interactions which can be studied repeatedly. It is through this repeated observation and familiarity with the details of talk that we are able to do our work. Early conversation analysts relied on audio tape recordings of face-to-face and telephone interactions. As technology developed, videotaping became a common method which expanded the ability of conversation analysts to study social life by providing access to nonverbal behaviors such as facial expressions, gaze direction, gestures and body orientation. These behaviors had been difficult to study systematically prior to the development of video recorders. Currently, with readily available digital video and audio recording technology, many different types of interactions can be recorded easily. The quality and comprehensiveness of the data available for study has thus improved markedly over the decades.

Protecting human subjects

It is essential to ask permission before tape recording or videotaping an interaction for research purposes. Institutions that conduct research (such as universities) have "Institutional Review Boards" whose job it is to ensure that data for research projects involving human subjects is collected in a manner that protects the safety and rights of the subjects. In particular, steps must be taken to obtain permission from your subjects and to protect their privacy. Your institution's Institutional Review Board will have specific requirements and guidelines to help you plan and conduct a research project involving human research subjects.

The importance of using naturally occurring data

Studying interaction in a laboratory setting is generally considered problematic for conversation analytic research (e.g. ten Have, 1999). However, since conversation analysts are ultimately interested in how people construct their interactions, many of the procedures participants use to do so could be studied adequately in a laboratory setting, as long as participants were allowed to speak as they wanted to without being constrained by rules imposed by the experimenter. In fact, some excellent conversation analytic research has been based on conversations collected in laboratory settings. Students who were strangers to each other and were asked to "talk and get to know each other" in a laboratory setting were tape recorded and became the basis of a quite well known body of research on interruptions in talk (e.g., West and Zimmerman, 1983). Many aspects of the ordinary procedures of talk can be adequately studied in laboratory settings because participants are not likely to be aware of or attempt to alter the mechanics of interaction (e.g. how they interrupt someone, when they change the topic of talk, how they select another to speak, and so on) simply because the interaction is occurring in a laboratory.

Nevertheless, naturally occurring interactions are the preferred type of data for conversation analytic studies, in part because they have the potential to teach us more about how people deal with real situations in everyday life. **Naturally occurring data** allows for more grounded explorations of how the context of talk is used by and becomes relevant for participants. When studying talk in workplace and other institutional settings, naturally occurring data are essential. The environment in which the talk occurs, its authenticity and the authenticity of its surroundings are likely to be critical to obtaining accurate examples of behavior in these settings. Such "naturally occurring" data, although more difficult to collect, have the advantage of being unimpeachably "real." The social context of the talk is the indigenous context of that setting rather than the artificial context of the laboratory.

Observer influence

Whether the data for a conversation analytic study comes from a laboratory or a naturally occurring setting, the issue of observer influence on the behavior of participants in the interaction must be considered. While observing interactions (whether in person or via tape recording or videotaping), does not irremediably disrupt the nature of the inter-action, the researcher should consider which method of recording or observing is likely to disrupt it the least. They should also consider what types of changes may have been made by participants because they know they are being observed. These changes are more likely to be in the content of the conversation than in the procedures used to conduct it. For example, depending on the image the participants want to project, they may alter their use of politeness conventions. Some people may be likely to curse less often, while other people will curse more often, depending on the image of themselves they are trying to project. The types of actions conversation analysts are interested in are relatively unlikely to be changed in a way that impedes our ability to analyze them, because the procedures used to organize talk are not typically noticed by participants as they are engaged in the interaction.

My experiences with data collection via observation combined with videotaping is that the effect on the data are minimal. I have several times had the experience while videotaping mediation sessions, of participants coming up to me afterwards and saying, "I forgot you were there," or "I forgot we were being videotaped." Today, videotaping is prevalent in many everyday contexts. Members of the general public are used to being videotaped whenever they go to a bank, ride a school bus, or shop at many stores. In some cities you may even be videotaped when you are in your car waiting for a red light. Because of these changes in our exposure to video recorders, being audio or video recorded does not create as much anxiety as it did previously. It is therefore unlikely to disrupt ordinary conversational routines and practices.

In addition, video recording technology has developed to a high level of sophistication, making the mechanisms used to record much less intrusive than in the past. Today's digital video and audio recorders are small and inconspicuous. Their small size allows for more creativity in the methods used to record data. For example, François Cooren and Boris Brummans have studied interactions between doctors and the refugees they serve by wearing a small video recording device in a medallion around their necks. This method minimizes the intrusiveness of the videotaping, and frees the researcher to observe and interact with the people he or she is studying in the most natural manner possible.

"Collections" of data

As mentioned above, traditional social science research differs from conversation analytic studies in several ways. At the time that conversation analysis was being developed, much social science research was done from a positivist perspective, which means that it was assumed that the truth is out there waiting to be discovered, and that if the appropriate measurement tools were used, scientists could accurately measure and explain social phenomena. This approach relies on theory building and testing via a deductive process involving the creation of hypotheses (educated guesses) about what is happening in the social world. Data are then analyzed to see if the hypotheses are supported, and theories are revised as necessary. In order to scientifically prove or disprove hypotheses, statistical techniques are typically used; these techniques rely on systematically derived samples from the population of interest. The types of samples required may vary, with random samples, representative samples, or stratified samples being suitable for different types of research questions, populations and statistical techniques. For traditional social science research, the sample must be created in a way that either removes or deals with any potential bias in the data so that when the relationship between variables is studied, accurate results can be obtained.

While this methodological approach is appropriate for testing statistical relationships between variables and for testing hypotheses, conversation analysts are not making statistical arguments about the relationships between variables. Instead of studying variables, we are studying human behavior directly. Whether and how an action is related to a subsequent action depends on the local context and is visible through direct observation of the interaction itself. Because of this, random samples are not necessary for conversation analysis. What is more useful for conversation analytic studies are **collections** of data. With a collection of many examples of the same type of interaction or interactional event, one can examine how actions are accomplished across a variety of participants and settings. For example, you might collect a number of examples of topic transitions, and use this collection of data to try to discover the techniques participants use to change topics in conversation.

In order to conduct a conversation analytic study, first decide what phenomenon you are interested in (e.g. how do people turn down invitations), and then collect as many instances as you can find (from a variety of speakers and social settings) of conversations in which people turn down invitations. You then analyze how this action is accomplished by studying the sequential actions of the participants in each example and looking for similarities from one conversation to the next.

Another way to create a collection of data is to decide on a specific type of interaction that one is interested in (e.g. emergency calls to the police, classroom interaction, doctor/patient interaction, or corporate board meetings), collect a number of examples of them and then analyze how interaction is done in that social setting.

For example, Schegloff (1979) used a collection of recordings of telephone calls to study how conversations are typically begun. This paper on telephone call openings is generally considered an exemplary application of the conversation analytic approach to the study of

Table 3.1 Comparison of traditional social science and conversation analytic approaches to research

Traditional Social Science	Conversation Analysis
Objective reality exists and can be measured	Participants construct reality through actions
Deductive approach	Inductive approach
(theory building, testing of hypotheses)	(based on direct observation of human action)
Random or systematic samples	Collections of data
Statistical analysis	Qualitative analysis of action in context

collections of data. Schegloff collected about 500 examples of telephone call openings, some from informal interactions between friends and acquaintances, as well as some service calls (e.g. calls to emergency telephone services such as "911"). It should be noted that because this paper was published in 1979, the telephone calls he studied were conducted on old-fashioned landline telephones, without such features as caller id or differentiated ring tones. As he analyzed the data, he first observed that the ringing of the phone served as a summons to bring the called party to the conversation. When the called party picks up the phone, they typically start by saying "hello." At first glance, this looks like the beginning of the conversation, and it also looks like a greeting. But Schegloff points out that what the person called is doing with this utterance is letting the caller know that they have picked up the phone, moved it to their ear, and are now ready to listen. The called person's "hello" is therefore the *second* turn in the interaction, not the first. It is an answer to the summons (the phone's ringing), rather than a greeting. Schegloff was able to discover this phenomena by observing a "deviant case" in which the phone rang and the caller heard the phone picked up, but no one answered. After a brief pause, the caller (instead of the person called) said "Hello." This example showed that while the called person *should* be the first to speak in a phone call, if they do not speak, then the caller can speak first and use their turn at talk to repair the absence of the called party's response.

Note that Schegloff's argument was not a statistical argument (for example, that in 499 out of 500 calls, the called person speaks first), but an *analytical* argument which incorporated all 500 excerpts, even the so-called "deviant case." The deviant case, in which the caller spoke first, nevertheless displayed an orientation to the rule that the called party should speak first, because the caller used their turn to try to repair the absence of an answer to the summons; they said "hello" in order to solicit this response.

Numerous other studies illustrate the process of creating a collection of data in order to study specific phenomena. For example, Arminen et al. (2010) studied ten hours of videotapes of simulated flights. Since they were interested in how aviation accidents can be avoided, they decided to study how cockpit crew and air traffic control personnel identified and repaired potential errors or misunderstandings during the flight. They therefore examined these data closely and created a collection of instances in which errors were repaired.

Single case analysis

Single case analyses are typically done with the goal of applying current conversation analytic knowledge to the understanding and explication of a single instance of interaction. These single cases are often chosen because the interaction was problematic in nature. The use of conversation analysis can be an effective diagnostic technique to discover the source of communication problems or failures in specific situations. Close analysis of a single case can lead to discoveries about ways to avoid or repair those types of problems or miscommunications. For example, Whalen et al. (1988) analyze an emergency phonecall to the police in which the caller became embroiled in an argument with the call taker. This and other problems in the call prevented them from successfully completing the business of the call (sending an ambulance to the caller's house to help his sick mother). Unfortunately, the delay caused by this argument meant that help did not get to the woman until she had already passed away. This case, which occurred during the 1980s, caused a great deal of media attention at the time. The public and the press argued that the call taker was incompetent and should have ordered the ambulance, because the caller had clearly indicated that his mother had one of the symptoms which is supposed to trigger a "priority one" response from ambulance services—"difficulty breathing."

However, what Whalen et al. (1988) were able to show through a painstaking sequential analysis of the entire call, was that the caller's claim that his mother was having difficulty breathing was not interpreted as a legitimate statement of her condition because the interactional context at that point was no longer that of a straight-forward emergency call. It had become "contaminated" by other activities—including the argument that had erupted between the caller and the call taker. Statements during arguments are interpreted in a different light than statements made when the participants are not engaged in arguing. Thus the authors were able to use a single case analysis to show how it was that the call taker could have not "heard" the caller's symptom description as automatically warranting a high priority response.

About a decade later, Garcia and Parmer (1999) reported on an emergency services call in which a man saw a friend shoot two undercover police officers at close range in the head. After the shooter fled, the witness called emergency services and attempted to get an ambulance for the fatally wounded officers. Again, due to specific aspects of the interaction, the call taker was not able to hear the caller's claim that two police officers were "down" as an authentic report of an actual emergency. She therefore did not give the call the high priority ranking it would have needed to be attended to quickly on that very busy night. As with the call Whalen et al. (1988) analyzed, the public and the press were quick to blame the call taker. While not denying that she held institutional responsibility for the correct completion of the call, Garcia and Parmer (1999) were able to show how the actions of the call taker were understandable, given the sequential organization of the call as it unfolded.

Summary

The methodological approach of conversation analysis differs from many other types of research in the social sciences. Conversation analysts typically rely on naturally occurring data rather than laboratory settings in order to obtain the most authentic data possible. They record the interactions to be studied with audio and or video recorders in order to preserve the interaction in detail so that it can be studied repeatedly, and so that the techniques participants used to construct and coordinate their actions are preserved for study. These recordings are then transcribed in detail using specialized conventions which we will study in the next chapter.

Conversation analysts started out studying ordinary conversations between friends and acquaintances for several reasons. First, the conversations of friends, family members and acquaintances were often relatively convenient and easy to record. Second, it soon became clear that the procedures used to accomplish every day interaction serve as the foundation for the construction of other types of interactions. For example, as we shall see in the second half of this book, the social organization of talk in institutional settings as trials, television news interviews, doctor-patient interactions and so forth are variations of the structure of ordinary talk. In addition, participants in workplace and other organizational settings also participate in ordinary conversations in the workplace; these ordinary conversations can be an important part of "getting the job done" (Koester, 2004; Whalen and Zimmerman, 2005). Because of this, it is advisable for students of conversation analysis to begin by studying ordinary conversations, and then progress to the study of talk in workplaces and other institutional settings after learning the basic procedures used to organize talk (such as turn-taking, topic organization, error correction, opening and closing interactions, and so on). After a chapter exploring the intricacies of the transcription of interactional data, it is these aspects of talk in every day settings that we will explore in the first half of this book.

Student activity

Schegloff's (1979) article on telephone call openings was based on traditional landline phones without caller id, distinctive ring tones, or other technological amenities. He found that the called party almost always spoke first, typically using "hello" as the answer to the summons of the ringing phone. Observe three phone calls that you conduct via cell phone or a landline phone with caller id. For each call, notice who speaks first and how they open the call. If Schegloff had been doing his research today, how would his conclusions have differed from what he found in his 1979 study?

Recommended sources

Have, Paul ten. (2007), *Doing Conversation Analysis: A Practical Guide, Second Edition.* London: Sage.

Maynard, Douglas W. (2003), *Bad News, Good News: Conversational Order in Everyday Talk and Clinical Settings.* Chicago and London: Chicago University Press.

McHoul, Alec and Rapley, Mark, (2001), *How to Analyze Talk in Institutional Settings: A Casebook of Methods.* London and New York: Continuum Press.

Schegloff, Emanuel A. (1987), 'Analyzing single episodes of interaction: an exercise in conversation analysis', *Social Psychology Quarterly,* 50, (2), 101–14.

—(2005), 'On integrity in inquiry… of the investigated, not the investigator', *Discourse Studies* 7(4–5), 455–80.

—(1996), 'Confirming allusions: toward an empirical account of action', *American Journal of Sociology,* 102, (1), 161–216.

Sidnell, Jack. (2010), *Conversation Analysis: An Introduction.* Oxford: Wiley-Blackwell.

Preparing the Data: 4
Transcription Practices

Chapter contents

Introduction

As we learned in Chapter 3, conversation analysts make audio and or video recordings in order to have precise and detailed records of the interactions they study. Since participants construct their talk with a great degree of complexity, we need access to these details in order to understand and analyze it. As a practical matter, these recordings must be transcribed in order for the researcher to work with a large collection of data and to study the details of the interaction carefully. Gail Jefferson developed a system for recording the details of speech, including such elements as timing, shifts in volume, pronunciation, stress, emphasis and intonation. While it is easy for us to understand why we must record the words spoken by participants if we are going to analyze and understand conversations, the need for very detailed notations of how people produced their utterances is less intuitively obvious. In this chapter we will first introduce the most common symbols Jefferson devised for making conversation analytic transcripts. We will then analyze several examples which demonstrate why these types of information must be recorded on the transcripts, and why they are essential for discovering how participants construct and coordinate their actions.

List of basic transcribing conventions

Some of the most commonly occurring transcription symbols that Jefferson developed are listed below. The list shows that conversation analytic transcripts include not only the words spoken, but any audible breaths, laughter, or other sounds produced. How speakers pronounced the words spoken, and whether they used techniques to express stress or emphasis, such as loudness or softness, or changes in pitch are also recorded. Pauses and simultaneous speech are also indicated on the transcripts. An extended list of Jefferson's transcribing conventions can be found in Atkinson and Heritage (1984, pp. ix–xvi).

A comparison of simplified and detailed transcripts

Conversation analysts are not the only types of researchers who make transcripts of talk. Social scientists and researchers in other disciplines (such as communication) may make transcripts of interviews or other research subjects' speech in order to record the data and facilitate analysis of it. Typically, these transcripts record only the words spoken and leave out the details of how the talk was produced. For example, when transcribing an interview with a research subject, scientists who are not working within a conversation analytic

Table 4.1 Simplified version of Gail Jefferson's transcription conventions

Symbol	Definition
.hh hh	Inhalations and exhalations, respectively
ta::lk	Colons indicate a syllable is drawn out
that-	Dash indicates a word was cutoff abruptly
lot	Underlining indicates stress or emphasis
YOU	Capital letters indicate increased volume
°cost°	Degree signs indicate decreased volume
(1.4)	Numbers in parentheses indicate length of pauses (in seconds)
(talk)	Words in parentheses are tentative transcriptions.
( )	Empty parentheses indicate non-transcribable talk or untimed pauses
.,?!	Punctuation generally indicates intonation, not grammatical structure.
heh, hunh	Laughter particles are transcribed as pronounced.
A: [a copy of it] B: [I have]	Brackets indicate simultaneous speech. Some transcripts use slash marks (e.g., "//") to indicate simultaneity.
A: yeah= B: =in order	Equal signs indicate one word is placed immediately after another without pause or overlap.
A: are yuh gonna?	Words spelled as pronounced.

framework would probably not transcribe pauses, errors in speech, hesitations or repetitions. They would record only the "important things"—the words produced that conveyed the subject's meaning. The details of *how* the words are produced are typically considered unimportant and irrelevant. For many non-conversation analytic research projects, these details may indeed be unnecessary. For example, if the goal of the researcher is to extract information and facts about a subject's life from an interview, they may be able get this information by transcribing only the words spoken. However, in order to understand the procedures people use to construct talk itself (which is the purpose of conversation analysis), these details are needed.

It should be noted that some non-conversation analytic researchers also argue for close attention to the details of subjects' speech. They find that details about how the talk is produced can be meaningful for the researchers in ways they might not have anticipated (e.g. Riessman, 1987; DeVault, 1990). We will now examine why several aspects of speakers' utterances—hesitations, pronunciation, laughter, breaths, and overlaps—can be transcribed, and how their transcription enriches our understanding of the interaction and the procedures participants use to produce it.

Transcribing hesitations and pronunciation

If you have ever taken a speech class, you have probably been advised to avoid saying "uh" or "uhm." These common sounds are often used by speakers to fill a pause in their utterance. They are typically considered a marker of poor speech, or a sign or awkwardness or uncertainty. It can indeed be annoying to listen to a speaker who constantly produces these "**filled pauses**." If you were transcribing an interview for a typical research project, you would probably leave them out of the transcript. However, Jefferson (1974) demonstrated that things like "uh" can be useful for interactants, and hence helpful to analysts trying to understand the meaning of the interaction. Let's first look at an example of an utterance as it would have been transcribed if we were just interested in writing down the words spoken:

Excerpt 1: [simplified transcript]
1   A: I told that to the officer.

In Jefferson's (1974) paper, she transcribes what Speaker A actually said as follows:

Excerpt 2: Jefferson (1974, p. 184)
1   A: I told that to thuh- uh- officer.

In Excerpt 2 we see that the speaker produced a **filled pause** or **hesitation marker** ("uh") before saying the word "officer." Note that the word "the" is spelled "thuh" instead of the orthographically correct "the." Jefferson's transcription system enables us to convey, at least roughly, how speakers pronounce words. In English, sometimes the word "the" is pronounced "thee", and some times it is pronounced "thuh." The dash marks ("-") after the words "thuh-" and "uh-" indicate that the speaker cutoff these words abruptly; they stopped suddenly in the middle of producing these words.

Jefferson (1974) demonstrates why these types of details are useful for understanding what was going in the interaction. Hesitation markers and cutoffs often indicate that a speaker is editing their utterance in progress or thinking about what to say next. Jefferson (1974) refers to this type of editing as error repair or error avoidance. In Excerpt 2 there are two clues that editing might be occurring: the use of the hesitation marker "uh" and the use of the cutoffs on "thuh-" and "uh-"). If these details had not been recorded in the transcript, the analyst would not have access to the information that the speaker was editing their utterance.

While in ordinary conversation, the fact that someone is editing their utterance may be only a curiosity or a minor frustration for the listeners, there are times when it can be consequential. For example, if a friend was telling you something very important, and used a number of cutoffs and hesitation markers, you would probably make inferences about their utterance or even their emotional state. For example, you might feel that they are uncertain about what they are saying or that they are unenthusiastic about saying it. In other words, their hesitation is accountable, and becomes part of the information (in addition to the words spoken) that you use to evaluate their utterance and determine what it means. If the hesitations were produced in a more formal interactional setting, for example a trial, they could well be quite consequential in terms of how that utterance is interpreted by the judge or jury.

Another difference between Excerpts 1 and 2 is how the definite article "the" was transcribed. Jefferson (1974) notes that people typically say "thuh" when the word that follows it begins with a consonant (as in "thuh book"), and "thee" when the word that follows it begins with a vowel (as in "thee airplane"). Since the speaker in this example used the pronunciation "thuh" prior to hesitating, and then completed the utterance with the word "officer," the question arises as to whether they replaced a word beginning with a consonant with a word beginning with a vowel.

Jefferson (1974) writes that this utterance was produced by a man who was defending himself against a ticket in traffic court. At least the judge, and possibly also the police officer who had given him the ticket, would have been present during the hearing. Given the social roles of the participants and the institutional context the utterance was produced in, it is possible that the speaker hesitated and revised his utterance. Since "thuh" does not match the word "officer", which begins with a vowel, it is possible that the speaker started to say "cop," but then substituted the more courteous term "officer," perhaps thinking that a formal approach would be more effective in this interaction with the judge in the context of a trial.

In short, the detailed version of the transcript in Excerpt 2 gives us information that is not contained in the simplified version of the transcript in Excerpt 1. First, we can learn something about the procedures participants use to construct their talk—the shared assumptions and commonsense knowledge that enables others to interpret their talk. Errors in speech (which will be examined more thoroughly in Chapter 10), can be corrected ("repaired") or avoided. Hesitation markers (such as "uh") are one of the actions that may reveal to listeners that repair work is being done.

Second, we may learn something about how the speaker defines the event or interaction they are currently engaged in. In Excerpt 2, the fact that the speaker apparently revised his utterance to replace an informal way of referring to the police officer with a more formal way, indicates something about how they defined the institutional context of traffic court. Most people would speak more formally in the context of a court hearing than they would in informal contexts such as conversations with friends and family members. In fact, the more formal nature of traffic court could be said to be created, in part, by choices made by participants, such as this speaker, to produce more formal speech.

Third, the details in Excerpt 2 may be useful to social scientists and other scholars who are interested in studying power and status differences. Perhaps the speaker is showing deference to the judge and/or to the police officer who gave him the ticket by means of this more formal language. In short, the details of interaction are relevant, first of all to the participants who use such details to construct their utterances and interpret the utterances of others, but also for conversation analysts, who can use this information to discover the procedures participants use to construct their actions.

As a practical matter, because the details of how words are pronounced (as in "thee" versus "thuh") are sometimes important, conversation analysts typically record perceptible deviations from standard pronunciation in the transcript. This is why many of the transcripts you will see in this textbook have what look like spelling errors—the transcriber is attempting to record, in a reasonably accurate manner, not just what the speaker said but the way that they said it. While not all of these details end up being useful or important for understanding interaction, it is impossible to know in advance *which* details will be important. Therefore it is the policy of conversation analysts to err in the direction of too much detail rather than too little.

Transcribing laughter

As with hesitation markers such as "uh", social scientists and other researchers often ignore other "extraneous" parts of the speaker's behavior when producing transcripts. Actions such as laughter, coughs or audible breaths are typically not recorded, because they are not deemed important for understanding what the speaker is saying. When any of these actions are transcribed, they tend to be simply noted as present rather than described in detail. For example, the following simplified transcript excerpt shows how participants' laughter might be referred to in a transcript produced by someone who was *not* doing conversation analytic research:

Excerpt 3: Jefferson (1979, p. 81)
1   Ellen: He said well he said I am cheap he said about the big things he
2   says but not the liddle things. (both laugh)

The simplified transcript of this utterance indicates that both participants laughed after Ellen completed her utterance. Compare Excerpt 3 with Excerpt 4, which shows how Jefferson (1979) transcribed the excerpt:

Excerpt 4: Jefferson (1979, p. 81)
```
1   Ellen:   He s'd well he said I am cheap he said .hh about the big things. he
2            says but not the liddle things, hhh HA HA [HA HA HA
3   Bill:                                              [heh heh heh
```

With the simplified version of the transcript in Excerpt 3 you would not be able to see that Ellen laughed first and Bill only joined in with laughter after she had already begun to laugh. The more detailed transcription of the interaction in Excerpt 4 is therefore more informative about what actually happened in the interaction. Jefferson's (1979) analysis of such detailed transcripts of interactions showed that the production of laughter is often quite a subtle interactional process. Speakers often laugh first, in response to their own utterance, thus signaling to their co-interactants that the utterance is a "laughable." The speaker's laughter works as an invitation to the listeners to laugh in response. While at times listeners laugh first, even without an explicit laugh "invitation," they often wait for the invitation. One benefit of waiting may be to avoid the awkward situation of laughing and then discovering that the speaker did not intend their utterance to be funny. If the speaker first displays their understanding of the utterance as a "laughable," there is less risk in responding with laughter.

Jefferson's (1979) analysis of laughter also reveals that the presence or absence of laughter is not a case of discrete, binary categories. There are gray areas; ways in which speakers can hint at laughter before plunging into it unambiguously. For example, notice that in Excerpt 4 Ellen first produces an extended exhalation ("hhh") at the end of line 2 of the transcript. In Jefferson's transcription system, the letter "h" indicates an exhalation, while an "h" preceded by a period indicates an inhalation (as in ".h"). The number of letters indicates the approximate length of the breath. Thus "hhh" is a longer exhalation than "h."

Ellen's utterance in Excerpt 4 has an extended exhalation which is followed by loud laughter particles ("HA HA HA HA HA"). Bill joins in with laughter after this escalated invitation has begun. The exhalation in Ellen's utterance is therefore a tentative invitation to laugh. When Bill does not respond to this tentative invitation, Ellen escalates to an obvious form of the invitation—laughter itself. Thus we can see that the timing of Bill's response to Ellen's utterance suggests that he does not find it as funny as she may be thinking he should. This detailed transcript of the laughter shows that Ellen invited Bill's laughter through a step wise process. This is a different type of interactional event than if both had started laughing together at the same time immediately after the utterance was completed. If a recipient's laughter is not produced until an invitation to laugh has been produced, that in itself may indicate a less enthusiastic reaction to the "laughable" than would be the case if the listener laughed without waiting for an invitation.

Finally, note that the detailed transcription in Excerpt 4 not only shows us when each participant laughed, it also shows us the *nature* of the laughter they produced. In conversation analytic transcripts, capital letters indicate increased volume (loudness), and lower case letters indicate the typical level of loudness for those participants in that interaction. Degree signs (as in "°quiet°") indicate when speakers are speaking noticeably more softly. In Excerpt 4 we see that when Bill does laugh, he laughs less loudly than Ellen did. Her laughter particles are transcribed in upper case letters ("HA HA HA HA HA"), indicating that they were louder than the surrounding speech, while Bill's laughter response ("heh heh heh") was transcribed in lower case letters, indicating that he was laughing in a softer volume than Ellen was. This indicates that his laughter response is less "enthusiastic" than hers. This difference in their responses to Ellen's utterance are not captured by the traditional transcript which merely notes "both laughed," thus implying that the participation of both in this activity was equal. But as we see from the conversation analytic transcript, that is not the case. We can thus learn something about how each participant perceives and interprets the actions of others from the detailed transcripts that conversation analysts produce.

Transcribing audible breaths and simultaneous speech

As noted above, conversation analytic transcripts also include audible inhalations and exhalations. The exhalation in Excerpt 4 which functions as an invitation to laugh illustrates one of the reasons why transcribing audible breaths might be important for our understanding of how interaction works. While people are breathing all the time, not all breaths are audible. Since not all breaths are audible, the question of why they are audible sometimes and not others becomes relevant. Audible exhalations can be used expressively as a "sigh." A common location for audible inhalations is prior to beginning a turn at talk. This use of audible inhalations is visible in line 2 of Excerpt 5. Excerpt 5 is from Bilmes' (2005) study of calls made by listeners to television talk shows. As the excerpt begins, the host of the show ("D") connects a caller who has been waiting on hold. He addresses the caller by the name of the city and state they are calling from ("Gulfbreeze Florida"). He follows this with a question ("are you there?"; line 2). The caller answers this question ("Yes" in line 2), and then immediately produces an audible in breath (".hhh"). This in breath suggests that the caller was getting ready to begin a turn at talk. The host begins speaking at this point, thus preventing the production of the caller's turn by talking over it (line 3). In his turn the host asks the caller to wait until after the "break" (lines 3–4). The brackets ("[") in lines 2 and 3 indicate that both parties began speaking at the same time.

There are two facts in this transcript which support the interpretation that audible in breaths often indicate that a participant is getting ready to begin a turn at talk. The first, in line 2, shows that the caller in fact began a turn after her in breath ("I-"). The second, in lines 3 and 4, is the host's response, the placement of which indicates that he may also have interpreted the caller's audible in breath as indicating that she was readying herself to take a turn. By beginning to speak immediately he forestalls her turn beginning. Note also that the caller cutoff her utterance abruptly (line 2) when the host began speaking (line 3). A number of conversation analysts have studied overlaps and interruptions in speech. The use of detailed transcripts captures details such as these and enables us to study this type of behavior. For example, West and Zimmerman (1983) studied how interruptions vary by gender of participant.

Excerpt 5: Bilmes (2005, pp. 159–60)
1 D: Gulfbreeze Florida are you there?
2 C: Yes .hhh [I-
3 D: [Okay I'll give you a chance. But I ask you to indulge us
4   this one break…

Summary

The examples discussed in this chapter have shown that when transcribing talk, details matter. While one can get at least a superficial sense of the content of the interaction without these details, the procedures used to construct the interaction, the relationship between the participants, and such issues as status differences or levels of involvement in the interaction, are not visible unless one has access to the details through which participants produce their utterances.

   It is worth noting that transcripts never totally complete. When transcribing, you will find that choices always have to be made about what details to include or not include. In general, it is better to err in the direction of too much detail rather than too little. For example, if you left out details such as the transcription of hesitation markers and laughter, you would not be able to discover how repair is done in interaction or how responses to utterances are invited by speakers.

   Compared to the types of transcripts used by linguists, conversation analytic transcripts are imprecise. Linguists use precise systems for notating pronunciation, and some also use sensitive equipment that can time pauses down to hundredths of a second. While this level of precision may be necessary for some types of research, for studies of ordinary interaction what is important is the relative amount of time that passes (Jefferson, 1989). While there have been some minor alterations and embellishments, Gail Jefferson's system of transcription has stood the test of time. It has been widely used by conversation analysts around the world since the 1970s. This system of transcribing talk is an effective means of recording not just the words spoken, but how they are produced, including the coordination of activity between speakers, such as through interruptions and the placement of silences.

Student activity

The two excerpts below show the same brief excerpt from a mediation session. Excerpt 6 shows just the words spoken, and Excerpt 7 shows the detailed transcription of the excerpt.

First read Excerpt 6 out loud. Then read Excerpt 7 aloud, attempting to reproduce as exactly as possible what the transcribing symbols indicate. How does your perception of the excerpt differ when you add the detailed information about how the words were produced and placed?

Excerpt 6: (Garcia and Fisher, 2011, p. 280, simplified transcript)

1	J:	Those are the things I'm concerned with. I'm just I worry and love
2		my children. And just want to see the very best for them. And
3		that's the part that I think that through. And I'm not saying I'm the
4		best daddy in the world but just in this particular case. I think I'm
5		the best parent right now.
6	MA:	Okay.
7	J:	But I don't know that we'll
8	MA:	Now you're home every day Susan?
9	S:	Mm hm
10	MA:	And the children are in school all day.
11	S:	Right.
12	MA:	So what happens after school. Will you be at work after school
13		John?
14	S:	Yes.
15	J:	There are times when I am now. Susan has left out a couple
16		things. She was working. And she quit, got laid off, however you
17		want to…

Excerpt 7: (Garcia and Fisher, 2011, p. 280)

1	J:	Those °are th' things° °°I'm concerned with!°° (0.4) °I'm
2		just,°<I w:orry?> (1.0) An' love? (0.6) °my children.° (0.6)
3		°An' just wanna see thuh very best for them.° (1.5)
4		°An' that's th' part° °that=I think that° .h (1.0) °through:°
5		°°An' I'm not s-°° °sayin' I'm thuh best Daddy in thuh world
6		but just-° (0.7) °°in 'is particular case°° °°°I think I'm
7		thuh best parent right now.°°°
8		(.)
9	MA:	°Okay.°=
10	J:	= °s-° (0.4) But I don't know that (we'll [( )]
11	MA:	[NOW YER]
12		HOM:E (0.6) every day Susan?
13		(0.3)
14	S:	°Mm hm?°
15		(.)
16	MA:	And um (1.2) th'children are in school all day.
17		(0.4)
18	S:	°Right?°
19		(0.5)
20	MA:	So, what happens after school.
21		(1.5)
22	MA:	M- Will=you be=at work after school John?
23		(1.0) ((Susan nods in pause.))

```
24  S:      °Y[es.°]
25  J:       [U:h ] there uh uh time when I am now-. (0.6) Susan='as:
26          left out uh couple things. She was working? (0.5) °A:n'°
27          (0.6) °she?° (1.0) °u:m° .h (1.2) >quit, got laid off, how
28          [ever=you=wanna=s-]
```

Recommended sources

Jefferson, Gail (1979). 'A technique for inviting laughter and its subsequent acceptance/declination', in George
    Psathas (ed.), *Everyday Language: Studies in Ethnomethodology*. New York: Irvington, pp. 79–96.

—(1985), 'An exercise in the transcription and analysis of laughter', in Teun van Dijk (ed.), *Handbook of Discourse
    Analysis, Volume 3: Discourse and Dialogue*. London: Academic Press, pp. 25–34.

—(2004b). 'A note on laughter in 'male-female' interaction', *Discourse Studies*, 6, (1), 117–33.

—(2010). 'Sometimes a frog in your throat is just a frog in your throat: gutturals as (sometimes) laughter-impli-
    cative', *Journal of Pragmatics* 42, 1476–84.

Potter, Jonathan and Hepburn, Alexa (2010). 'Putting aspiration into words: 'laugh particles', managing descriptive
    trouble and modulating action', *Journal of Pragmatics*, 42, 1543–55.

Part II
How Talk Works: The Social Organization of Human Action

5

The Turn Taking System

Chapter contents

Introduction

There are some activities that participants can or should do at the same time. For example, applauding is most effectively done in a group, with everyone in the audience coordinating their actions so that the applause becomes a collective rather than an individual response (Atkinson, 1984). Booing has a similar interactional structure. While an individual may start the process by booing independently, "successful" booing involves a group of people taking up the charge and booing together in a coordinated fashion (Clayman, 1993a).

However, many of the activities we participate in are not successfully accomplished unless people take turns. For example, we take turns when playing a game of cards or a game of baseball. When we go shopping, some stores may ask us to take a ticket with a number on it in order to determine our turn to be served. When going to a movie we may simply wait in line, with the people at the front of the line going in first.

Turn taking is also the convention in social actions involving talk. In some situations and types of activities the rules of turn taking are very explicit and routinized. For example, in a debate, the order of speakers is based on the role each participant will play in the debate.

The person taking the "pro" position speaks first, and the person taking the "con" position speaks second. In the television game show "Jeopardy" the first contestant to ring the buzzer gets to speak.

Turn taking procedures are also used in informal interactions in every day settings. The methods used to organize the exchange of turns at talk may vary with culture, the identity or social standing of the participants, and the nature of the activity the talk is embedded in. For example, in some societies there may be turn taking rules based on social status. Elders may be expected to speak first, men or women may be expected to speak first, or people with higher rank may be expected to speak first. Turn taking systems can also be related to social role or position in an institutional hierarchy. For example, if you were a private in the army, you would probably not speak to a general until he or she addressed you first. However, in ordinary conversation, the order of turns at talk is flexible and emerges during the inter-action rather than being predetermined.

In 1974 Sacks, Schegloff and Jefferson published a highly influential article on how turn taking in conversation is organized (Google Scholar lists over 5,000 citations for this article). Sacks et al. (1974) based their analysis of turn taking on a collection of tape recordings of many different conversations. The turn taking system they found operating in ordinary conversation solves two problems for interactants:

1. How do people know when to begin a new turn? Listeners pay attention to how speakers structure their turn as they are talking in order to figure out when the speaker is probably "done." This is what Sacks et al. (1974) refer to as the "**turn constructional**" component of the turn taking system.
2. If there are more than two participants in a conversation, how do people determine which of them will speak next? Sacks et al. (1974) refer to this as the "**turn allocational**" component of the turn taking system.

The turn constructional component

Sacks et al. (1974) note that turns at talk are made up of grammatical units of a variety of lengths. A complete turn at talk can be constructed out of one or more of the following types of units: a word, phrase, clause or sentence. Listeners try to project the possible completion of these units, in order to locate an appropriate place to take a turn at talk. Excerpt 1 is from a conversation between students in a college classroom. Excerpt 1 illustrates turns constructed out of a range of different types and sizes of units:

Excerpt 1: Conversation between Students

11	Roy:	What year are you?
12		(0.2)
13	Cindy:	I'm uh graduate student.
14		(0.2)
15	Roy:	Oh really!
16		(0.1)

```
17  Cindy:  °Yeah.°
18          (0.2)
19  Roy:    (Well okay) s'you uh soc major?
20          (0.3)
21  Cindy:  Yeup.
22          (0.6)
23  Roy:    Okay, (0.2) so u:m, what exactly do you plan on doing with
24          (that?)
25          (0.2)
26  Cindy:  Well, I'd like to teach!, one of these days,...
```

Constructing a turn out of a single word

In line 21 of Excerpt 1 we see Cindy using a single word to construct a turn at talk which is possibly complete in the context of Roy's question in the previous turn (line 19). Sacks et al. (1974) argue that turn transition is relevant at the end of such possibly complete units. Note that whether transition is relevant depends not just on the words produced or on the grammatical structure of the utterance. The speaker's intonation and the timing of their actions may also project whether their utterance is reaching completion or not. For example, Cindy's answer in line 21 was produced with "period" intonation (it sounded as if she was done). In addition, note that she stopped speaking after producing this one word, thus leaving space in the conversation for Roy to speak. Just because a turn constructional unit is *possibly* complete does not mean that turn transition will necessarily occur, only that it is relevant at this point in the interaction.

Constructing a turn with a complete sentence

There are several turns at talk in Excerpt 1 which are constructed out of grammatically complete sentences (lines 11, 13, 19, and 23–4). If you were a participant in this conversation, and you were listening to Cindy produce the turn in line 13 ("I'm uh graduate student."), you probably would not be able to project the completion of Cindy's utterance after the first word ("I'm") or the second word ("uh"). However, after the third word ("graduate"), you might be able to project the completion of her utterance, so if Roy's response ("Oh really!") had been placed immediately after "graduate," it would not have seemed out of place. Sacks et al. (1974) found that overlaps in speakers' talk often occurs at a point in the utterance where the current speaker's turn completion can be projected. In this instance, Roy waits until Cindy completes her turn and stops speaking before responding at a point where transition in speakership is clearly relevant.

Constructing a turn from a phrase or sentence fragment

Incomplete sentences (such as phrases, clauses, or other sentence fragments) are typically unacceptable in written language but are acceptable (and common) in spoken interaction, assuming that they are produced in an appropriate interactional context. Excerpt 2 shows Ann constructing a turn out of a sentence fragment. In the context of a response to Mark's "that's thuh longest three minutes of my [life.]" (line 1), Ann's sentence fragment "mine too:!," (line 4) is comprehensible as a complete turn at talk. Since utterances are interpreted in the interactional context they occur within, we can infer that Ann is referring to the same thing that Mark has referred to in his utterance—whatever it is that makes it "the longest three minutes" of Mark's life." Although it is an incomplete sentence, line 4 is not an incomplete turn.

```
Excerpt 2: Conversation between Students
1    Mark:     °that's thuh longest three minutes of my [life.°]
2    Ann:                                               [eh ] HENH! hih
3              (1.1)
4    Ann: ->  nhh mine too:! eh hinh hinh
```

In Excerpt 3 there are two examples of sentence fragments being used as complete turns at talk. After Ann says "oh! he was hidding on ev'ry body!" (line 1), a pause elapses and then Barb responds with laughter (line 3). Ann then produces another turn at talk: "=ev'ry girl.=" in line 4. This sentence fragment is hearable as a repair of her prior utterance, specifying that it is only the girls that he was "hitting on" rather than literally "everybody." After some more talk and laughter responses (lines 5 and 6), Barb produces a turn which assesses the person Ann is talking about: ".hh [dir]dy old man!" (line 7). While not a complete sentence, given the interactional context it occurs within this fragment is hearable as a possibly complete turn constructional unit.

```
Excerpt 3: Conversation between Students
1     Alice:    oh! he was hidding on ev'ry body!
2               ( )
3     Barb:     huh=huh=
4     Alice: ->           =ev'ry girl.=
5     Barb:                    =unh=hunh=hunh! .hh (some old man) hhhh
6     Alice:    yeah=unh honh honh honh!
7     Barb: ->  .hh [dir   ]dy old man!
8     Ann:          [yeah]
9               ( )
10    Barb:     .nhh! .n[hh!]
11    Ann:              [°ye]:ah!° (  ) °oh that was super fun though.°=
```

Summary of turn constructional component

These examples have shown that speakers can construct a complete turn at talk out of an utterance of any length or any combination of words, phrases or sentences. Whether an utterance is possibly complete or not depends on its interactional context. Because members of a culture share an understanding of how turns at talk are constructed, listeners can analyze a speaker's utterance-in-progress and "project" when the turn will be possibly complete

(Sacks et al., 1974). This projectability enables participants to identify viable places to take a turn, thus minimizing both interruptions and gaps (extended silences) in talk.

The turn constructional component of the turn taking system for conversation shows how listeners know when a current speaker might be reaching completion of their utterance. However, if there are several participants in the interaction, which of the two or more "listeners" will be the one to speak next? We now turn to the problem of turn allocation—how participants work out who will be the one to take the next turn at talk.

Turn allocation component

The **turn allocation** component of the turn taking system explains how participants determine who will speak next once a transition relevance place has been reached. In the following quote Sacks et al. (1974) describe the turn allocation process in ordinary conversation:

> The following seems to be a basic set of rules governing turn construction, providing for the allocation of a next turn to one party, and co-ordinating transfer so as to minimize gap and overlap.
> (1) For any turn, at the initial transition-relevance place of an initial turn-constructional unit:
>   (a) If the turn-so-far is so constructed as to involve the use of a 'current speaker selects next' technique, then the party so selected has the right and is obliged to take next turn to speak; no others have such rights or obligations, and transfer occurs at that place.
>   (b) if the turn-so-far is so constructed as not to involve the use of a 'current speaker selects next' technique, then self-selection for next speakership may, but need not, be instituted; first starter acquires rights to a turn, and transfer occurs at that place.
>   (c) If the turn-so-far is so constructed as not to involve the use of a 'current speaker selects next' technique, then current speaker may, but need not continue, unless another self-selects.
> (2) If, at the initial transition-relevance place of an initial turn-constructional unit, neither 1a nor 1b has operated, and, following the provision of 1c, current speaker has continued, then the rule-set a-c re-applies at the next transition-relevance place, and recursively at each next transition-relevance place, until transfer is effected. (Sacks et al., 1974, p. 704)

In short, Sacks et al. (1974) found three possible ways the transition to next speaker could be managed. First, a current speaker may select a next speaker. If that does not happen, a next speaker can select themself to speak at a **transition relevance place** in current speaker's utterance. If a next speaker does not select themself, a current speaker can select themself to continue their utterance or to produce another turn.

Participants attend to the current speaker's utterance-in-progress and listen for the end of a possibly complete turn constructional unit (the end of a word, phrase or sentence where the speaker's utterance may be considered possibly complete, given the context it occurs within). These are points in the conversation in which transition to a different speaker is relevant. At any transition relevance place, participants will first listen to see if the current speaker is selecting a next speaker. If they are not selecting a next speaker, then one of the participants may select themself to speak next. If none of the participants select themself to speak next, the current speaker may continue, effectively selecting themself for a second turn at talk. Every time a transition relevance place is produced, this cycling of the turn taking options repeats. We will now examine the techniques used for accomplishing turn taking via each of these options.

Current speaker selects next

A **current speaker may select the next speaker** by constructing their turn so that it solicits a response from only one participant out of the potential next speakers. This is often done by addressing a question to a specific person. Sometimes the recipient of the utterance will be addressed by name, but they can also be selected by nonverbal behaviors such as gaze direction or pointing. A current speaker can also select a next speaker by constructing an utterance to which only one listener amongst those present could reasonably respond. For example, if only one person is holding a book, and the current speaker asks "What are you reading?", this question could reasonably be taken to select the person who has the book as next speaker rather than one of the other persons present.

Excerpt 4 is from a mediation session in which the owner of a vehicle ("Don") is trying to get a refund for the cost of repairs which he believes the auto repair shop did not do correctly. "Rick" and "Steve" are representing the repair shop at the mediation session. There are two mediators facilitating the mediation, "Mediator A" and "Mediator B." As the excerpt begins, Mediator A has the floor:

> Excerpt 4: Garcia West Coast Mediation Data: Mobile Home, p. 21
> 1 MA: Let me ask you <u>this</u> Don?, (1.5) <u>what</u> hh (0.5) do you want <u>do:ne</u>
> 2   (0.4) put your ca::r (0.3) in thuh sha:pe,
> 3   (0.2)
> 4 Don: <u>nothing</u>!
> 5   (0.2)
> 6 MA: that=chou
> 7   (.)
> 8 Don: at Smith's Auto Dealership.

Mediator A's utterance in lines 1 and 2 accomplishes the selection of a next speaker by asking a question of a specific individual (identified by name). The question can also be heard as directed to Don rather than any of the other participants because of Mediator A's reference to "your ca::r" (line 2). Since Don is the one who is complaining about repairs to his car, and since Mediator A's question is about "your car," it can be heard as directed to Don (the owner of the car) rather than to Rick or Steve (the representatives of the repair shop).

Excerpt 5 is from the same mediation session. During this part of the session, the participants are examining the bills and other records of the repairs that have been made to the vehicle.

Excerpt 5: Garcia, West Coast Mediation Data: Mobile Home, p. 17
```
1    Rick:   the::re, should be some freon charged on it
2            (0.3)
3    MB:     °there is.°
4            (5.0)
5    MB:     .h did jou=know=thuh time you picked up thuh vehicle id had not
6            been road tested? (0.6) were you told that?
7            (0.1)
8    Don:    no, thuh guy (0.1) u:h Rick u::h called me aboud I think ih was uh
9            DA::Y before . . . said EV'RYTHING'S SET tuh go . . .
```

In lines 5 and 6, Mediator B selects Don as next speaker. This excerpt differs from Excerpt 4 in that the person selected as next speaker is not identified by name. Instead, Mediator B relies on the question format of her utterance (lines 5–6) along with the content of her utterance which again is clearly directed at Don (as the owner of the vehicle). In addition, notice that at the beginning of line 5 Mediator B stresses the pronoun "you" (".h did jou"). Previous research has shown that when multiple participants are present, speakers often use stress on the pronoun "you" to indicate that someone other than prior speaker is being identified by that pronoun (Garcia, 1989; Lerner, 1993).

Next speaker selects self

The **next speaker selects self** turn taking option only applies if the current speaker has not selected a next speaker. Excerpt 6 is an excerpt from a mediation session between "Roger" and "Cheryl". Roger is the owner of a carpet company that has installed wall-to-wall carpeting in Cheryl's home. Unfortunately, the installers placed the carpet so that a seam between two sections of carpet is clearly visible in the middle of her living room floor. Cheryl is trying to get Roger to agree to replace the carpeting in that room. However, carpet of the same dye lot is no longer available, so it would be impossible to match the color of the carpet exactly. In lines 1 and 2, Roger makes a suggestion to try to work around this problem:

Excerpt 6: Garcia, West Coast Mediation Data: PC, p. 11
```
1    Roger:   What if we took it out of your clo:set, (1.0) a:n' took this
2             piece an' put it in your closet. How would that affect you.
3             (1.4)
4    Cheryl:  .hh I don' know that we're going to, be any better o::ff!=
5    MA:                                                            =Now
6             your clo:sets are about two feet deep? (0.8) yih- you'd end up
7             with uh two foot strip, is=at what yer saying?
```

In line 2 Roger asks, "How would that affect you." Cheryl is able to hear Roger's question as directed at her because she is the owner of the house with the carpeting and the closets that he refers to in lines 1 and 2. When he says, "affect you" in line 2, "you" is hearably the same person that "your closet" referred to in lines 1 and 2. When Cheryl speaks in line 4, she is therefore doing so in response to another speaker's question, and has not selected herself to speak next. Cheryl reaches a possibly complete turn construction unit in her utterance after "better o::ff:!". Mediator A then selects himself to speak at this transition relevance place. He uses his turn (line 5) to ask questions about the possibility of using carpet from the closets to repair the carpet in Cheryl's living room.

Observe that there are equal signs between Cheryl's and Mediator A's utterances in lines 4 and 5, indicating that there was no gap or overlap between their turns—they were run together seamlessly. Why is it that Mediator A allowed no pause to elapse before responding? His promptness may be due to the fact that there are four participants in this interaction: Roger, Cheryl, Mediator A, and Mediator B. Sacks et al. (1974) found that if there are two or more "listeners" in a conversation, and a current speaker's utterance reaches a transition relevance place, the listener who starts speaking first is the one who typically gets the turn. Hence, there is a motivation for beginning a turn quickly. This explains some of the overlaps which occur at transition relevance places (Sacks et al., 1974).

Current speaker continues

The third turn exchange procedure can be used when a speaker reaches a transition relevance place in their utterance, but no one else is selected or selects themself to speak next. In this instance the current speaker can continue, either adding to their prior turn or selecting themself for a new turn at talk. Sacks et al. (1974) wrote:

> If the turn-so-far is so constructed as not to involve the use of a 'current speaker selects next' technique, then the current speaker may, but need not continue, unless another self-selects. (Sacks et al., 1974, p. 704)

At times the **current speaker continues** turn taking option is used when a pause follows a current speaker's transition relevance place. The pause indicates that other participants had an opportunity to select themselves as next speaker but passed on the opportunity to do so. The current speaker then selects himself to speak next.

Excerpts 7 and 8 show current speakers selecting themselves to speak next after a transition relevance place followed by a pause. Excerpt 7 is from a conversation between three students which was recorded in class. In line 4, "Bob" produces a possibly complete turn ("Yeah you weren't even out there.") with completion intonation (the period indicates falling intonation which sounded like the person was done speaking). While either Mark or Ken could have selected themselves to speak next during the pause following this utterance, neither does so (line 5). Bob then selects himself to speak again in line 6: "we had=uh s seven o'clock run…".

Excerpt 7: Conversation between Students
1   Ken: yeah it was <u>so:</u> co:ld when I walked [out this] morning.
2   Mark: [um hm]

```
3              (   )
4    Bob:      Yeah you weren't even out there.
5              (   )
6    Bob:      we had=uh s seven o'clock run it was free[zing,
7    Ken:                                               [yeahhhhh
```

In Excerpt 8, two college students are discussing a mutual friend. Liz completes a possibly complete turn in line 1 ("She's good."). Her cointeractant, Tina, does not select herself to speak at this transition relevance place. After a brief pause, Liz selects herself for another turn, and produces a second possibly complete unit ("She went back to school."; line 3). Tina does not respond to this utterance either, and after a pause Liz selects herself to speak again ("before I did."; line 5). This excerpt therefore contains two instances of a current speaker selecting themselves as next speaker.

```
Excerpt 8: Conversation between Students
1    Liz:    She's good.
2            (0.5)
3    Liz:    She went back to school.
4            (0.5)
5    Liz:    before I did. °so.°=
6    Tina:                  =weren't you going out to see her?
```

Summary of turn allocation procedures

When a current speaker's utterance reaches a transition relevance place:

1. If the current speaker's utterance selects a next speaker, that person may have the floor for a turn at talk.
2. If the current speaker does not select a next speaker, a next speaker may select themselves to speak next.
3. If a current speaker does not select a next and a next speaker does not select themselves, then the current speaker may continue.

Figure 5.1 Summary of Sacks et al. (1974) Turn taking procedures for ordinary conversation

Facts about conversation explained by the turn-taking system

Sacks et al. (1974) describe many of the commonly observed facts about ordinary conversation that are explained by the turn taking system:

1. Speaker-change recurs, or at least occurs.
2. Overwhelmingly, one party talks at a time.
3. Occurrences of more than one speaker at a time are common, but brief.
4. Transitions (from one turn to a next) with no gap and no overlap are common. Together with transitions characterized by slight gap or slight overlap, they make up the vast majority of transitions.
5. Turn order is not fixed, but varies.
6. Turn size is not fixed, but varies.
7. Length of conversation is not specified in advance.
8. What parties say is not specified in advance.
9. Relative distribution of turns is not specified in advance.
10. Number of parties can vary.
11. Talk can be continuous or discontinuous.
12. Turn-allocation techniques are obviously used. A current speaker may select a next speaker (as when he addresses a question to another party); or parties may self-select in starting to talk.
13. Various 'turn-constructional units' are employed; e.g., turns can be projectedly 'one word long', or they can be sentential in length.
14. Repair mechanisms exist for dealing with turn-taking errors and violations; e.g., if two parties find themselves talking at the same time, one of them will stop prematurely, thus repairing the trouble. (Sacks et al., 1974, pp. 700–1)

As Nofsinger (1991, pp. 87–90) summarizes, in conversation "[o]nly one participant usually speaks at a time, and overlap, when it occurs, is brief." This is not to say that interruptions never occur, but most of the time participants are able to organize their contributions to the conversation such that they do not overlap other's speech. Overlaps in speech commonly occur at transition relevance places, as potential next speakers try to start quickly in order to be first speaker and hence get the floor.

In ordinary conversation (unlike in debates which we considered at the beginning of this chapter), the order of turns and their distribution among participants is not determined in advance. The order and distribution of turns varies within and between conversations. As you can see from the turn allocation procedures described above, there is nothing and no one external to the conversation which controls when an individual contributes to the interaction. Any participant may become a current speaker at some point in the conversation. The role of next speaker can be claimed by any participant in the interaction if a current speaker does not select a next speaker. Therefore a defining characteristic of ordinary conversation is that participants are not constrained in advance as to how often or when in the conversation they will participate. Whatever pattern of participation emerges was created "organically" by the participants through their application of the turn taking procedures each time a transition relevance place was reached in a current speaker's turn. Sacks et al. (1974) refer to this process of emerging structure as **local management.**

Sacks et al. (1974) also note that the length of turns varies in ordinary conversation. Current speakers are free to construct their turns out of any type or length of grammatical units, and can even combine multiple units into an extended turn at talk by using timing, pausing, conjunctions and intonation to cue the listeners that any possibly complete units within the turn are not to be taken as transition relevance places.

In addition, notice that the turn taking system has nothing to say about what people are talking about. There are no assumptions or limits on what types of topics can be discussed, or what if any content has to be addressed in anyone's turn. Conversationalists typically end up discussing something, but what that topic is typically emerges through the joint action of participants rather than having been pre-specified (e.g. as in a debate).

Finally, Sacks et al. (1974) observe that speaker change occurs. Without transitions from one speaker to the next, it would not be a conversation, it would be a monologue, a speech or a failed attempt at a conversation. Nofsinger (1991, p. 92) notes that "[a] speaker who wishes to produce an utterance several units long is subject to losing the turn at each transition relevance place, where any listener may self-select." When a transition relevance place is produced by a current speaker, all potential next speakers are then put in a state of competition with each other for who is going to be the one to get the floor. Thus a motivation for listening is built into conversational structure. In order for a participant to know whether they have been selected by a current speaker as next speaker, or when a turn constructional unit in the current speaker's utterance is possibly complete so that they can select themselves to speak next, they must listen fairly carefully to the current utterance as it is being produced.

The fact that potential speakers can compete with each other to become next speaker indicates that the turn taking system of ordinary conversation is organized like an "economy" (Sacks et al., 1974). The scarce resource (turns at talk) gets allocated in ways that provides for competition for turns between current speakers and potential next speakers. Current speakers who wish to keep speaking have to "fend off" potential attempts to take the floor by constructing their turn-in-progress so that it either avoids possibly complete units or protects them from incursion (e.g., by strategic use of timing, intonation, conjunctions, and so on). Another technique that can be used to protect a multi-unit current turn from incursion by others at possibly complete unit types is the use of story projections or pre-sequences. These techniques will be discussed in Chapter 12.

Turn-taking in talk in institutional settings

As we will see in detail in the second half of this book, the turn taking system in ordinary conversation is a basic format which is then varied in systematic ways to produce the type of interactions that occur in a variety of organizational and institutional settings. Sacks et al. (1974) refer to these variations in procedures which lead to different structures of talk as "**speech exchange systems.**" Let us briefly consider the speech exchange system of television news interviews as an example of how talk in institutional settings differs from ordinary conversation.

Greatbatch (1988) found that the turn taking system in television news interviews differs systematically from that used in ordinary conversation. While in ordinary conversation the order of turns is not predetermined, in television news interviews the interviewer speaks first and the interviewee speaks second. In a conversation, the type of turns produced is not predetermined, with any one free, for example, to produce a question. However, in news interviews it is the interviewer who produces the questions and the interviewee who answers them. While in a conversation the topic of talk is free to vary and is determined by the participants, in television news interviews the interviewer selects the topic of talk. In short, the speech exchange system of news interviews varies in several key ways from ordinary conversation, and these differences are closely tied to the turn taking system. These variations in the turn taking system allow us to create interactions with very different structures in order to meet the needs of a wide range of institutional and organizational contexts. We will investigate the organization of various types of talk in institutional settings in the second half of this book. We now turn to furthering our understanding of the fundamental procedures used to create ordinary conversations as well as other types of speech exchange systems. The next chapter will address how participants use sequences of turns at talk to accomplish specific actions such as asking questions, making invitations, requesting favors, and so on.

Student activities

1. Sacks (1984) argued that by following routine procedures for everyday interactions one could "do being ordinary"; present oneself as a "normal," typical person. Similarly, Garfinkel (1967) wrote about the accountability of human action. When we do not follow routine procedures, such as those for turn taking, our behavior is noticeable and potentially problematic. What types of accounts might cointeractants make (explanations or excuses for behavior) given the following violations of turn taking procedures?
   a. One person is in the middle of an explanation and another person starts speaking before she has reached a possibly complete turn constructional unit.
   b. A speaker selects another to speak next by asking them a question, but that person does not respond.
2. Write a short dialogue involving three participants which includes the following:
   a. Examples of possibly complete turns consisting of only one word, one sentence and one phrase.
   b. At least one instance where a turn exchange occurs at a transition relevance place, and at least one where it does not.
   c. At least one example of each of the turn allocation options (current speaker selects next, next speaker selects self, and current speaker continues).

Recommended sources

Ford, Cecilia E. (2008), *Women Speaking Up: Getting and Using Turns in Meetings*. New York: Palgrave Macmillan.

Greatbatch, David. (1988), 'A turn-taking system for British news interviews', *Language in Society*, 17, 401–30.

Sacks, Harvey, Schegloff, Emanuel A. and Jefferson, Gail. (1974), 'A simplest systematics for the organization of turn-taking for conversation', *Language*, 50, (4), 696–735.

6 Adjacency Pairs, Preference Organization, and Assessments

Introduction

In Chapter 5 we noted that turns at talk are constructed out of a range of grammatical units of different sizes. Speakers can build complete turns at talk from very brief units, such as individual words or phrases, or from larger units such as sentences, sentence fragments or combinations of sentences (Sacks et al., 1974). These grammatical units can be thought of as the building blocks of turns. The fact that speech is built out of grammatical units is not a new insight; linguists have been studying the grammatical structure of language for decades. The ethnomethodological twist on this is to notice how the way turns at talk are constructed facilitates interaction. Participants use grammatical units as a resource to project when a current speaker may be done with an utterance, and hence when a transition in speakership may become relevant. Similarly, a current speaker can use turn constructional units to protect their hold on the floor if they want to continue speak, or to solicit a next speaker, if they do not. Turn constructional units thus provide structure to the conversation on a turn by turn level, and enable participants to exchange turns at talk. Individual turns at talk can also be designed to create longer sequences of turns through which complex interactional tasks can be accomplished. In this chapter we will begin to explore how sequences of utterances can be used as building blocks to create actions that take more than one turn at talk, and more than one participant, to be accomplished. The basic building block for most of these more complex structures is the adjacency pair (Schegloff and Sacks, 1973; Sacks et al., 1974).

Adjacency pairs

An **adjacency pair** is a sequence of two utterances in which the relationship between the utterances is closer than that between most turns at talk. Schegloff and Sacks (1973) define adjacency pairs as having the following characteristics:

1. A sequence of two actions each produced by a different person.
2. The two actions typically occur adjacently.
3. The two actions occur in a specific order.
4. The first action in the sequence is doing different work than the second action.

The technical terms for the two parts of an adjacency pair are "**first pair part**" and "**second pair part**." This terminology is intended to reference the fact that we are talking about a pair of utterances, one of which comes first (the first pair part), and the other of which comes second (the second pair part). Given a first pair part, only certain types of second pair parts are possible. Once a speaker produces a first pair part, the type of action that should come next is limited by the nature of the first pair part.

The following are examples of commonly occurring adjacency pairs:

summons/answer
question/answer
greeting/greeting
goodbye/goodbye
invitation/accept or decline
compliment/deny or accept
request/grant or refuse
accusation/deny or admit
offer/accept or refuse

Notice that specific types of second pair parts are tied to specific types of first pair parts. Thus a question is followed by an answer, not a return greeting (unless the greeting is used sarcastically, as in "hello?", to indicate that one has asked a dumb question). A goodbye is routinely followed with a return "goodbye," rather than a "hello." What type of second pair part is expected depends on which type of first pair part has been produced.

If the second pair part does not occur, its absence will be noticeable and accountable. We covered the concept of "accountability" in Chapter 2 of this text. Briefly, this ethnomethodological concept refers to the fact that participants make inferences by interpreting others' actions and evaluating whether they are consistent with routine norms, procedures and background knowledge shared by members of that culture. We noted that Garfinkel's (1967) breaching experiments revealed the fundamental accountability of human action by deliberately violating common sense procedures in order to observe how people reacted. Their emotional (or at least noticeable) reactions to these procedural violations indicated that the procedures were accountable.

Adjacency pairs have what Schegloff (1979) calls the property of "**conditional relevance.**" The property of conditional relevance is what makes a sequence a sequence, rather than just two utterances that happen to occur adjacently in a conversation. It is also what makes noticing the "absence" of a response possible. Schegloff describes conditional relevance as follows:

> [G]iven the first, the second is expectable, upon its occurrence it can be seen to be a second item to the first, upon its nonoccurrence it can be seen to be officially absent. (Schegloff, 1968, p. 364)

This means that when the first pair part is produced, it creates an expectation that an appropriately matched second pair part will be the next action in the interaction. And if it is not produced, its absence will be oriented to by the other participants, who may display this orientation in their response to its absence. For example, a participant may try to repair the absence of the second pair part by repeating the first pair part, thus giving the recipient a second chance to respond.

A summons and the answer to a summons are a commonly occurring type of adjacency pair. When we summon someone, for example by calling out a friend's name when we see them walking down the street, we expect that summons to be answered. If it is not answered, then the absence of that answer is accountable (Schegloff, 1968, p. 369). If we attempt to summon someone for a conversation by calling them on the phone, the ringing of the phone is a summons. If they do not respond, we may construct an account for the absence of the answer, such as perhaps the person we have called is not home or is asleep. If the telephone is picked up when it rings, but the called person does not say "hello," their answer to the summons is still missing. The caller may try to get them to respond by asking "Hello?" or "Are you there?" The caller will not start the conversation until the called person has displayed their availability for interaction by answering the summons.

The following examples illustrate how participants display an orientation to the conditional relevance of adjacency pairs. Excerpt 1 shows an interaction between two co-present individuals. Carol summons Anne by addressing her by name (line 1). When Anne does not reply (note the silence in line 2 of the transcript) Carol repeats the summons by addressing her again. The second time she produces the summons she stresses the name (as indicated by the underlining in the transcript). This second summons is successful in eliciting a response from Anne. She answers the summons with the word "What" (line 4), indicating that she has heard the summons and is available to talk.

Excerpt 1: (Nofsinger, 1991, p. 54)
1   Carol: Anne
2   ((silence))
3   Carol: <u>Anne</u>
4   Anne: What

Carol's repair of Anne's missing answer to the summons displays her orientation to the fact that an answer was expected. She thus shows the conditional relevance property at work, by indicating that Anne's failure to reply was accountable.

In Excerpt 2 from a call to the police, the dispatcher answered the summons of the ringing phone with the categorical identification "Police Desk" in line 1 of the call. He then waited for the caller to respond. When the caller did not respond, he produced a summons of his own to try to elicit a response from the caller (the second "Police Desk" in line 1). When this summons was also not answered, the dispatcher reissued the summons in line 2 and repeated the summons until it was answered. In line 3 the caller finally speaks.

Excerpt 2: (Schegloff, 1968, p. 369)
0   ((phone rings))
1   D: Police Desk (pause). Police Desk (pause).
2   Hello, Police Desk (longer pause). Hello.
3   C: Hello.
4   D: Hello (pause) Police Desk?
5   C: Pardon?
6   D: Do you want the Police Desk?

Excerpt 3 also illustrates the conditional relevance property of adjacency pairs, by showing a participant displaying an orientation to the expectation that if he is summoned he should answer that summons. There are apparently several people in a room, and Jim says in line 1 "Did somebody over there say 'Jim'?", thus showing his concern that he not be seen to be ignoring a summons. If he ignored the summons, people might think he was rude or inattentive. By checking to make sure that he does not accidentally ignore a summons Jim displays an orientation to the conditional relevance property of adjacency pairs.

Excerpt 3 (Nofsinger, 1991, p. 54)
((Jim turns from another conversation))
1   J: Did somebody over there say "Jim"?
2   U: No.
3   J: Oh ((turns back to the other conversation))

The concept of indexicality is also critical for understanding how adjacency pairs work, because what makes an utterance an adjacency pair second pair part is its position in the interaction. As an example, consider a relatively obscure joke. This joke requires the joke teller to have at least one confederate (a participant who already knows the joke and secretly plays along with the teller). The joke teller says something like "The elephant and the hippopotamus were taking a bath. And the elephant said to the hippo, 'Please pass the soap.' The hippo replied, 'No soap, radio.'" At this point the confederate (who is pretending that this is the first time they have heard this joke), starts laughing hysterically, as if the joke were very, very funny. The person who was told the joke is then left wondering why it is funny, and why everyone else "gets it," but they do not. Typically, the recipient of the joke will pretend to get it, and laugh along with the others, just so they won't look stupid. The joke teller and the confederate then laugh at the recipient for pretending to get it, because the joke is, in fact "ungettable." "No soap, radio" is not a punch line, it is a nonsensical statement which is not an answer to the request "Please pass the soap." Our attempts to interpret the utterance "No soap, radio" as a possible response to the request "Please pass the soap" derives from its placement after that request.

The three hypothetical adjacency pairs below illustrate how indexicality is relevant for the identification of adjacency pair first and second pair parts:

Excerpt 4 (Hypothetical)
1   A: Do bees make honey?
2   B: Yes.

Excerpt 5 (Hypothetical)
1   A: What do bees make?
2   B: Do bees make honey?

Excerpt 6 (Hypothetical)
1   A: Would you like a new car?
2   B: Do bees make honey?

In Excerpt 4 the sentence "Do bees make honey?" is used by Speaker A as a question (a first pair part in an adjacency pair), and receives the answer "yes." In Excerpt 5, the sentence "Do bees make honey?" is used as the answer to a question (a second pair part). It serves as a tentative answer, in which an answer is suggested, but the speaker also indicates that she or he is not sure whether this is the correct answer or not. The question format of the utterance, along with the rising intonation at the end of the utterance, signal this tentativeness. In Excerpt 6, the sentence "Do bees make honey?" is also used as the answer to a question, but in a very different way than it was used in Excerpt 5. In the context of the question "Would you like a new car?", the answer "Do bees make honey?" serves as a playful or sarcastic answer to the question. In this case it means "yes, of course" rather than providing a literal answer to the question.

These examples illustrate that the same utterance means very different things depending on where it is placed in the interaction (this is indexicality). Also, note that the same utterance can function as either a first pair part or a second pair part of an adjacency pair depending on how it is used in the interaction. Thus the identification of adjacency pairs, like the identification of any human action, is not possible without knowing the interactional context it occurs within. This context necessarily includes the immediately prior utterance as a primary context.

Preference organization

Recall from the list of adjacency pairs in the section above, that for some types of adjacency pairs, there are two categories of second pair parts rather than just one. For example, while a greeting is typically responded to with a return greeting, an invitation may be responded to with either an acceptance or a declination of the invitation. Similarly, a request may be either granted or refused, and an accusation may be either denied or admitted. We will consider the implementation of these alternative second pair parts in this section of the chapter.

While accepting or declining an invitation are logically equivalent choices, they are not socially equivalent activities. It is much easier and more comfortable to accept an invitation than to reject it. If you were to ask someone "Would you like to go to the movies with me?" and they simply said "Yes" or "Sure," their use of a simple one word response would probably not seem odd. However, imagine that you asked someone to go to the movies and they just said "No." Unless their declination of the invitation was mitigated in some way, for example if accompanied by an excuse or explanation (as in "I'd like to go to the movies with you, but I have to work tonight."), their rejection may seem insensitive or even downright rude. Thus while accepting an invitation can be accountably performed in a brief, straightforward utterance which is placed immediately after the invitation, declining an invitation is socially more complex and requires a different structure or "organization" in order to accomplish the work of rejecting the invitation.

Both acceptances and declinations of invitations are second pair parts to the adjacency pair first pair part, but they are not socially equivalent actions. Therefore, they are not typically done in the same way. Conversation analysts use the term "**preference organization**" to refer to these differences in how adjacency pair second pair parts are constructed.

The concept of preference organization is complex and has been used in different ways by different researchers (e.g. Pomerantz, 1984, Sacks, 1987a; Sacks and Schegloff, 1979; Schegloff, 2007a). While some of these other uses of preference organization will be discussed in later chapters (e.g. in Chapter 10 we will discuss how preference organization works when participants are repairing mistakes in their utterances), in this chapter we will first address how preference organization applies to the production of alternative categories of second pair parts of adjacency pairs, and then address how it works for responses to assessments.

We will begin by clarifying what preference organization is not. When conversation analysts use the concept preference organization, they are not talking about what a specific individual prefers. For example, consider the hypothetical case of Fred who is inviting people to a party. He may have any number of emotions or opinions about the people he is inviting. Hopefully, most of these people he really wants to attend the party. We might therefore say that he would prefer that these people accept the invitation. However, Fred may feel obligated to invite some people that he really does not want to come to the party. Perhaps he feels that if he does not invite his girlfriend's best friend he will be in big trouble, so he invites her even though he would rather she did not come to his party. In this case, he prefers that she not accept the invitation. While these individual preferences may be very real, they are not what conversation analysts mean by "preference organization." Preference organization in conversation has to do with what is interactionally preferred, what type of action is preferred within a specific culture or society, rather than what specific individuals prefer.

For example, in many cultures the acceptance of an invitation is more socially acceptable than declining the invitation. Acceptance is therefore considered a "preferred" second pair part, while declination is "dispreferred." There are a number of types of adjacency pairs for which the preferred response is a "positive" response.

Invitation:	Acceptance	(Preferred)
	Declination	(Dispreferred)
Request:	Grant	(Preferred)
	Refusal	(Dispreferred)
Offer:	Accept	(Preferred)
	Refuse	(Dispreferred)

Accepting an invitation, granting a request or accepting an offer are typically easier to do interactionally and are less problematic for the participants than the "negative" responses of declining an invitation, refusing to grant a request or rejecting an offer.

For some other types of adjacency pairs, a "negative" response is preferred:

Accusation:	Deny	(Preferred)
	Admit	(Dispreferred)
Self-Deprecating Remark:	Disagree	(Preferred)
	Agree	(Dispreferred)
Compliment:	Reject	(Preferred)
	Accept	(Dispreferred)

Admitting guilt in response to an accusation is a different type of action than accepting an invitation. If someone accuses you of something, admitting guilt could put you in an awkward situation, socially if not practically. Denying an accusation is therefore the preferred response (Atkinson and Drew, 1979; Garcia, 1991; Heritage, 1984).

Similarly, as Pomerantz (1984) points out, if someone produced a self-deprecating remark and the recipient agreed with it, this could also be interactionally problematic. A disagreement with a self-deprecation is therefore the preferred response. For example, of the two hypothetical examples below, Excerpt 7 is probably much more likely to occur. Agreeing with a self-deprecating remark may risk offending the person making the remark. It could also be taken to be a sarcastic rather than a genuine response. Because B's response in Excerpt 8 is dispreferred, it would probably not be formulated the way it is in the hypothetical example (unless B intended to offend or to be sarcastic).

Excerpt 7: (Hypothetical)
1   A: I'm such a klutz.   (Self-Deprecation)
2   B: No you're not.   (Preferred Second Pair Part)

Excerpt 8: (Hypothetical)
1   A: I'm such a klutz.   (Self-Deprecation)
2   B: Yes, you are.   (Dispreferred Second Pair Part)

For compliments, the polarity is analogous, with rejections of compliments being the preferred response (Pomerantz, 1978a). Accepting a compliment might be seen as arrogant or immodest.

Note that which type of second pair part is preferred may vary from one society to another. For example, Chong (2006) compares how gifts are offered and accepted in the United States and South Korea. In the United States, if one is given a gift, the preferred response is to accept the gift and thank the gift-giver (regardless of whether the gift is something you want or not). However, in South Korea the preferred response is to decline the gift at least several times before finally accepting it.

In a given society, certain types of actions can be performed without creating social awkwardness, without being "accountable." These preferred actions can be performed without delay, mitigation or explanation. However, actions that are dispreferred can not be performed in the same way. In order to perform these dispreferred actions, participants use procedures used to mitigate the threat to face (Goffman, 1967) or damage to the relationship that may occur if the matter is not handled delicately.

> Every person lives in a world of social encounters, involving him either in face-to-face or mediated contact with other participants. In each of these contacts, he tends to act out what is sometimes called a line—that is, a pattern of verbal and nonverbal acts by which he expresses his view of the situation and through this his evaluation of the participants, especially himself. Regardless of whether a person intends to take a line, he will find that he has done so in effect. The other participants will assume that he has more or less willfully taken a stand, so that if he is to deal with their response to him he must take into consideration the impression they have possibly formed of him. The term face may be defined as the positive social value a person effectively claims for himself by the line others assume he has taken during a particular contact. Face is an image of self delineated in terms of approved social attributes—albeit an image that others may

share, as when a person makes a good showing for his profession or religion by making a good showing for himself.

(Goffman, 1967, pp. 5–7)

Dispreferred responses may threaten the face of the co-interactant, or embarrass them or lessen their status. Therefore, participants tend to avoid dispreferred responses if possible. This is one of the reasons why **preferred second pair parts** are more common than **dispreferred second pair parts**. In order to minimize threats to face or social awkwardness that a dispreferred action might create, dispreferred responses are constructed differently than preferred responses. Dispreferred responses are typically preceded by some form of delay, are generally formulated indirectly and are typically formulated with mitigation techniques and/or accounts or explanations for the dispreferred response (Pomerantz, 1984; Schegloff, 2007a).

Excerpt 9 shows a dispreferred response to an invitation which is rejected by the invitee. As will be apparent, this example was collected prior to the invention of cell phones, answering machines, and call forwarding—in order to get the calls in response to her newspaper advertisement, Speaker A had to stay home to answer the phone:

Excerpt 9: (Pomerantz, 1978a, pp. 86–7)

```
1   B:   Uh if you'd care to come over and visit a little while this morning, I'll
2        give you a cup of coffee.
3   A:   Hehh! Well that's awfully sweet of you,
4        I don't think I can make it this
5        morning um, I'm running an ad in the paper
6        and- and uh I have to stay near the phone.
```

Speaker A uses several techniques to construct her declination of this invitation as a dispreferred response (Pomerantz, 1978a; Schegloff, 2007a; Sidnell, 2010). The first action she performs is a brief laughter particle ("Hehh!"; line 3). This serves as an audible "smile" (this is a phone conversation), which serves to soften the blow of the rejection. It also serves as a "filled pause" which delays the actual beginning of her utterance. When she does begin the utterance, she begins with "Well." Pomerantz (1984) and others note that "well" is disagreement-implicative, projecting that a declination of the invitation is coming. But what follows next is not a declination, it is a compliment: "that's awfully sweet of you," (line 3). The compliment also serves to delay the production of the actual rejection while at the same time working to mitigate the threat to face (Goffman, 1967) that may be created by the rejection. Compliments or other "gifts" often occur in the middle of dispreferred responses. Speaker A produces the actual declination following this compliment: "I don't think I can make it this morning." Note that Speaker A never actually says "no," instead she expresses this thought indirectly by saying she "can't make it." Notice also the uncertainty marker "think" (line 4) which makes A's rejection tentative instead of final and definite. After reaching a possibly complete turn constructional unit in line 5 after "morning," she uses a filled pause ("um") to hold the floor rather than creating a clear transition relevance place. She adds an explanation or account for why she can not accept the invitation: "I'm running an ad in the paper and-and uh I have to stay near the phone." (lines 5–6). This explanation also serves to mitigate the rejection, by showing that it is not lack of interest that makes her decline the invitation, it is that she has other obligations.

Participants use the structure of dispreferred responses to mitigate potential damage to the inviter's face or embarrassment to them by such means as delays, compliments, indirect refusals and accounts. Note also that this dispreferred construction does interactional work for the participants because it provides several opportunities for the inviter to revoke, repair, or revise his or her invitation prior to the production of the declination. If someone issues an invitation, and sees by the recipient's delay in responding that a dispreferred response (a declination) is projected, they may intervene to revise or retract their invitation. For example, they may suggest another day or make some other alteration to the invitation, in an attempt to get it to the point where it could be accepted. The revised invitation, if acceptable, may make production of the declination irrelevant. For example, in Excerpt 8, above, Speaker B could have intervened after Speaker A's "Well," or after the compliment ("that's awfully sweet of you,") in line 3, and said something like "If that's not convenient, we can do it another time." This hypothetical responses could have pre-empted Speaker A's production of the declination of the invitation, and made it unnecessary.

In mediation sessions participants sometimes produce proposals for how the dispute could be resolved. If the opposing disputant begins to produce a dispreferred response (a rejection of the proposal), mediators occasionally interrupt to try to pre-empt the impending rejection, in order to gain time for the proposal to be discussed (Garcia, 1989). This effort on the mediator's part may facilitate a successful resolution of the conflict by keeping potentially viable ideas on the table long enough for them to be carefully considered.

The preference for agreement

The most common type of adjacency pairs is the question/answer pair. Sacks (1987a) notes that for many types of questions, there is a preference for agreement. "Yes" answers occur more frequently than "no" answers, and questions are often structured to project a "yes" rather than a "no" response. If possible, the recipient will formulate their answer to the question as an agreement. For example, consider Excerpt 10 below. Speaker A's question in lines 1 and 2 is formulated to prefer agreement—a "yes" response. However, Speaker B's response is not a simple "yes," he or she seems to mean that the person they are discussing is not necessarily "permanently damaged." Speaker B is thus actually disagreeing with Speaker A. Notice that Speaker B handles this by first producing an agreement ("Apparently", in line 3), and then (after a filled pause, "Uh"), producing a disagreeing response ("he is still hopeful."). The disagreement is therefore produced in a dispreferred format (a delayed and indirect disagreement instead of an immediate, blunt disagreement).

Excerpt 10: (Sacks, 1987a, p. 57)
1   A: And it- apparently left her quite permanently damaged (I
2   suppose).
3   B: Apparently. Uh he is still hopeful.

If Speaker A had formulated the question to prefer a disagreement (a "no" response), it could have looked something like this:

Excerpt 11: (Hypothetical)
A: It didn't leave her permanently damaged, did it?
B: No.

Excerpt 12 below shows Speaker B producing a dispreferred response to a question that is structured to prefer a "yes" response (Sacks, 1987a). Note that Speaker B uses some of the same techniques for structuring a dispreferred response that we saw above in declinations of invitations.

Excerpt 12: (Sacks, 1987a, p. 58)
1   A: Yuh comin down early?
2   B: Well, I got a lot of things to do before gettin cleared up tomorrow. I
3   don't know. I w- probably won't be too early.

Note that B's response in line 2 does not begin with a "yes" response. Instead, the first thing Speaker B says is "Well," which Pomerantz (1984) notes is disagreement-implicative. The "well" serves not only to delay the production of the answer to the question, it also projects a negative response to come. The next thing that Speaker B does (line 2) is also not an answer to the question ("I got a lot of things to do before gettin cleared up tomorrow."). This utterance is an account or explanation for why a positive answer to the question can not be provided. The next item works as an uncertainty marker ("I don't know."), which in the context of dispreferred responses serves to soften or mitigate the effect of the impending "no" answer. Finally, when Speaker B eventually answers the question ("I w- probably won't be too early.") she or he answers it in an indirect way which avoids the blunt production of "no." Speaker B's response thus follows the procedures used for constructing a dispreferred response.

Agreeing and disagreeing with assessments

Speakers often use a turn at talk to produce an evaluation of something. This type of utterance is referred to as an **assessment**. Pomerantz (1984) notes that assessments often evaluate an activity one is participating in or is reporting about participating in. Assessments can be either positive or negative evaluations of something being referred to in the conversation. Pomerantz (1984) found that responses to assessments also have a preference for agreement. Excerpt 13 below (Pomerantz, 1984) is from a conversation between two people who were going swimming. When J comments on the water (line 1), R responds with an assessment ("It's wonderful…") in line 2. The second speaker agrees with the first assessment by also producing a positive assessment.

> Excerpt 13: Pomerantz (1984, p. 57)
> 1 J: Let's feel the water. Oh, it …
> 2 R: It's wonderful. It's just right. It's like bathtub water.

After one participant has produced an assessment, another participant often provides a second assessment which evaluates the same object or event that the first assessment evaluated. While the second assessment may agree or disagree with the first assessment, there is a preference for agreement (Pomerantz, 1984). Excerpt 14 is from a conversation between three students who were taping a conversation to be used as a class project. This example shows all participants in agreement as to their assessment of a movie they had been discussing.

> Excerpt 14: Conversation between Students
> 1 M: it's sup[posed tuh be goo:d.]
> 2 E: [°sounds like uh go]od movie.°=
> 3 H: =id i-h-s goo-h-h-d!

Excerpt 15, from Pomerantz (1984, p. 60) shows Speaker A ("Claire") agreeing with Speaker B's assessment of an activity both have participated in. Again, the second assessment (line 20) is in agreement with the first assessment (line 1):

> Excerpt 15: (Pomerantz, 1984, p. 60)
> 1 B: Well, it was fun Cla[ire,
> 2 A: [Yeah, I enjoyed every minute of it.

As with adjacency pairs, there are routine ways that participants can convey and position their second assessments as preferred (agreeing) or dispreferred (disagreeing) with the first assessment. Pomerantz (1984, pp. 65–70) notes that speakers often try to formulate their disagreement with an assessment as an agreement by making an "**upgrade**" or "**downgrade**" of intensity when they do not share exactly the same assessment as the prior speaker. This enables them to agree to the extent that their assessment has the same "polarity" as the first assessment (a positive or negative assessment). They use the degree of intensity of their assessment as a way to distinguish their assessment from that of the prior speaker. In short, a second assessment can either be the same as the first assessment, an "upgrade" of the first assessment, or a "downgrade" of the first assessment.

Excerpt 14 (above) illustrates second (and third) assessments at the same level of "enthusiasm" as the first assessment (all three evaluate the movie as "good."). Excerpt 16 shows an upgrade (from "beautiful" in line 1 to "gorgeous" in line 2) and Excerpt 17 shows a downgrade (from "beautiful" to "pretty").

Excerpt 16: Pomerantz (1984, p. 59)

1 J: Tsuh beautiful day out isn't it?

2 L: Yeh it's jus' gorgeous . . .

Excerpt 17: Pomerantz (1984, p. 58)

1 F: That's beautiful

2 K: Isn't it pretty

By means of upgrades and downgrades, a speaker can present a second assessment as an agreement with a first assessment even when they are not in complete agreement. When second assessments disagree with first assessments, Pomerantz (1984) found that typical methods of formulating dispreferred responses are generally used. For example, the disagreeing portion of the utterance can be delayed, either by silence prior to initiation of the turn or by preceding it with other material such as "well" or "uhm." Excerpt 18 shows a second assessment preceded by silence. Note that when Speaker B does produce her delayed response in line 4, it is not in agreement with Speaker A's assessment of the weather.

Excerpt 18: Pomerantz (1984, p. 70)

1 A: God izn' it <u>dreary</u>.

2   (0.6)

3 A: [Y'know I don't think-

4 B: [.hh It's <u>warm</u> though,

Excerpt 19 shows a disagreeing second assessment preceded by a disagreement-implicative preface ("We::ll,"; line 3).

Excerpt 19: Pomerantz (1984, p. 72)

1 C: I can' even send my kid tuh public school b'cuz they're so god

2   damn lousy.

3 D: We::ll, that's a generality.

In sum, although assessments and second assessments are not technically adjacency pairs, the formulation of second assessments typically follows the procedures for constructing preferred and dispreferred second pair parts. These responses, as Pomerantz (1984) has shown, indicate that there is a preference for agreement with assessments.

Summary

This chapter has shown how adjacency pairs can be constructed to create sequences out of individual turns at talk. These sequences can be used to accomplish a wide range of interactional tasks. The concept of preference organization describes how people construct their responses to first pair parts of adjacency pairs to coincide with social expectations.

Preference organization also applies to some categories of utterances that are not strictly speaking adjacency pairs, for example second assessments and agreements or disagreements with assessments. In the next chapter we will investigate how participants can use adjacency pairs as the building blocks of larger segments of talk.

Student activity

1. Some questions are constructed to prefer a "yes" response, and others a "no" response. For example, "Do you know where the library (grocery store, town hall, etc.) is?" prefers a "yes" response, "You don't know where the library is, do you?" prefers a "no" response. Ask a couple of people the first version of the question, and a couple of different people the second version. Note how each question is answered. Can you find systematic differences in how people answer questions that prefer yes or no answers?
2. Ask someone a simple favor such as lending you a book. Does their response follow the format for preferred and dispreferred responses to requests?

Recommended sources

Pomerantz, Anita. (1978a), 'Compliment responses: notes on the co-operation of multiple constraints', in J. Schenkein (ed.), *Studies in the Organization of Conversational Interaction*. New York: Academic Press, pp. 79–112.

—(1984), 'Agreeing and disagreeing with assessments: some features of preferred-dispreferred turn shapes', in Atkinson, J. M. and John Heritage (eds) *Structures of Social Action: Studies in Conversation Analysis*. Cambridge: Cambridge University Press, pp. 57–101.

Pomerantz, Anita. (1988), 'Offering a candidate answer: an information seeking strategy', *Communication Monographs*, 55, 360–73.

Sacks, Harvey. (1987a), 'On the preferences for agreement and contiguity in sequences in conversation', In Button, Graham and John R. E. Lee (eds) *Talk and Social Organisation*. Clevedon: Multilingual Matters, pp. 54–69.

Schegloff, Emanuel A. (2007a), *Sequence Organization in Interaction: A Primer in Conversation Analysis, Volume 1*, Cambridge: Cambridge University Press.

7 Sequential Organization: Interrogative Series, Insertion Sequences, Side Sequences, and Pre-Sequences

Chapter contents

Introduction

In Chapter 5 we learned how participants can use the turn taking system to organize individuals' actions into coherent conversations in which there is an orderly exchange of turns with a minimum of gaps and overlaps. In Chapter 6 we addressed how participants can combine turns at talk into adjacency pairs to create two-turn sequences within the conversation. However, we have not yet explored how participants can create sequences or units of talk longer than two turns in length. In this chapter we explore how adjacency pairs can be used as building blocks—as basic devices or techniques which, when combined in specific ways, enable participants to perform actions which extend beyond two-turn exchanges. We will first consider unexpanded and expanded action sequences, and then explore how side sequences, insertion sequences, interrogative series and pre-sequences can be used to accomplish different actions in the conversation. By learning how participants use adjacency pairs to create organization in talk beyond a two-turn sequence we set the groundwork for an understanding of story telling and topic development which will be explored in later chapters.

Unexpanded and expanded action sequences

While an adjacency pair consists of only two utterances, Jefferson (1977) found that participants can create three-turn **action sequences** by providing an acknowledgement after receipt of a response to an adjacency pair. This three-turn sequence begins with a speaker producing an action such as a question or a request. A second speaker responds to the first pair part by providing the requested action (e.g., answering the question or granting or refusing the request). The first speaker then acknowledges receipt of the second pair part. An unexpanded action sequence is shown in Excerpt 1. Jefferson (1977) analyzes this excerpt from a conversation between a boy selling newspaper subscriptions and several men who are sitting in the backyard of a house. After some conversation, the host directs the boy to ask his wife, who is inside the house, whether she wants a subscription to the paper. When the boy returns to the backyard he addresses Michael (who has just arrived), and tries to get him to take a subscription to the "Progress Bulletin":

> Excerpt 1: Jefferson (1977, p. 92)
>
> 1   Sales boy: Dju be innerested sir, ((addressed to Michael
> 2   who joined the ensemble in his absence))
> 3   ((pause))
> 4   Sales boy: -Taking the Progress Bulletin,
> 5   Steven: No, en *he* don' know nothin about it.
> 6   Sales boy: Okay.

The boy produces an adjacency pair first pair part in lines 1 and 4. Instead of Michael responding to the question, Steven responds on his behalf, providing both an answer and an explanation for why Michael does not want to get a subscription to the newspaper. The boy then provides an acknowledgement token in line 6 ("Okay."). By means of this acknowledgment he shows that he has heard and accepted the rejection of his request, thereby ending the sequence.

Jefferson (1977) argues that the end of the sequence is an alternative to another possibility, the expansion of the sequence. For example, the boy could have persisted in trying to get Michael to buy a subscription, perhaps by reissuing his request. Persistence of this type can occur, and would result in an expanded action sequence rather than in a single adjacency pair and its acknowledgement. Jefferson (1977) gives an example of an expanded action sequence from earlier in the same interaction, when the boy first approached the house:

> Excerpt 2: Jefferson (1977, pp. 87–8)
>
> 1   Sales boy: G'n aftuhnoon sir, W'dju be innerested in subscribing
> 2   to the Progress Bulletin t'help m'win a trip tuh Cape
> 3   Kennedy to see the astronauts on the moon shot. You
> 4   won'haftuh pay til nex'month en you get it ev'ry single
> 5   day en I guarantee you ril good service. Jus' fer a

6		few short weeks sir, tuh help me win my trip,
7	Richard:	Well I <u>live</u> in Los <u>An</u>geles. I don' live around here but
8		<u>these</u> fellas live here, you might- ask the:m, I don'
9		know,
10	Sales boy:	[W'd eejer- any of you gen,tuhmen be innerested in
11		subscribing to it,
12	Ted:	Whaddi<u>you</u> think uh Beany,
13	Steven:	[Na::w,
14	Steven:	Naw. I don't go faw it.
15	Sales boy:	[Plea:se, <u>just</u> fer a short weeks sir, Y'won'
16		haftuh pay t'l next <u>month</u>,
17	Ted:	[Well, you er uh, talk t'the <u>lady</u> of the house.
18	Steven:	Ye:h,
19	Sales boy:	[No. We knocked there no one w'z here.
20	Steven:	Well she's <u>here</u>,
21	Ted:	She's here alright.
22	Sales boy:	(Are you sure)?
23	Steven:	(Yeah.)
24	Sales boy:	(okay.)

This "**expanded action sequence**" begins in line 1 as the sales boy begins his pitch—an adjacency pair first pair part requesting that one of the men buy a subscription to the newspaper. Richard responds in line seven and produces a dispreferred response to the request—he declines to purchase a subscription. He then suggests that the boy ask the other "fellas." The boy immediately reiterates his request (lines 10 and 11); asking the others to subscribe. Instead of answering the request, one of the men (Ted) addresses another (Steven), and they discuss the request in lines 13–14. When the boy sees that they are tending towards refusing his request, he interrupts their exchange in line 15 to reiterate his request. At this point Ted directs the boy to talk to his wife instead of to him (line 17). The sales boy's initial adjacency pair first pair part (lines 1–6) thus leads not to an "unexpanded action sequence" of an adjacency pair followed by an acknowledgement, but instead to an extended sequence involving the talk of several participants, the reissue of the first pair part, and ultimately the transfer of the discussion to a third party who is not present (the wife of one of the men). All of this talk is in the service of getting an answer to the initial first pair part. The boy persists until it is clear that none of the men present will buy a subscription. This example thus serves to illustrate how adjacency pairs can lead to extended, expanded sequences. The property of conditional relevance, in which an adjacency pair first pair part creates an expectation for a particular type of second pair part, provides the boy with the warrant for pursuing the topic until a suitable response is produced. Note that this response does not have to be the preferred response (in this case buying a subscription); it can be either granting or refusing to grant the request. By means of the expanded action sequence the boy was able to extend his effort to get a positive response for his request.

Techniques for expanding sequences

There is a variety of different ways that action sequences can be expanded. In this section of the chapter we will discuss side sequences, insertion sequences, interrogative series and pre-sequences.

Side sequences

As we learned in Chapter 6, once the first pair part of an adjacency pair is produced, a second pair part is conditionally relevant. However, the response to an adjacency pair can be delayed if the intervening actions are somehow accountable in that interactional context. The **side sequence** is one type of action that can accountably displace or supplant a second pair part. Jefferson (1972; see also Schegloff, 2007a) uses the term "side sequence" to refer to attempts by participants to repair or comment on aspects of an ongoing sequence. Talk on the original trajectory can typically be resumed after this short interruption, hence constituting it as a "side sequence"—a brief repair or digression from the main line of talk which is then resumed after the sequence. However, side sequences can at times develop into lines of talk themselves which end up derailing the original action (Jefferson, 1972).

In Excerpt 3 Speaker A stops her own story-in-progress and pauses for four seconds (lines 1 and 2). When she starts speaking again in line 3, instead of continuing the story she requests help from Speaker B in remembering the name of the woman she is talking about. The two of them work to solve this problem in lines 5 through 10. Speaker A then resumes her story where she left off (line 11). Jefferson (1972) refers to the speaker's temporary departure from the story in order to recall the woman's name as a "side sequence."

Excerpt 3: Jefferson (1972, p. 302)
1   A: Uh, she asked me to stop by, she bought a chest of drawers from um
2   (4.0)
3   A: What's that gal's name? Just went back to Michigan.
4   (2.0)
5   A: Helen, um
6   B: Oh I know who you mean,
7   (1.0)
8   B: Brady- <u>Brady</u>.
9   A: Yeah! Helen Brady.
10   B: Mm hm,
11   A: And, she- she says she's uh never had a new bedroom set so she's
12   fixed this all up…

Insertion sequences

An **insertion sequence** is made up of one or more adjacency pairs which intervene between the first and second pair parts of another adjacency pair. The purpose of insertion sequences is typically to obtain information needed before the recipient of the first pair part can provide the second pair part. These can take the form of repair sequences, "sequences addressed to problems in hearing or understanding the preceding talk" (Schegloff, 2007a, p. 100). The structure of an insertion sequence is therefore a pair of embedded adjacency pairs, with one (or more) adjacency pairs inserted between the first and second pair parts of the original adjacency pair.

In Excerpt 4 below "Marge" asks a question of "Bea" in line 3 in order to clarify the name of the person she is asking about. Once Bea has provided this information (line 4), Marge is able to answer the initial question. The insertion sequence is thus embedded within the initial adjacency pair.

> Excerpt 4: Schegloff, et al. (1977, p. 368)
> 1 Bea: Was last night the first time you met Missiz Kelly?
> 2   (1.0)
> 3 Marge: Met whom?
> 4 Bea: Missiz Kelly.
> 5 Marge: Yes.

Insertion sequences are also common in talk in institutional settings. For example, when a caller makes a phone call to emergency services to request help, the call taker typically does not immediately grant the request (Zimmerman, 1984). The granting of the request occurs towards the end of the call, after the call taker has obtained all of the information needed to provide help. The first pair part of the adjacency pair (the request) is thus separated from its second pair part (granting or refusing to grant the request) by one or more adjacency pairs which do the work of information gathering.

Whalen and Zimmerman (1987) analyze the emergency service call in Excerpt 5. A caller describes a policeable problem ("somebody jus' vandalized my car,") in line 2 of the transcript, thus making an implicit request for help. The dispatcher responds not by granting the request, but by asking the caller first for their address, then whether it is a house or an apartment, then for their last name, and finally for the spelling of their last name. Only after the caller has provided the answers to all of these questions does the dispatcher say "Wull sen' somebody out to see you.", thus granting the request (line 11).

> Excerpt 5: Whalen and Zimmerman (1987, p. 174)
> 1 D: Mid-City Emergency
> 2 C: Um yeah (.) somebody jus' vandalized my car,
> 3 D: What's your address.
> 4 C: Thirty three twenty two: Elm.
> 5 D: Is this uh house or an apartment.
> 6 C: Ih tst uh house
> 7 D: Uh- your las' name.
> 8 C: Minsky,
> 9 D: How you spell it.

10 C: M. I. N. S. K. Y.
11 D: Wull sen' somebody out to see you.

This discussion of how action sequences can be expanded with insertion sequences provides an explanation for why the first and second pair parts of adjacency pairs not always adjacent. Other things can intervene between the first and second pair parts if they are analyzably relevant to the task of completing the adjacency pair. Although the two parts of the adjacency pair are not adjacent, the interactants still display an orientation to the property of conditional relevance by constructing an insertion sequence that can be seen to be in the service of completing the adjacency pair.

The interrogative series: "Chains" of adjacency pairs

Zimmerman (1984) coined the term "**interrogative series**" to refer to the series of adjacency pairs found in most emergency phone calls. The interrogative series is a question/answer chain: A series of question/answer pairs, with one person producing the questions and the other person producing the answers. The question/answer chain can be as brief as two adjacency pairs long, or it can go on for any number of exchanges. As Excerpt 5 (above) shows, the adjacency pair chain is functional for emergency service calls, because it lets the call-taker control the exchange of turns and the development of the topic. Each time the answerer uses their turn to answer the question, the questioner can select themself to speak again at a transition relevance place in the answerer's utterance. The questioner can then use their turn to ask yet another question.

Excerpt 6 is from an informal conversation between two students who recorded a conversation in order to be used as examples in the course. In this excerpt "Kay" is questioning "Art" about a date he recently had with a mutual acquaintance of theirs. Art repeatedly displays reluctance to talk about the date in this public setting, but Kay jokingly persists in questioning him about it. She uses a question/answer chain as a device to maintain control over the topic in spite of Art's efforts to avoid discussing it. Kay asks questions in lines 1, 5–7, and 11–12. Because of the classroom setting, Kay's questions are not entirely serious; she is playing with the public nature of a private discussion, and treating it as a humorous situation. While acknowledging the humorous tone of the exchange, Art repeatedly refuses to reveal information about the date.

Excerpt 6: Conversation between Students
1 K: You're=gonna take her out again?
2   (.2)
3 A: I DON'T KNOW, (.6) I don't know, (.3) °She wasn't very nice to
4   me.°=
5 K: =unhh! [hunh hunh] HEH HEH wh=hhh=heh=heh=y:
6 A: [(   )]
7 K: no=huh=huh=t:? hinh hinh=

```
 8   A:                              =Well, you know, ºI [don't want]
 9   K:                                           [.hhh      ]
10   A:  to get into [(                    º)]
11   K:               [Come on, WHAD'd] she do: that wasn't very nice?
12        You can share it with us!
13        (.1)
14   A:  No::,
```

These excerpts have shown how speakers can use adjacency pair chains to control the topic of the conversation.

Pre-sequences

Action sequences can also be expanded by preceding them with another sequence. A **presequence** is an adjacency pair first pair part which precedes (and projects) an action to come. Schegloff (1990) found that pre-sequences can fulfill a number of functions in the interaction. The presequence may be used to suggest that the action that is projected is "delicate" in some way; the recipient is thus alerted in advance that something delicate or sensitive is to be communicated or attempted (Schegloff, 1990). Pre-sequences can be used to check out the likelihood of success for a projected action, for example by finding out if someone might be receptive to an invitation.

Pre-sequences can also be used to get space in the interaction to produce longer utterances or actions than would normally be allowed for the holder of a single turn. These extended turns might be used to tell a story or provide background information necessary for understanding a question or request. For example, an action projection such as a pre-request is often not followed immediately by the request itself, but instead by some other material which explains, justifies, or otherwise sets up the hearer for the request. The **action projection** thus serves to get the speaker the floor to produce material *preliminary* to the production of the projected action.

For example, in Excerpt 5 a caller to a radio talk show sets up a question with a presequence (line 1, "I like tuh ask you something."). Schegloff (1980) argues that while utterances such as these appear to be asking for permission to speak, that is not typically their function. The caller uses this question as a presequence to prepare the audience (in this case the host and members of the show's listening public) for a projected action (a question) and to get time in the interaction to set up the question before it is produced. After the host's response in line 2 ("Shoot."—meaning "go on"), the next thing the caller does is not ask a question. Instead, the caller starts providing information which eventually leads up to a question. This information sets up the question and helps to make it comprehensible. The use of the presequence enables the recipient (the talk show host) to hear the information provided in lines 3, 5 and 6 as relevant to what will come next (the question in lines 7 and 8), rather than hearing it as off topic or irrelevant. Without the presequence, the caller would not have had space in the conversation to produce the preliminary information necessary to understand the question (lines 3–6).

Excerpt 7: Schegloff (1980, p. 105)

1 B: I like tuh ask you something.
2 A: Shoot.
3 B: Y'know I 'ad my license suspended fuh six munts,
4 A: Uh huh
5 B: Y'know for a reason which, I rathuh not, mention
6   tuh you, in othuh words, --a serious reason,
7   en I like tuh know if I w'd talk tuh my senator, or-
8   somebuddy, could they help me get it back,

Pre-Invitations. Pre-sequences can also be used to project actions such as invitations or requests. There are a variety of reasons why someone might want to set up an invitation with a presequence rather than asking it "cold". If the recipient is given a hint that an invitation may be coming they can act to pre-empt the projected invitation if they are unable or unwilling to accept it, thus saving the inviter from the awkwardness of having their invitation declined. Or, if the person making the invitation is able to discover in advance whether their invitation is likely to be successful, they can revise their invitation to increase its chances of success.

For example, in Excerpt 8 Nelson phones Clara and invites her out for a drink (line 6). However, before he produces the invitation he asks her a general question ("Whatcha doin'."; line 4). While this could be perceived as a purely informational question, it also works to discover whether an invitation, if produced, is likely to be successful. Thus it can be heard by both parties as being *prior* to the production of a (possible) invitation. Clare's answer to this question ("Not much."; line 5) displays that there is no obvious impediment to her being available to go out, so Nelson then produces his invitation with at least some confidence that the invitation can be accepted (as it is, in line 7). The question in line 4 is therefore a pre-invitation—a question that elicits information that informs the inviter's subsequent production of the actual invitation.

Excerpt 8: Schegloff (2007a, p. 30)

1 Cla: Hello
2 Nel: Hi.
3 Cla: Hi.
4 Nel: Whatcha doin'.
5 Cla: Not much.
6 Nel: Y'wanna drink?
7 Cla: Yeah.
8 Nel: Okay.

If Clare had not been available for (or interested in) an invitation from Nelson, it is likely she would have responded differently in line 5, perhaps by describing a prior commitment. If she had done that, it is likely that Nelson would not have produced the invitation in line 6. When these alternate scenarios are compared, the work done for the interactants by the presequence becomes clear. People can avoid the social awkwardness or threat to face

(Goffman, 1967) of a rejection by refraining from producing invitations when it has been made clear that they might not be accepted.

Excerpt 9 below illustrates how pre-sequences can be functional by showing how an invitation can be revised or retracted depending on what information is revealed in the response to the pre-invitation. Speaker A's question in line 1 is hearable as a pre-invitation. Speaker B's response in line 2 indicates they are not available. Instead of producing an invitation in line 3 Speaker A displays an understanding of why an invitation would not be successful.

> Excerpt 9: Terasaki (2004, p. 180)
> 1   A: Say what'r you doing.
> 2   B: Well, we're going out. Why.
> 3   A: Oh, I was just gonna say come out and come over here an' talk this
> 4   evening, but if you're going out you can't very well do that.

Pre-requests. Schegloff (1980) gives some examples of pre-sequences used as pre-requests. Excerpt 10 occurs in the middle of a telephone call Laurie has placed to Fred. After talking about other issues for a while, Fred produces a presequence in line 1. This pre-request gains time for Fred to produce background information to explain and justify his projected request. He introduces the topic of the blouse and explains why he needs help (he would do it himself, but his mother's buttonholer is broken). Notice that by use of the pre-request sequence, Fred is able to avoid producing the actual request. He never has to say, "Will you do the button holes for me?"), because Laurie can see that the request is the action that is projected and volunteers to do the button holes without being asked (Laurie's line 7). Thus the prerequest in this instance both prepares the ground for the request and obviates the need for its articulation.

> Excerpt 10: Pre-Request (Schegloff, 1980, p. 112)
> 1   Fre: Oh by the way ((sniff)) I have a bi:g favor to ask ya.
> 2   Lau: Sure, go 'head.
> 3   Fre: 'Member the blouse you made a couple weeks ago?
> 4   Lau: Ya.
> 5   Fre: Well I want to wear it this weekend to Vegas but my mom's
> 6   buttonholer is broken.
> 7   Lau: Fred I told ya when I made the blouse I'd do the buttonholes.
> 8   Fre: ((sniff)) but I hate ta impose.
> 9   Lau: No problem. We can do them on Monday after work.

Pre-Announcements. Another use to which pre-sequences can be put is as a preliminary to an announcement (Terasaki, 2004). Pre-announcement sequences serve to find out whether your audience has heard the news already or not. If they have heard the news, then the announcement does not need to be made. You can either change the topic or discuss the issue without announcing it. However, if you discover that the person you are talking to does not know the news yet, then you can produce the announcement. In Excerpt 11 below,

D learns that R has not yet heard the news, while in Excerpt 12 D learns that R has already heard the news he has to share.

> Excerpt 11: Terasaki (2004, p. 184)
> 1 D: Didju hear the terrible news?
> 2 R: No, what.

> Excerpt 12: Terasaki (2004, p. 184)
> 1 D: Hey we got good news!
> 2 R: I know.
> 3 D: Oh ya do?

In sum, pre-sequences can be used to do a wide variety of interactional work for the participants. They can be used to gain the floor for additional turns at talk to explain or set up a projected action, they can enable the speaker to determine the likelihood of success before producing a projected action (e.g. an invitation or an announcement), or they can set up the listener for something delicate or sensitive. As the examples above illustrate, how talk unfolds after a presequence will depend on what work that presequence is doing in the interaction. For pre-announcements and pre-invitations, the sequence typically consists of two adjacency pairs, the first pair part serving to project the action to come (e.g. inviting or announcing). For pre-sequences used to get space to provide background information prior to the projected action (e.g. prerequests), preliminary or background information will intervene between the first and second adjacency pairs.

Summary

The study of techniques for expanding action sequences reveals the detailed and subtle levels of structure in common, everyday interactions as well as in talk in institutional settings. This discussion has shown how participants can accomplish a wide range of actions through these aspects of sequential organization, and demonstrates that the structure of conversations are not limited to a simple series of turns at talk. Procedures exist to allow participants to accomplish a range of actions through the use of the techniques described in this chapter. Now that we have a basic understanding of how talk within interaction can be organized and how participants use interactional techniques to perform a variety of actions, we turn to the topic of how participants begin and end conversations.

Student activity

Throughout the day make a list of every pre-sequence used by yourself or those you are interacting with. What types of pre-sequences are most common (for example, pre-invitations, pre-announcements, pre-requests)?

Recommended sources

Drew, Paul. (1984), 'Speakers' reportings in invitation sequences', in J. Maxwell Atkinson and John Heritage (eds), *Structures of Social Action: Studies in Conversation Analysis*. Cambridge: Cambridge University Press, pp. 129–51.

Jefferson, Gail. (1972), 'Side sequences', in David Sudnow (ed.), *Studies in Social Interaction*. New York: Free Press, pp. 294–338.

—(1977), 'Some sequential negotiations in conversation: unexpanded and expanded versions of projected action sequences', *Sociology*, 11, (1), 87–103.

Schegloff, Emanuel A. (1980), 'Preliminaries to preliminaries, "Can I Ask You a Question?"', *Sociological Inquiry*, 50, 104–52.

Terasaki, Alene Kiku. (2004), 'Pre-announcement sequences in conversation', in Lerner, Gene H. (ed.), *Conversation Analysis: Studies from the First Generation*. Amsterdam and Philadelphia: John Benjamins, pp. 171–224.

Openings

Introduction

You might think that a chapter on opening conversations should be the first chapter in the book. However, in order to understand how people open conversations we need to understand the turn-taking system and the adjacency pair sequences that were discussed in previous chapters. In addition, identifying when a conversation begins and ends is not always a straightforward matter. Conversations do not always get neatly packaged into segments of continuous talk bounded by clear beginnings and endings. For example, if you are spending an evening sitting in the living room with your family, and occasionally someone says something or two people exchange a few words, is that talk the beginning of a new conversation or the continuation of a prior conversation?

In many situations there are specific techniques that can be used to mark an exchange as the beginning of a conversation. If you are walking down the street and see a friend, you might wave at them. If they respond, you might exchange greetings and begin a conversation. That would be an example of a conversation with a clear beginning. However, did you remember to bring your tape recorder or your video camera with you? It is not easy to collect instances of spontaneously emerging conversations with clear beginnings and endings. This is one reason why much of the early research on openings and closings in conversation was done by studying telephone calls. By attaching a tape recorder to the telephone, conversations could be recorded in their entirety and a large collection of complete conversations—including their openings and closings—could be created.

Much of the initial research on conversation analysis was conducted during the 1960s and 1970s. In addition to being long before *Skype* and text messaging, this was also before mobile phones, caller id, call waiting and other conveniences that we tend to take for granted today. Thus in order to understand and appreciate the initial research done on telephone call openings, we need to remember that callers at that time did not know who was calling them until they picked up the phone and talked to them. In this chapter we will review the early conversation analytic research on telephone call openings. In Chapter 16 we will look at recent studies of mobile phone calls, text messaging, and other technologies of communication, to see how they have changed the structure of conversations.

Another reason to focus our study of openings on telephone calls is that they provide a naturally occurring setting for studying two-person interactions. These types of interactions have a simpler structure than multi-party interactions which makes them easier to transcribe and to analyze than multi-party talk. Finally, because participants in phone conversations cannot see each other, they provide a naturally occurring setting in which one can legitimately focus on the verbal aspects of the interaction and not have to deal with nonverbal behaviors such as gaze direction, facial expression, gestures, and body orientation. Since these behaviors were not available to the interactants, they need not be available to analysts.

Every time a conversation is opened, regardless of whether it is face to face or over the telephone, there are several interactional tasks that must be accomplished by the participants. Parties must establish that they are available to communicate, and they must identify who they are talking to (or, they must know that it does not matter exactly who they are talking to, as when calling a store to find out what their hours are). They must be able to coordinate their entry into a state of talk so that the orderly exchange of turns can begin. In this chapter we will explore how people accomplish these tasks.

Schegloff's research on telephone call openings

Schegloff (1968) recorded telephone calls from a wide variety of sources. Many of these were ordinary conversations between friends, but his collection of data also included "service" calls. Service calls are telephone calls through which an organization, institution, or business provides a service to the public. Emergency phone calls to the police are a prime example of service calls, as are calls to a business' customer service line.

Schegloff's data set was extensive, consisting of over 500 taped telephone calls. Thus, he had sufficient examples of how telephone conversations were opened to be quite confident about the findings of his research. Schegloff wrote several papers on the telephone conversation data, one of which focuses primarily on the very beginning of the call—the ringing of the phone and the called person's answering of the phone (Schegloff, 1968). A later paper dealt with the entire opening sequence (Schegloff, 1979).

Schegloff found that openings in American phone calls typically have at least four sequences. A sequence is a series of two utterances, each produced by a different participant, which accomplishes a specific type of work in the interaction. The study of opening sequences in telephone calls is a good way to learn about what sequences are and how participants use them to accomplish specific tasks in interaction. The following example illustrates these four sequences from the opening phase of telephone calls: the summons/answer sequence, the identification/recognition sequence, the greeting sequence, and what Schegloff (1986; see also Sacks, 1987a) calls the "how are you" sequence (also referred to as the "exchange of initial inquiries").

> Excerpt 1: Schegloff (1986, p. 115)
>
> 1   ((telephone rings))
> 2   J: Hallo,
> 3   B: Hello Jim?
> 4   J: Yeah,
> 5   B: 's Bonnie.
> 6   J: Hi,
> 7   B: Hi, how <u>a</u>re yuh
> 8   J: Fine, how're <u>y</u>ou,
> 9   B: Oh, okay I guess
> 10   J: Oh okay.
> 11   B: Uhm (0.2) what are you <u>d</u>oing New Year's Eve.

*1. The **Summons-Answer Sequence**.* In the traditional landline telephone calls Schegloff (1968) studied, he discovered that when the phone rings the answerer speaks first. While it might seem logical that the person who called would be the one to begin the conversation, the answerer speaks first because although the caller can hear the sound of the phone being picked up, she or he does not know whether the phone has been brought to the answerer's ear so that they can hear the words spoken. Therefore, the answerer speaks first in order to communicate that they are now available for talk.

The very first thing that happens in Excerpt 1 is the ringing of the phone (line 1). Bonnie is calling Jim on the phone, so she cannot use a wave or a shout to attract his attention, as she might do if she saw him while walking down the street. Jim cannot see Bonnie or know that she wants to talk to him until the phone rings. The ringing of the phone serves as a summons to attract his attention and let him know that someone is placing a call. Remember that in these early telephone call studies, the phones in use were old-fashioned land line rotary dial phones. So when Jim picks up the phone in line 2 and says "Hallo," he is answering the summons—communicating that he heard the ring, picked up the phone, and now has the phone at his ear so that he can hear the other person on the line. Jim's "Hallo," in line 2 is therefore doing the work of answering the summons—displaying his availability to talk.

You may think that since Jim uses the word "hello" which is generally considered a greeting, that he must be greeting the person who has called him. But recall what Garfinkel (1967) said about the indexicality of human action. The meaning of an utterance comes from an analysis of that utterance in the context it occurs within. In this interactional context the word "hello" does the work of answering the summons, not of greeting the person who has called. If you think about it, it makes sense. Why would you greet someone if you did not yet know who you were talking to? Later on in this chapter we will discuss how phone calls are opened differently in some European countries; this comparison will make the distinction easier to see. Briefly, in some cultures the called person does not answer the phone with "hello"; they have other methods of answering the summons which make its status as an answer more obvious.

2. The **Identification/Recognition Sequence**. If the call is a conversation between friends or relatives, or colleagues in a workplace who know each other personally, the identification and recognition of the parties can often be accomplished through voice. As the called party picks up the phone and says "hello," a "voice sample" is provided to the caller, who may then recognize this person as the one he or she was calling. If the person who answers the phone is not the called party, or is not recognized by the caller, further work must be done in the interaction to establish the identity of the participants. For example, the caller could ask whether the person they are calling is there, or the called party could ask who is calling.

In American telephone phone call openings (at least prior to the days of caller id) people preferred to use voice recognition if possible. This means that if they could recognize the called party or the caller by their voice, they would let that suffice and not go through an explicit verbal identification sequence. However, if one or both of the participants failed to recognize the voice of the other, then verbal means would be used to establish their identities.

In Excerpt 1 the caller appears to recognize, or at least thinks she recognizes, the called party through his voice. We know this because in line 3 she proposes that he is in fact Jim ("Hello Jim?"). However, Jim apparently does not recognize the voice of his caller. His answer in line 4 ("Yeah,"), while clearly verifying that he is indeed Jim, noticeably omits a return display of recognition–he does not display that he knows who *she* is. Bonnie repairs Jim's failure to recognize her voice in her next turn ("'s Bonnie."; line 5). At this point the participants have established that they each are available for interaction (through the summons/answer sequence) and that they know who they are talking to (through the identification/recognition sequence).

3. The **Greeting Sequence**. The third sequence in the opening phase of ordinary telephone calls is the exchange of greetings. The greeting exchange is typically bilateral, with one party initiating the sequence and the other party reciprocating by returning a greeting. However, this sequence is occasionally elided or truncated, especially in cases where people call each other frequently. In Excerpt 1 the greeting exchange is in lines 6 and 7, where Bonnie and Jim exchange "Hi's."

You might be wondering why the greetings occur so late in the interaction rather than being the first thing that happens in the telephone conversation. After all, when we begin a face to face conversation, don't we typically begin by greeting each other? However, while it may seem that a greeting is the first thing that happens in a face-to-face interaction, this is actually a false impression. While an exchange of greetings may well be the first *words* that are spoken in a face to face conversation, prior to that exchange the participants have ascertained by visual means that they are both available for interaction. They have also identified each other, at least on a basic level. This does not have to be an explicit verbal identification such as an exchange of names, job titles or social roles. For example, you could strike up a conversation with someone while waiting on line in the grocery store without knowing their name. They have still, however, been identified. You know who you are talking to—the person in line behind you in the grocery store. So the work of the summons/answer and identification/recognition sequences is still done in face-to-face interactions, it is just not always done verbally. However, in a telephone conversation we cannot use visual means to identify each other or ascertain whether both parties are available for talk.

4. The "How Are You" Sequence. The "how are you" sequence (or "**exchange of initial inquiries**") is an optional sequence which is nonetheless extremely common in American telephone conversations. It consists of an exchange of queries such as "how are you?" or "what's happening?" These turns are typically exchanged bilaterally, although in some conversations they are not responded to explicitly. While generally considered a mark of politeness, another function of this sequence is to provide an opportunity for either participant to communicate something urgent or newsworthy very early on in the conversation.

In Excerpt 1 the exchange of initial inquiries occurs in lines 7 through 9. Jim answers Bonnie's "how are yuh" with the word "Fine," and reciprocates by asking, "how're you," (line 8). Bonnie answers this inquiry in line 9 ("Oh, okay I guess"). Schegloff (1986) notes that since these responses present no information that needs discussing, they make closing of the initial inquiry sequence relevant. If either party did have urgent or important information to convey (e.g., "I can't talk now because I'm on my way out the door"), this sequence provides a space to do so prior to the introduction of the first topic of discussion.

5. "Pre-topical" Talk. Maynard and Zimmerman's (1984) study of topical organization in face to face conversation found that when people were talking with someone they did not previously know they typically discussed a series of "pre-topical" items in order to find common ground on which to develop a conversation. These pre-topicals could be elicited through questions about where the other person worked, went to school, and so forth. For people who were previously acquainted, talk about prior experiences or about the setting they were currently interacting within often served as initial topics in conversation. In telephone conversations, preliminary topics may be discussed, or the caller may choose to go directly to the "reason for the call."

6. *The Reason for the Call.* Schegloff (1968) found that the person making the call typically produces the first topic in the call. Since Bonnie is the one who has called Jim, line 9 of the call would be the place in the conversation where she would be expected to introduce the first topic, but she does not do so. The person who places the phone call typically has a reason for the call, even if that reason is just to chat. Since Bonnie does not introduce a first topic, Jim could elect to introduce a topic of talk in line 10. However, he chooses not to do so, and instead simply responds to Bonnie's answer to his initial inquiry ("Oh okay."). At this point (line 11), Bonnie introduces the first topic, which seems to be the reason for her call. Her question about Jim's plans for New Year's Eve seems to set up an impending invitation. Often a story or news report, a request, an invitation, or some other type of action will be produced as the "business of the call." This can come right after the completion of the opening sequence, or may be delayed until later in the call.

Atypical phone call openings

Opening sequences such as the one in Excerpt 1 (above) are very common in telephone conversations between acquainted people. The similarities in how people open their inter- actions may make it appear that these opening sequences are "ritualistic" or script-like (as in a theatrical performance or a religious service). However, the goal with a ritualistic or scripted event is to produce the event exactly as scripted. Openings of conversations, on the other hand, although they may appear very similar, are not in fact scripted (Nofsinger, 1991, p. 139). Their similarities arise from shared procedures used to accomplish specific tasks in the conversation. One type of evidence for this claim is that participants in conversations adjust their actions to conform to each other's actions. For example, if the person you are calling recognizes your voice, you do not have to identify yourself by name. So whether there is name identification in the opening sequence of a phone call depends on whether one or both of the participants is successful in recognizing the other person by voice. Identification by name, when it occurs, occurs not because it is part of a ritual, but because voice recog- nition has failed. Second, note that if problems occur during the opening sequence (for example if one participant cannot hear what the other is saying, or if an urgent event occurs—like a pot boiling over on the stove), then the participants can repair, suspend, or alter the opening sequence to fit with ongoing events. This flexibility also shows that opening sequences are not performed automatically.

The non-scripted nature of telephone call openings can be illustrated by examining some atypical calls, to see how participants alter the opening sequence to fit specific situations (see

Schegloff, 1979). The creativity shown in these "deviant cases" reveals the work that is done through the opening sequences.

> Excerpt 2: Schegloff (1979, p. 30)
> 1   ((ring))
> 2   P: Hello::,
> 3   A: Are you awa:ke?

The phone call in Excerpt 2 begins in a typical fashion with a summons/answer sequence (the ringing of the phone is followed by the called party, "P," saying "Hello::,". However, after this point the call is no longer typical. Speaker A apparently uses voice recognition to identify who Speaker P is, and detects in his voice or intonation that it sounds like he's been sleeping. His answer to the summons is therefore ambiguous. While he has technically answered the summons, it is not clear that he is actually "available for interaction." Hence Speaker A asks "Are you awa:ke?" instead of initiating the greeting exchange that would typically follow.

Excerpt 3 begins with a routine summons/answer sequence in lines 1 and 2. The identification/recognition sequence is apparently accomplished through voice recognition, as the participants move directly from the answer to the summons (line 2) to a truncated (unilateral) greeting sequence (line 3). The exchange of initial inquiries is also elided. Instead, Speaker C moves directly to the reason for the call—her question in line 3 ("'r my kids there?"). Speaker C apparently feels that the purpose of her call is urgent enough that she can elide the greeting exchange and initial inquires. Her need to locate her kids will provide an account for the absence of these formalities.

> Excerpt 3: Schegloff (1979, p. 30)
> 1   ((ringing))
> 2   L: H'llo:,
> 3   C: Hi, 'r my kids there?

Excerpt 4 shows a telephone call opening which differs from the typical pattern of identification and recognition of participants.

> Excerpt 4: Schegloff (1979, p. 59)
> 1   ((ringing))
> 2   B: Hello,
> 3   A: Hi. Susan?
> 4   B: Ye:s,
> 5   A: This's Judith. Rossman.
> 6   B: Judith!

After Speaker B answers the summons in line 2, the caller says "Hi. Susan?" showing that she at least tentatively identifies Susan by her voice. However Susan's response in line 4

("Ye:s,") indicates that she does not yet recognize the voice of the person who has called her. The caller attempts to repair this trouble in line 5 with "This's Judith." Note the "completion intonation" after the name—it sounded as if Judith was done with her utterance at this point. However, Susan's absent response to this self-identification indicates that Judith's first-name-only identification was not sufficient. Judith then adds her last name ("Rossman."). This second repair move is successful, and Susan responds in line 6 with "Judith!." thus (finally!) displaying that she recognizes the caller.

Cross-cultural comparison of telephone call openings

Those of you who have travelled abroad will probably have noticed considerable cross cultural variation in how telephone calls are answered. Recall first that the research we are covering in this chapter is the "pre-caller id" and "pre-mobile phone" research (we'll cover those technologies in Chapter 16). For pre-caller id calls, when people in England received a phone call at home they often answered the phone by reciting their telephone number rather than by saying "Hello." Recipients of phone calls in Sweden and the Netherlands typically answered the phone with explicit self-identifications rather than with "Hello." Lindström (1994) found that in both these countries call recipients typically said their name in the first turn of the call, rather than saying "Hello." In these calls the self identification does double duty as the answer to the summons.

While in the United States there is a preference for voice recognition, in Sweden call recipients choose to identify themselves by name even when they can recognize the person calling them from their voice. While in the U.S., failing to recognize someone's voice when you know them is sometimes embarrassing, this failure would clearly not have the same meaning in Sweden.

Excerpt 5 shows the called party answering the summons by self-identifying in his first turn (line 2).

Excerpt 5: Lindström (1994, p. 238)
(Grandmother calls her grandson Henrik; English translations in parentheses)
1   ((phone rings))
2   H: Hej de e He:nri:k,   (Hi it's Henrik)
3   G: Ja hej de va mormo:r?   (Yes hi it was (maternal)grandmother)
4   H: Hej,   (Hi)

The caller then identifies herself in line 3 of the call. Even though Henrik presumably knows what his grandmother's voice sounds like, she does not rely on voice recognition and instead explicitly identifies herself. Lindström (1994) also points out that in Swedish calls the initial exchange of inquiries rarely occurs, while it almost always occurs in American calls.

"Service call" openings

One common category of business call is the "service call," when a member of the public calls an organization in order to access a specific type of help or service. Examples of service calls include calls to emergency services, telephone directory assistance or customer service lines. The interactional organization of conversations between friends differs from the organization of telephone calls in business and other organizational settings because the purpose of the calls differs. In this section we will explore the openings of telephone calls in institutional contexts; in Chapter 25 we will explore the structure of the body of the call as well as the closing sections of these calls. The excerpts below illustrate how the openings in these calls differ from telephone conversations between friends.

Excerpt 6 shows the first two turns in a call to emergency services. The dispatcher ("D") answers the phone with the words "Mid-City Emergency," which is a pseudonym for the city where the data were collected. The dispatcher thus uses an institutional identification to answer the summons rather than a "Hello" or some other device (Whalen and Zimmerman, 1987). This method of answering the call serves two purposes. First, it immediately communicates to the caller that they have reached emergency services, so that if their call is urgent they can go right to the business of requesting help. Second, by not using "hello" to answer the summons the dispatcher signals that this is a business rather than a personal call and that he is ready to conduct the call in as efficient a way as possible. In the second turn of the call (line 3), the caller begins by saying "Um yeah." This type of beginning to caller's first turn is typical for emergency service calls. As Whalen and Zimmerman (1987) point out, by saying "yeah" or "yes" at the very beginning of their first turn, the caller acknowledges that she or he did intend to reach the emergency services. The caller then goes on to describe the problem she is calling about ("somebody jus' vandalized my car."). This statement of the problem informs the dispatcher of the type of assistance she will be requiring, and at the same time provides a warrant for her use of the emergency services number—her call is about a problem which is demonstrably a police-relevant matter.

Excerpt 6: Whalen and Zimmerman (1987, p. 174)

1 ((phone rings))
2 D: Mid-City Emergency
3 C: Um yeah (.) somebody jus' vandalized my car.

Notice also what is *not* present in the opening segment of the emergency phone call. In addition to the absence of "hello" in the call taker's first turn, there is no greeting sequence or exchange of initial inquiries. The dispatcher has produced an *institutional* identification ("Mid-City Emergency"), but is not expected to identify himself as an individual. The caller will be asked her name and address during the course of the call, but this information is not essential in the opening phase. While in a personal phone call, you need to know who you are talking to in order to carry on a conversation, in a business or service call you only need to know that you have reached the correct service. The participants have to align themselves in terms of their social and interactional roles (dispatcher and caller) rather than in terms of their individual identities. Also notice that there are no preliminary topics in emergency service calls. The participants go directly to the reason for the call or the request for help (Whalen and Zimmerman, 1987).

Calls to directory assistance are also examples of service calls. Their purpose (and hence their structure) is different from that of calls to emergency services. Wakin and Psathas (1994; see also Wakin and Zimmerman, 1999) found that since telephone companies want the calls to be completed as quickly as possible, call takers are taught how to answer calls in the most efficient manner possible. The operators begin by asking the caller for the city of the phone number they need, so that they can open that file on their computer while the caller is giving them the name of the person whose number they are looking for. They can then quickly enter the name and direct the computer to recite the number for the customer. Meanwhile, the call taker gets off the line to answer another call.

Excerpt 7 shows a call to directory assistance (Wakin and Psathas, 1994). Notice that the caller seems momentarily unsure of how she should respond to the operator's question in line 1 ("What city plea:se"). She first says "hi" (line 2), then produces a hesitation marker ("uh), and then states the city ("in Fairfield"). Instead of asking for the name, the operator then says "yes," confirming receipt of the name of the city. The caller then immediately produces the name (without being asked), and spells it (again without being asked). The caller thus shows that they are cooperating with the goal of completing the business of the call in the shortest amount of time possible. The operator then moves to close the call by saying "thank you." After the caller's return "thanks" in line 6, the operator pushes the button to play the phone number for the caller and disconnects from the call.

Excerpt 7: Wakin and Psathas (1994)
0   ((phone rings))
1   O: What city plea:se
2   C: hi uh in Fairfield
3   O: yes
4   C: Callhan c a l l h a n, the first name is Jack
5   O: thank you
6   C: thanks

In service call openings participants determine mutual availability to talk, align the identities of the participants, and perform any other actions that need to be performed prior to conducting the business of the call, but do so in a way that differs from openings in calls between friends or other acquainted persons.

Openings in face-to-face interactions

As explained above, opening sequences in face-to-face interactions may be shorter than those in telephone calls because some functions can be performed visually. In addition, the nature of the opening will vary depending on the context and purpose of the interaction. For example, Mondada (2009) studied how people approach others in public places to ask for information. She refers to these techniques for opening an encounter "pre-beginnings." This encounter is in French, with English subtitles below each line in italics:

Excerpt 8: Mondada (2009, p. 1981)

```
1   E   excusez-moi madame, je cherche l'église saint-roch
        sorry madam, I'm looking for the church of saint Roch
2       (0.6)
3   L:  euh: (.) elle est là.
        ehm: (.) it's here.
```

Speaker E uses an apology to summon the attention of Speaker L. The apology also serves to display an orientation to Speaker E's lack of acquaintanceship with the person addressed. Her request for directions then provides a justification for speaking to a stranger.

Pillet-Shore (2011) studies how people conduct introductions in face-to-face interactions. In Excerpt 9, Olexa (a college student who belongs to a sorority) arrives at a sorority event with her brother. Olexa then introduces her brother to her sorority sisters. Note the ways in which the opening of the interaction is similar to and different from the telephone call openings we considered above. Since it is a multi-party interaction, some actions are performed by two or more people, rather than just one. For example, the greeting exchange in lines 1 to 3 involves three people, and Olexa's introduction of her brother receives responses from four people (lines 5–8). Since the participants can see each other, a separate summons/answer sequence is not needed. Explicit self-identifications are also not required, except for the introduction of people who do not know Olexa's brother.

Excerpt 9: Pillet-Shore (2011, p. 79)

```
01   Kelsy:   He[y Olexa,
02   Olexa:      [Hello, huh huh.hh
03   Trish:   Hi:a[:y,
04   Olexa:       [Thisiz my little brother.hheh!
05   Jenel:   Oh wo[:w hi:.
06   Trish:        [Hi[:,
07   Sher:           [Hi:ee,
08   Kelsey:  He['s welcome.
09   Olexa:      [.hhh This is Trisha, Jenelle, Kelsy,
10   Olexa:   [an' Sher.
11   Jenel:   [Hi,
```

The opening sequences of face-to-face interactions in institutional settings differ in several key ways from the informal interactions between friends and strangers illustrated above. For example, consider Excerpt 10 which shows the opening sequences of a doctor/patient consultation (Pappas and Seale, 2009). In this excerpt the participants greet each other, then the doctor invites the patient to come in and sit down. After she does so, the doctor asks the patient how he can help her. There is no "how are you" sequence. The doctor moves instead straight to the business of the visit.

Excerpt 10: Heath (1986, p. 26; also cited in Pappas and Seale, 2009, p. 1232)

```
1   Dr:  Hello
2   P:   Hello
3   Dr:  Come in Misus Lebling
4        (3.3)
5   Dr:  Sit down please
6        (9.0)
7   Dr:  Yes (.) what can I do for you?
8   P:   .hhh well (.) since urm (.5) last Friday I've not been very
9        well Doctor Jarousa
```

Talk in institutional settings between acquainted persons who are all affiliated with the organization unfold differently than those between employees and clients (as in Excerpt 10 above). For example, consider Excerpt 11 from Mirivel and Tracy's (2005) paper on "pre-meeting" talk, which shows how coworkers initiate an interaction with each other while gathering for a meeting. In this excerpt the parties greet each other and exchange initial inquiries, but they do not do any identifications. The "how are you" sequence leads to pre-topical talk about Ernest's cold. The participants display the nature of their relationship and the informality of the pre-meeting talk with these actions. The social roles of colleagues in a workplace are different from those of a doctor and a patient in an office visit for a consultation. These different social roles and relationships are both displayed and created by how participants organize their talk in these settings.

Excerpt 11: Mirivel and Tracy (2005, pp. 9–10)

```
1   Jim:      good morning (.) How are you doing?
2             (.)
3   Ernest:   good how are you
4             (.)
5   Jim:      you gotta cold?
6             (1.0)
7   Ernest:   yes sir I do.
8   Jim:      oh: darn.
9             (2.3)
10  Frank:    that stinks du::de
11            (1.0)
12  Ernest:   I hear you.
13            (3.1)
14  Frank:    you're down with that huh?
15  Ernest:   ((smiles and chuckles))
```

Summary

Schegloff (1968) discovered that participants rely on the sequencing of events in telephone call openings so that the conversation can begin in an orderly manner. They use shared techniques and procedures at specific places in the call in order to solve the problems of establishing availability to talk and the identity of participants, and to introduce topics of talk in a way which is appropriate to the interactional context of the call and the relationship between the parties. Examining the structure of traditional phone calls reveals much about how interactions in general are begun. They make the work done by opening sequences visible. Participants vary the structure of opening sequences as needed to accomplish openings in a wide range of interactions, whether between acquainted people or strangers, and in both informal and institutional contexts. In later chapters we will examine how contemporary technological innovations (such as mobile phones, video phones and caller id) transform the nature of telephone call openings.

Student activities

1. Notice how friends answer the phone when you call them on a cell phone or a landline telephone with caller id. How do those openings differ from the openings in the traditional land line phone calls Schegloff (1968) studied?
2. Observe people arriving at work or school in the morning and note how face-to-face interactions are opened. Is saying hello the first thing that happens? What other types of conversational openings do you observe? How do people in this face to face setting summon one another to speak, or otherwise indicate they are available for interaction?

Recommended sources

Lindström, Anna. (1994), 'Identification and recognition in Swedish telephone conversation openings', *Language in Society*, 34, 231–52.

Mirivel, Julien C. and Tracy, Karen. (2005), 'Premeeting talk: an organizationally crucial form of talk', *Research on Language and Social Interaction*, 38, (1), 1–34.

Pappas, Yannis and Seale, Clive. (2009), 'The opening phase of telemedicine consultations: an analysis of interaction', *Social Science & Medicine*, 68, 1229–37.

Pillet-Shore, Danielle. (2011), 'Doing introductions: the work involved in meeting someone new', *Communication Monographs*, 78, (1), 73–95.

Schegloff, E. (2002a), 'Beginnings in the telephone', in J. Katz and M. Aakhus (eds) *Perpetual contact: Mobile communication, private talk, public performance*. Cambridge: Cambridge University Press, pp. 284–300.

—(2002b), 'Opening sequencing', in J. Katz and M. Aakhus (eds) *Perpetual contact: Mobile communication, private talk, public performance*. Cambridge: Cambridge University Press, pp. 326–85.

Sun, Hao. (2004), 'Opening moves in informal Chinese telephone conversations', *Journal of Pragmatics*, 36, pp. 1429–65.

9 Closings

Introduction

In Chapter 8 we studied how participants open conversations, and noted that before a conversation can begin participants must determine that all participants are available for talk and identify the participants (even if only by role, category, or location rather than by specific identity). Thus in ordinary telephone conversation openings, the greetings were not the first action performed. Greetings typically occurred in the third or fourth turn of the conversation, and were preceded by the summons/answer sequence and the identification and recognition sequence. Similarly, in closing a conversation there is quite a bit of interactional work that must be done to prepare the ground for farewells. In this chapter we will explore the interactional work that has to be done to terminate a conversation in an accountable and "ordinary" manner.

The work done by the terminal exchange

Ordinary conversations are typically ended with an exchange of goodbyes (a "farewell sequence"). The interactional work accomplished by the first "goodbye" is to propose suspension of the turn exchange system (Schegloff and Sacks, 1973). Recall from Chapter 5 that the turn taking system for ordinary conversation provides for the exchange of speakership via three turn taking options (Sacks et al., 1974). Briefly, when a current speaker reaches a transition relevance place, they can select a next speaker. If the current speaker does not select a next speaker, a next speaker may select themself. And, if a next speaker does not select themself, the current speaker may continue. These turn taking options recur each time a transition relevance place is reached. Therefore, the exchange of turns at talk *could* continue indefinitely unless something is done to stop it. Although participants are not required to speak (unless selected by another for a turn), simply being silent at a transition relevance place would be noticeable as the absence of a turn. It displays that a participant has declined to take a turn at talk at a place where turn transition is relevant (Sacks et al., 1974). Therefore, there needs to be an "off" button—something that provides a way of exiting from the turn taking system so that no one is expected to take a next turn, and the conversation can end.

By saying goodbye, a speaker proposes the suspension of the turn taking system. If the other participant responds with a return goodbye, they are in effect agreeing with the suspension of the turn taking system. The second goodbye shows the person who produced the first goodbye that their move to terminate the conversation has been heard, understood and accepted. Through the completion of the terminal exchange the participants display their orientation to the fact that they are no longer obligated or expected to take another turn at talk. If one party continues talking instead of saying goodbye, a new place for turn exchange will be produced, and the conversation will not end.

Locations for terminal exchanges

Terminal exchanges cannot be placed just anywhere in the conversation. For example, it would not be relevant to say goodbye immediately after the summons/answer sequence that opens a telephone call—at least not without appearing rude. The summons/answer sequence creates a space for a conversation (of whatever length) to occur; it does not create a space for a goodbye. Schegloff (1968) referred to this feature of the summons/answer sequence as its "nonterminality." Consider this hypothetical example in which a speaker says goodbye immediately after the summons/answer sequence:

Excerpt 1: Telephone Call (Hypothetical)
1   ((phone rings))   (Summons)
2   A: Hello?   (Answer)
3   B: Goodbye.   (Terminal Exchange)

As you can see from this hypothetical example, a terminal exchange could not accountably be placed immediately after a summons/answer sequence. It would be seen as either deliberately rude or interactionally incompetent.

Even after the opening sequence has been completed, there are any number of places in conversations where "goodbyes" are not relevant. For example, if someone asks a question, a goodbye is not relevant prior to the answer to the question. In Excerpt 2, a phone call to emergency services, the participants say goodbye in lines 8 and 9. However, imagine that the caller said "goodbye" after line 5, where the call taker had just asked the caller to verify the location of the fire being reported. This location would not have been suitable for a farewell, because the dispatcher's question creates an expectation that the question will be answered (as it is, in the caller's line 6). Because line 5 is constructed to elicit a response, a goodbye cannot accountably be placed after it.

> Excerpt 2: Raymond and Zimmerman (2007, p. 40)
> 1 CT: Nine-one-one emergency,
> 2 C: My name is Todd Fillmore=I live at thuh Vista del Monte Ranch,
> 3   and I wanna report uh <u>fire</u> [(uh)]
> 4 CT: [OK] is it in thee area of Two Thirty Five
> 5   and Mountain Glade or Old San Pedro,
> 6 C: Right.
> 7 CT: Okay we're on thuh way we'll be there in just uh minute
> 8 C: Thanks you=By-
> 9 CT: Okay=Bye

What we learn from this example is that not every location within a conversation is suitable for initiating the closing of a conversation. Something has to be done to prepare the ground for the goodbyes. The work of preparing the ground for the terminal exchange is typically done through what Schegloff and Sacks (1973) call the "preclosing sequence."

Pre-closing sequences

Terminal exchanges are typically preceded by one or more **pre-closing sequences**. Through pre-closing sequences participants display that they have nothing more to contribute to the current topic, and hence possibly, to the conversation as a whole. Preclosing moves typically consist of one word utterances such as "yeah" or "okay" which do not contribute anything to the topic of the conversation. They function as "passed turns," in which the speaker indicates they have nothing to say at this point in time. The following hypothetical exchanges illustrate the types of utterances that typically comprise pre-closing sequences:

> Excerpt 3: Hypothetical Pre-Closing Exchanges
> a. A: Well,
>   B: Okay
>
> b. A: Yeah
>   B: Right

    c. A: Okay
        B: Okay

Excerpt 4 below is from the end of an ordinary telephone conversation between acquainted persons. It begins with Speaker G reviewing arrangements for the next time they will get together (lines 1 and 2). Speaker E then confirms these arrangements in line 3 ("Yeah."). Following this, Speaker G produces a preclosing move in line 4 ("Okay."), which Speaker E responds to with a second preclosing move ("Okay dear,"; line 5). They then move to the exchange of goodbyes in lines 6 and 7 and end the phone call.

> Excerpt 4: Button (1987, p. 102; also cited in Nofsinger, 1991, p. 141)
> 1   G: I'll be down there, oh en you'll-
> 2   you'll be aroun' then when I [(come in)]
> 3   E: [Yeah.   ]
> 4   G: Okay.
> 5   E: Okay dear,
> 6   G: Buh Bye,
> 7   E: <u>Bye</u> bye,

A conversation may have only one preclosing sequence, as in Excerpt 4, or it may have a series of preclosing sequences, as in Excerpt 5 below (Schegloff and Sacks, 1973). There are several turns in Excerpt 5 which are possible pre-closing sequences. In lines 1 and 2, Speaker B is summing up the import of a story she or he has been telling. In line 3, Speaker C produces a listener response in overlap at a possibly complete turn constructional unit. Speaker C then produces a preclosing move in the clear (line 4), which receives a return preclosing move from Speaker B in line 5. The participants then produce another exchange of preclosing moves in lines 6 and 7 ("Yeah" and "Alrighty."). Speaker B then goes on to review arrangements for their next meeting (lines 7 and 8), ending this utterance with a tag question ("Okay?"), which Speaker C answers in the affirmative (line 9). Speaker B then produces another preclosing move ("<u>Al</u>righty.") in line 10, followed by Speaker C's return preclosing move in line 11 ("Okay."). After one more very brief review of arrangements in line 12 ("We'll see you then."), which Speaker C confirms in line 13 ("Okay."), they exchange goodbyes and end the call. The purpose of these multiple pre-closing sequences is to allow time for either participant to bring up any topic or unfinished business they want to before the conversation is ended.

> Excerpt 5: Schegloff and Sacks (1973, p. 318)
> 1   B: Well that's why I <u>said</u> I'm not gonna say anything, I'm
> 2   not making <u>any</u> <u>com</u>ments [about anybody.]
> 3   C: [Hmh   ]
> 4   C: Eh yeah
> 5   B: Yeah
> 6   C: Yeah
> 7   B: <u>Al</u>righty. Well I'll give you a call before we decide

```
 8        to come down. Okay?
 9   C:   Okay.
10   B:   Alrighty.
11   C:   Okay.
12   B:   We'll see you then.
13   C:   Okay.
14   B:   Bye bye.
15   C:   Bye
```

When a preclosing move is used, the speaker shows that they are passing on the opportunity to produce "topical" talk. However, in some interactional contexts an extended silence can function as a preclosing move. An extended silence, or "gap" makes termination of the conversation relevant by displaying that neither party has anything more to say (see Sacks et al., 1974). Even so, the conversation will rarely move from an extended silence directly to the terminal exchange of farewells. Typically at least one sequence of preclosing moves will be produced prior to the goodbyes. An extended silence is thus best thought of as a suitable location for preclosing moves rather than a preclosing move itself. It is to the locations for preclosing sequences that we now turn.

Locations for preclosing sequences

In general, preclosing sequences occur at points in the conversation where participants have nothing else to contribute to the current topic of talk, or possibly to the conversation itself. As mentioned above, an extended silence (or "gap") in a conversation can serve as a location for a preclosing sequence, by displaying that no one has anything more to say at that point. Another typical location for preclosing sequences is reviewing arrangements, as we saw in Excerpts 4 and 5 (Button, 1987). Reviewing arrangements for the next time the participants will talk or see each other makes closure of the current conversation relevant. If a preclosing sequence follows the reviewing of arrangements, the participants may then move to a terminal exchange.

The third major location for preclosing moves is at topic boundaries. We will cover topic organization in detail in Chapter 11, but for now let's just consider several of the ways particip- ants can work to bring a topic of talk to closure. Three common techniques for bounding topics include assessments, summaries, and aphorisms or clichés.

Assessments. Assessments are short turns which work to assess or evaluate something such as a prior utterance, story, topic or event (Pomerantz, 1984). As a hypothetical example, imagine that someone is telling the story of how their car got a flat tire, and a story recipient responds with an assessment such as "That sounds awful." Assessments respond to the story but in a way that does not add new information or make more on-topic talk relevant. Assessments make transition to another topic (or to closure of the conversation) relevant.

Summaries. Participants can bring topics to closure by "wrapping up" a topic with a summary or drawing the "upshot" of a story or a subject of discussion. While not precluding further development of the topic, summaries indicate that at least one participant considers the topic potentially complete at this point, thus making a preclosing sequence relevant. Excerpt 5 (above) shows Speaker B summarizing the prior topic in lines 1 and 2.

Aphorisms or clichés. Aphorisms, maxims, pithy sayings, or clichés (such as "it never rains, it pours") can also be used to close down a topic (Schegloff and Sacks, 1973).

> Another 'topic-bounding' technique [...] involves one party's offering of a proverbial or aphoristic formulation of conventional wisdom which can be heard as the 'moral' or 'lesson' of the topic being thereby possibly closed. Such formulations are 'agreeable with'. When such a formulation is offered by one party and agreed to by another, a topic may be seen (by them) to have been brought to a close. (Schegloff and Sacks, 1973, p. 306)

These sayings make closing relevant by providing a "last word" on the topic of discussion.

> Excerpt 6: Button (1991, p. 255; also cited in West, 2006, p. 385)
> 1   A: Yeah well, things uh always work out for the best
> 2   B: Oh, certainly. Alright, [Bea
> 3   A: [Uh huh, okay,
> 4   B: G'bye
> 5   A: Goodnight

It is important to note that while preclosing sequences can be made relevant by one of these methods of closing down a prior topic, participants are not required to produce them. Participants always have the option of continuing the conversation by returning to topical talk or introducing a new topic (Button, 1987). Similarly, when a preclosing sequence is produced, participants do not necessarily move to terminate the conversation. Preclosing moves can serve as an interlude between topics during which participants think of further topics to develop or introduce.

For example, Excerpt 7 below shows a portion of an extended phone call between two acquainted people. They have already been talking for a while when this segment occurs. This excerpt shows participants "moving out of closings" (Button, 1987). At the beginning of the excerpt they had begun closing-relevant actions by reviewing arrangements for the next time they will meet. This turns out to be more complex than anticipated, because Speaker A is not available for the type of event that Speaker B was planning. A preclosing move is potentially relevant after reviewing arrangements for their next meeting. However, after completing the talk about arrangements in line 20, Speaker A begins another unit type ("I=huh::"). She then hesitates (1.2 second pause in line 21), and goes on to introduce a new topic, which ends up being the topic of Ada's death. In short, not every opportunity to begin a closing sequence is carried through. Participants may discover they have more things they need to discuss.

Excerpt 7: Schegloff and Sacks (1973, p. 320)

1 A: I mean b'cause l=eh you're going to this meeting at twelve
2   thirdy, and I don't want to uh inconvenience <u>you</u>,
3 B: Well, even if you get here et abayout eh ten thirty, or
4   eleven uh' clock, we still have en hour en a half,
5 A: Okay, <u>A</u>lright,
6 B: Fine. We c'd have a bite, en[(talk),]
7 A: [Yeh,] Weh-No! No,
8   <u>don't</u> prepare any [thing]
9 B: [And uh-] I'm not gonnah pre<u>pare</u>, we'll
10   juss whatever it'll [be, we'll (   )]
11 A: [<u>No</u>! No.   ] I don't mean that.
12   I mean- because uh, <u>she</u> en I'll prob'ly uh be spending the
13   day together, so uh: we'll go out tuh lunch, or something
14   like that. hh So I mean if you:: have a cuppa cawfee or
15   something, I mean [that uh that'll be fine. But] uh-
16 B: [Yeah.   ]
17 B: Fine.
18 A: Other than that don't [uh   ]
19 B: [Fine.]
20 A: Don't bothuh with anything else. l=huh::
21   (1.2)
22 A: l=uh::: I <u>did</u> wanna tell you, and I didn't wanna tell
23   you uh:: last night. Uh because you had entert-uh, company.
24   I- I- I- had something- <u>terrible</u> t'tell you. So uh
25 B: How terrible <u>is</u> it.
26 A: Uh, tuh- as worse it could <u>be</u>.
27   (.8)
28 B: W'y- mean Ada?
29 A: Uh yah
30 B: Whad'she do, die?
31 A: Mm

Button (1987) showed that participants can "move in and out of closings" (begin preclosing sequences and then revert to topical talk) many times before ending the conversation by moving to a terminal exchange.

Terminal exchanges

Terminal exchanges are adjacency pairs, and as such, once a first "goodbye" is produced, an expectation is created that a return goodbye will be the next event in the interaction. Given a first goodbye, a second goodbye is conditionally relevant. The absence of the second goodbye in the sequence could be taken to display rudeness or anger (Schegloff and Sacks, 1973). If this norm is violated we draw inferences about the person—their failure to reciprocate with a return "goodbye" is noticeable and accountable.

However, whether an absent return "goodbye" is accountable depends on the type of interaction being engaged in and the specific circumstances as they unfold. If one is angry, and walks away in a huff without saying goodbye, that will likely be interpreted as an intentional snub. However, imagine that you are chatting with a friend and their mobile phone rings at the instant they were supposed to have been saying "goodbye" to you. If they instead answered the phone call, their failure to produce the goodbye would be accountable, and probably not problematic. In addition, there are some types of interactions in which goodbyes can be accountably unilateral or even elided altogether. For example, in emergency phone calls to the police the second goodbye in the sequence may be either not produced or the call taker may terminate the call before it is produced. This is most likely to occur when the call taker needs to quickly make themselves available to receive another incoming call.

In addition to the time constraints emergency service call takers operate under, police calls differ from ordinary conversations because they are "**monotopical**" as opposed to potentially "multi-topical." While an ordinary conversation may end up having only one topic, there is no limitation or requirement for how many topics participants in ordinary conversation should produce (Sacks et al., 1974). One of the functions of the preclosing sequence is to allow any participant the opportunity to re-open topical talk and either revisit a prior topic or raise a new topic for discussion. But for police calls, there is only one topic of talk: the problem the caller is calling about (Zimmerman, 1984). Within the context of this topic, the discussion may touch on many different things as the caller and call taker work together to get the information needed to provide help. However, all of this talk serves the purpose of the overall topic of the caller's problem. When this problem has been dealt with, there is nothing left to discuss, and the conversation can be brought to a close. Excerpt 8 shows the ending of an emergency service call about a noisy fight in an alley way. The call taker responds to the caller's problem by offering to send help (line 6). After a very truncated closing sequence (lines 7–8), the call taker says "Bye." and then cuts the connection to free her line to take another call.

> Excerpt 8: Whalen and Zimmerman (1990, p. 475)
> 1   C: What iz happening is that a woman has been screaming for thuh last
> 2   twenty five, thirty minutes "give me my money, give me my money"
> 3   heh! .hh and uh (.) it's just kept up too long and uh they're- they're
> 4   assaulting each other physically and uh:, I don't know what thuh
> 5   problem is there.
> 6   CT: Okay, we'll get somebody there=
> 7   C: ='kay thank you ma'am
> 8   CT: Umhm. Bye.

Closing sequences in calls to emergency services thus differ from those in ordinary telephone calls in that they are likely to be brief and truncated.

Summary

As with opening a conversation, closing a conversation involves the participation and cooperation of both (or in multi-participant conversations, all) of the participants in the conversation. The participants share assumptions about when it is relevant to close a conversation, and use shared techniques and procedures (such as pre-closing sequences) to set up a location for the termination of a conversation. The procedures used allow participants in ordinary conversation maximum flexibility in deciding whether to move to close the conversation or "open up the closing" in order to resume topical talk, whereas participants in institutional contexts may be under additional constraints (e.g., to limit the call to one topic).

Student activity

1. Notice how friends end telephone calls. Are these closings similar to or different from the closings sequences of telephone calls between friends and acquaintances described in this chapter?
2. Observe people ending conversations at the workplace or at school. What do people do before they say goodbye? Are the methods people use to close these face-to-face interactions similar to or different from the ways people typically close telephone conversations?

Recommended sources

Button, Graham. (1987), 'Moving out of closings', in G. Button and J. R. E. Lee (eds) *Talk and Social Organization*. Clevedon: Multilingual Matters, pp. 101–51.

Schegloff, Emanuel A. and Sacks, Harvey. (1973), 'Opening up closings', *Semiotica*, 8, 289–327.

West, Candace. (2006), 'Coordinating closings in primary care visits: producing continuity of care', in John Heritage and Douglas W. Maynard (eds.) *Communication in Medical Care: Interactions between Primary Care Physicians and Patients*. Cambridge: Cambridge University Press, pp. 379–415.

Error Avoidance and Repair

10

Chapter contents

Introduction

Nofsinger (1991, p. 124) defines repair as the "processes through which we fix conversational problems." Conversational problems can include specific types of errors in speech (such as errors in pronunciation, grammar, or word choice), interactional problems (such as neglecting to answer a question), or social problems (such as saying something impolite or offensive). For example, a speaker may discover that they have produced a grammatical error, and may edit their utterance to correct that error. However, not everything which speakers repair is an actual error. A participant can edit or revise their utterance regardless of whether an actual error has been produced, and can also choose *not* to correct actual errors. Correcting an unimportant error could unnecessarily interrupt the flow of the interaction, or draw attention to the speaker in a negative way. Participants may therefore choose to ignore errors if they are unimportant, or if correcting the error would challenge the speaker's "presentation of self" (Goffman, 1959).

Schegloff (2000) explains the more general term "**trouble source**," which includes both actual errors and "non-errors" which participants may choose to repair:

> [T]he sorts of actions underwritten by the practices of repair are not limited to 'correction', nor are their targets limited to 'errors'—hence the use of the terms 'repair' and 'repairable' or 'trouble-source'. There can be 'trouble' grounded in other than mistakes—the unavailability of a word, such as a name, when needed (or of a name *recognition* on the recipient's side); hearing problems engendered by interference by ambient noise; an uncertain hearing or understanding in search of confirmation, and the like. And on the intervention side there can be practices directed to other than correction—for example, searching for a word, requesting repetition, or offering a candidate hearing or understanding for confirmation or replacement (Schegloff et al. 1977: 362–3). (Schegloff, 2000, p. 209)

In this chapter we will first examine a range of interactional events that can be sources of trouble in talk, and then examine how participants avoid or repair these types of troubles.

Some common types of repairables

Jefferson (1974) describes a number of common types of repairables in her paper on error correction. We will review several of them here:

Grammatical errors

Excerpt 1 shows the production of a grammatical error. In line 3, Anna (the mother of a new-born baby) says "Yea:h he sleep- he slept very early." She first produced the phrase "he sleep-", (note the dash indicating the word sleep was cutoff abruptly), then replaced it with the past tense of the verb ("he slept…"). After a brief pause, she repairs her utterance again ("fell asleep at- nine thirty"). The recipients of this utterance may interpret the cutoff and the hesitation as indicating that Anna is editing her utterance-in-progress. They can thus understand Anna's utterance to be "He fell asleep at nine thirty," rather than "he sleep he slept very early fell asleep at nine thirty."

Excerpt 1: Conversations between Students
1   Cara: how was thuh sleep last night? can you get any sleep?
2   (0.4)
3   Anna: Yea:h he sleep- he slept very early (0.4) fell asleep at- nine thirty

Word choice errors

Excerpt 2 shows a hypothetical example of a word choice error of the type that Jefferson (1974, p. 187) calls a "contrast class" error. "Tom" announces that he is Carol's sister, then abruptly cuts off the word "sister-", produces a filled pause ("uh"), and then says "brother."

Excerpt 2: Jefferson (1974, p. 187)
Tom: Hi. I'm Carol's sister- uh brother.

Pronunciation and other speech production errors

Pronunciation errors and other malapropisms also occur fairly often. In Excerpt 3, Ernie misspeaks, saying "savorite-". After a brief filled pause ("uh") he says "favorite," thus displaying that "favorite" is a correction of the mis-spoken "savorite-".

Excerpt 3: (Hypothetical)
Ernie: Which horse is your savorite- uh favorite?

Violation of social norms

In addition to errors in the production of language (whether grammatical, semantic, or phonetic), there are social errors that can be made, including violation of rules of politeness or other social norms. These types of errors may lead a speaker to edit their utterance to repair or avoid the social implications of the violation. Excerpt 4 shows a defendant in traffic court speaking to the judge. As we explained in Chapter 4, Jefferson (1974) argues that the hesitation in the speaker's utterance conveys that the utterance was being edited, and that the mismatch between "thuh" and "officer" suggests that the speaker had been preparing to say "cop" and then replaced it with "officer." In English there are two ways of pronouncing the definite article "the." People typically say "thuh" when the article precedes words that begin with consonants, and "thee" when the article precedes words that begin with vowels (Jefferson, 1974). In the formal court setting, the defendant may have realized that the term "officer" was more polite and appropriate than the informal "cop." The editing of this utterance, while a simple instance of hesitation or a possible word search, may also display for us the social organization of the setting it occurs within. The relative powerlessness of the speaker in the context of a court session, and the formality of the setting may reflexively reflect and help construct the interaction as talk in a specific institutional setting.

Excerpt 4: Jefferson (1974, p. 184)
A: I told that to THUH- UH- officer.

Placement errors

The placement of utterances can also be a source of trouble in the interaction. For example, long gaps in talk can indicate the failure of a participant to take a turn at talk, and may prove awkward or embarrassing for participants. Interruptions can be problematic both practically (in terms of making it hard to be heard) and socially (in terms of implications of lack of consideration for others). Participants do sometimes take steps to repair troubles in talk caused by problematic placement of utterances. Jefferson (2004c) found that participants can use partial repeats of turn beginnings to ensure that a turn which began in overlap can be produced "in the clear." This repetition can be seen as a repair of overlapped or simultaneous speech. In Excerpt 5 Speaker B begins talking in line 3 while Speaker A is still finishing his or her utterance. Note that the first part of Speaker B's utterance is produced in overlap with Speaker A's turn. Once Speaker A stops speaking, Speaker B repeats part of her simultaneous turn ("I didn' know...") in the clear, to make sure it was heard.

Excerpt 5: Jefferson (1987, pp. 80–1)
```
1   A:   Yeah my mother asked me. I says I dunno. I haven't heard from her.
2        I didn't know what days you had [classes or anything.°
3   B:                                   [Yeah an I ddin' know° I didn'
4        know when you were home or- [I was gonna.
```

The correction of "non-errors"

There are many different types of "errors" possible. When conversation analysts talk about errors, they include the "correction" of things that are "correct." You can "correct" something just because you want to change it. This is why we often refer to "potential trouble sources" in the conversation rather than "errors" or "mistakes."

Excerpt 6 is an example of a speaker correcting a "non-error" (Schegloff et al., 1977). Ken replaces one word with another, not because one is wrong (they both mean essentially the same thing in this context), but as a matter of choice. In Excerpt 6, Ken first says, "later the bell r-", cuts off the last word abruptly, and then completes the utterance with ("the doorbell rang..."). He thus replaces "bell" with "doorbell."

Excerpt 6: Schegloff et al. (1977, p. 363)
```
Ken:    Sure enough ten minutes later the bell r- the doorbell rang...
```

The repair of errors: A two-part process

Jefferson (1974) observes that we can often distinguish between the **initiation of repair** and the repair itself. The initiation of repair is the process of identifying or locating the trouble source in the utterance. The repair itself is the fixing of the trouble source by replacing it with something else. Note that in practice, these two procedures often cannot be separated. The process of replacing the error with something else is done via locating the error by marking it with pauses, hesitation or other perturbations of speech. For example, consider Excerpt 7 below from a phone call to a poison control hotline:

Excerpt 7: Frankel (1989, p. 214; also cited in Nofsinger, 1991, p. 125)
```
1   P:   She tasted it? is it l- (0.1) in a liquid for:m?
2   C:   Ye:s
```

The Poison Control Center call taker ("P") produces the first part of an utterance in the middle of line 1 ("is it l-"). She then hesitates briefly ("0.1"), and produces a replacement for what went before the hesitation and micro-pause: "in a liquid for:m?". The completed utterance can be understood to be "She tasted it? Is it in a liquid for:m?" The cutoff on liquid ("l-") and the micro-pause ("(0.1)"), are the initiation of the repair. They stop the utterance in progress and mark the utterance as problematic. When the call taker resumes with "in a liquid for:m?", the caller can hear this as replacing "l-". Note that without the hesitation which initiates the repair, it could be difficult to tell which part of the utterance is the repairable and which part is the repair.

The recipient of the utterance hears the replaced item along with the hesitation markers. They may in fact draw inferences about the speaker from the fact that they made and corrected an error—this behavior is accountable. The production and repair of the error is part of the speaker's "presentation of self", to use Goffman's (1959) terminology, in which how we behave in public is viewed by others and used as a source of information about us.

Self and other repair

The error repair format involves first producing all or part of an error, hesitating, and then producing the correct word or phrase. This procedure provides a concise and efficient way of editing the utterance so that recipients can understand that the corrected item replaces the error. The importance of the distinction between the initiation of repair and the accomplishment of repair becomes clear when we start examining the role each participant plays in the repair process.

The initiation of repair can be done by the person producing the trouble source or by another participant in the conversation (Schegloff et al., 1977). In Excerpt 7 (above), the same person produced the trouble source, initiated the repair, and performed the repair. This is an instance of "self repair." Another typical pattern is for a current speaker to produce a trouble source, and another participant to initiate repair by identifying the trouble source. The original speaker then actually performs the repair. Excerpt 8 shows an example of **other-initiated repair**.

Excerpt 8: Nofsinger (1991, p. 125)

```
1   B:   Why don'cha flick on the lights. (0.9) I've (0.6) discovered
2        th't (0.3) I'm in the dark
3        (0.9)
4   C:   hhuh .hh
5   B:   hh .hh Which actually is: (0.6) an enlightening experience
6   C:   hh heh heh heh .hh t' discover it? or t'be.
7   B:   t'discover it.
```

In line 5 Speaker B produces a trouble source (an utterance which Speaker C finds ambiguous). Speaker C initiates repair by asking "t' discover it? or t'be." (line 6), thus referring to the prior utterance and asking for clarification of it. Speaker B then repairs the error by providing the clarification Speaker C asked for ("t'discover it."; line 7).

Nofsinger (1991, p. 126) notes that "repairs are overwhelmingly done in close proximity to the turn containing the trouble source." There are three main reasons for this. First, the more time (and talk) that intervenes between the trouble source and its repair, the more complicated it is to identify or locate the trouble source. Second, the farther away the talk gets from the trouble source, the less relevant the error may be to the conversation, so the less need there is to correct it. Third, in some cases, the further away the conversation gets from the trouble source before it is corrected, the more damage is done by the error. A very old *Saturday Night Live* skit with Gilda Radner illustrates the problematics of the delayed repair of misunderstandings. Ms. Radner's character was a commentator on a TV news show who has been asked to discuss the problem of violence on television. However, she mishears the question as referring to "violins on television," and therefore spends a couple minutes arguing that children should not be prevented from hearing violin music on television. Eventually she is interrupted by the person who initially asked the question, and informed of her mistake. Occasionally, a conversation will continue for a long time without a critical misunderstanding being resolved. Schegloff (1992) gives a fascinating example of a conversation which proceeded for several minutes before the participants realized they were talking about two different historical events. Normally, these types of misunderstandings are resolved quickly, typically by the third or fourth turn in the sequence, so such extended misunderstandings can be avoided.

Error avoidance

The difference between error avoidance and error repair is that with error avoidance, the speaker catches the "error" or trouble source before it is spoken, so no error is actually produced. The only evidence that the speaker may be editing their utterance-in-progress is the hesitation, pause or repetition that the speaker may produce while they take the time to consider what to say next. The error avoidance process may result in an utterance which is seamless except for a slight (or not so slight) hesitation or perturbation of speech. The recipient of the utterance (or the observer or analyst) can note the hesitation and infer that an error was avoided.

In short, hesitations, pauses and repetitions can be evidence that indicate a speaker has recognized a potential error or trouble in talk *before* producing it. In Excerpt 9 Speaker A begins an utterance, produces a filled pause ("uh-"), and then completes the utterance. When the utterance is read without the hesitation, you can see that nothing was obviously replaced or "corrected." The utterance simply continues after the hesitation. Perhaps the hesitation was due to the speaker doing a word search or needing to think about how to end the utterance. By gaining more time, the speaker was able to avoid an error.

Excerpt 9: Jefferson (1974, p. 183)
Leslie: I'll have yer uh g-garment uh- at thuh jeweler's next door…

Note that in our discussion of error repair and error avoidance we have not discussed the emotional state of the speaker. People often assume that if someone is hesitating or producing a lot of filled pauses (e.g., "uh"), that this indicates they are nervous or upset. It may well be that when we are upset or nervous there are more perturbations and pauses in our speech. However, notice that when you examine transcripts of interactions, the hesitations and perturbations are not randomly placed. They can often be seen to be linked to speakers' editing of their utterance-in-progress. It is not necessary to know or assume the emotional state of a speaker in order to discover what work the hesitations or perturbations are doing in the interaction.

Locations for self-initiated repair

Opportunities to initiate and accomplish repair of troubles in talk are not distributed equally between participants in a conversation. Current speakers have more opportunities to repair their utterances than do other participants, because they already have the floor when the "error" is produced. The current speaker can initiate repair of their utterance-in-progress in the same turn as the trouble source. Other participants typically wait for a transition relevance place (or a later turn) to initiate repair of a current speaker's utterance.

For example, in Excerpt 10 there are three instances of self-initiated repair in lines 4 and 5 of the transcript. Liz starts to say "another girl an then the-", cuts herself off after "the-", replaces it with "my fiancé an three-", cuts herself off after "three-" and replaces it with "two other guys". The current speaker has both initiated and accomplished repair of her own utterance-in-progress.

Excerpt 10: Conversations between Students
1   Liz: an::so:: (0.9) this wasn't <u>planned</u> but we ended up=like hh hh it
2   would=of been like a purfect play station commercial where some
3   were=like (0.2) .hh sittin aroun my friends apartment were play-
4   =like (1.0) there's me:: an (0.4) uhm: another girl an then the- my
5   fiancé an three- two other guys

If a current speaker does not self-repair in the same turn, their next opportunity to self-repair is at the transition relevance place at the end of their utterance. In Excerpt 11 Ruth completes an utterance (".h so what did ja get in::? (0.2) our other class,") in line 1. Immediately after the completion of this possibly complete turn constructional unit, Ruth clarifies which class she is referring to with the phrase "what sociology of thuh family °or whatever°." The juxtaposition of these two parts of her utterance enables the recipients of the utterance to hear the later phrase as clarifying or repairing the first. Perhaps Ruth thought that "Our other class" was too vague. Replacing this with the more specific "sociology of the family or whatever" narrows the field of potential courses to other sociology courses they both have taken.

Excerpt 11: Conversations between Students
1   Ruth: .h so what did ja get in::? (0.2) our other class, what sociology of
2   thuh family °or whatever°

Self-repair of errors can also occur in what is referred to as the "third turn position." The third turn is the current speaker's *next* turn after another speaker has had the floor (Schegloff et al., 1977).

First Turn	(Speaker A produces turn with "error")
Second Turn	(Speaker B)
Third Turn	(Speaker A initiates repair of error in the first turn)

Figure 10.1 Self-repair of error in third turn position

Excerpt 12 shows Speaker L completing a turn in line 1, using the word "today." Speaker M then responds with a question in line 2. In line 3, Speaker L begins his turn not with an answer to Speaker M's question, but with the self initiation of a repair. He replaces "today" (from line 1) with "w'll not today, maybe yesterday, aw who knows when, huh,". After this repair, Speaker L then answers Speaker M's question ("it's called Dragon Stew."; lines 3–4).

Excerpt 12: Schegloff et al. (1977, p. 366)
1   L: I read a very interesting story today,
2   M: uhm, what's that.
3   L: w'll not today, maybe yesterday, aw who knows when, huh, it's
4   called Dragon Stew.

Another form of "third turn repair" occurs when it is the recipient's *response* to the first turn which is problematic, rather than the first turn itself (Schegloff, 1992). When the first speaker detects that the recipient's understanding of their utterance was problematic, they may then initiate a third turn repair in order to clarify their initial turn. This happens in Excerpt 13, where Dan can tell from Louise's response that she is thinking of something different than what he was thinking of. He repairs this misunderstanding in line 3 ("No, I mean Al.").

Excerpt 13: Schegloff (1992, p. 1303)
1   Dan: Well that's a little different from last week.
2   Louise: heh heh heh Yeah. We were in hysterics last week.
3   Dan: . No, I mean Al.
4   Louise: Oh. He…

Locations for other-initiated repair

The primary opportunity for other-repair is the next turn after the trouble source (Schegloff et al., 1977). There are several different techniques available to next speakers to initiate repair of another speaker's prior utterance. One common technique is to initiate repair by locating a trouble spot in the prior speaker's utterance with a brief request for clarification such as "what?" "who?", or even "huh?". Excerpt 14 illustrates this method of other-initiation of repair. This excerpt is from a psychiatric intake interview between a doctor and a client. In line 3 the doctor asks, "Have you ever tried a clinic?". For whatever reason, the client finds this question problematic. Perhaps he had trouble hearing the question, or perhaps he was momentarily distracted. In line 4 the client uses a request for clarification ("What?") to initiate repair by identifying line 3 as a trouble source. The doctor responds by repeating the question in line 5, which the client then answers. Note that while the client has initiated the repair in the next turn position, the doctor actually produces the repair, by re-issuing the question.

Excerpt 14: Schegloff et al. (1977, p. 367)
1 D: Were you uh you were in therapy with a private doctor?
2 C: yah
3 D: Have you ever tried a clinic?
4 C: What?
5 D: Have you ever tried a clinic?
6 C: ((sigh)) No, I don't want to go to a clinic.

Another common technique for other-initiation of repair is what Schegloff et al. (1977) call "partial repeat of the trouble source." The next speaker repeats all or part of the prior utterance, typically with questioning intonation, thus identifying the prior speaker's utterance as problematic. In Excerpt 15 from a conversation between three students recording a conversation for a class, the subject of movies has been introduced. Rose says that she saw a movie called "Nell" ("i saw ne:ll?"; line 4). After a brief pause in line 5, Rick initiates a repair of Rose's utterance with a repeat of the trouble source with questioning intonation (line 6). Rose then repairs her utterance in line 8 by repeating the title of the film.

Excerpt 15: Conversations between Students
1 Rick: haven't seen uh movie in uh long time. [have] you?
2 Mary: [(aye-)]
3   (0.4)
4 Rose: i saw ne:ll?
5   (0.4)
6 Rick: nell?
7   (0.2)
8 Rose: ne[ll.]
9 Rick: [was] that good?

```
10        (0.2)
11 Rose:   ih=was preddy goo:°d.°=
```

While typically the recipient of an utterance will *initiate* repair (as in the examples above) and let the person who produced the problematic utterance *make* the repair, at times the recipient produces the repair themselves. This is shown in Excerpt 16, when Norm replaces "Wednesday." from Larry's line 1 with "Tomorrow." in line 2.

Excerpt 16: Jefferson (1987, p. 87)
```
1  Larry:  They're going to drive ba:ck Wednesday.
2  Norm:   Tomorrow.
3  Larry:  Tomorrow. Righ[t.
4  Norm:                 [M-hm,
5  Larry:  They're working half day.
```

Repair and preference organization

Recall that when we were studying adjacency pairs in Chapter 6, we noted that for some adjacency pairs there are two possible categories of responses, with one preferred and the other dispreferred. The term preference organization was not used to refer to the emotions or opinions of the participants engaged in the interaction, but rather to social or societal preferences for one type of response over another. We also noted that there is a structural component to preference organization, with participants using different techniques to formulate their preferred and dispreferred responses. Preferred responses tend to be formulated quickly, simply, and directly, while dispreferred responses are characterized by delay, indirectness, explanations and mitigations. It is also the case that the preferred responses are produced more frequently than dispreferred responses.

In terms of how preference organization applies to the repair of troubles in talk, there are both similarities and differences to the preference organization of adjacency pairs. Schegloff et al. (1977) discovered that there is a preference for self repair of errors. One reason for this is because two of the three locations for self repair occur before recipients of the utterance have even one chance to initiate repair. A current speaker has three primary locations for self-repair: within their current turn, at the transition relevance place at the end of their turn, and in the third turn of the sequence. A next speaker has two primary locations to initiate other-repair: in the second turn position (after the problematic turn is completed), or in the third turn position. There is a good chance that an error that needs repairing will be self-repaired by the speaker before the recipient's turn, thus increasing the proportion of errors that are self-repaired. Second, when the recipient does get a chance to initiate repair, they typically initiate the repair by identifying the problem and locating it. The original speaker is generally the one to produce the repair itself, thus also increasing the proportion of repairs that are self-repairs as opposed to other-repairs.

Summary

Interactional resources exist for the correction or revision of errors or other non-error troubles in talk. A speaker may revise their own utterance, or a recipient may initiate repair of the speaker's utterance. When self-repairing, speakers typically initiate the repair by a pause or hesitation marker, which then enables listeners to interpret what follows as a replacement of the problematic part of the utterance. When initiating other-repair, participants typically use a question or partial repeat of the prior turn to locate the object needing repair. Because current speakers' opportunities to repair their own utterances occur *before* other participants have a chance to intervene, instances of self-repair are more common than instances of other-initiated repair. There is therefore a "preference" for self repair (Schegloff et al., 1977).

Student activity

Compare the two excerpts below. Which excerpt illustrates error avoidance, and which illustrates error repair? Explain why.

Excerpt 17: (Conversation between Students)
7   A: i=don'=know how i've <u>done</u> it all thes:e (0.3) past few <u>ye</u>ars.

Excerpt 18: Jefferson (1974, p. 185)
Desk: He was here lay- uh earlier, but 'e left-

Recommended sources

Jefferson, Gail. (1974), 'Error correction as an interactional resource', *Language in Society*, 13, (2), 181–99.

Schegloff, Emanuel A. (2000), 'When "Others" Initiate Repair', *Applied Linguistics*, 21, (2), 205–43.

Schegloff, Emanuel A., Jefferson, Gail, and Sacks, Harvey. (1977), 'The preference for self-correction in the organization of repair in conversation', *Language*, 53, 361–82.

11 Creating Topical Coherence

Chapter contents

Introduction

When we think about topics of talk, our minds immediately go to what people talked about—the "content" of the conversation. But for conversation analysts, the "topic of topics" does not have as much do with *what* people talk about as it has to do with *how* the subject matter of talk is organized. If you examine a conversation carefully, you will quickly realize that any attempts to categorize the content of the conversation seem arbitrary and potentially infinite. For example, if someone mentions their dog "Rover," should the topic of conversation be characterized as Rover, dogs, German Shepherds, pets, animals or typical dog names?

As Schegloff (1990) points out, the source of topical coherence in a conversation is more often due to the types of actions people are producing and how they organize and structure their talk, rather than to any inherent "relatedness" of the subject matter being discussed. For conversation analysts, therefore, the topic of "topics" is about the procedures people use to organize their talk, which then result in different patterns of topic development. In this chapter we will examine how participants work to develop or refocus a current topic, close down a topic, or initiate a new topic.

Creating topical continuity

Participants can formulate utterances to display their connection with prior talk (thus creating **topical continuity**) or to display its divergence from prior talk. What we are calling "topical continuity" occurs when a series of utterances are organized so that their topical cohesiveness is apparent. Excerpt 1 (below) is from a mediation session between two brothers ("Bob" and "Ron") who had inherited a house from their mother. They were in disagreement over whether they should sell the house and split the proceeds, or let Bob buy the house from Ron. The mediation session is facilitated by two mediators ("MA" and "MB"). As you read the excerpt, notice the different subjects or "topics" that are touched upon as they talk.

Excerpt 1: Garcia West Coast Data Set, Mediation 5, pp. 80–1

```
 1  MA:   . . . let's assu:me u:h u::h s:mutually satisfactory price, could be
 2          arrived at, (.) for Bob to buy=out your interest=in=it. (  ) how
 3          could you accomplish tha:t? (  ) I take it chou have very little
 4          income?
 5  Ron:   °(ri:ght.)
 6          (  )
 7  Bob:   How could I accomplish thuh buy=out (  ) I would hah- I
 8          would haf to=u::hm hhm I'd have to start generating income. (  )
 9          an' I would have to=u:hm (  ) call=in my presen' investments, .h
10          (  ) u::h (.) fer=fer=thuh- I could- (.) ya=know?, uh- (  ) do
11          fordy!, (  ) I=could=give='em thuh fordy cash, .h an' make
12          payments on thuh re::st? (  ) u::h
13  MA:    .hh could you go to an institutional, (  ) lender, (.) for example,
14          .h
15          (  )
16  Bob:   I do[ubt it.]
17  MA:        [and to]MO:RROW,
18          (  )
19  MA:    u::h
20          (  )
21  MB:    could=you=gedduh loan?
22          (.)
23  Bob:   it'd=haf to be private money!, twe:lve percent!,
24          ya=know?,=an'=I'd=have=°tuh- (.) an' I'd have to really
25          scra:mble?, to do=it, you=know? an'=
26  MA:                                    =(in=other=words), you
27          know, he's not gonna wanna=be tied up °with °u:::h (  ) with
28          any kine=of=uh no:te from you? (  ) .h he's gonna want his
29          ca::sh, 'cause he's got his own things he has to do=he needs thuh
30          money! (  ) tch now, I don't think he'd have thuh sli:ghdest
31          problem, if he had (reached uh) mutually satisfactory PRICE!,
32          (  ) if you were cashed (out)! (  ) tch=and you continued to live
```

33	there=the only way I would see that <u>ha:</u>ppening? ( ) .hhh (.)
34	would=<u>be</u>- ( ) for <u>you</u> duh go an' get .h ( ) uh loa:n in
35	addition to thuh ca:sh you HA:Ve, ( ) buy=im <u>out</u>? . . .

Many different things were discussed in this excerpt, including buying or selling a house, income, investments, payments, loans, and cash. All of these things are part of the "topic" of the conversation. One way of characterizing the topic of this excerpt could be "how can Bob buy out his brother's share of the house?" The many things that are discussed are the issues that came up while the participants were trying to answer that question. How could Bob generate the income necessary to pay for the house? How large a down payment could he afford to pay? Could Bob qualify for a loan from a bank? What are his brother's financial needs? Does his brother need to be paid in cash, or could Bob pay with a promissory note? Some of these issues are raised by Bob and some by the mediators. Taken together, they constitute a discussion of whether Bob can buy out his brother's share of the house. Therefore, "topical continuity" is not as simple as saying only one subject is talked about, because many different subjects can be talked about while still being part of the same line of talk. Excerpt 1 shows that topical continuity is created by *how participants organize their talk*, rather than how many subjects they touch on in the course of that talk. We will now examine some of the basic techniques participants use to organize their talk such that it has topical continuity—so that the different things that are discussed can be seen to be related to each other.

Questions and answers

In Chapter 7 we described how a speaker can control the topic by asking a series of questions to create a question-answer chain or "interrogative series" (Zimmerman, 1984; Whalen and Zimmerman, 1990). Questions can create topical continuity because the conditional relevance of the first pair part creates an expectation that the addressed party will use their turn to provide an answer to the question—hence typically producing two utterances in a row on the same topic of talk. In Excerpt 1 the mediators used a series of questions to elicit information from Bob to discover whether Bob can afford to buy out his brother's share of the house. The first two questions are produced by Mediator A in lines 1–4, 13 and 17. Mediator B adds a question in line 21, but her question is really an "other repair" of Mediator A's prior question rather than an independent line of questioning. Because of their role as facilitators of the mediation session, Mediators A and B work as a team and produce the question/answer chain together, thus collectively controlling the topic and eliciting information from Bob which develops this topic (Garcia, 1994).

Pronouns and other indexical expressions

Pronouns and other indexical expressions can be used to convey that a current utterance is referring to prior talk, and thus work to create continuity in the talk (Sacks, 1992a; West and Garcia, 1988). For example, in line 2 (above) Mediator A refers to the brothers' house as "it," thus requiring participants to understand his utterance as referring to prior talk in the mediation session (in which they discussed the house). In line 23, Bob says "it'd=haf to be private money!," in response to Mediator A's question about whether he could get a loan or not. Bob uses the indexical expression "it" to refer to the loan, thus tying his utterance to Mediator A's prior utterance and displaying continuity between the two turns.

There are several instances in this excerpt where pronouns are used to refer to others. In line 11, Bob uses the pronoun "them" to refer to his brother and sister-in-law. Using pronouns or other indexical expressions conveys that an utterance is related to prior talk, because the recipient must refer to prior utterances to figure out who or what is being referred to.

There are several points in Excerpt 1 (above) where participants made explicit references to talk that occurred earlier in the mediation hearing. Note that Bob says "thuh fordy cash" (line 11) rather than "fordy cash", thus referencing a point earlier in the session in which he revealed that he had forty thousand dollars to invest in the house (not shown). Another instance is Mediator A's utterance in lines 3 and 4 ("I take it chou have <u>very</u> little income?"). This question proposes an "upshot" of what Bob has told them earlier in the hearing about his life style and employment history (not shown).

Format tying

Continuity with prior talk can also be constructed through **format tying** (Goodwin and Goodwin, 1987). Format tying involves repeating part (or occasionally, all) of a prior speaker's utterance in the response to it. While format tying is often used in argument sequences, it can also be used in non-arguing contexts to display the current utterance's relationship to prior talk. For example, in line 3 of Excerpt 1 (above) Mediator A asks "<u>how</u> could you accomplish tha:t?". Bob replies with "How could I accomplish thuh buy=out", thus repeating Mediator A's phrase "how could you accomplish…" (with the appropriate pronoun change). Similarly, in lines 3 and 4 Mediator A asks "I take it chou have <u>very</u> little income?". Bob responds in lines 7 and 8 with "<u>I</u> would hah- <u>I</u> would haf to=u::hm hhm I'd have to start <u>g</u>enerating income." Bob uses format tying to connect his utterance to Mediator A's by repeating the word "income" while creating a contrast with Mediator A's position ("you have very little income" vs. "generating income"). By means of these techniques Bob is able to create continuity with the prior utterance. Individual words are repeated several times in this segment (e.g. Mediator A's "buy=out" in line 2 and Bob's "buy out" in line 7).

In short, the techniques detailed above show some of the ways participants can create topical continuity. In Excerpt 1, many issues were talked about, but the exchange was organized in such a way as to contribute to one over-arching general topic (how can Bob buy out his brother's share of the house). In the next section we examine how participants can bring a topic to a close to allow for the introduction of a new topic.

Topic closure and topic change

A topic change is a point in a conversation where a transition to a new topic is constructed, typically at a point where the prior topic has been "bounded" or closed down. As noted in Chapter 9, topic closures can be accomplished by a variety of techniques: summaries or assessments of the topic, maxims or aphorisms (Schegloff and Sacks, 1973, p. 306), passed turns or preclosing moves (Schegloff and Sacks, 1973), or lapses in talk (West and Garcia,1988; Maynard, 1980). Schegloff and Sacks (1973) describe one technique for creating a space in a conversation for the introduction of a new topic:

> The first proper way of initiating a closing section that we will discuss is one kind of (what we will call) 'pre-closing'. The kind of pre-closing we have in mind takes one of the following forms, "We-ell…", "O.K.….", "So-oo", etc. (with downward intonation contours), these forms constituting the entire utterance. These pre-closings should properly be called "POSSIBLE pre-closing', because providing the relevance of the initiation of a closing section is only one of the uses they have. One feature of their operation is that they occupy the floor for a speaker's turn without using it to produce either a topically coherent utterance or the initiation of a new topic. With them a speaker takes a turn whose business seems to be to 'pass,' i.e., to indicate that he has not now anything more or new to say, and also to give a 'free' turn to a next, who, because such an utterance can be treated as having broken with any prior topic, can without violating topical coherence take the occasion to introduce a new topic, e.g., some heretofore unmentioned mentionable. AFTER such a possible pre-closing is specifically a place for new topic beginnings. (Schegloff and Sacks, 1973, pp. 303–4)

Maynard (1980) describes new topic beginnings as follows:

> A class of such utterances can be considered as topic changes; they are unrelated to the talk in prior turns in that they utilize new referents, and thus they implicate and occasion a series of utterances constituting a different line of talk. (Maynard, 1980, pp. 263–4)

Excerpt 2 illustrates the difference between topical continuity and topic change (West and Garcia, 1988). Note that from lines 1 to 8 each utterance is constructed to relate to prior talk. After topic bounding-implicative "upshots" and assessments (lines 7 and 8), there is a long silence (line 9). In line 10, Andy produces a question which is not tied to prior talk, it instead opens up a new line of conversation (West and Garcia, 1988).

Excerpt 2: West and Garcia (1988, p. 557)
01 Andy: … So I have to run all the way over here. (.6) .h
02   Make sure I wouldn' be late. How- how long have you
03   been here anyway?
04   (0.3)
05 Beth: Oh just a few minutes. (0.7) 'Bout ten minutes.
06 Andy: Oh! Jus' ten minutes! °heh-heh-heh Oh.

07 Beth: I[t does]n' [matter.   ]
08 Andy: [Well.]   [So I didn't] blo::w it too long.
09   (1.7)
10 Andy: Where do you cOME from.
11   (0.7)
12 Beth: Ventura. Not too fa:r from home.
13   (0.3)
14 Andy: No not at all you go home every weekend?...

In Excerpt 3, "Mark" and "Alice" are students in a college course who are recording their conversation for a class project:

Excerpt 3: Conversation between Students
1   Alice: ='specially when: [the university] can't find thuh=money tuh
2   put salt down on thuh ground? hih=hih! [.h henh] henh .h=
3   Mark: [u:h,   ]   =he
4   has uh [(financial) problem.]
5   Alice: [THAT general   ] he: thi:ng?, you wonder what's
6   goin' on. i don' know! eh hunh hunh hunh!
7   (0.2)
8   Mark: yea:h that's: (0.2) that's uh problem, gettin' stuff done around
9   here i know. henh hunh!
10   (0.1)
11 Alice: YEE=up! uh huh huh hunh!
12   (2.1)
13 Alice: take any more foreign language classes? lately?

In lines 1–11 of the excerpt Mark and Alice discuss their university and complain about it. In lines 8 and 9 Mark draws an upshot or makes a summary of the import of the topic, a common topic closing move. Alice then provides an agreement token in line 11 and accepts Mark's invitation to laugh at the university's problems. After a fairly long pause in line 12, Alice introduces a new topic ("take any more foreign language classes? lately?"). Schegloff (2007a) refers to this type of topic introduction as a **"topic proffer,"** because it suggests a new topic but then leaves it to the recipient to develop the topic or not. Since they are both students, their shared university experience is a likely choice of subject matter for this conversation (Maynard and Zimmerman, 1984), but the topic of what classes they are taking is clearly different from the discussion of their university's ability to handle problems. No work is done by either participant to tie these two topics together. The relevance of the topic does not have to be justified, because Mark and Alice are previously acquainted. They already know that they share the experience of taking language classes.

Excerpt 4 is from a conversation between three students in a college classroom setting. Prior to this excerpt, the students had been discussing the television show *Star Trek*. As the excerpt begins, they continue this discussion in lines 1–7.

Excerpt 4: Conversation between Students
```
 1   Ed:     .hh my pa-h-rents (say) i probably know more, .hh about stahr
 2           trek than anybody else.
 3           (0.2)
 4   Harry:  really? (0.3) wo::w. (0.7) i haven't seen=thuh- (0.4) star
 5           trek movies er anything.
 6           (0.5)
 7   Mark:   .h °i=don' either.° (0.5) so=are you guys: grad students?,
 8           undergra:d?
 9           (1.2)
10   Harry:  i'm an undergra:d.
```

In the middle of line 7, Mark introduces a new topic by asking "so=are you guys: grad students?, undergra:d?". The use of "so" is consistent with its use as a transition marker (Jefferson, 1984; Schegloff and Sacks, 1973). No work is done to tie the new topic of student status to the prior topic of the Star Trek show. It is constructed as the beginning of a new topic of discussion (Maynard, 1980).

Soliciting New Topics. The examples we have considered above are instances where a current speaker introduces a new topic themself. However, current speakers can also solicit new topic beginnings from other participants in the conversation. Button and Casey (1984) describe the use of **topic initial elicitors** for accomplishing this work. The topic initial elicitor is the first turn of a sequence through which participants work together to solicit, propose, and agree upon new topics for discussion. The speaker who begins the sequence solicits a report of a "newsworthy event" from another. This turn works not only to elicit a potential new topic for discussion, but marks the beginning of the new topic as discontinuous from prior talk. In the second turn of the sequence the person addressed can suggest a potential new topic. In the third turn of the sequence the original speaker can choose to "topicalize" it by soliciting further talk on that topic.

Excerpt 5 shows a complete topic initial elicitor sequence, in which Speaker A is successful in eliciting a potential next topic from Speaker B.

Excerpt 5: Button and Casey (1984, p. 167)
```
1   A:   Whaddiyuh kno:w.
2   B:   .hh Jis' got down last night.
3   A:   Oh you di:d?
4        ((talk continues on topic))
```

In line 1, Speaker A uses a topic initial elicitor to solicit a new topic from the other participant. Speaker B responds to the solicit by providing a "news report" (line 2). This is considered a positive response to the solicit. Speaker A then topicalizes this news report in line 3 ("Oh you di:d?"). The **topicalizer** is an utterance which expresses interest in the topic suggested by the news report and solicits more talk on it (Button and Casey, 1984). The participants continue talking on that topic (not shown). The new topic has been successfully proposed and "ratified."

The range of types of topics that can be solicited by topic initial elicitors is broad but not limitless. Button and Casey (1984, p. 170) state that, "they provide an open, though bounded, domain from which events may be selected and offered as possible topic initials."

Recipients of topic initial elicitors can respond negatively by making "no-news" reports. Excerpt 6 shows Speaker H declining to suggest a new topic by producing a "no news report" in line 3:

Excerpt 6: Button and Casey (1984, p. 168)
1   N: What's doin,
2   (.)
3   H: aAh:, nothi:n:,

If the recipient of a topic initial elicitor declines to produce a news report, the initiator of the sequence can make a second attempt to elicit a potential topic. One method of doing this is what Button and Casey (1984) call "recycling" the no news report. In Excerpt 7, Speaker P provides a no news report in line 2. Speaker M repeats the no news report in line 3, adding a tag question as a way of making a second request for news.

Excerpt 7: Button and Casey (1984, p. 184)
1   M: How are things goin?
2   P: oh-h-h-h nothin' doin.
3   M: Nothin' doin' huh?

Another typical response to a "no news" report is to suggest a topic oneself. Button and Casey (1984) call this "topic nomination." In Excerpt 8, Speaker N responds to Speaker H's no news report with a question about what Speaker N has been doing ("Y' didn't go meet Grahame?="; line 4); this question serves to "nominate" the topic of the meeting with Grahame.

Excerpt 8: Button and Casey (1984, p. 186)
1   N: What's doin,
2   (.)
3   H: aAh:, noth[i:n   ]
4   N: [Y'didn't g]o meet Grahame?=
5   H: °pt° hhhhhah Well I got ho::me,=
         ((continues on topic))

The techniques described above provide mechanisms for introducing a new topic of talk which is marked as separate from prior talk—a topic change. In the next section we discuss how transitions in topic can be made in ways that maintain connectedness with prior talk.

Topic refocusing

An ongoing line of talk can be refocused to introduce new subject matter in a way that ties it to previous talk rather than creating a separate line of talk (as with the topic initial elicitors and topic proffers discussed above). Participants can use a variety of techniques to refocus the conversation from one set of features to another set of features of the same object or general topic. Schegloff and Sacks (1973) refer to this as "**topic shading**":

> Not all topics have an analyzable end. One procedure whereby talk moves off a topic might be called 'topic shading', in that it involves no specific attention to ending a topic at all, but rather the fitting of differently focused but related talk to some last utterance in a topic's development. (Schegloff and Sacks, 1973, p. 305)

Sacks (1992b) refers to this process as a step-wise transition to a new topic. Instead of one topic being wrapped up neatly, and then a new topic being introduced, speakers can link new topical material to prior.

Excerpt 9, from a conversation between two friends who were recording a conversation for a class assignment, illustrates topic refocusing.

Excerpt 9: Conversation between Students

```
 1   Ann:   =now I=was=saying I had (  ) thee most (  ) boring, summer.=I
 2          worked:. (  ) well I worked,=
 3   Lee:                             =(for [Tee)]
 4   Ann:                                   [at  ] Tee
 5   Ann:   Bee Gees!, fer fordy hours uh week. (  ) and then I worked on
 6          at Grocery Cen[tral?]
 7   Lee:                 [(ye  ]ah?)=
 8   Ann:                           =for like- (  ) twenny hours uh week.
 9          (  )
10   Ann:   that's all. I hardly did a[nything °else.°]
11   Lee:                            [Isn't-     did]n't Donna work there?
12            (  )
13   Ann:   Yeah! she still [works for there,] yeah.=
14   Lee:                   [oh she (      )]      =how'd she do?
15          (.)
16   Ann:   She's good. (  ) She went back to school. (  ) before I did.
17          °so.°=
18   Lee:     =weren't you going out to see her?
19          (  )
20   Ann:   yeah=I::=
21   Lee:        =did jou?
22          (.)
23   Ann:   yea:h, [I mean I:    ] dro:ve to Indiana?
24   Lee:          [(oh uh hunh)]
25          (  )
```

```
26  Ann:   one weekend? (  ) and, o:h! my gosh you=kno=huh=w=hhh!
27         (  ) her apartment, (  ) is like, (  ) you have never seen
28         anything like that befo[re.=like-     ]
29  Lee:                          [oh=like- eight] twelve?
30         (  )
31  Ann:   Yeah! it['s::       ] okay she's got (  ) two roo:mmates?, (  )
32  Lee:          [Chuh hunh]
33  Ann:   a:nd, (  ) their whole apartment is just=like (  ) beaudiful.
34         (  )
35  Ann:   it's nicer than my house at home. and it's so: nice. (  ) like you
36         wa:lk i:n, and they have like uhm, (  ) wooden?, (  ) like
37         couches?, (  ) you=know=what=[I=mean?]
38  Lee:                              [unh=    ]=hunh
39         (  )
40  Ann:   like (when) [there's cus]hions?, sidding in thuh wooden
41  Lee:               [yeah (  ) ]
42  Ann:   thing?,
43         (  )
44  Lee:   right.
```

You will note that the topical organization in Excerpt 9 has both similarities and differences from Excerpt 1 which we discussed in the beginning of this chapter. As in Excerpt 1, a variety of different things are talked about in Excerpt 9. However, while in Excerpt 1 all of the topics discussed had to do with the over-arching question of how Bob could buy out his brother's share of the house, in Excerpt 9 the topics discussed, although related, do not fit under one larger umbrella topic. The two friends started out talking about Ann's "boring summer," but by the end of the excerpt they are discussing the furniture in a mutual friend's apartment. How did they get from the first topic to the last one? There is no point in the excerpt where there is an abrupt change of topic. Instead, the participants link each utterance to a prior utterance, thus gradually shifting from one topic to another rather than displaying a break with prior talk. They use two main techniques for accomplishing this topic refocusing: 1) asking questions which carry over elements of prior talk and tie them to a new angle or aspect of the subject, and 2) elaborating or developing tangents of previously introduced topics.

Using questions to refocus topics

A question can be used to ask about previously mentioned aspects of a topic while tying it to a new angle or aspect of the subject. For example, in line 11 Lee asks, "Isn't- Didn't Donna work there?". This question ties the prior topic of Ann's workplace to the related topic of a mutual acquaintance who worked in the same place. Once the co-worker ("Donna") has been introduced, Lee uses another question to develop discussion about her (line 18, "=weren't you going out to see her?"). This question ties the prior topic of Donna to the related topic of visiting Donna.

Elaborating or developing tangents of topics already introduced

Ann begins developing the topic of Donna's apartment which was previously introduced in response to a question from Lee. Sacks (1987a, p. 61) refers to this method of shifting topic as a step-wise topic shift. The topic shifts can occur within one speaker's turn, for example by adding new topical material to the answer to a question. Note that while the subject of the apartment is a tangent relative to the prior topics, both participants know how they got to that point, and at every step of the way the new content was connected to prior utterances. By the end of the excerpt, Ann is describing the furniture in Donna's apartment (lines 36–42).

The example of topic refocusing in Excerpt 9 illustrates the choices people make during conversations and how they negotiate what will be talked about. For example, at the beginning of the excerpt, Ann mentioned a number of things that *could* be topicalized, such as her boring summer, where she worked, and the hours she worked. Out of these possibilities, Lee chose to topicalize one aspect of Ann's utterance, the place she worked. Thus both parties have a role in the development of the topic. Their coordinated actions led to the transition from the topic of the boring summer, to the work, to the coworker, to visiting the coworker, to the coworker's apartment, to the furniture in the apartment, and so on.

Chapter summary

In this chapter we have examined how the topic of talk is shaped by the actions of participants. Participants can use a range of techniques to create topical continuity, shift from one topic to the next, or close a topic down and either introduce a new topic or solicit a new topic from another participant. Participants' actions, rather than the nature of the subject matter, are what create topical coherence.

Student activity

With a friend, do two role plays of a brief conversation in which you talk about the following three things: chocolate cake, airplanes and hats. The first time you have the conversation, work to display topical discontinuity between these three things, and the second time work to display topical continuity. Notice what techniques you use to display continuity and discontinuity.

Recommended sources

Button, Graham and Casey, Neil. (1984), 'Generating topic: the use of topic initial elicitors', in J. Maxwell Atkinson and John Heritage (eds) *Structures of Social Action: Studies in Conversation Analysis*. Cambridge: Cambridge University Press, pp. 167–90.

—(1985), 'Topic nomination and topic pursuit', *Human Studies*, 8, 3–55.

—(1988/89), 'Topic initiation: business-at-hand', *Research on Language and Social Interaction*, 22, 61–92.

Goodwin, Charles. (1995), 'The negotiation of coherence within conversation', in Morton Ann Gernsbacher and T. Givón (eds) *Coherence in Spontaneous Text*. Amsterdam and Philadelphia: John Benjamins Publishing Company, pp. 117–37.

Jefferson, Gail. (1993), 'Caveat speaker: preliminary notes on recipient topic-shift implicature', *Research on Language and Social Interaction*, 26, (1), 1–30.

Maynard, Douglas W. and Zimmerman, Don H. (1984), 'Topical talk, ritual, and the social organization of relationships', *Social Psychology Quarterly*, 47, (4), 301–16.

12 Story Telling and the Embodied Nature of Face-to-face interaction

Chapter contents

Introduction

This chapter on story telling focuses on two themes. The first theme is a continuation of the work we've done in the last few chapters on how people accomplish actions that require more than one turn at talk. We learned that turns at talk are the basic building blocks of interaction and that adjacency pairs are the primary device by which participants can combine turns into sequences of actions. Adjacency pairs can then be combined into larger units of talk in order to do things that require more than one turn, for example by constructing pre-sequences, question answer chains, or insertion sequences. Story telling is another way that a participant can produce an action which is longer than a single turn at talk. By getting the floor to tell a story, a speaker can then hold the floor for an extended period of time. The second theme of this chapter is how people integrate physical actions (such as facial expressions, hand gestures and gaze direction) with talk. We will explore these two themes by examining a story analyzed by Charles Goodwin.

Story telling procedures

Goodwin (1984) discovered how participants work together to tell stories, and how they integrate verbal and embodied action to accomplish the tasks they are engaged in. He identified six interactional techniques that participants use to facilitate the telling of stories: story prefaces, story solicits, preliminaries to the story, parenthesis within a story, story climax and story appreciation. Each of these devices provides a solution to a different set of problems involved in getting stories told.

Story prefaces and story solicits are two methods of initiating stories and aligning participants as either story teller or story recipient. **Story prefaces** are produced by the story teller and work as an announcement that the speaker has a story to tell. The preface is used to discover if there is any interest among potential story recipients in hearing the story. **Story solicits**, on the other hand, are used by a potential member of the audience to a story. Participants can solicit a speaker's story in a variety of interactional locations, including after a story preface.

Once the speaker has gotten the floor to tell a story, whether through a positive response to a story preface or through a story solicit from a co-interactant, they typically begin the story with preliminary background information. This preliminary information sets the stage for the story and provides information the audience needs to understand and appreciate the story. The preliminary information is not always presented in a seamless way. Goodwin (1984) uses the term "**parenthesis**" to describe the situation when a story teller temporarily breaks off a story-in-progress to insert information that will help with the telling or comprehension of the story.

Goodwin (1984) uses the term "**story climax**" to refer to the conclusion, main point or "punch line" of the story. While stories have different structures, and conventions about story telling differ from one culture to the next (e.g., Young, 1982), stories in many cultures end with a climax of sorts. The **story appreciation** is the audience's reaction to the story. It can be either a positive or a negative response. The story appreciation may include such actions as laughter, comments or questions about the story.

Goodwin (1984) used the story in Excerpt 1 below to illustrate how participants use specific techniques to get space in the conversation to produce their stories and make them comprehensible to their audience. This story was told at a picnic where several adults were sitting around a table while eating dinner and talking. Ann tells the story of what happened when she and her husband Don visited their friend Karen's new house for the first time.

Excerpt 1: Goodwin (1984, pp. 225–6)

1	Ann:	Well- ((throat clear)) (0.4) We coulda used a liddle, marijuana. tih
2		get through the <u>week</u>end.
3	Beth:	What h[appened.
4	Ann:	[Karen has this new <u>hou</u>:se. en it's got <u>a</u>ll this like- (0.2)
5		ssilvery:: g-go:ld wa:llpaper, .hh (h)en D(h)o(h)n <u>s</u>a(h)ys, y'know
6		this's th' firs' time we've seen this house.=<u>Fif</u>ty five thousn dollars in
7		Cherry Hill.=Right?
8		(0.4)
9	Beth:	Uh hu:<u>h</u>?
10	Ann:	Do(h)n said. (03.) dih-did they ma:ke you take this

```
11              [wa(h)llpa(h)p(h)er? er(h) di[dju pi(h)ck    ]=
12   Beth:      [hh!                          [Ahh huh huh]
13   Ann:       [[i(h)t ou(h)t.
14   Beth:      [[huh huh huh [huh
15   Don:                     [Uhh hih huh hu[h
16   Ann:                     [UHWOOghghHHH!=Y'kno(h)w
17   Ann:       that wz [like the firs' bad one.
18   Beth:              [Uh: oh wo::w hh
19              (0.2)
20   Don:       But I said it so innocuously y'know.
21   Ann:       Yeh I'm sure they thought it wz- hnh hnh
```

Story Preface. In lines 1 and 2 Ann produces what Goodwin (1984) calls a story preface. This is like a "teaser" that introduces some information about a story that could be told, in order to gauge the interest level of the audience in hearing the story. Ann uses a comical way of suggesting that their weekend was stressful: "Well- ((throat clear)) (0.4) We coulda used a liddle, marijuana. tih get through the <u>weekend</u>." This preface sets the hearers up for a story to come, and allows co-interactants to express or withhold interest in hearing the story. If the story teller is given the floor to tell the story, they then have the floor for an extended turn or series of turns. Instead of turn transition being relevant at the end of every possibly complete unit type, the transition out of the role of story teller will occur after the story is done.

Story Solicit. Beth responds to Ann's story preface with a solicit in line 3 ("What h[appened."). With the solicit Beth both accepts Ann's offer to tell the story, and specifically solicits the story. Note that Karen begins telling the story in overlap with this solicit, projecting the end of the solicit from the first word, and beginning the story immediately.

Preliminary to the Story. Ann responds to the story solicit by providing background information to set up the story for the audience (lines 4 and 5, "[Karen has this new <u>hou</u>:se. en it's got <u>all</u> this like- (0.2) ssilvery:: g-go:ld wa:llpaper,"). This is background information necessary for the audience to understand the story to come. Recall that in Chapter 7 we learned that one of the functions of pre-sequences was to get space to produce information necessary to understand the projected action. In this excerpt, the preface functions as a pre-sequence (a pre-story). The story solicit responds to the pre-sequence, and the preliminary information which follows precedes the projected action (the story itself).

Parenthesis. The parenthesis is preliminary (background) information which is out of place in the story. The story teller interrupts her story to add this information because it is important for the understanding and appreciation of the story. After the preliminary information, Ann continues with the story, saying ".hh (h)en D(h)o(h)n <u>sa</u>(h)ys," (line 5). However, instead of telling us what Don says, Ann switches back to providing details to set up the story: "y'know this's th' firs' time we've seen this house.=<u>Fifty</u> five thousn dollars in Cherry Hill.=Right?". This information is the same type of information that is presented in the preliminary segment of the story, but Ann marks it as out of place by breaking off her story-in-progress to insert it.

Story Climax. Stories often reach what Goodwin (1984) refers to as the story climax. This is the punch line of the story (if it is a humorous tale, as is the one we are considering here), or it could simply be the main point or conclusion of the story. In this excerpt, Ann constructs the story climax to signal that it is humorous by the use of breaths and hints of laughter in her utterance: "Do(h)n said. (03.) dih-did they ma:ke you take this [wa(h)llpa(h)p(h)er? er(h) di[dju pi(h)ck]=[[i(h)t ou(h)t." The aspirations in Ann's speech are laughter-implicative, and hence function as an invitation to laugh (Jefferson, 1979). She thus produces the punch line to the story she has set up with her preliminary information, at the same time signaling to her audience that laughter is an appropriate "appreciation" of the story.

Story Appreciation. The story appreciation is the work audience members do to communicate their response to the story. The story appreciation can consist of a number of different types of actions, for example laughter or comments or questions about the story, and can be either positive or negative. In Excerpt 1 the story appreciation consists largely of laughter. Beth produces laughter in lines 12 and 14, and Don joins in with laughter in line 15. Note that Beth's laughter occurs in overlap with Ann's story climax, thus showing an enthusiastic response. Ann then joins in with a reaction to her own story (lines 16 and 17). Note that in lines 17 and 18 she also produces what looks like a story preface for a second story. This utterance is followed by more comments from Beth and Don.

In sum, the story in Excerpt 1 contains the following: a story preface, a story solicit, background information to set up the story, the beginning of a story climax that is aborted, the insertion of parenthetical information, a story climax that is completed, and several appreciations of the story. In order to create this structure the participants used the verbal techniques described above. In addition, the participants used physical actions ("nonverbal behaviors") to help facilitate transitions from one part of the story to another, and to coordinate speaker and listener roles. We now review Goodwin's (1984) examination of how participants use nonverbal behaviors such as gestures, body orientation and manipulation of objects to communicate and help create story structure.

Story telling and embodied action

Goodwin (1984) describes the storyteller's physical actions while telling the story. As you read this description, think of Sacks' (1992a) instruction to conversation analysts to pay attention to the question "why that now?" The body movements and gestures that Ann makes during the telling of the story are not randomly placed. Goodwin explains how they coordinate with and support the different phases of the story and types of work being done in it (as analyzed in the section above).

First, Goodwin observes from his analysis of the videotape of the interaction that Ann marks the beginning of the story preface by pausing in the act of eating, thus signaling a switch to a new activity. Before she begins her story preface in line 1 (in Excerpt 1 above), she puts her fork down and raises her head. While producing the preface (lines 1 and 2), Ann changes her posture, adjusts her hair and glasses, and moves her drinking glass to the other side of her plate. Goodwin (1984) observes that these actions seem to be preparatory to her story. When the story proper begins she switches to new embodied actions, thus displaying for her recipients the transition from one type of activity (the preface) to another (the story proper). They also serve to prepare her to be the focus of attention as she tells her story.

After Beth solicits her story in line 3, Ann begins her story telling with preliminary information, changing her body posture as she does so (lines 4–5). She puts her elbows on the table and leans toward Beth. She thus marks the transition from the story preface to the beginning of the story, and treats Beth as the primary recipient of the story. She keeps her elbows on the table until the story ends. In addition, as she starts this preliminary phase of the story, Ann begins gesturing with her hands. However, when Ann begins the parenthetical part of her story at the end of line 5, she changes to a different hand gesture, which visually differentiates the parenthesis from the story-in-progress. The hand gesturing, in addition to signaling the phase of the story she is engaged in, also serves to convey to her audience that she is not yet ready to relinquish the floor. This new gesture ceases after she completes the parenthesis; she stops gesturing as she produces the climax of the story (lines 10–11, 13), thus signaling its end by this embodied "retreat" from the gestures she had been making previously. Ann's embodied actions throughout the story thus mirror and reinforce the transitions in the story she is constructing, and help to communicate the work she is doing with each utterance to her audience.

In sum, Ann's physical movements, gestures and manipulation of objects communicate information to her recipients. The information communicated is about the structure of her story and how it is organized rather than about the content of her talk or how she feels about it. Her embodied actions reinforce the spoken structure of her story, such as when she shifts from preliminary material to parenthesis, or to the climax of the story. These actions make it easier for the story recipients to follow the structure of her story.

Gaze direction

People talking on the telephone can successfully coordinate turn exchange without difficulty, even though they cannot see each other and cannot tell where the other party is gazing. Thus eye contact is not necessary for turn transition to occur. As in face-to-face conversation, participants in telephone calls can monitor each other's utterances-in-progress and locate transition relevance places by projecting where the utterance is possibly complete.

They can also attend to intonation, pauses, and the pacing of speech to project whether a current speaker's utterance is possibly complete or not. Goodwin (1984) found that during face-to-face interaction, gaze direction and eye contact are used by participants to monitor each other's turns-in-progress and to coordinate turn exchange at transition relevance places (Goodwin, 1984).

When engaged in a face-to-face interaction, it is not necessary for all participants to be constantly gazing at each other. However, Goodwin (1984) found that gaze direction is clearly coordinated with turn exchange. While participants can look away or engage in other activities during the interaction, participants typically restore mutual gaze direction prior to turn transitions, as well as at other points during a speaker's utterance. Goodwin (1984) also noticed that speakers and listeners have different responsibilities or expectations about when they are to be gazing at each other. Specifically, when restoring mutual gaze, the listener should bring their gaze back to the face of the current speaker *prior* to the speaker returning their gaze to the listener. If the speaker gazes at the listener and finds the recipient looking elsewhere, he or she may use hesitation, repetition, stuttering or other perturbations in speech to indicate that there is a problem. These hesitations and verbal perturbations can serve to delay the completion of the current speaker's utterance until gaze is restored, thus ensuring that the speaker has the listener's attention when the remainder of the utterance is produced. They also initiate a repair of the listener's absent gaze.

Note that it is not always easy to determine what hesitations or repetitions mean in the context of a specific utterance. As we discussed in Chapter 10, it may be a case of error avoidance, with the speaker trying to get more time to decide how to complete their utterance, or editing the utterance as they produce it. In order to tell the difference between error avoidance and an attempt to restore listener's gaze, it is necessary to closely observe the interaction. This can be done either with a video recording or at least a transcript with gaze direction shifts transcribed. With these types of data it is possible to determine whether the hesitations occur when recipient's gaze is absent, and stop when the gaze is restored. If it is not the gaze direction that is causing the problem, then it might be a word search or other type of error avoidance.

Goodwin (1984) developed a system for transcribing gaze direction which enables us to track when participants are gazing at each other. The system he uses involves displaying the gaze of the current speaker above the transcript of their utterance, while the gaze of the other participant (or participants) is displayed below the speaker's utterance. Dotted lines indicate that a participant is moving their gaze from somewhere else towards the participant's face. An "X" marks the spot in the transcript at which the gaze reaches the other's face, and a comma is used to indicate when the speaker moves their gaze away from the other's face. A solid line indicates that the participant is gazing toward another participant's face. Length of pauses are indicated by dashes within parentheses, with each dash equaling about a tenth of a second. Thus (----) equals a .4 second pause.

Excerpt 2 shows how Goodwin (1984) transcribed the gaze direction of the partici-pants in the story we have been working with in this chapter. Both participants were looking elsewhere during the beginning of Ann's turn in line 2, but first Beth and then Ann move their gaze toward each other (as indicated by the periods in lines 1 and 3). Beth initiates her move first, quickly turning her head to gaze at Ann's face during the 0.4 second pause. Beth maintains her gaze at Ann's face throughout the remainder of her turn (indicated by the solid line underneath her turn in lines 3 and 6). Ann turns her gaze toward Beth's face slightly later (she starts turning at the end of "coulda" in line 2), and finds Beth's gaze already fixed on her. She completes her utterance without incident. This pattern of gaze shift is consistent with what Goodwin (1984) found to facilitate smooth turn production.

Excerpt 2: Goodwin (1984, p. 231)
```
1   Ann:                                          . . . .X_____
2   Ann:    Well- ((throat clear)) (----) We coulda used a liddle, marijuana. tih
3   Beth:                          . X_____

4   Ann:                          . X____
5   Ann:    get through the weekend.
6   Beth:         _____
```

Goodwin (1984) notes that if these procedures for coordinating gaze direction are not followed, the current speaker may attempt to repair the lack of recipient gaze by using hesitations, restarts, or stuttering to initiate the repair. The current speaker can also use solicits to verify that the intended recipient of the utterance-in-progress is attending to their utterance, even though their gaze may be elsewhere. A recipient may respond to a solicit with restored gaze or with such actions as nods or minimal responses to indicate their attention.

Recall that during the preface to the story, Beth gazed steadily at the story teller (Excerpt 2, above). However, during the body of the story, Beth turned her gaze away from the teller (line 3 in Excerpt 3). However, as Ann continues her utterance (line 5), Beth turns her gaze toward Ann, and again holds it steadily toward her face.

Excerpt 3: Goodwin (1984, p. 235)
```
1   Ann:    _____
2   Ann:    Karen has this new hou:se. en it's got all this like- (0.2) ssilvery::
3   Beth:    _____,,,                    ((nod))

4   Ann:    _____
5   Ann:    g-go:ld wwa:llpaper, .hh (h) en D(h)o(h)n sa(h)ys, y'know this's th'
6   Beth:    . . . . . . . X_____     ((Nod))_____

7   Ann:    _____
8   Ann:    firs' time we've seen this house.=Fifty five thousn dollars in Cherry
9   Beth:    _____((Nod))__, , , ,
```

```
10 Ann:      _____
11 Ann:      Hill.=Right?
12 Beth:
```

Technically, this example violates the procedure for coordinating gaze which Goodwin outlines, since the current speaker (Ann) was gazing at the listener (Beth) before Beth gazed at her. However, since this discussion occurred at a picnic, where all participants were engaged in eating and related activities, it is not as problematic for Beth to look away at times. Also recall that since Ann is telling a story, she may have the floor for an extended period. Audience members are not expected to continuously hold their gaze at speakers; they may look away and back again, as Beth does in Excerpt 3. Goodwin (1984) notes that the rule about gaze direction during speaker's turns is relaxed during extended, multi-unit turns.

However, Goodwin (1984) notes that there are several ways Ann's utterance may be responsive to Beth's patterns of gaze. At the end of the parenthetical section of the story (line 11), Ann adds a tag question soliciting a response from Beth. This question may serve to solicit Beth's gaze or to check her attention to the story-in-progress. Note also that although Beth does not provide continual eye contact in response to Ann's gaze, she does provide several nods which serve as minimal responses indicating her attention to the speaker. These nods (in lines 3, 6, and 9) all occur shortly after possibly complete unit types, regardless of whether Beth is gazing at Ann (as in lines 6 and 9) or not (as in line 3).

In sum, both participants showed an orientation to the conventions around gaze direction and turn exchange. Nonverbal listener responses, including gaze direction and nods, are a key way listeners display their attention to the story-in-progress. Other types of non-verbal behaviors are also consequential for interaction. Goodwin (2000) shows how hand gestures can facilitate communication. Forrester (2008) analyzes how communication can be accomplished through a combination of words and gestures, and gazes. Excerpt 4 shows a small child (1 year and 8 months old) using a combination of a single word repeated several times with coordinated nonverbal behaviors to request a food item from her father ("F").

Excerpt 4: (Forrester, 2008, p. 107)

```
1   F:    = ye::a
2         (1.8)                                   ...........(sits down on chair)
3   F:    and baby can have some
4         (0.5)
5   F:    beans in a minute if she wants =        (positioning himself in chair)
6   E:    = beans:: minute                        (looks towards bowl of beans
                                                  at end of utterance)
7         (2.5)                                   (E drops spoon)
8   E:    beans::                                 (looks towards bowl and
                                                  stretches out arm towards it)
9         (0.3)
10  E: →  Beans                                   (E begins to open and close
                                                  outstretched hand)
```

```
11        (0.4)
12  E: →  bean:: ↑NYA: [:::    ]              (hand movement increases)
13  F:                [do you] want
          some beans [darling] ?              (turns and looks at E)
14  E:                [(nods) ]
15        (0.2)
16  E:    yea
```

Note that Ella ("E") repeats the word "beans" in lines 8, 10 and 12. The first time she repeats the word she looks toward the bowl and stretches her arm out toward it (line 8). When her father does not respond to this embodied request, she repeats the word beans and gestures with her hand (line 10). After her third request in line 12 the father asks her whether she wants the beans, and she responds with a nod. Although her ability to form sentences and make verbal requests is limited at this age, she attempts to communicate what she wants through a combination of words, gestures and gazes toward the desired object.

Summary

There are a variety of techniques speakers use to facilitate the telling of stories and other actions. These techniques span the verbal and nonverbal realms of communication. They work to help the story teller hold the floor for the duration of their story, and to coordinate audience responses and story teller's transitions from one part of the story to the next.

The material in this chapter clearly illustrates the interactional nature of talk. When we speak, we tend to think of our utterance as shaped by ourselves and ourselves alone, but actually what we say, and when and how we say it are also shaped by the actions of those in interaction with us—if only because it is through their remaining silent that we are able to speak. This characteristic of talk becomes very clear in the material on story telling, as every aspect of the story is produced with the cooperation and participation of the audience members to that story.

Student activity

1. Sit down opposite another student and engage in a conversation with them for about five minutes. Try to conduct the entire conversation without gazing at each other's faces. Notice how hard it is to do this. At what points in the conversation did you find yourself wanting to gaze at the other person? At what points was it more comfortable to gaze away?
2. Repeat the exercise above, except instead of attempting to control gaze, keep your hands still and folded in front of you during the entire conversation. Again, note the points in the conversation where it is most difficult to refrain from gesturing.

Recommended sources

Goodwin, Charles. (1984), 'Notes on story structure and the organization of participation', in J. Maxwell Atkinson and John Heritage (eds) *Structures of Social Action: Studies in Conversation Analysis*. Cambridge: Cambridge University Press, pp. 225–46.

—(1989), 'Turn construction and conversational organization', in Brenda Dervin, Lawrence Grossberg, Barbara J. O'Keefe, and Ellen Wartella (eds). *Rethinking Communication, Volume 2: Paradigm Exemplars*. Newbury Park, CA: Sage, pp. 88–102.

—(1995), 'The negotiation of coherence within conversation', in Morton Ann Gernsbacher and T. Givon (eds). *Coherence in Spontaneous Text*. Amsterdam and Philadelphia: John Benjamins, pp. 117–37.

Goodwin, Marjorie Harness. (2007), 'Participation and embodied action in preadolescent girls' assessment activity', *Research on Language and Social Interaction*, 40(4), pp. 353–75.

Cuff, E. C. and Francis, D. W. (1978), 'Some features of "invited" stories about marriage breakdown', *International Journal of the Sociology of Language*, 18, 111–33.

Jefferson, Gail. (1978), 'Sequential aspects of storytelling in conversation', in *Studies in the Organization of Conversational Interaction*, Jim Schenkein (ed.), New York and London: Academic Press, pp. 219–48.

Lerner, Gene H. (1992), 'Assisted storytelling: deploying shared knowledge as a practical matter', *Qualitative Sociology*, 15, (3), 247–71.

Stivers, Tanya. (2008), 'Stance, alignment, and affiliation during storytelling: when nodding is a token of affiliation', *Research on Language and Social Interaction*, 41, (1), 31–57.

13 Referring to Persons

Chapter contents

Introduction

Whether telling a story, conducting a telephone conversation, or engaging in an informal conversation at home, we continually find ourselves referring to people. In this chapter we examine how this work of referring to others is done, and explore how consequential it can be for interactions in both ordinary conversations and institutional settings. The chapter begins with an explanation of membership categorization analysis, an approach to the study of participants' methods for referring to persons. We will then examine how participants use "membership categorization devices" in telephone conversations, legal proceedings and workplace interactions.

Membership categorization analysis

There are many different ways that individuals can be mentioned, referred to, or characterized during the course of interaction. If the person being referred to is someone that could be reasonably expected to be recognized by your co-interactant, you could use a "recognitional" term, such as the individual's name (Sacks and Schegloff, 1979). For example, in the story analyzed in Chapter 12, the story teller uses her husband's name ("Don") as a recognitional term to refer to him. He is present during the story telling, and all the people present know him and know that his name is Don, so using this recognitional term suffices to identify the person referred to during the story.

However, in some interactional contexts, recognitional terms cannot be used (such as when referring to someone who is unknown to your interactants), or is not optimal for the purpose at hand. In those cases other methods of referring to persons may be employed. A common technique for doing so is the use of **membership categories** (Sacks, 1972; 1974) through which a person is identified by means of a group or category of persons to which he or she belongs. For example, the story teller in Chapter 12 could have used the membership category "husband" rather than the recognitional term "Don" to refer to him. Note that it is not just that a recognitional term can be used because it is an informal conversation among friends, but that using a recognitional term (as opposed to a categorical identification) is one way the interaction is constructed as an informal interaction—the participants are "doing being friends" by displaying and orienting to their familiarity and common knowledge of each other.

There are many different types of membership categories that can apply to a given individual. The examples below give an idea of the wide range of ways individuals can be categorized:

> Membership categories, as defined by Sacks, are classifications or social types that may be used to describe persons. By way of illustration an occasioned list of such categories might include 'politician,' 'gravedigger,' 'pimp,' 'nerd,' 'astronaut,' 'skinhead,' 'boozer,' 'former boy scout leader' and 'grandmother.' (Hester and Eglin, 1997, p. 3)

> The categories at issue here are ones like men, women, Protestants, minors (or miners), professors, goalies, adults, cellists, conservatives, vegetarians, merchants, murderers, 20-year olds, cat-people, technicians, stamp collectors, Danes, 'looky-loos' (people who slow down on the highway to stare at an accident), lefties (both politically and handedly), surfers, Alzheimer's, etc. (Schegloff, 2007b, p. 467)

By their choice of referents, speakers can convey different types of information and create different types of impressions about the individual to which they are referring. Speakers can work to make different aspects of the individual relevant for that particular interaction. The categories can also be used to link individuals with others.

The social structure of a given society (for example how family, work, or social institutions are organized) is reflected in common sense understandings about how people are grouped or organized. At the same time, participants "do social structure" by the use of these categories—the relationship between social structure and human action has the property of reflexivity. The membership categories can therefore be used to invoke relevant "**collections**" of categories (Hester and Eglin, 1997; Sacks, 1974). For example, McHoul (2007, p. 461) lists "postman," "butcher," and "professor" as categories in the collection "professions," and "Australian," "Albanian," and "Afghan," as categories in the collection "nationality." Hester and Eglin (1997) list "father," "son," and "daughter" as categories in the collection "family."

Some categories can belong to more than one collection. For example, while the category "professor" can be seen to be included in the collection "professions," it could also be seen to be included in the collection "teachers" (including, for example, preschool teachers, elementary school teachers, high school teachers and college professors). Similarly, Hester and Eglin (1997) note that some of the categories in the "family" collection (for example "child"), could also belong to the "phase of life" collection: (baby, child, teenager, adult, senior citizen). Given that a category can belong to more than one collection, how is the listener to tell which collection is being referred to when a category is used? Sacks (1974) discovered a set of procedures for using and interpreting categories and collections which he referred to as "rules" and "maxims." Collections of categories in conjunction with the rules or procedures used for assigning members to collections are often referred to as '**membership categorization devices**.' Sacks defines membership categorization devices as follows:

> any collection of membership categories, containing at least a category, which may be applied to some population containing at least a member, so as to provide, by the use of some rules of application, for the pairing of at least a population member and a categorization device member. A device is then a collection plus rules of application. (Sacks, 1974, pp. 218–19)

Sacks (1974, p. 219) notes that "a single category from any membership categorization device can be referentially adequate." In other words, even though many categories may apply for a given individual, a speaker only needs to use one category in order to adequately identify that person. Sacks refers to this as the "**economy rule**." So for example, even though a person may simultaneously be a student, an elder brother, a son, a gymnast, a pianist, etc., it is not necessary to use all of these categories in order to adequately identify that person in a conversation. Typically one category is sufficient.

One you have used a category from a collection (e.g. the category "baby" from the collection "family"), other categories from the same collection become relevant (e.g. the category "mommy" from the collection "family"). Sacks calls this the "**consistency rule**":

> if some population of persons is being categorized, and if a category from some device's collection has been used to categorize a first member of the population, then that category or other categories of the same collection *may* be used to categorize further members of the population. (Sacks, 1974, p. 219)

Closely associated with the consistency rule is the "**hearer's maxim**":

> if two or more categories are used to categorize two or more members of some population, and those categories can be heard as categories from the same collection, then: hear them that way. (Sacks, 1974, pp. 219–20)

What this means is that if a speaker uses two categories from the same collection (e.g., "baby" and "mommy"), the hearer can reasonably assume that the speaker intended those individuals to be heard as both belonging to the collection "family," rather than hearing one as a member of the collection "family" and the other as a member of another collection (e.g. stage of life). If the speaker does not want the hearer to assume they belong to the same collection, they may describe them in such a way that the relevance of a second collection is apparent. In other words, the rules and maxims describe the default interpretations.

When speakers use membership categories they do not always do so by naming the category. They can reference activities typically performed by members of that category, either instead of or in conjunction with naming the category itself (Stokoe, 2012). Sacks (1974, p. 222) referred to these activities as "**category-bound activities**" (also sometimes referred to as "**category-predicates**"). Categories are "inference rich"—if a person belongs to a category, there are things you can assume are true about them. These assumptions come from common sense knowledge of what people in that category do. For example, the category-bound activity of crying is associated with babies, the category-bound activity of lecturing is associated with professors and the category-bound activity of arresting people is associated with the police. The work of referencing the category membership of an individual can therefore be done by means of the category itself or "by mentioning that person's doing of an action that is category bound" (Schegloff, 2007b, p. 470). Stokoe (2012) uses the term "designedly ambiguous" to refer to occasions on which participants use the inference-rich capacities of categories to convey information obliquely. Stokoe (2012) also notes that participants can claim different implications from categories, and can resist the implications claimed by others' use of categories.

Membership categorization analysis ("MCA") therefore refers to the work participants do to manage and interpret the references to persons in their talk. As Hester and Eglin (1997, p. 3) note membership categorization analysis is both a members' practice and a potential resource for analysts of interaction. Members' use of membership categorization analysis both invokes and reveals their commonsense knowledge of social structure. Stokoe (2012) makes recommendations for how to conduct membership categorization analysis:

> Look for evidence that, and of how, recipients orient to the category, device or resonant description; for the interactional consequences of a category's use; for co-occurring component features of categorial formulations; and for the way speakers within and between turns build and resist categorizations. (Stokoe, 2012, p. 280)

In the remainder of this chapter we will consider several examples of how membership categorization analysis can be used in a variety of different types of interactions.

Membership categorization analysis in a telephone call

Stokoe (2009) analyzes how a person who called a mediation center to make a complaint about a neighbor uses membership categories as she formulates her complaint. During the call she claims that the neighbor's child is making too much noise too late in the evenings. Excerpt 1 shows a portion of her call. The caller refers to her own daughter in line 4 by saying "I: have a little girl." By using the categorical identifier "little girl" the caller is able to concisely convey her role as a mother and the child's status as her daughter, while at the same time giving a rough indication of the child's age. Since the caller and the call taker are not acquainted, the call taker has no way of knowing the child's name. Therefore if the caller had used a recognitional term to refer to her daughter, the call taker would not have been able to understand who that person was or why she was being mentioned.

```
Excerpt 1: Stokoe (2009, p. 76)
1   C:    Um:: an' some- uh- [sometimes:
2   M:                       [((sniffs))
3         (0.6)
4   C:    Because I- I: have a little girl who's the s-
5         (.) exactly the same age actually.
6   M:    Oh ri:ght.
7   C:    Um: (0.3) an'- an:, (.) an' I usually get her
8         into bed for half past eight.
9         (0.2)
10  C:    An,=
11  M:        =Yeah.
12        (0.3)
13 -> C:  By that ti- a- cos I'm a single mother,
14 -> M:  M:mm.=
15  C:             =By that time, (0.3) I'm ti:red
16        (0.2)
17  C:    .hhh
18  M:    Yeah.=
19  C:    An' I don't have many resources left for
20        co:ping with things.
```

The caller then invokes the category of age in line 5, noting that the child whose noise she is calling to complain about is the same age as her daughter. She does not state either child's age, but she has already characterized her child as a "little girl." The age of the children may be seen to be related to the category-bound activity of "making noise." Children of different ages can be expected to produce different types and amounts of noise. Babies produce crying, older children produce loud noises while playing or running around, and teenagers may produce loud music. The argument the caller is developing is that her little girl (although the same age as the neighbor's noisy child she is complaining about), does not make noise in the evening, because she puts her to bed early (lines 7–8). Putting children to bed is a category-bound activity associated with the category of parent (in this case, the mother). By reporting that she puts her child to bed early, the caller is displaying her proper performance of the role of a good parent, while implicitly claiming that her neighbor's family does not do good parenting.

As the caller continues her explanation of her complaint, she invokes a separate collection of categories related to marital status (e.g., single, married, divorced, widowed). By specifying that she is not just the mother of a little girl, but "a single mother" (line 13), Stokoe (2009) notes that she is invoking a realm of "features" or "predicates" that are typically tied to the category single mother:

> The use of the indefinite article "a" produces the category as something with known-in-common meanings. C ties "being tired" and "not having many resources for coping" to the category "single mother," moving from naming a category to unpacking its incumbent features or "predicates." The category "single mother" works to explicate why C does not have "resources" for "coping"—she has no partner to share the load of additional problems. (Stokoe, 2009, p. 77)

Stokoe (2009) is arguing that by categorizing herself as "a single mother" and invoking specific features of this category the caller constructs a justification of her complaint. It is not just that the child next door makes too much noise late at night, this noise is a problem for her because of her social status and life situation, which she has concisely conveyed via her use of categories and category predicates. The caller thus makes use of the membership categorization devices "family," "age," and "marital status," specific categories within those devices ("mother," "little girl," and "single mother"), and category-bound activities or predicates associated with those roles or social statuses (e.g. putting a child to bed or being tired).

Membership categorization analysis in legal procedures

Winiecki (2008) analyzed the use of membership categorization devices and their associated "predicates" or category-bound activities to convey and contest the status of an expert witness in a trial. The trial was about whether creationism (the theory of "intelligent design") was a valid scientific perspective that should be taught in public schools along with the theory of evolution. The witness needed to defend his claim to be a scientist in order to be considered a scientific expert in the trial. In Excerpt 2 the attorney uses a series of questions designed to get the witness to agree to statements that, taken together, constitute a challenge to his status as a scientific expert. The attorney's overall strategy is to demonstrate that the conventional way scientists display the value of their research is through publication in scientific journals, rather than informal advocacy among segments of the lay public. Since (as is shown elsewhere in the trial), the witness does not have any publications in scientific journals and has tried to advocate his position amongst nonscientists, if the witness agrees with these statements he is in effect agreeing with the attorney's challenge to his status as a scientific expert. His claim to the category "scientific expert" is thereby challenged by his failure to participate in the category-bound activity of "publication in peer reviewed journals" and his participation in non-scientific actions of advocacy among lay groups.

> Excerpt 2: Winiecki (2008, p. 768)
>
> 01　Q.　Drs. Crick and Watson won a Nobel Prize for the conclusions they drew from that other scientist data, correct?
>
> 02　A.　Correct.
>
> 03 -> Q.　… the way they did that is, they published… in peer reviewed scientific journals for the scrutiny of their colleagues, true?
>
> 04　A.　In a one page article in 1953 in *Nature*, right…
>
> 05 -> Q.　*Nature*, that's a peer reviewed scientific journal?
>
> 06　A.　It is.
>
> 07　Q.　Is that the probably the number one most respected peer reviewed scientific journal in the world?
>
> 08　A.　I think *Nature*, *Science*, *PNAS*, *Cell*, would all fit in that.
>
> 09　Q.　Now Dr. Crick and Watson didn't win a Nobel Prize by trying to convince school boards, average citizens, lawyers, the press?
>
> 10　A.　I made that clear yesterday…
>
> 11 -> Q.　Well, it's important to publish your scientific conclusions in peer reviewed journals so that other scientists, people who are qualified to evaluate those conclusions and the evidence… and determine whether they make sense or not?
>
> 12　A.　I agree.

As Excerpt 2 begins the attorney mentions two well-known, high-status scientists (Drs. Crick and Watson), and notes that they have won a Nobel Prize. This accomplishment documents the quality of their work and ratifies their status as scientists. After obtaining the witness's corroboration of this information (line 2), the attorney asks him to confirm that Drs. Crick and Watson won the prize for work published in peer reviewed scientific journals. Instead of immediately confirming this information, the witness prefaces his answer with the statement "In a one page article in 1953 in <u>Nature</u>," then answering "right…" (line 4). The preface works to qualify the attorney's claim about their publication in peer reviewed scientific journals. It minimizes their accomplishment by pointing out the article was only one page long. In addition, the preface showcases the witness's knowledge of the scientific literature by his recall of the length of the article and the year it was published. Displaying his knowledge of the relevant publications is an alternative way of trying to establish his claim to the status of scientific expert.

In response to the question in line 7 about whether *Nature* is "the number one most respected peer reviewed scientific journal in the world?" (line 7), the witness again provides more information than was asked for by the question. The question was designed to prefer a "yes" answer. While not denying that *Nature* is a highly respected journal, the witness claims that three other journals are of equally high status (line 8). Again, the witness is not denying the accomplishments of scientists such as Watson and Crick, but he is working to downgrade the prestige of their publication. At the same time, he works to establish himself as a scientific expert by displaying his knowledge of which journals are important in the field. He is resisting the attorney's claim that a real scientist would be publishing in scientific journals (implying a necessary connection between the category scientist and the category-bound activity of publishing in peer reviewed journals) by claiming membership in the category scientist by displaying his knowledge of other scientist's work and the relevant journals in the field.

The attorney goes on to contrast Drs. Crick and Watson's actions with the witness's actions. Previously in the hearing it had been revealed that the witness was using informal networks to get his point across; this is contrasted with the way the professional scientists communicated their theories. The witness begins to resist this characterization (line 10), and the attorney intervenes to reiterate the point about publishing in peer reviewed journals, this time adding that this enables "people who are qualified" to "determine whether they make sense or not?" (line 11). This formulation removes the "school boards, average citizens, lawyers, and the press" referred to in turn 9 from the category of "people who are qualified to evaluate those conclusions." The witness agrees with this statement (line 12), thus acknowledging the attorney's point that these category-bound activities are part of the scientific process rather than something lay people do. Winiecki's (2008) analysis thus shows how the attorney successfully problematized the witness's claim to the status of scientific expert. This was done through a contest over which category-bound activities are most relevant.

Halkowski (1990) used membership categorization analysis to explore how roles were used by participants in Congressional hearings held in the late 1980s regarding the "Iran-Contra" scandal. The witness in Excerpt 3 is Colonel Oliver North, who was asked to defend a number of his actions, including the shredding of important documents that could have provided evidence to assist in the investigation. Note that in his response below he uses two different methods of referring to the same person. At times he uses a categorical identifier (job title) and at times a recognitional identifier (the individual's name). In line 40 he referred to the attorney general by his job title ("thee Attorney General"), but he then reformulates this identification in line 42, using his name ("Mr. Meese"). By using different methods of referring to the same person, the witness can create different implications for the meaning of his actions.

Excerpt 3: (Halkowski, 1990, p. 572)

40 thet thee Attorney General,

41 (0.5)

42 in his r:ole as (0.4) Mister <u>Meese</u>.

43 (0.2)
44 NOT (0.2) thet thee Attorney General is gonna come <u>by:</u>
45 (0.2)
46 an' do ah full fledged investig<u>a</u>tion.=thuh word
47 investigation wasn't <u>used</u>.
48 (0.6)
49 Thet
50 (0.2)
51 Mister Meese
52 (0.3)
53 had been a:s:ked to do aye fact finding <u>inquiry</u>.

The witness's use of membership categorization devices and recognitional terms to refer to Mister Meese provides an effective defense against the acts he has been accused of (Halkowski, 1990). Note that category-bound activities are also key to Colonel North's claims. While a "full fledged investigation" is a category-bound activity for an Attorney General, a "fact finding inquiry" could be done by someone other than an attorney general; it is not an official legal procedure. Mr. North is claiming that the "Attorney General" was not conducting a "full fledged investigation" of his activities (which perhaps might imply wrongdoing on Mr. North's part), but that "Mister Meese" "had been a:s:ked to do aye fact finding <u>inquiry</u>." (line 53). The witness's reformulation to a "fact finding inquiry" is much less ominous than the "full fledged investigation"; the shift from "Attorney General" to "Mister Meese" helps him make this reformulation.

Membership categorization analysis in the workplace

Membership categorization devices can be used in a variety of ways in workplace and other institutional settings. They can be used to perform and differentiate institutional roles, to accomplish work-related tasks, and to facilitate the organization of turn exchange during meetings.

Oak (2009) uses membership categorization analysis to explore how participants in a building design meeting perform their roles of architect and client. One way in which categories affect interaction is in terms of what actions are associated with each role. So for example, the architect is the one who leads the meeting and determines what work will be done in it. He asks questions of the clients to elicit the information he needs to do his work (Oak, 2009). The nature of the responses to the questions display the clients' orientation to their role as clients. They differentiate their responses from the architect's role by displaying an orientation to his areas of professional competence. Oak (2009) presents an example in which the clients express a desire for a room to be larger. They speak in general terms instead of stating a specific size or length for the building, leaving the architect to articulate a specific size for the room. By these means the clients display an orientation to the architect's professional role.

McHoul (2007) analyzes a military incident in which American fighter pilots fired on British vehicles and troops who had been mistakenly identified as enemy troops. He shows how the categories and category predicates invoked by the American fighter pilots enable them to do the work of killing without claiming those actions and the moral accountability that would come with them, if not warranted by their institutional role. When the category-bound activities of a category (killing as part of the job of fighter pilots) is morally problematic, actions can be described in ways that defuse or avoid the moral implications of the actions. For example, the fighter pilot crew "engaged" the convoy rather than targeted them (McHoul, 2007).

Markaki and Mondada (2012) show how membership categorization analysis works in conjunction with turn-taking procedures to accomplish the selection of next speakers in a group setting. The meeting they analyze is conducted within a multinational corporation. Representatives from several countries are present as the chair leads them through discussion of a number of issues. Individuals present display an orientation to their role as "representatives of their countries" as they introduce themselves to the group at the beginning of the meeting, and as they respond to the chair's ongoing talk during the meeting. When the chair mentions one of the countries represented, she typically uses gaze direction and pointing or other gestures to indicate the representative of that country. That individual will then typically respond, thus displaying their orientation to their status as country representative. Thus selection of next speaker is accomplished via reference to their membership in the category of representative of a specific country rather than their individual identity, job category, or other characteristic.

Markaki and Mondada's (2012) analysis shows how turn-taking procedures intersect with membership categorization analysis in order to produce the smooth flow of interaction in this meeting in a way which facilitates and displays its status as a multinational meeting. Excerpt 4 shows how the participants choose to specify the country they represent as they introduce themselves, even though they have only been asked to produce a name. This displays their orientation to the relevance and importance of the category "country they represent" for the work to be done in this meeting.

Excerpt 4: Markaka and Mondada (2012, p. 36)

```
1   CLA   oké. so just eh:: ery quick: eh:: °>roundtable<° so that you
2         can put eh a name on each (0.3) face:,
3         (1.2)
4   VER   oké. vernoique lemaitre, from lyon:, i work with claire:: and i'm in
5         charge of: quality assurance and: (0.7) scientific affairs:.
6         (0.5)
7         you know me: (°at [least]° haha ahh hh
8   RIC                  [°yeah of course°
9   ARI   you don':::, kn- >don't< know me:,
```

```
10       (0.5)
11 ARI   eh: arianna rocci legal affairs:, italy.
12 RIC   °o:key.°
13       (1.2)
14 JUL   julia dupont (.) legal affairs, i work with marie:
15       (1.3)
16 MAR   marie charpin, legal affairs france
17       (0.5)
18 PIL   pilar frias, legal affairs spain
```

During the meeting speakers used gaze direction, pointing, or the mention of the country in conjunction with the pronoun "you" to select the next speaker, rather than relying on names of individuals (Markaka and Mondada, 2012). The individual identified by these categorical procedures then typically speaks in response to the utterance, while the other participants in the meeting remain silent and will typically turn their gaze toward the selected speaker.

In some occupational settings, the work of categorizing people is itself part of the work of the organization. Mazeland and Berenst (2008) analyze a staff meeting held at a school in the Netherlands. The purpose of this meeting was to decide which school their students should be promoted to: a higher level academic secondary school ("HAVO"), a lower-level academic school ("MAVO"), or a vocational school. The teachers at the meeting use membership categorization devices to do this work as they discuss students' academic strengths and weaknesses. For example, in Excerpt 5 the chair ("MA") solicits the geography teacher's ("Bert") perspective on a student. English translations appear below the Dutch transcription.

```
Excerpt 5: (Mazeland and Berenst, 2008, pp. 70–1)
1   MA:    Bert? ((Bert is the geography teacher))
2          1.5
3   GE:    e:h ('n aanta-) ook wat eh steekjes lateh valleh
           u:h (a numbe-) made some minor uh mistakes too
4          zie ik. (0.6) hè ik e:h (0.6)
           I see.        you know. u:h
5          a'k 'm zo zie zitteh< denk ik nou:,
           if I look at him, I think, well,
6 ->       goeje (hè?) heel goede (.) mAvo leerling.
           good (you know) very good MAVO pupil.
7          1.5
8 ->       maar: e::h niet meer dan dat.
           but u::h no more than that.
```

In turn 6, Bert concludes that the student would be a good "MAVO" student (the lower-level academic school). The evidence he has given to support this conclusion is that the student has made some "minor mistakes" (turn 3). For a student to qualify for the higher level school he or she must be a truly excellent all-around student; making minor mistakes are activities that link them to the lower-level school rather than the higher level school. The students' academic performance is thus treated as a category-bound activity linked to the category "MAVO" student, "HAVO" student, or vocational student.

Membership categorization analysis in informal settings

There have been some studies of membership categorization analysis in informal settings. Hester and Hester (2012) analyze how participants use and transform categories and collections of categories in the conversation that occurred during a family dinner. This excerpt also serves to illustrate how membership categorization analysis can be applied to objects as well as to people. In Excerpt 6 the mother "Jen" starts serving the food to her two children, 13-year-old "Russell" and 7-year-old "Maggie." As the excerpt begins, Jen is offering Russell potatoes and asking him which type of potato he wants. Her utterance thus treats potatoes as a collection and red potatoes and white potatoes as two categories within that collection.

> Excerpt 6: From Hester and Hester (2012, pp. 571–2)
> 001   J: do you want a potato (0.5) do you want a red potato or
> 002   a white potato?
> 003   R: a normal potato [please]
> 004   J: [hhhh.] ((sighs)) they are both
> 005   normal but one's a red potato and [one's a white one]
> 006   R: ((falsetto voice))   [a white one please]

However, by his response in line 3, Russell proposes a different type of collection of categories potatoes: normal potatoes and the implied category of potatoes that are not normal. This transformation of the categories implies a value judgment, with the "normal" potatoes (as we see in line 6) defined as the white potatoes. The mother contests his categorization of the red potatoes as "not normal" by first sighing, and then characterizing both red and white potatoes as normal. Russell then conforms to her categorization of the potatoes as he produces his revised response to her offer in line 6 ("a white one please"). The mother therefore declines to adopt Russell's alternative collection (normal/not normal), instead rearticulating her formulation of potatoes categorized by color (red or white).

Summary

Membership categorization analysis is a resource for participants to manage and interpret references to persons and objects during interactions in both informal and workplace settings. Speakers can use categories, collections of categories, and category-bound activities to identify and claim characteristics for persons or objects mentioned, and these claims can be contested or resisted by other participants. In the chapters that follow, social statuses such as institutional role or job category are made visible and relevant in the talk, in part through the use of membership categorization devices.

Student activities

1. List 10 different categories of which you are a member. List at least 2 "category-bound" activities that are associated with that category.
2. Can you write a short story (one paragraph) in which two people go to a store to buy something and get into an argument without using any categories? Can you write a story using only categories and no category-bound activities?

Recommended sources

Hester, Stephen and Eglin, Peter (eds). (1997), *Culture in Action: Studies in Membership Categorization Analysis.* Washington, DC: International Institute for Ethnomethodology and Conversation Analysis & University Press of America.

Jayyusi, Lena. (1984), *Categorization and the Moral Order.* Boston: Routledge & Kegan Paul.

Mazeland, Harrie and Jan Berenst. (2008), 'Sorting pupils in a report-card meeting: Categorization in a situated activity system', *Text & Talk*, 28(1), 55–78.

Sacks, Harvey. (1974), 'On the analysability of stories by children', in R. Turner (ed), *Ethnomethodology.* Harmondsworth: Penguin.

Schegloff, Emanuel A. (2007b), 'A tutorial on membership categorization', *Journal of Pragmatics*, 39, 462–82.

Stokoe, Elizabeth. (2010), ' "I'm not gonna hit a lady": Conversation analysis, membership categorization and men's denials of violence towards women', *Discourse & Society*, 21(1), 59–82.

Part III
Technologically Mediated Interaction: Work Done Through and with Technology

14 Routine Service Calls: Emergency Calls to the Police

Chapter contents

Introduction

While in the first half of this book we focused our attention on the study of ordinary conversation, with this chapter we begin our formal examination of talk in the workplace and in institutional settings more generally. We begin by considering the types of work that can be done over the telephone, because in contemporary society much workplace interaction is technologically mediated, either by telephone, computer or a combination of technological devices. For some types of employees, for example emergency service call takers, customer service representatives, marketing researchers, and so on, the work day largely consists of talking to people on the phone. We will begin our examination of phone calls in work settings by examining what are called "**service calls.**" Service calls are typically made by the public or by clients or customers of an organization or business in order to obtain information or a specific service.

In this section of the chapter we examine how emergency service call takers and callers work together to accomplish the work of the call in a timely and efficient manner. We will compare the organization of emergency service calls to that of ordinary conversational telephone calls, in order to gain a better understanding of how both types of interaction work. We will then examine how calls to emergency services unfold when intense emotion is displayed in the call.

While phone calls to emergency services are answered by call takers who have had at least a short training course, many of those who call emergency services are calling for the first time. Even though emergency service callers have some type of problem they want help with or even an urgent emergency, most emergency service calls are handled in a surprisingly calm and mundane way.

The interactional organization of emergency telephone calls

The opening/identification sequence

Because of the urgency of many emergency service calls and the time constraints call takers work under, the emergency service call opening is truncated in order to get to the business of the call as quickly as possible. While both emergency service calls and ordinary telephone calls begin with a summons/answer sequence, in emergency service calls the identification sequence is collapsed with the answer to the summons.

The emergency service call taker answers the summons by producing an institutional identification such as "Emergency Services" rather than responding with "hello" as callers do in ordinary phone calls (Zimmerman, 1984). This institutional identification serves to notify the caller that they have reached emergency services so that they can begin to talk immediately. The identity of the specific individual answering the phone is not relevant to the provision of emergency services, but it is important for the caller to know that they have reached the correct service.

In Excerpt 1 the call taker answers the phone with the institutional identification "Mid-City Emergency," thus combining the answer to the summons with the identification. The caller responds with "Uh: yes." (line 2). This is a typical opening for caller's first turns and works to display the caller's receipt of the institutional identification and their acknowledgement that they want to talk to emergency services (Whalen and Zimmerman, 1990).

> Excerpt 1: Zimmerman (1992b, p. 45)
> 1   CT: Mid-City Emergency
> 2   C: Uh: yes. I would like tuh speak with someone abou' havin' uh car
> 3   come out to thuh <u>An</u>drews Hotel please hh=

The caller does not have to identify themself in the opening phase of the call, but if they do not, the call taker will often ask for this information later on in the call. When a caller does identify themselves in the opening phase of the call, they usually provide an institutional identification rather than their name (as in Excerpts 2 and 3 below). The use of an institutional identification provides a warrant for the call. It accounts for how they know about the problem and why they are concerned.

Excerpt 2: Zimmerman (1992a, p. 456)

```
1   D:   Midcity emergency.
2        (  )
3   C:   Uh: this is uh: da g .h Knights of Columbus Hall: at tuh nine twunty three
4        west Haverford? north=
5   CT:                      =Umhm [keyboard]
6   C:   .hh Uh: we had some uh women's purses uh: stolen?
```

Excerpt 3: Zimmerman (1992a, p. 447)

```
1   D:   Midcity emergency{?,}
2        (  )
3   C:   .hhh! This is thuh Noonlight clu:b, on fordy one ten? (Penn:)(ten: )?
```

Another difference between the opening sequences in emergency service calls and ordinary telephone calls is that there is no exchange of greetings or initial inquiries (Whalen and Zimmerman, 1987). There is also no pre-topical talk (Maynard and Zimmerman, 1984). While in ordinary conversation participants may discuss a variety of preliminary topics before getting to the reason for the call, in emergency service calls there is only one topic to be discussed—the problem for which the caller needs help. The reason for the call is typically produced in the caller's first turn, immediately following their acknowledgment of the institutional identification. The opening sequences of emergency service calls thus differ markedly from those in ordinary telephone calls.

The reason for the call

The caller typically uses their first turn to produce the reason for the call (Zimmerman, 1984). This first turn may be framed as an explicit request for help or as a statement of a problem which functions as an implicit request for help (Whalen and Zimmerman, 1987). The trajectory of the call differs depending on how the caller formulates their opening turn. In both types of openings, the dispatcher hears the first turn as a request for help, because that is why people call emergency services. The request can be inferred by the action of calling emergency services and stating a policeable problem.

The caller in Excerpt 1 (above) follows his acknowledgement of the institutional identification with a request for a police car to come to the hotel (lines 2–3). The caller in Excerpt 4 also makes an explicit request for help:

Excerpt 4: Whalen and Zimmerman (1990, p. 481)

```
1   D:   Midcity emergenCY:?
2        (.)
3   C:   Yes Uh: I=need thuh paramedics please?
4        (.)
5   D:   Where to.
```

In Excerpt 5, the caller begins with a report of the problem:

> Excerpt 5: Zimmerman (1992a, p. 424)
> 1   D: Midcity emergen<u>cy</u>?hh
> 2   (.)
> 3   C: <u>Yes</u>. I'd <u>l</u>ike tuh repor' uh dee<u>stur</u>:bance, in an <u>a</u>:lleyway, (.) Be<u>h</u>ind are
> 4   building?
> 5   (.)
> 6   D: Oka<u>h</u>y, <u>Whu</u>t's thee=address (sir/there)?=

If the caller is not making an urgent call or a request for help, they typically communicate this immediately.

> Excerpt 6: Zimmerman (1992a, p. 463)
> 1   D: Midcity emergen<u>CY</u>:?
> 2   (.)
> 3   C: <u>HI</u>: Uhm:: I don't- think this is, really uh<u>mer</u>[gency   ]
> 4   D: [Well then] <u>HO</u>ld on
> 5   please.
> 6   ((caller put on hold))

If the caller in an emergency service call does not state the reason for the call in their first turn the call taker will later ask. "What's the problem?" In Excerpt 7 the caller uses their first turn to repeat the phone number of the person who referred him to emergency services (perhaps to justify calling emergency services for a minor problem—a noisy party—by showing that another police official had told him to call). When no reason for the call is given, the call taker asks "Whut's thuh <u>pro</u>blem sir?" in line 6 of the call. The caller then provides the reason for the call in line 8.

> Excerpt 7: Whalen and Zimmerman (1987, p. 176)
> 1   D: Midcity emergency .h
> 2   (.)
> 3   C: Uh: Yeah: Ah=wuz=<u>juss</u>' given this <u>number</u> by (   ) Three four eight (.)
> 4   three two: (   ) ((noise in pause)) UH:::: uh- uh:m three four=eight (.) two
> 5   eight three two:=
> 6   D: =<u>Yes</u>. Whut's thuh <u>pro</u>blem sir?
> 7   (.)
> 8   C: Well Ah <u>want</u> tih reeport uh <u>par</u>:dy goin'=(on/at) Six fifteen
> 9   twel<u>th</u>=avenue=<u>SOU</u>:th, Marl[aire:.]
> 10 D: [.hhh]=We=<u>HA</u>:ve thuh call.

The response to the request

The response to the request for help comes in a very different place in emergency service calls than it typically does in an ordinary conversation. Recall from our discussion in Chapter

6 that in ordinary conversation, responses to adjacency pair first pair parts typically occur immediately after the first pair part. If the response does not occur, participants will attempt to repair or account for its absence. However, in emergency phone calls, if the first turn is a request (as in Excerpt 1), the call taker's next turn is typically <u>not</u> a granting of the request, even though granting a request is the preferred second pair part of this type of adjacency pair. This is because before the request can be granted, the call taker must elicit additional information from the caller. At the very least, the call taker needs to know the location of the problem and enough about the nature of the problem to determine what type of help to send, where to send it, and what priority to give the call. Contemporary emergency service call systems utilize caller identification software to display the location of calls from landline phones (and in some areas, cell phones as well) on the call taker's computer screen. The address therefore does not have to be given as much attention today as it did in these earlier emergency service calls. However, there will still be a series of questions asked by the call taker prior to the granting of the request.

The risk in first granting the request by promising to send help is that the caller might then hang up before critical information is obtained. This is because once the "reason for the call" has been accomplished (the granting of the request for help), closing the call becomes relevant (Zimmerman, 1984). In fact, the granting of the request initiates the preclosing sequence in emergency service calls. This is because emergency service calls are monotopical (Wakin and Zimmerman, 1999). When the purpose of the call has been achieved, there are no more potential topics to discuss, so participants typically move immediately to a truncated closing sequence after the granting of the request (see below).

The interrogative series

The interrogative series (Zimmerman, 1984; Whalen and Zimmerman, 1990) comes after the caller's request for help or statement of the problem. It is an insertion sequence, typically comprised of more than one question/answer pair, and thus constitutes an inserted question/answer chain. The call taker asks the questions and the caller provides the answers. Thus in addition to being monotopical, the body of emergency service calls differs from ordinary conversations in its structure—a consistent pattern of questions and answers instead of the wide variety of participation and turn exchange patterns that can occur in ordinary conversation (Sacks et al., 1974).

The interrogative series in Excerpt 8 begins with the dispatcher temporarily asking the caller to hold and then verifying the location of the problem (lines 4 and 5), and where in the hotel the officers should go when they arrive (line 7). The caller answers these questions quickly and concisely. The call taker then asks, "What's thuh problem there." (line 9). The caller responds by telling the story about the tenant whose actions have prompted the call (lines 10–14). The call taker needs to know what type of problem help is being requested for in order to decide whether help is warranted, and if it is, what type of help should be sent (e.g. police, fire, or ambulance). Note that as soon as the request is granted (line 15), the participants move to close the call.

Excerpt 8: Zimmerman (1992b, pp. 45–6)

```
1   CT: Mid-City Emergency
2   C:  Uh: yes. I would like tuh speak with someone abou' havin' uh car
3       come out to thuh Andrews Hotel please hh=
4   CT:                                    =Hold on sir. ( ) Ah-
5       thuh Andrews hotel?
6   C:  Right.
7   CT: In thuh lobby?
8   C:  Correct.
9   CT: What's thuh=problem there.
10  C:  Thuh problum iz, that we have a tendent here that uh didn't pay
11      thuh rent We went up to her room tuh askt her tuh either leave or
12      (whatza callu,) .hh an whan thee uh security guard knocked on the
13      door tuh tell ur (.) she threatened tuh (tow) thuh security ta guards
14      heads off wif a gun.
15  CT: O:kay will get somebody=there right away.=
16  C:                              =Okay thank you
17  CT: Thank you.
```

Closing the call

As noted in Chapter 9, participants in ordinary conversation do work to end the conversation—by moving a topic to closure and preparing for the exchange of goodbyes with a preclosing sequence. If both parties have nothing more to say, closure is relevant. If they do have more to say, closure can be postponed.

The procedures used to close down police calls are the same as those used in ordinary conversation, but the institutional context of the call leads the process to unfold somewhat differently. In Excerpt 8 (above) the caller completes his explanation of "what the problem is" in line 14. The caller was able to successfully convey that the problem was both a policeable matter and serious enough to warrant sending a police car. The call taker then grants the request (line 15). The caller then produces an acknowledgment and a thank you (line 16), which is responded to by the call taker's "Thank you" in line 17. At this point the call taker cuts the connection to answer another call.

While in ordinary conversations the terminal exchange is always bilateral, in emergency service calls the call taker may end the call prior to the terminal exchange if there are time pressures (such as other incoming calls). However, the pre-closing is always bilateral, to give each party a chance to remember something that needs to be dealt with before ending the call.

The work done by the preclosing sequence becomes visible when it is used by participants as a last chance to mention something prior to closure. Excerpt 9 is from a call from the manager of a club who has called to report that the door to a Laundromat near by is open past the time it should be. After communicating the address and other information, the call taker moves to close the call by granting the request (we'll get somebody there).

However, instead of moving to closing, the caller raises the issue of whether the owner of the Laundromat should be notified; this reopens some locational issues which they work to resolve. When Excerpt 9 picks up the conversation, this work to resolve the locational issues is being wrapped up (lines 1 and 2). The call taker then reiterates the granting of the request (line 3), thus making closing relevant. Note that the call taker signals the end of the interrogative series by repeating the granting of the request, thus reopening the closing sequence. This time the closing sequence is completed and the call is terminated.

Excerpt 9: Zimmerman (1992a, p. 447)
```
1   CT:  .hh Okay you're eighty one nineteen Pine Avenue North arn't=ch=
2   C:   =That's correct=
3   CT:                =O:kay we'll get somebody=there
4   C:   O:kay? Thank you=
5   CT:                 =Mnhn bye.
```

Summary

The table below summarizes research by several researchers on the similarities and differences between emergency service calls and ordinary conversations conducted via telephone (e.g., Zimmerman, 1984; Whalen and Zimmerman, 1987; Schegloff, 1968, 1979).

1. Ordinary telephone calls begin with a summons/answer sequence, emergency service calls with a combined summons/answer and identification sequence.
2. Ordinary telephone calls have an identification/recognition sequence in the next turns of the opening, typically followed by a greeting sequence and the exchange of initial inquiries; emergency service calls do not have these sequences.
3. After the full opening sequence, the first topic or reason for the call is typically produced in ordinary phone calls. In emergency service calls the caller produces a brief acknowledgment of the institutional identification of the call taker and the reason for the call (either a request for help or a statement of the problem).
4. In ordinary calls participants may discuss a number of topics, in emergency service calls there is one topic; the body of the call consists of an interrogative series.
5. In ordinary calls there may be an extended pre-closing and closing sequence, in emergency service calls the granting of the request for help makes the closing relevant; preclosing sequences are brief and terminal exchanges may be truncated or elided.

The organization of emergency service calls differs in several ways from ordinary telephone conversations. Participants use the basic procedures and techniques for organizing talk, such as summons/answer sequences, adjacency pairs, insertion sequences, and closing sequences, to accomplish the work done in that institutional setting. The choices made about how to structure the interaction differ because the purpose of the call and the institutional context, roles, and responsibilities differ from those in ordinary phone calls.

The display of emotions in emergency service calls

In the ordinary emergency calls discussed above, although there are moments when the callers' emotion is apparent, for the most part all participants interacted in a calm and controlled manner. However, callers to emergency services do not always remain calm. Whalen and Zimmerman (1998) showed that displays of hysteria create problems for emergency service call takers by interfering with the business of the call. At the same time, these emotional displays provide an account for the caller's incompetence in completing the call. This display works to justify their need for police assistance by providing evidence that the emergency is real. When the caller's behavior is such that a call taker can describe them as "hysterical," this provides a warrant for the call taker to take steps to get the caller back on task. Whalen and Zimmerman (1998) explain that this is because emotions are accountable—we assume that there is an underlying reason for the display of emotion.

> In the case of hysteria, then, one must be hysterical *about* something, usually some feature of a situation in which one finds oneself. Some callers to emergency numbers display themselves as emotionally responsive to their particular situation; it may be the business of the 9-1-1 call taker to hear about and respond to this situation.[…] Because the caller's circumstances are not directly available to the call taker, these vocal expressions and displays by the caller provide an assessment of the seriousness of events at the other end of the phone line. With the concept of situated display we emphasize that these various vocal behaviors are produced as actions in the sequence of activities making up the call for help, and that the call taker assesses and responds to them as such. (Whalen and Zimmerman, 1998, pp. 143)

Thus the problem for the caller is to convey the source of their emotion in a way that the call taker can understand and find credible. The problem for the call taker may be to help the caller control their emotional state, at least to the extent that the communication of essential information is facilitated.

Displays of hysteria thus present two types of problems for the call taker. One, to accurately interpret the caller's emotional display as information indicating the seriousness of the incident being reported, and two, to successfully manage the call so that the caller's display of emotion does not interfere with the transmission of information—the work of the call. We will now examine some of the examples from Whalen and Zimmerman's (1998) analysis in order to show how call takers manage caller's emotional displays. Excerpt 10 shows a caller who is hysterical, judging by tone of voice, loudness of speech, and content of the utterance (e.g. shouting "GO::D!,", and adding "HURRY U:::::P!" to the end of his first turn (lines 3–5).

Excerpt 10: Whalen and Zimmerman (1998, p. 146)

1　CT:　Nine one one what is yur emerg- ((cutoff by static))
2　　　　(0.2)
3　C:　((howling/shrieking voice)) GO::D!, MY WIFE (JUST SHOT

```
4        HERSELF)! (0.3) THIRTY EIGHT FIFTY NINE ( ) AVENUE
5        HURRY U:::::P!
6        (0.2)
7   CT:  What happened?
8        (0.2)
9   C:   ((howling/shrieking voice)) (AR:::)=SHE JUS SHOT
10       HERSE::LF!=
11  CT:          =SHE FELL?
12       (0.2)
13  C:   SHE SHOT HER SELF WITH A SHOTGUN!
```

However, note that in spite of this caller's obvious emotional distress, he still follows the routine procedures of emergency service call openings. He waits to begin speaking until the call taker has answered the summons. He then produces a clear statement of a policeable, high priority problem in the first line of his turn, and he gives the address. His hysteria is thus available to the call taker as evidence of the seriousness of the situation and in a sense documents his claim that someone has been shot—his emotional display is consistent with the seriousness of the event. However, he still manages to construct his initial turn in a routine fashion and to communicate all the information needed for the call taker to provide help.

Whalen and Zimmerman (1998) contrast this with another caller with an equally serious emergency to report, who also displays emotion and hysteria. However this caller's emotion and distress impede her ability to complete the tasks required in the call.

Excerpt 11: Whalen and Zimmerman (1998, p. 148)

```
1   CT:  Nine=one=o[ne, what is your emergency?
2   C:           [HUHHHHH .HHHHHH HHHHHHH .HHHHH
3        HUHHHH .HHH ((loudly gasping/out of breath))
4   CT:  Hello?
5   C:   we(HHH)- .HHHH we've(HHH)- HUHHH .HHHH HEEHHH- the
6        address- HHHHH .HHH we need (ambu-Ln-) .HHH HHHHH
7        hee[hhh
8   CT:     [What?
9   C:   we=need=an=ambula(HH)nce- .H[UHHH HHHH HEEHHhh
10  CT:                               [>What's the address?<=
11  C:   =(ehdmmhmm) (.) .HHHUHHH an explo::sion! H[HH
12                                               [Ma'am?
13  CT:  I['ll (need ya tah) take a deep breath, I can't=
14  C:   [.hhh my- hh
15  CT:  =understa:nd you, what is the address?
16  C:   HHHH .HUHH (twenty) two .HHUHH ↑fou:r ↓one five
17       hhh .HHHH Kasman(hh) ↓Road .HHHHH[(I'm)
18  CT:                                    [(Ta- ta- [ta-)
19  C:                                              [There's
20       a ↑fire .hh huhh and we don't kno:w .HHUH where my
21       husband is:! .hhh hh
```

In this excerpt the caller's first turn consists of loud sounds of breathing and gasping, as if she is out of breath. The call taker responds by saying "Hello?" in line 4, as a way of summoning her to respond. At this point she is able to articulate at least a few words mixed in with her breathing and gasping, so the call taker knows that she is trying to communicate with him (lines 5–7). However, the call taker is not able to understand her words, and initiates a repair of her utterance in line 8 with the word "What?", thus concisely and quickly asking her to repeat her statement. As soon as the caller articulates her request for help in line 9, the call taker overlaps her gasping breaths with a request for the location of the problem (line 10). However, instead of providing the address, the caller states that there has been an explosion. At this point the call taker steps away from the interrogative series to do repair work on the caller's emotional state and the quality of her communications. The call taker then repeats his request for the address (lines 12–13, " Ma'am? I['ll (need ya tah) take a <u>deep</u> breath, I <u>can't</u>=under<u>sta:nd</u> you, what is the ad<u>dress</u>?"). The caller takes his advice and produces one more deep breath (line 16), and then provides the address. So while functional for the call in terms of providing evidence for the severity of the situation she is reporting, her hysteria is also <u>dysfunctional</u> in that it impedes the production of vital information and her ability to answer the call taker's questions. However, after the call taker's intervention she is able to communicate clearly enough to provide the critical information about the location of the problem.

In this final excerpt, the caller still displays emotion, but the level of emotional display is much lower and does not impede his participation in the call.

Excerpt 12: Whalen and Zimmerman (1998, p. 149)

```
 1  CT:  Nine one-on:e what is yur emergen[cy        ]
 2  C:                                    [>Oh m]y
 3        God ( ) gunshot=hh<
 4        (0.3)
 5  CT:  Whe:re
 6        (0.3)
 7  C:   Uh:m (0.1) eighteen ten Halston Street .hh apartment
 8        (0.2) three fourteen=hhh[.hhh        ]
 9  CT:                          [Anybody] shot?=
10  C:   =Ye:s we've go:tta hh .hh <my roommate's (hurt)
11        Oh: my: Go:d ple:a[se co-  ]
12  CT:                    [Okay ju]st stay on the li:ne,
13        is the gun- <is the gun put away?
14        (0.2)
15  C:   YE:S
16        (0.9) ((background voice heard))
17        Oh my God, please come. ((delivered in dazed monotone))
```

The very beginning of the caller's first turn is atypical, beginning with "Oh my God" instead of an acknowledgment of the institutional identification or a statement of the problem. However, after this brief exclamation, the caller is able to produce one word ("gunshot"; line

3) which suffices as a statement of a serious, policeable problem. Since the caller has stated the problem in the first turn, the call taker does not need to ask, "What's the problem?" The call taker goes immediately to the issue of location ("Whe:re"; line 5), which after a brief pause and hesitation, the caller is able to produce.

For all three of these excerpts analyzed by Whalen and Zimmerman (1998), the emotion displayed by the callers was of a specific type—their exclamations, breaths, and other statements communicated anxiety, upset and hysteria rather than irritation or some other emotion. In addition, in all three cases, the incidents that were reported were consistent with the production of the types of emotion that were displayed. Hence in these instances the emotion displayed contributed to the credibility of the callers, rather than detracting from it.

Summary

The interactional organization of emergency phone calls has both similarities and differences from ordinary telephone calls. The differences that we observe (such as truncated opening sequences, delayed responses to the request for help and the interrogative series) occur systematically because participants use them to achieve the goals of the call. Differences in the organization of interactions in institutional contexts (as is the case with emergency service calls) are related to the goals and constraints of that context, as well as the differential responsibilities assigned to the holders of institutional roles. While most callers are able to competently manage their participation in emergency service calls, some caller's displays of emotion may interfere with their performance in the calls. In Chapter 15 we will examine several additional types of interactional problems that can arise in emergency phone calls, and discuss how these interactional problems can lead to problems in providing help to those who need it.

Student activity

Choose a 911 call from the Los Angeles Police Department website:
http://www.lapdonline.org/communications_division/content_basic_view/27361
Compare the call you have chosen with the calls analyzed in this chapter. What similarities and differences do you find in the call's opening sequence, formulation of the request for help, interrogative series, or closing sequence? Do you believe the caller and the call taker did a good job communicating during the call?

Recommended sources

Wakin, Michele A. and Zimmerman, Don H. (1999), 'Reduction and specialization in emergency and directory assistance calls', *Research on Language and Social Interaction*, 32, (4), 409–37.

Whalen, Jack and Zimmerman, Don H. (1998), 'Observations on the display and management of emotion in naturally occurring activities: the case of "hysteria" in calls to 9-1-1', *Social Psychology Quarterly*, 61, (2), 141–59.

Whalen, Marilyn R. and Zimmerman, Don H. (1987), 'Sequential and institutional contexts in calls for help', *Social Psychology Quarterly*, 50, (2), 172–85.

—(1990), 'Describing trouble: practical epistemology in citizen calls to the police', *Language in Society*, 19, 465–92.

Zimmerman, Don H. (1984), 'Talk and its occasion: the case of calling the police', in Deborah Schiffrin (ed.) *Meaning, Form and Use in Context: Linguistic Applications. Georgetown University Roundtable on Language and Linguistics 1984*. Washington, DC: Georgetown University Press, pp. 210–28.

—(1992a), 'The interactional organization of calls for emergency assistance', in Paul Drew and John Heritage (eds) *Talk at Work*. Cambridge: Cambridge University Press, pp. 418–69.

15

Problematic Emergency Service Calls

Chapter contents

Introduction

In Chapter 14 we learned that participants in routine emergency service calls use procedures and techniques common to ordinary conversation, but adjust their use according to the expectations of their role (caller or call taker), and the interactional context of calling emergency services. These calls therefore end up having a very predictable structure which efficiently and concisely accomplishes the work of the call so that help can be provided when needed. However, on rare occasions a call may be unsuccessful. In this chapter we explore several types of interactional problems that can emerge in emergency service calls and threaten the ability of the call taker to provide help when needed.

A problematic emergency service call

Whalen et al. (1988) analyze a problematic emergency service call in which the caller did not succeed in obtaining an ambulance for his mother who was seriously ill. Unfortunately, because of the delay in providing services which resulted from this problematic interaction, the caller's mother died before an ambulance could reach her. While the media and the public were understandably unhappy with the call taker's job performance at the time this tragic incident occurred, Whalen et al. (1988) note that the reasons for the failure of communication were not yet accurately understood. They analyzed the call using the techniques of conversation analysis and discovered the sources of the breakdown in communication between the caller and the call taker. We will review several of these sources of trouble in talk in this section.

When this call occurred the city had recently switched to a system where all medical calls were transferred to a nurse dispatcher who would determine whether the emergency warranted an ambulance and prioritize the call in terms of the severity of medical need. Therefore, when the call taker discovered that the caller was requesting an ambulance, he transferred the caller to the nurse dispatcher. Unfortunately, the caller became frustrated with the interaction with the nurse and got into a dispute with her. After an extended disagreement, the caller eventually ended the call, saying he would call a hospital directly to get an ambulance from them. A few minutes later, the caller's roommate called emergency services a second time and was transferred to that same nurse. This second caller was able to avoid many of the problems that happened in the first call, and this time the nurse dispatcher did order an ambulance. Unfortunately, so much time had elapsed that the patient died before the ambulance reached the house (Whalen et al., 1988). Members of the press argued that "the caller had provided enough information about his stepmother's condition to warrant the immediate dispatching of an ambulance" (Whalen et al., 1988, p. 340). Whalen et al. (1988, p. 340) note that "the nurse who handled this call was fired and several of her supervisors were reprimanded or demoted."

The transcript for this call is in Appendix A at the end of this chapter. Examine it closely and then read the following analysis of the call which is based on the findings in Whalen et al.'s (1988) article. Whalen et al. (1988) note that there is a "social organization" to calls to emergency services; a routine set of procedures, background assumptions, social roles, and expectations that when implemented correctly, result in a successful call.

Whalen et al. (1988) observe that the caller produced several *"informings"*—statements about his stepmother's condition which describe a serious medical state. For example, at one point he says that his mother has difficulty breathing (lines 50–1), and at another point he says that it is a life threatening emergency (lines 77–8). However, as we learned in Chapter 2 when discussing the indexicality of human action, the meaning of an utterance depends on the context it occurs within. A critical component of this context is the sequential environment—the immediately prior utterances in the conversation. Whalen et al. (1988) refer to this as the "primacy of sequential context." The question then becomes not what words or phrases did the caller produce during the call, but how did the caller and nurse fit their actions together, and what sense do they make of each other's actions? Whalen et al. (1988) analyze the sequential context of this call more closely.

Recall from Chapter 14 that the organization of routine emergency phone calls is accomplished through the following components: a truncated opening sequence, a request for help (either formulated as an explicit request or one that is implicit in the description of the problem and the act of calling emergency services to report it), an interrogative series in which the call taker obtains the information needed to provide help, and a response to the request for help which opens up the closing of the call. In the call Whalen et al. (1988) analyze, although the caller begins with a request for help in his first turn, he fails to provide the requested description of the problem when asked by the dispatcher (Excerpt 1) and (later on in the call) the nurse (Excerpt 2):

Excerpt 1: Whalen et al. (1988, p. 336)

```
6   D:   What's thuh problem sir?
7   C:   I: don't know, n'if I knew I wouldn't be ca:lling
8        you all
```

Excerpt 2: Whalen et al. (1988, p. 337)

```
45  N:   And whatiz thuh problem there?
46  C:   I don't kno:w, if I knew I wouldn't be needin'
47       [y-
```

Whalen et al. (1988, p. 346) ask "How could [the caller] come to hear the problem probe as pressing him to provide knowledge that he could not be expected to possess?" It may be that he assumed that the call takers were requesting a medical diagnosis, which he was not able to provide. This belief may have been reinforced by the subsequent transfer to the nurse dispatcher.

Heritage and Robinson (2006, p. 55) analyze an excerpt from an acute primary care visit to a physician (Excerpt 3). In this excerpt the patient appears to interpret the doctor's question (line 1) not as a request for a <u>description</u> of the problem she is experiencing, but as a request for a <u>diagnosis</u> of the problem. Note that the patient's response in lines 2 and 3 is very similar to that of the caller in the Whalen et al. (1988) emergency service call.

Excerpt 3: Heritage and Robinson (2006, p. 55)

```
1   DOC:   What's ha:ppenin' to ya Clarisse
2   PAT:   I don't know sir=if I knew that I wouldn't
3          h[ave [(ta)
4   DOC:        [You [wouldn't be here. [hu:h?
5   PAT:                                [Yeah. This is true. .hh I- I asked …
```

Whalen et al. (1988) also note that there are different types of service calls, each with different sets of expectations. A "Type I" service call is what happens in situations such as ordering a pizza for delivery to your home. When you call to order a pizza, you are not expected to explain why you want a pizza. For "Type II" service calls an account or explanation is necessary in order to receive the service. Emergency service calls are Type II calls. However, the caller acts as if his call to emergency services is a "Type I" call. The caller's display of surprise at being asked "what's the problem" shows that he expected his request to be granted as soon as it was made. He also clearly did not anticipate being transferred to the nurse dispatcher, and when the nurse repeated the question "what's the problem" later on in the call (Excerpt 2, above), his answer displays that he still did not expect to be required to provide an explanation. Whalen et al. (1988, p. 346) note that "there is a fundamental misalignment of C and D concerning the "ground rules" of the exchange; they refer to this as "interactional asynchrony." They note that once the caller has stated that he does not know what the problem is, he can not easily retract that position and give an answer—to do so would display an inconsistency in his responses which would be problematic.

> As Clayman (1985:36) has observed, displaying realignment by modifying a prior position cannot be done wholly at random; such modifications must occur for some demonstrable reason and be heard as ultimately consistent with what was previously said. (Whalen et al., 1988, p. 352)

Not all of the problems in the call emerged from the caller's misunderstandings or actions. The nurse's handling of the call was also, at times, problematic. For example, in Excerpt 4, when the caller expresses his frustration in line 65, instead of ignoring the utterance or trying to refocus the caller back onto the business at hand, the nurse focuses the topic of her utterance on his cursing (line 67). She characterizes it as a curse directed at her, and admonishes the caller for it (see Whalen et al., 1988, p. 352).

> Excerpt 4: Whalen et al. (1988, p. 337)
> 64 N: <u>Why</u> is she inco<u>her</u>ent?
> 65 C: How thuh hell do I:: kno::w
> 66   (.)
> 67 N: Sir <u>don</u>'t curse <u>me</u>

Whalen et al. (1988) note that the nurse's "Sir <u>don</u>'t curse <u>me</u>," in line 67 treats the caller's line 65 as an oppositional move. By providing a return oppositional move, the nurse dispatcher maintains or even escalates the state of arguing between them. Arguing is done through the exchange of oppositional utterances, through what Goodwin and Goodwin (1987) call recycling, "with each of the opposing parties repeating their prior position" (Whalen et al., 1988, p. 353).

As noted above, the caller, on several occasions, produced "informings," which when taken out of context, constitute statements of his mother's condition that appeared to justify a high priority medical response. However, as Whalen et al. (1988) explain, the interactional context they occurred within (an emerging argument between the caller and the nurse call taker), led to their being interpreted not at face value but as oppositional moves in a dispute. One technique through which disputing is accomplished in ordinary conversation is through what Goodwin and Goodwin (1987) refer to as <u>format tying</u>:

> In producing a subsequent argumentative move participants tie their utterance not only to the types of action produced by the last speaker, but also to the particulars of its wording, thus reusing the materials provided by prior talk to shape a counter to it. (Whalen et al., 1988, p. 354)

Excerpt 5 illustrates how the emerging argument creates a sequential context for the interpretation of subsequent utterances.

Excerpt 5: Whalen et al. (1988, pp. 337–8)
64 N: <u>Why</u> is she inc<u>o</u>herent?
65 C: How thuh hell do I:: kno::w
66   (.)
67 N: Sir <u>don't</u> curse <u>me</u>
68   (.)
69 C: Well I don't care, you- ya- ya-stupid ass
70   (anit-) questions you're asking
71   (3.0)
72 C: <u>Gimme</u> someone that knows what they're <u>doin'</u>,
73   why don't you just send an <u>ambulance</u> out here?
74   (0.6)
75 N: Sir, we only come out on <u>life</u> threatening
76   eme:<u>r</u>[gencies, okay?]
77 C: [Well <u>this</u> is <u>li</u>]fe threatening
78   e<u>mer</u>gency=
79 N: =hold on sir, I'll let you speak with
80   my sup- uh <u>officer</u>

Because of the interactional context it occurs within, the caller's utterance in lines 77–8 is heard not as a legitimate "informing" about his stepmother's condition ("life threatening emergency"). Instead, the nurse hears it as a contradiction of what she has just said—in short, another oppositional utterance in a *series* of such utterances in what has been transformed from a service call into a dispute (Whalen et al., 1988, p. 354). Whalen et al. (1988, p. 354) refer to this process as "activity contamination."

> The sequential development of an activity in talk is critical for the determination of its status and consequences… Consequently, seemingly informative utterances occurring in different types of sequential contexts may not function or be registered by participants as in the first instance informings, but as other types of activity, e.g., rejoinders, accusations, excuses, and so on. (Whalen et al., 1988, p. 354)

Another source of conflict within this emergency call was the caller's frustration with the questions the nurse was asking about the condition of the patient. Recall from Chapter 14 that the interrogative series is a routine part of ordinary emergency service calls. In the current instance, however, some of the nurse's questions seem unnecessary for the purpose of deciding whether to provide help. For example:

Excerpt 6: Whalen et al. (1988, p. 338)
114 N: Does thuh la:dy have history of any kind of lung
115   di<u>sease</u>?
116   (0.3)
117 C: No. She has rheumatoid arthritis, a <u>broken</u> hip
118   and a <u>broken</u> e:<u>l</u>bow.
119   (0.5)

```
120  N:  Okay, how did she get thuh broken hip en thuh
121      elbow, did she fa:ll?
122  C:  Yes she did.
123      (0.2)
124  N:  Whe:n?
125      (0.3)
126  C:  Oh, back in August of: ah:- last year.
```

A study by Frankel (1995) on how doctors conduct clinical interviews with their patients may shed some light on how the interrogative series in this call contributed to the conflict between the participants. Frankel notes that while doctors may ask a number of questions, and that the connection between these questions may not always be apparent to the patient, patients typically accept these questions unproblematically. However, if the questions appear to ignore an urgent condition in favor of a less urgent one, the patient may find the questions problematic:

> To illustrate, suppose a patient comes to a physician concerned about chest pain and during the course of the encounter the physician asks a lot of questions about lifestyle that seem unrelated. I would argue that the physician's specialized knowledge and the contingent nature of the activities that occur between the problem identification and the proposed solution provide a warrant for the patient to continue to answer what may seem like unrelated questions. By contrast, suppose that the same patient comes to a physician concerned not only about chest pain but about committing suicide. If the physician inadvertently focuses on the patient's first problem to the exclusion of the second (as happens frequently according to our research, Beckman and Frankel, 1984) then the clinical activities that follow as well as the proposed solution may be inadequate to the overall task of developing a complete data base. (Frankel, 1995, p. 248)

This may be what has occurred in the Whalen et al. (1988) call. If from the perspective of the caller, the nurse's questions seem irrelevant to the problem at hand, they may further damage her credibility as a competent call taker and further increase the caller's level of frustration with the process.

Whalen et al. (1988) thus conclude that when the call is analyzed in its sequential context using the conversation analytic perspective, the roles both the caller and the call taker played in the failure of call become clear. We can also see how the call taker could have come to doubt this caller's legitimacy. We now turn to a second emergency service call in which problems in the communication between the participants also led to the failure to provide timely service. In this second call the primary issue was the failure to develop trust.

A problematic service call: failure to maintain trust

Garcia and Parmer (1999) use conversation analysis to investigate why an emergency service call taker failed to treat a caller's report that two police officers had been shot as a high priority emergency. Unlike the call analyzed above, this call taker did order a police car to the address to check out the situation. However, she did not give it a high priority ranking, so the police response was delayed. During this call "Melvin Smith" (a pseudonym) made an heroic effort to get an ambulance for the dying officers, under very traumatic circumstances. However, several aspects of his actions during the call apparently aroused and maintained the skepticism of the call taker. The complete transcript of this call is in Appendix B of this chapter. Examine it closely and then read the following summary of Garcia and Parmer's (1999) analysis of the interactional problems that occurred in this call.

The importance of context

Four friends were socializing in an apartment when two undercover police officers knocked on the door to serve a warrant to the tenant. Tragically, instead of letting himself be arrested, the man shot the two officers in the head at close range, mortally wounding them. The man then ran from the apartment, taking the gun with him. When about a block away from the apartment, off-duty police officers saw him running with a gun and began chasing him. He then fatally shot himself with the gun, only a block away from the apartment where the shooting took place. Meanwhile, two of the three guests ran from the apartment, while the third, Mr. Smith, stayed behind and called emergency services. Before he made his emergency service call, calls had already come in about the shooting on the next block. In addition to some atypical actions taken by the caller (which will be described below), the call taker's job is complicated by her prior knowledge of the unfolding events around the suicide that occurred a block away. Instead of assuming that the caller is calling about a different event, she apparently assumes that the shots he heard were the same shots that the shooter used to kill himself only a block away from the apartment. Given this assumption, her ability to hear Mr. Smith's reportings as related to a different event are compromised. Even so, she tried several times to determine whether the shots he heard could have been from a separate event. All addresses and phone numbers have been replaced with pseudonyms.

```
Excerpt 7: Garcia and Parmer (1999, p. 300)
01  CT:  ((click))=°nine one one.°
02        (0.4)
03  MS:  nine one one? 'h=needs U::H (0.2) .h i need=uh (0.3) uh shots fired at
04        uh twenny two west hanover street. ((Caller's voice sounds rough
05        and slightly slurred))
06        (0.4)
07  CT:  twenny two? ((sounds bored))
08        (0.2)
09  MS:  yehs. (0.2) ple:ase. ple:ase. (there's) two police down.
10        (0.2)
11  CT:  are you ou:tside?,
12        (0.2)
13  MS:  no i'm inSI::'e!
```

14		(0.3)
15	CT:	well how do you know they're down?
16		(0.2)
17	MS:	because they're in fron' uh MY FA::CE! ((last two words in
18		anguished shout))

When the call taker asks in line 11 "are you ou:tside?,", and the caller replies with a very emphatic "no i'm inSI::'e!", she then asks how he knows they are "down" (line 15). When Mr. Smith responds "because they're in fron' uh MY FA::CE!" (line 17), this informing is colored by the sequential context of his prior utterance. In line 3 he reported "shots fired" rather than "two police down." The call taker's perceptions are also most likely affected by her knowledge of the shots that were fired outside, a block away from the apartment Mr. Smith was calling from. This leads to her assumption that if he is inside he has limited knowledge of what is actually happening.

The importance of callers' opening turns

Callers' opening turns are critically important to the success of emergency service calls. As Zimmerman (1984) noted, how the caller's first turn is structured affects the trajectory of the call in several important ways. In this call, the hesitant and uncertain nature of the caller's first turn, the error avoidance and repair work evident, along with the caller's slurred speech, all conveyed a lack of urgency. When the caller does produce his request for help, it is formulated as a statement of the problem ("shots fired") rather than as a request for specific services (line 3 in Excerpt 7, above). "Shots fired" implies that he heard shots fired, not that someone was shot.

Mr. Smith's failure to specify that he needs an ambulance, especially given his later claims that two police officers have been shot, sets the stage for a "hard sell." Once the problem has been formulated as "shots fired," it is very difficult to upgrade it to "two police down" without an account or explanation to rationalize the disjuncture between these two positions (Clayman, 1985). The caller's first turn, therefore, rather than justifying the need for help to the call taker, instead raises questions as to what has actually happened.

The problematic nature of unresolved disjunctures

In addition to the disjunctures between the caller's first turn and his subsequent formulations of the reason for the call, there are several other instances where the caller produces disjunctures which the call taker is not able to resolve through investigative questioning. For example, in line 9 (Excerpt 7, above) Mr. Smith claimed that two police officers were "down." Excerpt 8 (below) shows that after the call taker asks "well how do you know they're down?" (line 15), the caller answers "because they're in fron' uh MY FA::CE!" (line 17). However, in line 38 Mr. Smith claims that he didn't see anybody. Immediately after claiming that he did not see anybody, he says "THEY IS DYIN' (0.3) THEY IS DYIN'!=", thus raising the question of how both of these things can be true.

Excerpt 8: Garcia and Parmer (1999, pp. 300–1)

15 CT: well how do you know they're down?
16   (0.2)
17 MS: because they're in fron' uh MY FA::CE! ((last two words in
18   anguished shout))
19   (0.3)
20 CT: what's your name sir.=
21 MS: =(melry/melvin) SMI::th! PLEASE (come) i
22   don' wanna be in thuh (theh- thuh-) I DON't wanna be named
23   involved wit' this. PLEASE [NO!]
24 CT: [(   )] if you're in thuh HOUSE you're
25   not involved, okay? what's yer phone number?, (0.2)
26 MS: please (uhm) six four three two (0.2) two five nine uh four six. (0.3)
27   .hhh please. ple~ase don't cause i don't want to go to jail, please.
28   [(come)]
29 CT: [why] would jou go to JAIL?, (sir?) you just called in to report it.
30   Are you- are you INVOLVED?
31   (0.4)
32 MS: NO I'M NOT IN[VOLVED.]
33 CT: [(then)] CA:Lm down and give me some
34   information, okay?
35   (0.2)
36 CT: if you're INside thuh house you're pretty safe. did you see any body?
37   (0.4)
38 MS: NO:::. .nh hh (0.7) THEY IS DYIN' (0.3) THEY IS DYIN'!=

These types of unresolved disjunctures occur throughout the call. The apparently contra-
dictory nature of the caller's statements contribute to the call taker's doubts that he is a
credible witness.

The problematics of multi-topic emergency service calls

Phone calls to emergency services are typically monotopical or monofocal (Wakin and
Zimmerman, 1999), but in this call the caller introduces several issues which are not
directly related to the business of the call (getting help for the officers who have been
shot). For example, in lines 22–3 (in Excerpt 8 above) Mr. Smith introduces the issue of
not wanting to be "named involved in this," a theme which he returns to in line 27. His
introduction of this topic distracts the call taker from her work of determining whether
a policeable problem exists, and if so, what priority to give it, thus impeding her ability
to successfully complete the call. These types of topic shifts rarely occur in emergency
service calls. By mere virtue of its atypicality, these shifts serve to reinforce the existing
evidence that this caller is not a typical caller. These differences from typical emergency
service calls further reinforce the call taker's emerging skepticism about the credibility
of the caller.

The problematics of concealment in emergency service calls

Based on what we know from newspaper reports about the incident, at several points in the call the caller appears to conceal information from the call taker. Concealing information impedes the call taker's efforts to verify the caller's credibility. When Mr. Smith says "NO I'M NOT INVOLVED." (line 32 in Excerpt 8 above), this is not strictly speaking true. While he is not responsible for the shooting, he is involved in the sense that he was a witness to the event and he knows what happened and who was involved.

It may be that Mr. Smith was reluctant to reveal this information because he did not want to get his friend (the shooter) in trouble. If instead of saying I'm not involved," he had said "I saw…" or "I witnessed…", the call taker would have been able to understand his relationship to what happened and how he knew what he was claiming to know. In addition, Mr. Smith says he did not see anybody else, which is clearly not true (Excerpt 9, line 52). There were three other people in the apartment at the time the shooting occurred, but he reports seeing no one.

> Excerpt 9: Garcia and Parmer (1999, p. 301)
> 45 CT: <u>whut</u> do you <u>see</u>?
> 46   (0.3)
> 47 MS: i see two undercover cops layin' in fron' of my face an' (0.8)
> 48   (<u>bleeding</u>/with bullets) they DEA::D (LO::RD!!)
> 49   (1.2)
> 50 CT: .hh two undercover. you don't see anybody else?
> 51   (0.3)
> 52 MS: NO::::!
> 53   (0.4)
> 54 CT: No?
> 55   (0.3)
> 56 MS: UNH UNH!

The lack of a coherent story or narrative

While Mr. Smith produced various "informings" (Whalen et al., 1988) at various points in the call, at no point does he weave these informings together into a story or narrative that explains what happened. For example, compare Mr. Smith's call with the call below from Zimmerman's (1992b) article:

> Excerpt 10: Zimmerman (1992b, pp. 45–6)
> 1 CT: Mid-City Emergency
> 2 C: Uh: yes. I would like tuh speak with someone abou' havin' uh car
> 3   come out to thuh <u>A</u>ndrews Hotel please hh=
> 4 CT: =Hold on sir. ( ) Ah-
> 5   thuh Andrews hotel?
> 6 C: Right.
> 7 CT: In thuh lobby?
> 8 C: Correct.

```
 9   CT:  What's thuh=problem there.
10   C:   Thuh problum iz, that we have a tendent here that uh didn't pay
11        thuh rent We went up to her room tuh askt her tuh either leave or
12        (whatza callu,) .hh an whan thee uh security guard knocked on the
13        door tuh tell ur (.) she threatened tuh (tow) thuh security ta guards
14        heads off wif a gun.
15   CT:  O:kay will get somebody=there right away.=
16   C:                                  =Okay thank you
17   CT:  Thank you.
```

In the emergency phone call in Excerpt 10, the caller very quickly and efficiently tells a story that communicates not just what happened, but how he knows what happened (lines 10–14). In line 10 the caller conveys that he works for the hotel, thus justifying his role in calling the police. In lines 11–14, he conveys that he witnessed these events himself, which shows *how* he knows what he knows (e.g. "We went up to her room tuh askt her tuh either leave…"). When he says "she threatened tuh (tow) thuh security ta guards heads off wif a gun." (lines 13–14), he communicates that the problem is clearly a policeable, and potentially serious, matter, thus justifying his request for a police car to be sent.

In the Garcia and Parmer (1999) call, on the other hand, at no point does the caller present a narrative, however brief, of what happened. His first formulation of the problem ("shots fired"), leaves open the question of who fired the shots or what they were fired at, and also fails to communicate how he knows that shots were fired. This leaves the call taker to assume that he heard shots fired from a location that prevented him from seeing who or what was fired at. Similarly, when he says "two police down", he implies that the officers were shot, but he provides no information as to how that might have happened or how he knows what happened—there is no story, scene, or setting described which could give these informings the context needed to make them understandable. The absence of a story or narrative is fatal to his attempts to get help for the dying officers.

In short, although the call taker made several attempts to do her job, the caller did not provide her with enough accurate, consistent information in order to enable her to treat this caller unskeptically. While she can be criticized for not giving him the benefit of the doubt, a significant portion of the work of emergency service call takers is screening calls, a large portion of which end up being non-emergencies or even hoax calls. Thus, by evaluating the credibility of this caller, determining that his call was probably referring to the shooting a block away, and assigning it a low priority ranking, the call taker was doing her job in an appropriate manner. Unfortunately, in this tragic instance, she was wrong.

Summary

This chapter has shown how misunderstandings and mistakes in interactions can be caused by participants' actions during the call. Both caller and call taker are relying on commonsense everyday procedures for both constructing their own actions and interpreting the actions of others. The context of each utterance, in particular the immediately prior utterance but also other utterances in the interaction, provide the sequential context in which the utterance is interpreted and understood. In the first problematic emergency services call analyzed in this chapter, the transition into an arguing framework was the major source of trouble in the call. In the second call, the caller constructed his contributions such that the call taker was unable to verify what he was saying. In both cases, an understanding of what went wrong in the calls was achieved by a detailed, sequential analysis of the interactions using the techniques and research findings of conversation analysis. The goal of theses types of analyses is to explain how problems in talk emerge so that such problems can be avoided in the future.

Student activity

Examine the complete transcripts of the two calls analyzed in this chapter in Appendices A and B. For each call, identify which you feel is the most problematic utterance the caller and the call taker produce. What could have they said instead of these problematic utterances? How would the remainder of the call unfolded differently if they had produced these improved utterances instead of what they actually said?

Appendix A: Transcript of Emergency Services Call (Whalen, et al., 1988, pp. 336–9)

```
1    D:   Firedepartment
2         (0.8)
3    C:   Yes, I'd like tuh have an ambulance at forty one
4         thirty nine Haverford please
5         (0.5)
6    D:   What's thuh problem sir?
7    C:   I: don't know, n'if I knew I wouldn't be ca:lling
8         you all
9         (0.5)
10   D:   Are you thuh one th't needs th'ambulance?
11   C:   No I am not. It's my mother.
12        (1.1)
13   D:   Lemme letya speak with thuh nurse
14        (0.3)
15   C:   Oh, bu:ll shit!
16        (1.7)
17        ((in background)) Nurse, line one (1.0) Nurse, line one
18        (1.2)
19   N:   This is thuh fi:re department nurse, what iz thee
20        address?
21        (0.3)
22   C:   Forty one thirty nine Have:ford
23        (1.4)
```

24	N:	For[ty-] (.) one thirtynine what's thuh street?
25	C:	[Driv]e
26		(0.3)
27	C:	Haverfo:rd Drive ((spoken with irritated tone))
28		(0.3)
29	N:	H. a. v. e. (c.) o. r. [d.
30	C:	[No, H. a. v. e:.
31		r. f. o. r. d. Drive ((exasperated tone))
32		(1.6)
33	N:	Okayiz thisuhhouse or n' apartmen'?
34	C:	It- it is a ho:me
35		(0.6)
36	N:	What street crosses Haverford there onthuh corner?
37		(0.4)
38	C:	Uh: it's Lincoln, you (cn'cut) off at Lincoln
39		(1.9)
40	N:	And thuh pho:ne number?
41		(0.6)
42	C:	Thuh phone number, three two nine, three two
43		two fi:ve.
44		(0.8)
45	N:	And whatiz thuh problem there?
46	C:	I don't kno:w, if I knew I wouldn't be needin'
47		[y-
48	N:	[Si:r:, I- eh- would you answer my questions
49		please? whatiz thu[h problem?]
50	C:	[She is hav]ing difficult in
51		breathing
52		(.)
53	N:	How old is this person?
54	C:	She is sixty years old.
55		(1.1)
56	N:	Where is she now?
57		(0.3)
58	C:	She is in thuh bedroom right now
59		(0.4)
60	N:	May I speak with her, please?
61	C:	No you ca:n't, she's (ch-) she's (.) seems
62		like she's incoherent.
63		(0.5)
64	N:	Why is she incoherent?
65	C:	How thuh hell do I:: kno::w
66		(.)
67	N:	Sir don't curse me
68		(.)
69	C:	Well I don't care, you- ya- ya-stupid ass
70		(anit-) questions you're asking

71		(3.0)

71   (3.0)
72 C: <u>Gi</u>mme someone that knows what they're <u>doin</u>',
73   why don't you just send an <u>am</u>bulance out here?
74   (0.6)
75 N: Sir, we only come out on <u>life</u> threatening
76   eme:r[gencies, okay?]
77 C: [Well <u>this</u> is <u>li</u>]fe threatening
78   em<u>er</u>gency=
79 N: =hold on sir, I'll let you speak with
80   my sup- uh <u>of</u>ficer
81   (10.8)
82 S: Hell<u>o:</u>
83   (.)
84 C: .hh Ye:s, what do I hafta do to get an
85   ambulance out tuh this house?
86   (0.2)
87 S: You hafta answer thuh nurse's questions=
88 C: =Allright.
89   what <u>are</u> they before she <u>dies</u>, would you <u>please</u>
90   <u>tell</u> me what thuh hell you <u>want</u>?
91   (1.9)
92 S: Well I'll tell you=what. If you <u>cuss</u> one more
93   time I'm gonna hang up thuh phone
94 C: Well I'll tell <u>you</u> what, what if it was <u>your</u>
95   mother in there and can't breathe, what would
96   <u>you</u> do?
97 S: ((slightly louder)) <u>You</u> answer that nurse's
98   questions and we'll get you some help
99 C: Sh'having <u>diff</u>icult in <u>breath</u>ing. She <u>can</u>not
100   talk, [she (   )
101 S: [Awright, she's back on- she's back on
102   there n'don't you cuss her a<u>gi:n</u>
103   (1.1)
104 C: Well you put 'er on then
105 S: (say) <u>what</u>?
106   (0.5)
107 C: Well then put-er <u>on</u>
108   (0.2)
109 S: She's on there.
110   (0.2)
111 N: Sir, this is fire department nurse a<u>gain</u>
112   (0.2)
113 C: Yes
114 N: Does thuh la:dy have history of any kind of lung
115   di<u>sease</u>?
116   (0.3)
117 C: No. She has rheumatoid arthritis, a <u>broken</u> hip

118   and a <u>bro</u>ken <u>e:l</u>bow.
119   (0.5)
120   N: Okay, how did she get thuh broken hip en thuh
121   <u>e</u>lbow, did she fa:ll?
122   C: Yes she did.
123   (0.2)
124   N: Whe:<u>n</u>?
125   (0.3)
126   C: Oh, back in <u>Aug</u>ust of: ah:- last year.
127   (0.3)
128   N: Okay <u>sir</u>, I need to <u>talk</u> to her still
129   C: You <u>ca:n't</u> she is inc<u>oh</u>e:rent
130   (0.2)
131   N: Let me <u>talk</u> to her sir
132   (0.3)
133   C: thhh:
134   (1.0)
135   C: ((to third party in background)) Would you
136   please tell her that she's <u>inc</u>oherent, that she
137   <u>can</u>not talk?
138   (1.1)
139   C: She <u>can</u> <u>not</u> talk at [all
140   N: [WHY:?
141   (0.7)
142   C: Well how am I s'posed tuh <u>kno:::w</u>?
143   (.)
144   N: Well then <u>give</u>'er thuh <u>pho:</u>ne
145   (1.0)
146   C: hhhh .hh
147   (0.3)
148   C: ((to his roommate in background)) Give'r thuh
149   phone in there (.) give'r thuh phone in there so
150   that she- (0.3) I <u>know</u> she can't talk, but they
151   want ta talk to <u>her</u> (.) but she can't talk
152   (1.7)
153   C: ((to nurse-dispatcher)) Uh forget it, I'll call
154   an am- uh hospital around here, all right?
155   N: 'kay, b'bye

Appendix B: "Mr. Smith" Emergency Service Call (Garcia and Parmer, 1999, pp. 300–2)
01   CT: ((click))=°<u>nine</u> one one.°
02   (0.4)
03   MS: nine one one? 'h=needs U::H (0.2) .h i need=uh (0.3) uh shots fired at
04   uh twenny two west hanover street. ((Caller's voice sounds rough
05   and slightly slurred))
06   (0.4)
07   CT: twenny two? ((sounds bored))

08   (0.2)
09   MS: yehs. (0.2) <u>ple:ase</u>. <u>ple:ase</u>. (there's) two police down.
10   (0.2)
11   CT: are you <u>ou:t</u>side?,
12   (0.2)
13   MS: no i'm inSI::'e!
14   (0.3)
15   CT: well how do you know they're down?
16   (0.2)
17   MS: because they're in fron' uh MY FA::CE! ((last two words in
18   anguished shout))
19   (0.3)
20   CT: what's your name sir.=
21   MS: =(melry/melvin) SMI::th! PLEASE (come) i
22   don' wanna be in thuh (theh- thuh-) I DON't wanna be named
23   involved wit' this. PLEASE [<u>NO</u>!]
24   CT: [( )] if <u>you're</u> in thuh HOUSE you're
25   <u>not</u> involved, okay? <u>what's</u> yer phone number?, (0.2)
26   MS: please (uhm) six four three two (0.2) two five uh four six. (0.3) .hhh
27   please. ple~ase don't cause i don't want to go to jail, please.
28   [(come)]
29   CT: [why] would <u>jou</u> go to JAIL?, (sir?) you just called in to report it.
30   Are you- are you INVOLVED?
31   (0.4)
32   MS: <u>NO</u> I'M NOT IN[VOLVED.]
33   CT: [(then)] CA:Lm down and give me some
34   information, okay?
35   (0.2)
36   CT: if you're INside thuh house you're pretty safe. did you <u>see</u> any body?
37   (0.4)
38   MS: NO:::. .nh hh (0.7) THEY IS <u>DYIN</u>' (0.3) <u>THEY</u> IS DYIN'!=
39   CT: =who's
40   dying?
41   (0.3)
42   MS: THUH POLI:C:E! (0.7) they're DETECTIVES! (1.6) .h hh
43   PLEA:SE!
44   (1.2)
45   CT: <u>whut</u> do you <u>see</u>?
46   (0.3)
47   MS: i see two undercover cops layin' in fron' of my face an' (0.8)
48   (bleeding/with bullets) they DEA::D (LO::RD!!)
49   (1.2)
50   CT: .hh two undercover. you don't see anybody else?
51   (0.3)
52   MS: NO::::!
53   (0.4)
54   CT: No?

```
55        (0.3)
56   MS: UNH UNH!
57        (0.2)
58   CT:  we'll sen' 'em there sir. what's yer APARTMENT number.
59        (0.3)
60   MS: chuh chuh ONE!
61        (0.3)
62   CT:  d'you live in thirty two west nicholson?
63        (0.2)
64   MS:      UNH HUNH!
65        (0.2)
66   CT:  an' you live in apartment number one?
67        (0.3)
68   MS: unh hunh. NA::H i'm (three) (0.3) i was juss' (0.3) visi'ing my
69        fri:end.
70        (0.4)
71   CT:  in apartment number one.
72        (0.4)
73   MS: yehhs.
74        (0.2)
75   CT:  ALL right. we'll send someone there sir.=you need to stay on thuh
76        phone with me, okay?
77        (2.2)
78   CT:  OKAY?
79        (0.2)
80   MS: (yeahs/al'rih')=
81   CT:              =(this is uh police matter/i'm gonna send the police)
82        now you stay on thuh phone with me.
83        ((long gap))
84        ((CLICKING NOISES, background noises))
85   MS: HELLO?
86        (1.6)
87   CT:  i'm still here.
88        ((TAPE ENDS))
```

Recommended sources

Baker, Carolyn D., Emmison, Michael, and Firth, Alan (eds), (2005), *Calling for Help: Language and Social Interaction in Telephone Helplines*. Amsterdam and Philadelphia: John Benjamins.

Whalen, Jack and Zimmerman, Don H. (1998), 'Observations on the display and management of emotion in naturally occurring activities: the case of "hysteria" in calls to 9-1-1', *Social Psychology Quarterly*, 61, (2), 141–59.

Whalen, Jack, Zimmerman, Don H. and Whalen, Marilyn R. (1988), 'When words fail: a single case analysis', *Social Problems*, 35, (4), 335–62.

Technological Transformations and Talk on the Telephone

16

Introduction

In our discussion of how conversations are opened in Chapter 8 we examined early research on telephone call openings. This research was done before the technological innovations we take for granted today. The landline telephone of days gone by did not provide the range of affordances that contemporary telephones provide, such as mobility and the widespread use of caller id on both mobile and landline phones. Some users take advantage of distinctive ringtones which can be used to signal who is calling by the sound of the ring. Some users send pictures or texts over the phone in addition to making phone calls, and some use Skype or other video-conferencing software to conduct phone calls on the computer. While interactions between users of traditional landline telephones that did not have these features have been studied extensively by conversation analysts (see, for example, Hutchby, 2001, Schegloff 1968; 1979; 2002a; 2002b), research on how talk on the telephone has been changed by transformations in technology is relatively recent. In this chapter we examine how the features of these contemporary telephones (e.g. mobility, caller id, photo and video capability, and text messaging) affect the nature and structure of interactions between the people using them.

Knowing who is calling and the opening sequence of the call

Weilenmann (2003) notes that how people open telephone calls has changed over the last couple of decades as technology has transformed how and where people make phone calls:

> It is important to remember that certain features of mobile-phone technology have an impact on how identification and recognition are dealt with in telephone conversations. The mobile phone (often) makes it possible to see the telephone number of the person calling, or the name of the person—if this had been registered in the mobile phone's address book (known as caller ID). Also, some telephones give the option of choosing ring signals which are specific to a group of people, or just one person; for example, one's best friend or husband could have a unique ring signal. This allows the answerer to tell from the summons—the ring signal—who is calling. In some of the instances collected for this paper, it is likely that technological features, such as caller ID and ring signals, play a part in the opening sections. (Weilenmann, 2003, p. 1595)

Recall from Chapter 8 on how telephone conversations are opened, that typical opening sequences in traditional landline phone calls have the following structure:

1. Summons/Answer Sequence (the ringing of the phone and an answer to the summons, e.g., "hello")
2. Identification/Recognition Sequence
3. Greeting Exchange
4. Exchange of Initial Inquiries ("How are you" sequence)

With traditional landline telephones, the called party does not know who is calling until after they have answered the summons and the caller has begun speaking. This is why the identification/recognition sequence occurs after the summons/answer sequence, and the greeting exchange occurs after identification and recognition of the parties has been accomplished.

The organization of mobile telephone call openings differs substantially from traditional landline telephone call openings (Arminen, 2005; Arminen and Leinonen, 2006).

> A new type of summons-answer sequence has emerged. The answerer orients to a personalized summons that conveys information about who is calling. Correspondingly, the phone answers have diversified, as they no longer are responses to a neutral summons. Moreover, summons have also become variable, as calls from unknown callers or from silent numbers do not reveal the identity of the caller, merely informing the answerer only about the unknown or silent number. The answers to the summonses have become tailored through recipient-design, unlike the analogue telephone system, on which summonses were uniform. Further, the greeting opening on the mobile phone differs from the voice sample 'hello' opening of the landline call. When a mobile call is initiated with a greeting, the caller does not consider the greeting as simply an answer to a summons and a voice sample, but a greeting that makes a return of the greeting relevant. Since the anchor position for the reason of a call is established after the return of the greeting, the opening sequence is systematically reduced from earlier analogue landline openings. (Arminen, 2005, pp. 650–1).

Arminen and Leinonen's (2006) study of openings in Finnish mobile phone calls shows that the opening sequences of mobile calls are substantially different from landline phone call openings. Traditional Finnish landline phone calls (like the Dutch and Swedish phone calls we reviewed in Chapter 8), typically open with the called party answering the summons of the ring by identifying themself (Arminen and Leinonen, 2006, p. 340; Houtkoop-Steenstra, 1991; Lindström, 1994). However, in Finnish mobile call openings "the answerers have adopted a new opening practice, a greeting response to the summons" (Arminen and Leinonen, 2006, p. 340). This change in social practices has occurred because mobile phone call recipients can identify the caller prior to answering the call. The answerer's initial "hello" thus has a dual purpose. It is indeed an answer to the summons of the ring, through which the called party displays that they have answered the phone and are ready to listen. However, because the identification issues have been dealt with prior to the answering of the call, the next action in the opening sequence is a greeting. In the Finnish mobile phone calls, the caller typically responds to the greeting with a return greeting. For example, in Excerpt 1 the recipient of the call answers the phone with a greeting which is returned by the caller in line 2. After a very brief pause (line 6), the caller moves right to the reason for the call, a question in line 5. In the excerpts in this chapter the English translation appears below each line of the Finnish transcript.

> Excerpt 1: Arminen and Leinonen (2006, p. 346)
> 1 R: no   moi,
>   []   hi
> 2   (0.3)
> 3 C: no   mo:i,
>   []   hi::,
> 4   (.)
> 5 C: ooks sää lähössä,
>   are you leavin,
> 6   (.)
> 7 R: e,
>   no,
> 8   (0.3)

Arminen (2005) found that the intonation of the caller's opening "hello" also provided evidence that it was functioning as a greeting as well as an answer to the summons. When mobile phone call recipients answer the phone with a "hello," the intonation of this hello tends to differ from that used in traditional landline calls. Specifically, in landline calls the recipient answers the summons with a "hello?" with rising ("questioning") intonation, while in mobile phone calls the "hello" typically has a flat intonation (Arminen, 2005). The called party's "hello?" on traditional phones is produced as an answer to the summons of the phone ringing. Since the called party does not know who is calling at that point, their answer in effect solicits the caller's first move. In the mobile calls, or any phone calls with caller id, the called party's opening "hello" is both an answer to the summons and a greeting of a known caller. The opening sequence thus omits the "identification/recognition" sequence, because this work already has been accomplished prior to the beginning of the call.

Arminen (2005, p. 655) found that not only the identification/recognition sequence, but the greeting exchange as well could be omitted without causing problems in the call. When the parties were acquainted, and the caller was identified via the technology prior to the call being answered, participants sometimes skipped the exchange of greetings (shown in Excerpt 2).

> Excerpt 2: Arminen (2005, p. 655)
> (SB = Answerer; Kisha = caller)
> 1   ((summons))
> 2   Kisha: >Wha' time you finishin' uni<
> 3   SB: °Ummh wot's wrong. °
> 4   Kisha: ↑Huhh?
> 5   SB: °Why what's wrong°

In Excerpt 2, Kisha answers the phone with a question for the caller ("uni" in line 2 is short for "university"). She thus displays an orientation not only to the fact that she has already identified her caller via technological means prior to answering the phone, but that her familiarity with her caller (and perhaps the frequency with which they engage in contact via their mobile phones), has obviated the need for an exchange of greetings each time the phone is answered. As an analogy, consider what typically happens in repeated face-to-face encounters. When you get to work in the morning, the first time you see a colleague in the hallway you may be expected to exchange greetings. However, if you pass each other several times during the course of the work day you are not expected to greet each other every time you see each other. Similarly, acquainted people who make repeated calls over a short span of time may be able to omit the greeting exchange without its absence being problematic.

The importance of "location" for mobile phone calls

When making a phone call from one landline phone to another, the caller typically knows where the called person is located. The called person, if they know the caller, may also know where that person is calling from. However, with mobile to mobile or mobile to landline calls, at least one and sometimes both parties do not know where the other person is. Arminen (2006) analyzes the importance of location for the interaction in mobile phone calls. The location of participants is a more prominent, relevant, and necessary component of conversation in mobile phone calls than it is in traditional landline phone calls. Arminen and Weilenmann (2009) use the call in Excerpt 3 to illustrate how important location can be for calls involving mobile phones. In line 16 the caller asks whether the person he has called is at home. The reason for this question is to determine if the called party is available to join him at a restaurant for a drink. His location (specifically, its distance from the restaurant) is relevant to whether he would be able to travel to the restaurant to meet the caller. If the called party had been on a landline phone, the caller would have known his location before he called, and the location would not need to be discussed.

Excerpt 3: Arminen and Weilenmann (2009, p. 1910)
(A = answerer; C = caller)

```
1   A:  tjena,
        hi,
2   C:  tja::,
        he::y,
3   A:  >hallå vad gör du<
        >hello what are you doing<
4       (0.1)
5   C:  sitter å tar en gin å tonic faktiskt
        sitting having a gin an' tonic actually
6   A:  o↑j det är inte illa
        o ↑h that's not bad
7   C:  nä::, [(.) du själv då
        no:: [(.) what about yourself
8   A:        [(xxx)
9   A:  nej jag tar det lugnt sitter och surfar lite,
        no I'm chilling and surfing a little,
10  C:  surfar du porr igen
        are you surfing porno again
        ((laughter in the background))
11  A:  ja:, sorm alltid vettu,
        ye:s, like always you know,
12  C:  ja (.) det är det enda du gör
        yes (.) that's the only thing you do
13  A:  ja,=
        yes,=
14  C:  =du?
        =listen?
15  A:  =ja?
        =yes?
16  C:  du eh::: va va gör du i- va är du hemma?
        listen eh::: what what are you doing to- what are you at home?
17  A:  ja
        yes
18  C:  a ska du me::d (ut) till Lilla London och käka lite
        yeah will you come (out) to Little London to have a bite
19      (senare)
        (later)
```

```
20  A:  nej det går inte jag och tjejen har jubileum:::
        no that's not possible it's me and my girlfriend's anniversary:::
21      (0.1)
22  C:  jubileum?
        anniversary?
23  C:  nja:::: ((said with a teasing voice))
        oh::::
```

While knowledge of participants' location is not always essential for accomplishing the business of the call, Arminen (2006) found that a discussion of the participants' location is a typical component of mobile phone calls. Since some callers are literally in motion while calling (either in a vehicle or walking), location can be especially problematic because it may be changing during the call. If a participant expects their location to be problematic for the call they typically mention their location in the opening sequence. For example, the call recipient may be in a noisy location or may be soon cutoff from cell phone service (as might happen when entering a train). Participants typically mentioned their location when making arrangements for meeting (Arminen 2006). Excerpt 4 shows the location of participants in a mobile to mobile call as the first order of business. The participants use their phones to help them locate each other.

```
Excerpt 4: Arminen and Leinonen (2006, p. 358)
1   R:  joo?
        yes?
2       (0.2)
3   C:  terve,
        hello,
4       (.)
5   C:  no,
        huh,
6       (0.8)
7   R:  miss ä s ä oot,
        where are you,
8       (.)
9   C:  täälä <ruokalassa,     >h
        here <in the cafeteria, >h
10      (0.2)
11  R:  nii minäki,
        so am i:,
12      (0.2)
13  C:  aha ([yvä,)
14      o:h (g[ood,)
15  R:        [(-)
15      (0.4)
16  R:  no nii mä nään sut. (h)e
        oh yeah I see you.  (h)e
```

Integrating mobile phone calls and interaction with co-present parties

Arminen and Weilenmann (2009) explore how social action is accomplished when participants engage in mobile phone calls while at the same time participating in face-to-face interactions with others. They analyze how Finnish and Swedish participants in mobile phone conversations engage in these concurrent interactions.

> [M]obile messages and talk can be appropriated as a part of local interaction and mobile communication can be shared by taking turns in talking on a mobile phone between group members, or sharing text messages within a group (Weilenmann and Larsson, 2002). The accomplishment of mobile action, however, requires the party to make the relevant frame of action and its changes recognizable so that the distant party can follow communication and understand "why that now" to discern the relevant messages from local contingencies. (Arminen and Weilenmann, 2009, p. 1908)

Excerpt 5 illustrates how people in a group face-to-face setting can construct the opening of a mobile phone call to convey who is present.

```
Excerpt 5: Arminen and Weilenmann (2009, p. 1908)
(C = caller, A = answerer)
1   C:  päi: vää,
        goo:d afternoon,
2   A:          päi: vä[ä.
        goo:d afternoo[on.
3   C:                  [(h)(h)e (h)e (h)e (h)e
4       anteeks että herätän vahing[oss.
        sorry to wake you up by     [accident.
5   A:                              [se pitkähiuksinen
                                    [the longhaired
6       kaveri j[oka-
        guy  w[ho-
7   C:          [(h)e (h)e (h)e noh mitäs
                    so what's
```

After the opening sequence (lines 1–2), the caller begins an utterance in line 3 which the answerer interrupts (line 4). This interruption is used to make a reference to "the longhaired guy who-". By this description, the answerer informs the other people in the room who he is talking to on the phone. Presumably, the people he is with will know who the "long haired guy" is based on this description. At the same time, this action conveys to the caller ("the long haired guy…") that there are other people in the room with him (hence his announcement of who is calling). The answerer thus makes the ongoing mobile phone call relevant to the co-present face-to-face interaction, rather than having it merely be an interruption of it.

Taylor and Harper (2003) conducted an ethnographic study of how students in England used mobile phones. They observed frequent integration of face-to-face interaction with phone calls and/or text messaging. This excerpt from their field notes illustrates the central place these technologically mediated exchanges can play in the social life of the students:

> Lisa and Sarah are sitting at different tables both with their heads down looking at their displays—both seem to be 'texting'. Lisa walks over to Sarah. Sarah shows Lisa her display—Lisa takes Sarah's mobile and reads the display. They talk briefly, looking intermittently at Sarah's phone, and then Lisa returns to her seat. Lisa looks towards me and says: "We're addicted to these phones!" and then looks down to her phone's display to interact with her phone. Lisa goes back to Sarah and they both start to talk to each other. As they're talking Lisa receives a message. She reads it and then shows it to Sarah. As they talk, Lisa writes something on her display and shows it to Sarah. I assume she shows her a message she is preparing to send. Later on Lisa holds the mobile. She seems to be 'coveting' it as she speaks to Sarah. (Taylor and Harper, 2003, p. 280)

This excerpt from Taylor and Harper's article shows the extent to which mobile telephone technology (whether being used for voice or text) is integrated into the ongoing flow of interaction in daily life.

Integrating mobile phone calls with other activities

Just as participants using the telephone can be engaged in interaction with co-present individuals at the same time, they can also be simultaneously engaged in other types of activities. One area of concern that has attracted some research attention is the combination of mobile phone use with driving. Arminen and Weilenmann (2009) analyze a videotaped interaction between a person who is driving a call and talking on his mobile phone at the same time. They explain how the driver balances his attention between the phone call and the activity of driving. While continuously engaged in both activities, the driver switches between "foregrounding" one activity or the other at any given point in time. In the quote below, the authors explain how the driver manages these competing activities:

> The driver balances between focusing on traffic and driving, and on the conversation (see also Haddington and Keisanen, 2009). At times, he lets the person at the other end know that he is driving and is in a tricky situation. By sharing information about what is going on at his end the recipient can understand his situated communicative challenges, thereby loosening his communicative obligations temporarily. Mobile contextual configuration allows a person to foreground the phone talk or the handling of the ongoing situation alternatively. The sharing of the present activity accounts for features of communication that might otherwise be considered inadequate, e.g., long pauses, repetition of words, etc. (Arminen and Weilenmann, 2009, p. 1908)

The driver in their data uses several techniques to manage the integration of driving with talking on the mobile phone (Arminen and Weilenmann, 2009, p. 1909). One technique is the repetition of easy phrases (such as "yes yes yes"; p. 1909) which do not take much effort to compose during times when the driving demands are more complex. Another technique is to listen rather than speak during points at which the demands of driving are more complex. The driver also sometimes uses intonation strategically—stretching out words to give him more time to think about how to complete a sentence (e.g., "What was I going to say::::"; p. 1909). He also at times alerts his co-interactant that he needs to pay attention to the driving (using an idiomatic expression meaning "I have to be careful"; p. 1909). He also provides an account for his inability to focus completely on the conversation ("I'm at Västermalm where it's so damn narrow"; p. 1909). While he manages to participate in the conversation, at least to a minimal extent, and communicate to his co-interactant why he can not speak more freely at times, one can also see how the mobile phone conversation may easily interfere with a driver's ability to focus on the task of driving.

Esbjörnsson et al. (2007) found similar results in their video graphic and observational study of drivers using mobile phones:

> When the traffic situation became more complex, and Anders needed to focus more on maneuvering the car to ensure safe driving, he made the traffic situation available in the phone conversation. Accordingly, when more attention is demanded on the traffic, conversational strategies are used to keep the conversations going with minimal contribution from the driver. (Esbjörnsson et al., 2007, p. 44)

Given these findings, it is not surprising that some research has found that using mobile phones while driving increases the chance of having an accident (Svenson and Patten, 2005). Many states are creating laws limiting mobile phone use while driving.

The role of technology in social relationships and social networks

Access and availability

Harper and Taylor (2009) note that in face-to-face interactions people use often glances to determine whether a co-present party is available for talk. For instance, you might be sitting in your living room and glance at a family member before deciding whether to speak to them. If they are engrossed in a book, you might decide to wait until later to talk to them. However, perhaps they are just tidying the coffee table, staring into space, or tying their shoes. You might then decide to ask them a question or initiate a conversation. In short, in a face-to-face encounter you can use a glance to determine whether another person is available for talk. This use of a glance to check on someone's availability for talk could be considered a "pre-summons." If the person you have glanced at notices your glancing at them, it can become a two way interaction. If they do not react to your glance, that may indicate that they are not interested in interacting at that point in time. If they do react, they could react in a way that indicates receptivity to interaction (e.g., "What?"), or in a way that indicates a lack of receptively (e.g. hunkering down even more intensely over their book, or saying "Not now.").

However, when you call someone on the telephone, whether a mobile or landline phone, you usually do not know whether they are available to talk on the phone or what they are doing until the call is connected. Harper and Taylor (2009) explored how the cameras on a mobile phone could be used to answer these questions about access and availability. Interaction between a mutually chosen group of acquainted people (e.g., family members, colleagues or friends) could be facilitated if an electronic "glancing" mechanism could be added to the affordances of telephones. Until you dial someone's number and get them on the phone, you do not know whether this is a good time for the interruption of a phone call. An electronic "glance" could provide you the information needed to determine whether this is a good time to call or not.

Harper and Taylor (2009) describe a field test of the prototype of a "glance phone." The purpose of this phone is to let geographically distributed people perform technologically mediated glancing in order to determine if someone is available for interaction prior to calling them. If a member of the group was willing to be "glanced at" by another member of that group, they would set their phone up vertically using an attached base. This action instructed the phone to take a picture of them which would then be shown to any of the group members who used their glance phones to see what that person was doing. For example, if you were home in your living room, you could set the phone up on the coffee table to show yourself sitting on your couch. If any of the friends that you had designated to have this "glancing" privilege wanted to see what you were doing, they could use their glance phones to see this picture. They would then know roughly what you were doing and where you were (e.g., alone or with others, at home, in a restaurant, or at work at the office). The intended purpose of the glance phone was so that people could check out other's activities to determine whether it was a good time to call them.

Several years ago Harvey Sacks (1989) observed that there are multiple social uses and meanings of the act of glancing in face-to-face interaction. For example, in addition to checking availability for interaction, one could share an assessment of something with a co-interactant or check to see who has entered the room. Harper and Taylor (2009) found that people also used the glance phone creatively to accomplish a range of uses, not just the one intended by the designers of the technology. The people in their field study primarily used the glance phone for other purposes. One common use of the glance phone was to share humorous scenes with friends. Other group members used it for "showing off" (e.g. showing their friends that they were having dinner in a fancy restaurant). People did not tend to use them for the intended purpose of making a well-timed initiation of a phone call. In short, people approached the ability to electronically glance at members of their phone group creatively, and used the affordance for a variety of purposes.

Text messages as "gift giving"

Taylor and Harper (2003) use ethnography and the analysis of recorded phone conversations to study how young people use mobile phones. They conclude that one use of the phones by this age group constituted a "gift exchange." While text messages are a way of communicating information quickly and efficiently, the fact that they can be saved has led to a variety of social uses of the messages that go beyond immediate communication. The messages sent were valued not just because of the information in the message, they were treated as gifts sent, received, saved and shared. They thus allowed the users to both display and reinforce the relationships between the participants as well as their status in the group.

> Young people… use text messages, call-credit and mobile phones themselves as forms of gifts. We will contend that these gifts are exchanged in performances that have specific meanings in young people's daily lives and are played out with the intent to cement social relationships. (Taylor and Harper, 2003, p. 271)

The fact that text messages can be saved makes them more valuable to these users. The recipient can keep the messages and read them again later. The excerpt below from Taylor and Harper's (2003) field notes illustrates the importance of text messages in the social life of young people. In this excerpt Alex interviews two students, Jennifer and Susan, about why text messages are important to them:

> Jennifer: Plus you can read them [text messages] as well later. Like I can keep them and read them later.
> Alex: Why do you want to read them later?
> Jennifer: I don't know—if it's a nice message or something.
> Susan: Yeah, Peter sends me loads of nice messages and I want to keep them all. It's so sad cause he sends me so many nice ones and I have to delete some. I feel horrible.
> Jennifer: I know and then you feel really sad.
> Susan: And like I really don't want to give the phone back because it's got so many little memories and things on. And it's not the same having them written down so I'm sending them to my other phone.
> Alex: Why is it not the same?
> Susan: I don't know. I know it sounds stupid but…
> Jennifer: They don't look the same.
> Susan: It's just not the same cause it's not from him anymore. It's just like me writing it down. It's just really sad. Maybe I'm just over emotional about my text messages.
> Jennifer: And it's even the same when you put them in the 'outbox' and they lose all the time and they lose who it's from and everything.
> Susan: That's why I think we should have memory cards because I would buy millions, really I would… I really hate deleting messages that are nice you know. Like when someone's said something that's really sweet or just like really personal or something. (Taylor and Harper, 2003, p. 273)

These fields notes show that the text messages their friends send to them have an emotional meeting that goes far beyond the practicalities of communication. For these students, text messages are therefore not just a convenient way to communicate, but a way of maintaining and experiencing friendships. Because they can be saved, read again and shared with friends, they are more valuable to the recipients than are telephone calls.

Summary

The technological changes reported in this chapter are relatively recent. Both the technologies and users' practices for using the technologies are likely to keep continually evolving. Further research is needed on a number of the topics in this chapter, as well as other issues around the use of mobile phones and telephone technology in general. For example, when talking on mobile phones, if two people talk at the same time, one is cutoff in order to avoid simultaneous speech. How this function affects the rhythm of the conversation, the timing of turn exchange, and the listener's ability to use minimal responses effectively should be investigated.

Student activity

Try to play a challenging video game while engaging in a mobile phone call with a friend, and then play it again while not engaged in a phone call. Are you able to focus on the game better without the distraction of the phone call? What are some ways the phone call was disrupted or adjusted to accommodate the simultaneous playing of the game?

Recommended sources

Arminen, Ilkka. (2006), 'Social functions of location in mobile telephony', *Personal Ubiquitous Computing*, 10, 319–23.

Arminen, Ilkka and Leinonen, Minna. (2006), 'Mobile phone call openings: tailoring answers to personalized summonses', *Discourse Studies*, 8, (3), 339–68.

Arminen, Ilkka and Weilenmann, Alexandra. (2009), 'Mobile presence and intimacy--reshaping social actions in mobile contextual configuration', *Journal of Pragmatics*, 41, 1905–23.

Esbjörnsson, Mattias, Juhlin, Oskar, and Weilenmann, Alexandra. (2007), 'Drivers using mobile phones in traffic: an ethnographic study of interactional adaptation', *International Journal of Human Computer Interaction*, 22, (1), 39–60.

Harper, Richard and Taylor, Stuart. (2009), 'Glancephone: an exploration of human expression', *MobileHCI'09*, September 15–18, Bonn, Germany. ACM 978-1-60558-281-8.

Air Traffic Communication

Chapter contents

Introduction

In terms of the risk of fatal accidents, air traffic is a very safe mode of transportation, and has become increasingly safer in the last several decades (Arminen et al., 2010). When fatal plane accidents do occur, human error is likely to be a factor. While human error can involve a variety of factors, the nature of the interaction between crew members in the cockpit of the airplane, with the air traffic control tower, and with the complex equipment and technology in air craft itself can be a source of trouble.

> It is worth noting here that the world's worst airline accident, in terms of loss of life, was a 1977 runway collision of two Boeing 747 jumbo jets where there was confusion in one cockpit over whether or not takeoff clearance had been received (Cushing, 1994). Taking off without a clearance is very dangerous, and a serious professional lapse. Each pilot must know, and know that the other pilot knows, that takeoff clearance has been received. (Nevile, 2001, p. 65)

Nevile (2001) notes that the cockpit crew works in one of the most technology-intensive workplaces today. The work of flying a commercial air plane is an example of both a geographically distributed and a technologically mediated workspace. Flying a plane is not simply a matter of manipulating technology, it is a complex combination of verbal interaction and embodied action. While the pilot and copilot are working together in the cockpit of the airplane, they are using and talking about the plane's controls, indicators and other technology as they fly the plane. They are also often communicating via radio with the Air Traffic Control tower ("ATC"). The job of the ATC is to prevent airplanes from getting too close to each other and to facilitate the efficient flow of traffic along air routes and into and out of airports (Harper and Hughes, 1993). The work of ATC is made more complex by the fact that planes in the air are in constant motion. These different sets and types of interactions need to be coordinated carefully in order to be successful.

In this chapter we will examine the interactional work done in the cockpit to successfully fly the plane. This discussion will center on how crew members and ATC staff manage routine interactions as they do their work. We will examine how scripted talk, sequential organization, pronouns and "and-prefaces" are used to identify professional roles and accomplish the tasks involved in flying an airplane, so that problems in air traffic communications that may cause or contribute to errors and accidents can be avoided.

Interactional procedures in routine air traffic

There are several routine interactional problems that the cockpit crew has to manage in order to successfully accomplish their work. Crew members have to establish and maintain knowledge about which person is doing which tasks during the flight. They have to communicate information obtained from the equipment on the flight deck to each other, and coordinate their actions as they manipulate the machinery. They also have to monitor radio communications with ATC, responding to them when addressed and initiating communications with them when necessary. We will now consider how crew members use talk to accomplish these goals.

Identifying professional roles through scripted speech and pronouns

Nevile (2001) notes that since there is a division of labor in the cockpit, crew members have to establish and share knowledge about which crew member is playing the role of lead pilot (called "Pilot Flying" or "PF") and which is playing the role of co-pilot (called "Pilot Not-Flying" or "PNF"). This work role typically shifts from flight to flight and is not tied to the rank or seniority of the crew member (e.g. a Captain has a higher rank than a First Officer, but could play either the PF or PNF role during a given flight). The PF takes most of the responsibility for the control of the air craft (including steering the plane with the "yoke"), while the PNF assists the PF and takes responsibility for radio communications with ATC.

This division of labor is functional both practically and interactionally. Since the PNF is the only crew member to use the radio to communicate with ATC, ATC knows that they can rely on that person to have knowledge of their previous exchanges with that flight. This division of labor also prevents the crew members from sending conflicting messages. The plane speaks with one voice--that of the PNF. Nevile (2001) notes that:

> It is only the PNF who will speak to the controller, and so he will speak as the representative of that flight, on behalf of all those on board. The work of the controller depends on this. The controller is concerned with the location and movement of a particular plane, identified as a flight with a particular call sign. For the controller, the relevant participant 'identity' is 'alpha november romeo', and it is not relevant or helpful for the controller to distinguish between the individual persons who happen to be flying that plane. All talk to and from the controller is identified as to or from Flight X; for example, it is X that the controller will clear for takeoff. (Nevile, 2001, p. 64)

Nevile (2001) found that cockpit crews use a range of interactional techniques to distinguish the PF and the PNF roles, in order to successfully maintain the appropriate division of labor during the flight as well as to effectively coordinate the contributions of both participants to the process of flying the plane.

Much of the interaction in the cockpit is scripted. Pilots are trained as to what they need to say at given times and how they need to phrase things (Nevile, 2001). Interaction in air traffic work is therefore only partly "locally managed," to use Sacks et al.'s (1974) terminology. This scripted portion of the talk is integrated into the ongoing interaction via everyday interactional procedures such as turn taking, adjacency pairs and repair.

Nevile (2001) found that the cockpit crew uses a scripted interactional routine to distinguish which role is being invoked during the flight. They use pronouns to clarify referents and make sure all crew members understand the role each is playing in flying the plane. As Gronn (1983) and others have argued, the talk that occurs in this and other work settings is not an incidental part of the actions of the crew. The talk itself is a large part of the work being done and is critically important to the safe operation of the aircraft. In Excerpt 1, which shows a crew preparing for take off, the captain says "my go:" (line 2) to signal that he is taking the role of PF. When the copilot responds with "check" (line 9), this signals that he acknowledges that the captain is PF for this flight. This scripted routine also confirms his own role as the PNF. This routine interactional procedure thus prevents misunderstandings or ambiguity between crew members as to which officer is responsible for which tasks during the flight.

```
Excerpt 1: Nevile (2001, p. 62)
1          (6.6)
2    PF:   and it's ah my go: wi:th (.) go-around ASE:L left (0.2)
3          autopilot command=
((three lines of transcript deleted))
8          (0.5)
9    PNF:  check
10         (3.2)
```

Similarly, in Excerpt 2 Nevile (2001) notes that the Captain uses the scripted utterance "my yoke" (line 4) to indicate that as PF, he will be the one using the yoke to "steer" the plane.

Excerpt 2: Nevile (2001, pp. 65–6)
```
1              (1.7)
2   FO/PNF    that's sixty knots, (.) a::nd powers are normal
3              (1.1)
4   C/PF      ( ) my yo::k:e,
5              (0.5)
6   FO/PNF    check
7              (8.0)
```

Again, the PNF responds with "check" (line 6), thus signaling that he understands that the Captain will be the one using his yoke to control the plane.

Sequential organization in cockpit talk

The sequential organization of talk in the cockpit is often quite different from that in ordinary conversation or in most other types of institutional settings. The open radio contact with ATC is one of the main reasons for this difference. Because radio communications with ATC are audible by all planes in the sector, cockpit communications can be interrupted by radio transmissions at any point. The work of the PF and PNF is therefore frequently interrupted, and adjacency pairs between PF and PNF are not always adjacent due to ATC communications which may intervene.

The ATC begin their utterances with the call sign of the plane they are addressing. This alerts the PNF in the addressed plane to attend to the utterance and respond to the ATC, and also signals to other planes in the area that they can ignore the communication. Excerpt 3 illustrates how ATC communications can affect the sequential organization of cockpit interaction.

Excerpt 3: Nevile (2001, pp. 66–7)
```
1              (7.5)
2   C/PF      gea:r up,
3              (7.4)
4   FO/PNF    a:nd the gear's up,
5            · (2.8)
6   C/PF      flaps up,
7              (1.4)
8   WZG       Big City tower (  ) whiskey zulu golf
9              (3.4)
10  FO/PNF    flaps up,
11  Tower     whiskey zulu golf ([  ) make your approach (
12  C/PF                         [yeah what I was about to say was I'll
                leave=
13  Tower                                     )]
14  C/PF      =takeoff power on for] a whi:le.
15             (0.5)
16  FO/PNF    okay (  )
```

The cockpit crew do not respond to ATC exchanges that are not relevant for them (e.g. lines 8, 11, and 13), and continue their ongoing interaction as if the interruption had not occurred. The PF takes the lead role in flying the airplane by giving commands (e.g. in lines 2 and 6) which the PNF then executes. When the command has been executed, the PNF indicates this verbally (lines 4 and 10).

Note that in line 12 the PF waits until the first part of the ATC's utterance has been completed ("*whiskey zulu golf*"). After hearing this call sign, they know that the ATC's utterance is not addressed to their plane. The PF places his utterance at the first possible point after the ATC produced the call sign (line 12). PF's utterance is thus placed in overlap with the ATC's utterance, but this simultaneous speech is not problematic because ATC's utterance is addressed to another plane.

Both the division of labor between the two pilots and the use of the "call and response" method of requesting and confirming that each step has been completed are procedures designed to prevent errors (Nevile, 2001). If the pilots did not verbalize each of these steps as they completed them, a mistake might be made without either of them noticing it. Doing these tasks cooperatively and providing bilateral verbal confirmation is a "checks and balances" system that ensures that both pilots are engaged in the process and are checking up on each other.

And-prefacing to maintain and restore sequentiality

If the work of an airline pilot is done in the wrong order, or if something is left out, the results could be catastrophic. In addition to the interactional resources described above, "**and-prefacing**" is used by cockpit crews to display a joint orientation to the sequencing of actions necessary for doing their jobs. Heritage and Sorjonen (1994) explored the use of and-prefaces in medical settings, and found the device used to indicate that a question was part of a sequence of questions for accomplishing an activity. Nevile (2006) found and-prefacing used by pilots to show where they are beginning or ending a task, or for soliciting shared awareness of both pilots to an ongoing action.

> *And*-prefacing presents a new action as adding to something prior, as some relevantly next thing to do. By initiating an action with an *and*-preface, a pilot can make maximally hearable that something prior is completed or somehow past, that it is here-and-now appropriate to move to some next action, indeed even to *the* next one. (Nevile, 2006, p. 282)

Excerpt 4 has two instances of "and-prefacing," in lines 11 and line 17. In line 17, the and-preface is used to mark an utterance as the completion of a sequence that was begun earlier in the interaction. Its completion was delayed because other actions intervened before it could be completed.

Excerpt 4: Nevile (2006, p. 287)

1		(9.2)
2	C/PF:	flaps ten.

```
 3              (2.6)
 4   C/PF:      nine miles.
 5              (3.1)
 6   FO/PNF:    checked ah:: (0.3) at descent point (0.3) you're on profi:le.
 7              (0.3)
 8   FO/PNF:    nine miles (.) >twenty< nine hundred.
 9   C/PF:      set the (minimum overshoot) thanks,
10              (0.2)
11   C/PF:      and I'll have (1.0) VS wi::th (.) ASEL.
12              (0.6)
13   FO/PNF:    che:ck.
14              (3.7)
15   FO/PNF:    nine miles, (.) twentynine hundred.
16              (3.8)
17   FO/PNF:    and you have flaps ten.
18              (0.8) ((repeating alert tone continues))
19   C/PF:      thanks you.
20              (3.7)
21   FO/PNF:    on profi::le, (0.3) eight mi:les (.) twentysix hundred.
22              (22.3) ((repeating alert tone continues))
```

Nevile (2006) explains the detour from completing the task initiated in line 2 as follows:

> During a descent at night the C/PF calls for the FO/PNF to position the wing flaps to position 'ten' (line 2). As the FO/PNF moves the lever to set the flaps as asked, the C/PF talks to announce that the plane has reached a particular point in the descent and approach ('nine miles', line 4). This announcement initiates talk in reply from the FO/PNF (line 6, line 8), before talk from the two pilots on other tasks (lines 9–13). Some 3.8 seconds after these exchanges the FO/PNF makes the required response to the earlier call for flaps ten ('and you have flaps ten', line 17). (Nevile, 2006, p. 288)

Thus when the PNF says "and you have flaps ten" in line 17, he is using the "and-preface" to indicate that this utterance refers back to the previously begun sequence which is only now being completed, rather than referring to the immediately prior utterance.

In addition to displaying the sequencing of actions by marking completion or initiation of a sequence, Nevile (2007) notes that "and" prefaces can be used by pilots to initiate other-repair or to inform or remind the pilot of something that should be done at that point in time. If a pilot has omitted, or at least not performed quickly enough, an action that should be done, an and-preface enables the quick and efficient repair of the missing action without foregrounding the pilot's "forgetting" or making it obvious than a repair has been done. For example, Excerpt 5 shows the PF managing the process of approaching an airport for landing. In line 20 the PF uses an "and-prefaced" request to prompt the PNF to let the air traffic controller know that they are approaching the airport. This is a critical step in coordinating their descent with the air traffic control. The PNF responds by making the radio announcement (line 22).

Excerpt 5: Nevile (2007, p. 239)

```
15  C/PF:     okay I'm going to hand [fly from here.
16                                 [((aural alert indicating autopilot is
              disengaged))]
17            (0.5)
18  FO/PNF:   check.
19            (4.3)
20  C/PF:     and (if) you could let him know we're approaching.
21            (1.3)
22  FO/PNF:   Airline One Two is approaching seven thousand.
```

Coordinating talk with embodied action

In order to understand the sequential organization of talk in cockpit interactions it is necessary to observe how participants accomplish the integration of verbal action with physical actions as they manipulate the equipment to accomplish the joint activity of flying the plane. Physical actions are referred to as "embodied actions," and include the use of technology, tools and artifacts as well as gestures, gaze direction, and facial expressions. Nevile (2004a) uses the example of how the cockpit crew accomplishes the "approach briefing" to illustrate the integration of embodied action with verbal exchanges between the PF and PNF during the flight. The approach briefing is work done to prepare for the impending landing:

> The aim of *approach briefings* is for the pilots to develop a shared understanding of how the descent, approach, and landing will proceed [...] The precise details to be covered will vary for every flight, and so the *approach briefing* is an opportunity for matters to be raised and discussed, clarified, and even for details to be amended when necessary according to particular circumstances (e.g., changed weather conditions) [...] Although the briefing itself is a task that involves certain activities, its primary role is to form the basis for new shared understandings that will be a guide and warrant to the conduct of later tasks [...] A Pilot-Flying typically leads the briefing, with the other pilot's contribution, often consisting only of an acknowledgment to confirm understanding and to accept the briefing, coming only at the end. (Nevile, 2004, pp. 453–4)

Excerpt 6 shows the initiation of an approach briefing by the PF:

Excerpt 6: Nevile (2004a, p. 457)

```
1             (13.4)
2   FO/PF:    okay we need to plan hh- so the plan shall be:::, (3.4) go downhill
3             at (0.2) f::orty: (0.3) eight (0.4) mi::les:: er::: (0.4) south of
4             Smalltown (0.3) on DME on the GPS, (1.6) we'll expect to be
5             visual within twentyfive miles make a visual approach:, (1.7) to
6             join left downwind for left circuit landing runway one ei::ght::.
7             (0.3) the airfield elevation is eighteen (.) circuit height a thousand
8             feet is bugged on the altimeter. (0.9) visual procedures left circuit:.
9             (1.9) we'll be landing flap twentyfi::ve with a:: ah
```

10		(2.2) Vref of ninety:ni:ne and (0.2) seventeen point seven (ton),
11		(1.2) carry ten for a hundred and ni::ne (0.9) and Vfr Vcl's a
12		hundred and nine and fourtee:n (1.3) <and they're all se:t:.>
13		(0.8)
14	C/PNF:	°set° (°crosschecked°).
15		(0.8)

The First Officer initiates the approach briefing by first using "okay" (line 2) as a pivot to transition from the state of silence to the new activity (Nevile, 2004a). He then refers to the approach briefing as a plan rather than invoking the formal name of the process. Because of their familiarity with the work involved in flying a plane, both pilots know that at this stage of the flight the relevant "plan" is the approach briefing. The PF uses the collective pronoun "we" to display that the approach briefing is something that the two of them do together (even though the PF does most or all of the talking). When the PF begins to articulate the plan ("so the plan shall be:::, (3.4)"; line 2), he extends the word "be," thus indicating that he is not done. The PNF displays an orientation to the fact that the PF is not done by remaining silent throughout the pause in line 2. The PF's hesitations in line 2 and elsewhere in the approach briefing have to do with his coordination of embodied action with the verbal construction of the briefing.

As Nevile's (2004a) analysis of Excerpt 7 shows, when descriptions of the crews' actions and movements obtained from the videotape are added to the transcript, the production of speech is coordinated with the embodied action involved in flying the plane and preparing it for the approach to the airport for landing. In line 6a the PF begins to direct his gaze to the control yoke, anticipating his need for the information displayed there. Meanwhile, he is engaged in completing an earlier part of the "plan" (line 6, "join left downwind for left circuit landing runway one ei::ght::."). After shifting his gaze to the control yoke (line 6a), he then reads the information on the control yoke (line 7b). Thus the PF's actions coordinate with his talk and the pauses in his utterances so that the PNF can understand what he is doing and how he is getting the information he is citing.

Excerpt 7: Nevile (2004a, p. 464)

6 FO/PF:	join left downwind for left circuit landing runway one ei::ght::.
	↑_>
6a FO/PF:	((looks down to control yoke))
7 FO/PF:	(0.3) the airfield elevation is eighteen (.) circuit height a thousand
	>__↑
7a FO/PF:	((continues looking down to control yoke))
	↑_____↑
7b FO/PF:	((reads from chart on control yoke))
	↑____↑
7c FO/PF:	((reaches for bug on altimeter))

8 FO/PF: feet is bugged on the altimeter. (0.9) visual procedures left circuit:.

↑___>

8a FO/PF: **((moves hand away from
altimeter, leans back in seat))**

9 FO/PF: (1.9) we'll be landing flap twentyfi::ve with a:: ah

These embodied actions also provide accounts for the placement of pauses in his utterance. When the embodied action is observed in conjunction with the transcript of the verbal exchange, the pauses can be accounted for by the transitions in actions involving physical and visual attention to the equipment being manipulated to prepare for the approach (such as in lines 7 and 8).

There are a variety of interactional techniques and resources cockpit crews can use to accomplish the technologically mediated and geographically distributed task of flying an airplane. These resources enable them to coordinate a complex sequence of actions in a way that minimizes the possibility of error, allows both pilots to be aware of and check each other's work, and enables the discovery and repair or errors before they become problems. The work of airline pilots is thus not just a mechanical or technological job. Talk in inter-action is an integral part of the work of flying a commercial airplane.

Summary

The "miracle on the Hudson," occurred on January 15, 2009, when U.S. Airways Flight 1549 lost both engines due to bird strike shortly after taking off from LaGuardia Airport in New York City (e.g. McFadden, 2009). The pilot was rightfully congratulated on his skill in landing the plane safely in the Hudson River without losing a single life. Part of the miracle was due to the skill of the pilot, and part was due to the "miracle" of the routine production of talk in the cockpit and in the air traffic control tower.

When Flight 1549's engines were knocked out by a flock of birds, the cockpit crew was able to safely land the plane in the Hudson River in part due to routine interactional procedures reviewed in this chapter. For example, when the engines failed, the Captain of Flight 1549, who had been serving as PNF, used a scripted formula to take over the PF role from the First Officer. He used pronouns to quickly and efficiently communicate his decision to take over:

> Captain Sullenberger, who has been hailed by the mayor and the president for his skill and bravery, was not at the controls at takeoff. Instead, the plane's first officer, 49-year-old Jeffrey B. Skiles, was in control; a 23-year veteran of the airline, he had just 35 hours of flying time in this particular kind of craft, the Airbus A320.
>
> But as soon as the plane encountered the birds and the engines quit nearly simultaneously, Captain Sullenberger, 58, took over.
>
> "My aircraft," he announced to his first officer, using the standard phrasing and protocol drilled into airline crews.
>
> "Your aircraft," Mr. Skiles responded.

> With little thrust, and with the plane's airspeed falling sharply, Captain Sullenberger lowered the nose to keep his plane from falling out of the sky. And he set his co-pilot to work at moving through a three-page checklist of procedures for restarting both the engines. (Wald and Baker, 2009)

The story of Flight 1549 provides just one example of how the appropriate use of routine interactional procedures in air traffic can facilitate safe operation of planes and help crew members respond to emergencies in the most effective way possible.

Student activity

Visit the website of the Federal Aviation Administration (http://www.faa.gov/data_research/accident_incident/1549/) and listen to one of the audio recordings from the Flight 1549 incident (for example, "New York Tracon Audio"). How many of the interactional techniques and procedures discussed in this chapter can you find being used in the recording?

Recommended sources

Arminen, Ilkka, Auvinen, Petra and Hannele Palukka. 2010, "Repairs as the Last Orderly Provided Defense of Safety in Aviation." *Journal of Pragmatics* 42(2): 443–65.

Frankel, Richard. (2000), '"Captain, I was trying earlier to tell you that you made a mistake": Deference and demeanor at 30,000 feet', in J. K. Peyton, P. Griffin, W. Wolfram, and R. Fasold (eds). *Language in Action: New Studies of Language in Society: Essays in honor of Roger W. Shuy*, Cresskill, NJ: Hampton, pp. 289–301.

Nevile, Maurice. (2004b), *Beyond the Black Box: Talk-in-Interaction in the Airline Cockpit*. Aldershot: Ashgate.

Part IV
Talk in Medical Settings

18 Doctor/Patient Communication and the Delivery of Bad News

Chapter contents

Introduction

While most would agree that the most important thing about the practice of medicine is the treatments prescribed, there is also evidence that the doctor/patient consultation itself, if appropriately conducted, can be beneficial to the patient. Research has shown that the doctor/patient consultation can have an effect on patient outcomes (Miller, 2002; Silverman,1987, 1997; Heritage and Maynard, 2006b). Some doctors (and patients) believe that the interaction between the doctor and the patient has the power to heal (Meldrum, 2010). Shorter (1985, p. 157) argues that the consultation has the power to heal if "the doctor shows active interest in the patient [...] [and] the patient has the opportunity to tell his/er story in a leisurely, unhurried manner." While there may be debate about the source of this healing power, Shorter notes that it could be the power of suggestion or a cathartic effect. The patient's conflicts and anxieties could be lessened by the act of sharing their concerns with someone else, which could have a beneficial effect on overall health. There is a biological basis of thoughts and emotions, so our mental and emotional states can have an impact on our physical condition (Novak, 1995); this is often referred to as the "mind/body" connection.

There is a considerable body of evidence which suggests that the ideal conditions for healing are unlikely to be met by most doctor/patient interactions. While patients may want the doctor to listen to their problems, doctors frequently do not allow patients to tell their stories and often interrupt them before they have had a chance to explain their concerns.

> Beckman and Frankel (1984, 1985) conducted a study of 74 visits to a primary care internal medicine practice to determine how physician participation in soliciting and responding to the patient's major concerns influences the further expression of concerns. They found that the average interruption by the physician occurred 18 seconds after the patient began to speak. Following this interruption, the physician took control of the visit by asking questions that effectively halted the spontaneous flow of information. (Lazare et al.,1995, p. 9).

Doctors also tend to underestimate the amount of information patients want, and to overestimate the amount of information they give patients (Waitzkin, 1984; Waitzkin and Stoeckle, 1972).

It seems clear from these studies that real doctor/patient interaction differs significantly from an ideal communication event. One consequence of this may be that patients do not sufficiently understand or remember the doctor's recommendations. A study by Tuckett et al. (1986) found that a significant portion of patients do not understand what the doctor tells them or cannot remember treatment and preventative recommendations after the consultation. While medical care in the United States is among the most expensive in the world, health outcomes are not the best in the world. One reason for this may be inadequate communication between doctors and patients which lead to relatively low levels of compliance with doctor's orders (Frankel and Beckman, 1989).

> Nonadherence is an astonishingly common problem. An estimated 20% to 80% of patients do not follow the recommendations of their providers (Di Matteo & Di Nicola, 1984; Sackett & Snow, 1979). (Frankel and Beckman, 1989, p. 63)

In some cases the failure to follow a doctor's advice or treatment recommendation is due to not understanding that advice. However, in some cases the patient understands the advice but decides not to take it. Reasons for deciding not to follow a doctor's advice can include cost, convenience or personal reasons. For example, in Vise's (1999) study of doctor/patient consultations, she videotaped a doctor explaining to a diabetic patient why it was essential for her to follow the special diet he had previously recommended to her. He then left the room to get some more information, leaving the wife alone in the examining room with her husband. While they were alone, the wife told the husband that she was not going to follow the special diet, because she would have to cook different meals for them both. While the doctor was in the room, the patient had given no indication that there was any problem with the advice he was giving her.

This example raises several questions about the nature of the interaction between them. Was the patient too in awe of the doctor's authority to challenge his advice to his face? Was there too weak a relationship between them for her to share the practical details of her life? Did the compressed time frame of today's typical doctor/patient consultation lead her to believe that the doctor would not have time to listen to her explanation? While we do not have the answers to these questions for this particular patient, there is reason to suspect that had the interaction between the doctor and patient been conducted differently, a different outcome could have been achieved. For example, when the doctor discovered that she had not been following the diet he had recommended on a previous visit, instead of just repeating his advice that she follow the diet, he could have asked her *why* she had not yet begun implementing the diet. If the doctor had pursued this topic, perhaps more patient cooperation with the treatment plan could have been obtained.

In this chapter we will explore the nature of the interaction in doctor/patient consultations. We will first discuss some of the problems that can occur in the consultation, and then address how doctors accomplish an important part of their job—the transmission of diagnostic news.

Physician's competence in communication with patients

Although how doctors are educated has been evolving over recent years, the current approach to the selection and training of future physicians still works against their acquisition of effective communication techniques and strategies. Medical education still focuses primarily on the science of medicine and medical treatments, while de-emphasizing the doctor/patient interaction itself. When medical students are explicitly taught how to communicate with patients, they may be taught what information to communicate, but generally not *how* to do so. For example, Clark (1995) advises doctors what they should tell patients, but not how or when to say it. He recommends that doctors memorize a list of items to be communicated to the patient during the consultation, if they believe the patient has a problem with drugs or alcohol. Organized around the mnemonic device "DR HELPS CD" (Chemical Dependency), each sentence conveys information the patient should be given during the consultation:

> **DR HELPS CD** (Chemical Dependency)
> You are **D**ependent on the drug alcohol.
> Come for a **R**eturn visit on…
> **H**elp is necessary and available.
> The **E**vidence that tells me you're in trouble is…
> **L**eave alcohol (and mood-altering drugs) behind; abstain.
> Your **P**erspective is limited; you can't see the reality.
> This predicament **S**neaked up on you; no one asks for it.
> I'm **C**oncerned and worried about you because you're ill.

Your **D**epression and despair result from not living according to your own values, hurting people you love, and not living up to your potential. (Clark, 1995, p. 292)

Clark provides only general advice for doctors on how to use this information about chemical dependency in the consultation:

Adjustments should be made to individual situations. The information just listed should be spread throughout the encounter and appropriately accompanied by relationship-building statements, apologies, and pauses while the patient digests and responds. (Clark, 1995, p. 192).

This advice begs the question of how to apply this knowledge in a specific interaction. Both social and pragmatic factors are important. Who is the patient, and how well does the doctor know them? What are the reasons the doctor suspects chemical dependency? Has the patient raised the issue, or the doctor? Is the patient likely to be receptive to this information? Is the patient likely to be in legal trouble if they admit to taking certain substances? Such aspects of the social and relational context are largely ignored by this type of general advice.

In addition, the pragmatics of interaction are taken for granted by this type of advice. How should this information be communicated? At what point in the interaction? What types of questions should the patient be asked? How should the patient's reactions to this information be responded to? These interactional skills are not explicitly taught to doctors. However, substantial evidence indicates that doctors often have poor interactional skills. The two excerpts below from Lewis and Pantell (1995) are from pediatrician's examinations of child patients. A parent is in the room in both instances. Excerpt 1 shows a physician communicating effectively with a child patient. Excerpt 2 shows a doctor with very poor communication skills. While it is likely that extreme examples such as this one are rare; it is disturbing that it happened at all.

Note that in Excerpt 1 (below) the doctor addresses the patient directly, asks for his perspective on his medical problem, checks frequently to see if the patient understands what he is saying, and demonstrates that he is listening to the patient and has understood him. In the final line of the excerpt the doctor compliments the patient. The patient in this encounter is likely to feel good about the interaction. The groundwork has been laid for a good relationship between the pediatrician and the patient, which should facilitate future cooperation.

Excerpt 1: Lewis and Pantell (1995, pp. 209–10)
(D = Doctor; P = Patient)
1   D: You can put on your T-shirt and let's talk about how we need to
2   manage your problem, OK?
3   P: You mean a plan?
4   D: Yeh. Why don't we make a plan that we can both live by. OK? That
5   I can live by so you don't get too sick. And that you can live by so
6   you stay healthy. OK?
7   P: OK.
8   D: What makes you know that your asthma's started?

9   P: When I can't breathe.

10 D: What things cause asthma for you? You told me sport. What about

11   when you get a cold?

12 P: Yes.

13 D: What else?

14 P: [Walks over to doctor and whispers in doctor's ear.]

15 D: OK, let's just say when you get active at school. What should you do

16   when your asthma starts up?

17 P: Take my medicine. Also get a lot of sleep.

18 D: That's very smart for a boy your age to be able to say.

Excerpt 2 illustrates poor communication techniques. The physician creates a great deal of unnecessary distress in the child patient. He addresses the mother and ignores the child's contributions to the conversation. When he does speak to the child it is only to give commands or criticize her. He makes no attempt to build rapport with the patient, and after the child becomes upset he criticizes her in an unfriendly and inappropriate way. This type of interaction will likely make the child very resistant to visiting this pediatrician in the future.

Excerpt 2: Lewis and Pantell (1995, p. 210)

(D = Doctor; C = Child (the patient); P = parent)

1   D: How often are you giving it to her--the cough medicine?

2   P: Usually in the evening.

3   C: Sometimes she would give it to me, usually in the afternoon, or

4   sometimes in the morning. [The doctor does not look at the child

5   while she is offering this information.]

6   D: [To mother] Well, from what you've said, I'm not concerned she's

7   seriously ill, but let me check. [To child as he places the stethoscope

8   in his ear: his first interaction with the child] Take off your top.

9   [Child slowly begins pulling off top.]

10 D: Take it off. [Impatiently moves forward with the stethoscope.]

11 P: Don't resist; take it off. (Child begins crying.)

12 D: [While examining the child] Just breathe in and out; I'm not through

13   yet. Breathe in and out. Now you can put your top back on.

14 P: [To child] Let me fix your collar.

15 C: I can do it myself.

16 D: How old are you, Susan?

17 C: Six and a half.

18 D: Well, then, you shouldn't behave like that, not like a baby. You're not

19   a nice girl when you do that. Why are you not a nice girl? Why are

20   you so angry? [Child does not respond.]

21 D: Did I make you angry? [Child looks away.]

22 D: Look at me when I speak to you, Susan!

23 C: [Sobbing] I never want to come here again!

24 P: She was in a good mood till you came in, seriously!

25 D: I can't understand it, she must be premenstrual.

While many medical schools have improved how they teach doctors communication skills over the last few decades, most medical students are still not explicitly taught how to communicate with patients. Some medical schools have only one course that even touches on the doctor/patient relationship. While medical students do get practical experience interacting with patients as part of their training, these interactions often cause considerable anxiety for the students (Smith and Kleinman, 1989). Their inexperience and lack of knowledge of appropriate interactional techniques may create awkwardness in the interaction which could affect the quality of care. Fallowfield and Lipkin (1995) quote a physician recalling how his lack of training in communication skills affected his job performance when he was a young doctor:

> I was 25 years old and working in an emergency department. A young boy was brought in with severe head injuries following a traffic accident. We tried to resuscitate him, but it was obviously useless. I had to go out and tell his parents. I'd never told anyone before that their child was dead and didn't have a clue what to say. I just blurted it out and the mother started screaming—I didn't know how to handle this situation. I just said "Sorry" and ran out of the room. I can still hear that woman's screams. That was over 30 years ago and I don't think things are really much better in terms of helping young doctors learn how to break bad news. (Fallowfield and Lipkin, 1995, p. 317).

Mistakes such as these are not only upsetting for the doctor, they can be traumatic for patients and their families as well. There is evidence that physician's improper communication styles can lead to bad patient outcomes. Fallowfield and Lipkin (1995) cited examples showing that how medical news was delivered affected patient satisfaction. In fact, in one study which compared how doctors and police officers delivered bad news, the police officers were seen as significantly more sympathetic than the doctors (Finlay and Dallimore, 1991).

Recent research by conversation analysts and others shows that even very small changes in what doctors say to patients can make a big difference in patient care. Heritage et al. (2007) conducted an experimental study of how doctors solicit additional concerns from patients at the end of consultations. They discovered a significant difference between asking whether patients had "anything else?" or "something else?" they wanted to discuss. Asking whether the patient had "something else?" they wanted to discuss was 78 percent more effective in getting unasked questions on the table than was asking "anything else?". This indicates that even very small and subtle differences in the nature of the doctor/patient interaction can be consequential, not just for the interaction, but for patient care.

The research reviewed in this section clearly shows that problems in communication between doctors and patients are common. The job of conversation analysis is to discover how doctor/patient interactions are conducted in a variety of medical settings, and to investigate what types of communication problems emerge and what causes them.

Talk as work in medical practice: Good and bad news delivery

Doctors often find the giving of bad news difficult, even though it is an important part of their job. One way of handling this difficulty is simply to avoid telling the bad news. Glaser and Strauss (1965) reported that during previous decades it was the norm to not tell terminally ill patients that they were dying. At that time it was considered unhelpful medically for the person to know that there was no hope of a recovery. There was also a greater degree of stigma associated with terminal illnesses such as cancer than there is today. Roter and Hall (1993) verified this finding, but also pointed out that medical personnel may avoid talking about dying because it is difficult and uncomfortable for them.

> The doctor may be particularly reluctant to give information that may be bad news, ostensibly for the patient's own good, but sometimes for more self-serving reasons. In cases of poor patient prognosis, physicians have been found to withhold information for the sole purpose of patient management. In a study of fourteen families with children suffering from polio, it was found that after two years, only one family was given a prediction of the likely clinical outcome (which was very favorable), while the remaining families (whose children were, in fact, considerably handicapped) were not told anything about what they might expect (Davis 1972). While the prognosis for full recovery of a child suffering from this disease is in doubt for about six weeks, the pretense of uncertainty was maintained long after the outcome was no longer uncertain. The purpose of maintaining this uncertainty was so that the physician could avoid "scenes" with patients and avoid "having to explain to and comfort them," tasks which were viewed as onerous and time-consuming. One staff member told the investigator: "We try not to tell them [parents] too much. It's better if they find out for themselves in a natural sort of way. (Roter and Hall, 1993, p. 99).

Fallowfield and Lipkin (1995) also address the challenges of giving bad news in medical interactions. They report that sometimes doctors neglect to give bad news. When they do give it, it may be communicated too briefly or casually, or in a way that is not sensitive to the needs of the patient. Explanations may be too full of medical jargon, or may fail to directly articulate the news (see also Lutfey and Maynard, 1998). Doctors also often fail to realize that the patient receiving bad news may be too emotionally distraught to process the information given, and therefore may need a written summary or an opportunity to ask questions later.

Researchers have found that giving bad news in a sensitive way can improve the results. Fallowfield and Lipkin (1995, pp. 317–18) cite a study done by Cunningham et al. (1984) in which parents given bad news about their children's health were far more likely to be satisfied with the way the medical personal communicated the news when the practitioner was trained to give the news in an "unhurried, honest, balanced, emphatic manner." In the next section we examine specific interactional techniques that can be used to deliver bad news in such a way that it minimizes emotional upset for both parties, while communicating the information in a way that the patient is more likely to accept.

Appropriate techniques for conveying diagnostic news

Maynard (1989; 1992) found that both lay people and medical personnel can use what he calls the "**perspective display sequence**" to facilitate the telling of bad news. Instead of producing the news themself, the person with bad news to tell solicits the recipient's perspective on the problem. The recipient may then state the bad news themselves. If not, they typically state enough of a perspective on the topic so that the person delivering the bad news can then merely confirm their suspicions, rather than having to deliver the bad news themselves. Maynard (1992, p. 333) notes that "a bringer of bad news may have difficulty stating the news outright. By avoiding the pronouncement and simply confirming a recipient's inference, a teller can manage the conveyance as a joint activity."

The perspective display series consists of at least three turns produced by two different speakers. In the first turn of the sequence the clinician asks the patient to share their perspective on the problem. In the second turn the patient may present their perspective on the problem. In the third turn, the clinician responds to the patient's characterization of the problem by assessing it and elaborating on it.

Maynard (1992) analyzed consultations in which clinicians conveyed diagnoses of severe developmental delays or disabilities to the parents of children who have undergone psychological testing. He gives examples of how participants used each turn in the perspective display series.

Turn One: The Perspective-Display Invitation. The physician can begin the bad news delivery with either a "marked" or "unmarked" perspective-display invitation. In a marked invitation, the clinician conveys a problem or difficulty, while the unmarked invitations do not (Maynard, 1992). Excerpt 3 shows the doctor producing a marked invitation (line 1).

Excerpt 3: Maynard (1992, p. 335)
1 Dr: What do you see? as- as his difficulty.
2   (1.2)
3 Mo: Mainly his uhm: (1.2) the fact that he doesn't
4   understand everything (0.6) and also the
5   fact that his speech. (0.7) is very hard to
6   understand what he's saying.

Excerpt 4 shows the doctor producing an "unmarked invitation." The doctor solicits the patient's perspective without indicating that there is a problem (lines 1–3).

Excerpt 4: Maynard (1992, p. 335)
1 Dr: Now that you've- we're been through all this I
2   just wanted to know from you::. (0.4) .hh how
3   you see Judy at this time
4   (2.2)
5 Mo: The same.

```
6        (0.7)
7   Dr:  Which is?
8        (0.5)
9   Mo:  Uhm she can't talk…
```

The choice of a marked or unmarked invitation allows the clinician to calibrate their initiation of the perspective display sequence according to what they think the parent's level of awareness is about their child's disability.

Turn Two: The Patient's Reply. The second turn in the sequence is where the parents display their views on their child's condition. In Excerpt 3 (above) the mother provided her perspective on her child's condition which showed that she believed her child had problems (lines 3–6). However, in Excerpt 4 (above), the mother's reply in line 5 does not clearly display that she understands that there is something wrong with her child. The doctor therefore repairs this missing problem formulation with a repair initiation in line 7. The mother then provides her perspective on her daughter's problems (line 9).

Turn Three: The Diagnostic News as Confirmation. If the perspective display invitation was successful in getting the parent to display that their child had problems, the clinician would confirm the parent's perspective in the third turn of the sequence (Maynard, 1992). However, at times the parent's perspective on their child's condition is very different from the doctor's. If this happens, the doctor cannot agree with the parent. On the other hand, if the doctor were to suddenly produce a diagnosis which was much more serious than the parent's perspective, the parent might not be ready to accept it. The doctor has to work to gradually bring the parent around to his or her way of thinking.

Excerpt 5 shows a mother responding to the doctor's unmarked invitation with what looks like a "no problem" report. As she talks about how well her son has been doing in school (lines 2–11), she seems to reject the possibility of a problematic diagnosis for her child.

Excerpt 5: Maynard (1992, p. 339)

```
1   Dr:  How's Bobby doing.
2   Mo:  Well he's doing uh pretty good you know
3        especially in the school. I explained the
4        teacher what you told me that he might be
5        sent into a special class maybe, that I was
6        not sure. And he says you know I asks his
7        opinion, an' he says that he was doing
8        pretty good in the school, that he was
9        responding you know in uhm everything that
10       he tells them. Now he thinks that he's not
11       gonna need to be sent to another school.
12  Dr.  He doesn't think that he's gonna need to be
13       sent
```

14 Mo: Yeah that he was catching on a little bit uh
15   more you know like I said I- I- I <u>know</u> that
16   he needs a- you know I was 'splaining to her
17   that I'm you know that I know for sure that
18   he needs some special class or something.
19 Dr: Wu' whatta you think his <u>pro</u>blem is.
20 Mo: Speech.
21 Dr: Yeah. yeah his main problem is a- you know a
22   <u>lang</u>uage problem.
23 Mo: Yeah language.

Because the mother's response in lines 2–11 seems to suggest a "no problem" perspective on her child's condition, the doctor withholds confirmation of her perspective, and refrains from agreeing with her (Maynard, 1992). Instead, in line 12 he produces a reformulation of her statement. The mother agrees with the doctor's formulation of the teacher's perspective, but then goes on to reveal that her perspective is different from the teacher's; the mother does believe her son will need special education. Once the mother has revealed that she knows there is a problem with her child (lines 17 and 18), the doctor again solicits her perspective on her child, this time using a marked version of the perspective display invitation (line 19). When the mother responds to this second invitation with a specific problem ("Speech."; line 20), the doctor produces an agreement token "Yeah" (line 21), thus confirming her perspective.

In other consultations, the parent starts out with an understanding that their child has a diagnosable problem, but their characterization of the problem is not as severe as the doctor's. Excerpt 6 shows an interview in which the doctor upgrades the mother's understanding of her child's problem to a more serious diagnosis. Before this excerpt began, the mother had already stated that she knew her child was not functioning on the appropriate level at school, and that "she is kinda slow" (Maynard, 1992, p. 341).

Excerpt 6: Maynard (1992, p. 341)
1   Mo: … and I have seen no progress, from
2   September to June. For her learning
3   ability, she is slow.
4   (0.6)
5   Dr: That's what we uh:: also found on- on
6   psychological testing. .hhhh That she was
7   per- <u>not</u> performing like a normal (0.2) uh:::
8   six and a half year old uh (0.4) should.
9   Mo: mm hmm
10 Dr: And that she was performing more uh (0.3)
11   .hhhh what we call as a borderline (0.4)
12   rate of retardation .hhh uh:::m
13   (2.2)
14 Dr: For a <u>nor</u>mal (0.4) kind of might use a

15   number .hhhh it's usually about hundred
16   (0.2) or more. (0.6) and anywhere between
17   uh:: (0.3) eighty two and (1.2) uh::::: (0.4)
18   ninety is kind of uh:: (0.4) borderline
19   (0.6) kind of uh:: (0.2) .hhh functioning.

Note that the physician begins his response by displaying agreement with the mother's description of her child's problems ("That's what we uh:: also found…"; line 5); thus confirming the mother's perspective. He then characterizes their shared perception of the child as "not performing like a normal (0.2) uh::: six and a half year old uh (0.4) should."; lines 7–8). The doctor thus upgrades the diagnosis, describing the child's problem by introducing the label "not normal" to the discussion. Note that the mother provides only a minimal response to this statement (line 9), thus indicating that she is still listening, but that she is withholding either agreement or disagreement with the doctor's utterance. The doctor then upgrades the diagnosis from "not normal" to "borderline rate of retardation" in lines 10–12. Note that the mother does not reply to this utterance, thus suggesting that she may be not ready to accept this more serious characterization of her child's condition. Her delay in responding may indicate a dispreferred response—in this case, a disagreement). Given her lack of response, the doctor then backpedals slightly in his extended explanation in lines 14–19, this time refraining from using the label "retarded," and instead talking about "borderline functioning." The doctor thus appears to retreat to a less extreme depiction of the diagnosis given the mother's lack of acceptance of the more extreme version.

Given the high stakes of this type of interaction, in which the patient's willingness to accept the diagnosis and recommended treatment plans can have a major impact on the health of the patient, doctors would be well advised to learn about and practice appropriate techniques for the delivery of bad news.

Summary

Maynard's research on how to deliver diagnostic news effectively is just one example of how conversation analytic research can produce information that is directly relevant to teaching doctors how to practice medicine effectively. When appropriate interactional techniques are skillfully used, the doctor can be much more successful and efficient in doing their job. Patient outcomes are likely to be better, because patients will be better prepared to understand and accept what the doctor is telling them.

Student activity

The procedures for telling bad news in an effective way can be used in a wide range of interactions, not just in medical encounters. Conduct two role plays with a fellow student in which one of you plays the role of a manager who needs to tell an employee they are being laid off. The first time use the "perspective display sequence" as you communicate this information to the "employee." The second time through, try to communicate the news without using the perspective display sequence. Which method is more effective and more comfortable for the participants?

Recommended sources

Heath, Christian. (1992), 'The delivery and reception of diagnosis in the general-practice consultation', in Paul Drew and John Heritage (eds) *Talk at Work: Interaction in Institutional Settings*. Cambridge: Cambridge University Press, pp. 235–67.

Kinnell, Ann Marie K., and Maynard, Douglas W. (1996), 'The delivery and receipt of safer sex advice in pretest counseling sessions for HIV and AIDS', *Journal of Contemporary Ethnography*, 24, (4), 405–37.

Lutfey, Karen and Maynard, Douglas W. (1998), 'Bad news in oncology: how physician and patient talk about death and dying without using those words', *Social Psychology Quarterly*, 61, (4), 321–41.

19 The Primary Care Consultation: Diagnostic Interviews and Medical Advice

Chapter contents

Introduction

Much of the frontline work of physicians occurs during the medical consultation. During this encounter the doctor both examines the patient physically and asks them questions to elicit information that will help them diagnose medical problems and make treatment recommendations. Physicians are trained in medical school to conduct diagnostic interviews. They know which questions to ask in order to narrow down the diagnosis of a set of symptoms. The patient's answer to each question leads to another set of possibilities to be checked out. While the doctor is doing this work of diagnosis, the patient also has concerns, which they may raise at some point during the consultation. The research in this chapter examines both how doctors do the work of diagnosis and how patients intervene in this work and in the treatment recommendation process in order to get their own concerns addressed.

Attending to patients' concerns

Frankel (1990) found that question-answer chains were prevalent in medical consultations, with doctors controlling the development of topics by assuming the role of questioner. Excerpt 1 shows a typical question/answer chain from a consultation in which the doctor is taking a family history.

Excerpt 1: Frankel (1990, p. 239)

1   D: Does anybody have tuberculosis?
2   P: No, not that I know of
3   D: Heart disease
4   P: No
5   D: Diabetes
6   P: No
7   D: High blood pressure
8   P: My father had that
9   D: Did you ever have whooping cough
10 P: Yes
11 D: Scarlet fever
12 P: No

Doctors have a great deal of discretion in terms of whether they chose to develop a topic raised by the patient's responses to their questions. They may keep the interaction closely focused on the question/answer chain, or may temporarily abandon it in order to address topics or concerns, including emotional issues, that might be raised by the patient (Frankel, 1995). In some cases the doctor may choose an empathic response, in which he or she expresses concern for the patient and addresses their subjective experience of their troubles, while in other cases the doctor may refrain from responding to patients' concerns and instead continue on with the diagnostic series. Frankel (1995) argues that choices doctors make during the consultation are based in part on the overall purpose or goal of the interaction:

> To illustrate, suppose a patient comes to a physician concerned about chest pain and during the course of the encounter the physician asks a lot of questions about lifestyle that seem unrelated. I would argue that the physician's specialized knowledge and the contingent nature of the activities that occur between the problem identification and the proposed solution provide a warrant to the patient to continue to answer what may seem like unrelated questions. By contrast, suppose that the same patient comes to a physician concerned not only about chest pain but about committing suicide. If the physician inadvertently focuses on the patient's first problem to the exclusion of the second (as happens frequently according to our research, Beckman & Frankel, 1984) then the clinical activities that follow as well as the proposed solution may be inadequate to the overall task of developing a complete data base. My point is that the various activities that make up the clinical encounter are "nested." Delivering an accurate diagnosis and effective treatment plan depends on establishing a therapeutic relationship with the patient, and prior to that, finding out all of the reasons they are seeking health care. (Frankel, 1995, p. 248)

Frankel's (1995) research shows that physicians who ignore patient's subjective experience and reasons for coming to the doctor may miss important information. They may also end up with a patient who is not satisfied with their diagnosis or treatment plan. This finding is emphasized even more strongly in Frankel (2001) which shows that unless physicians solicit patients' beliefs about what is wrong with them, there is a greater likelihood that the patient will not accept or be satisfied with the diagnosis. This is true even if the diagnosis declares them to be in good health. Frankel (2001) cites a tragic case in which a patient was given a clean bill of health and then committed suicide after the consultation. This outcome suggests that the doctor's finding that she was in good health did not resolve the patient's concerns. Had the doctor addressed her concerns about what she believed was wrong with her during the consultation, it may have been possible to deal with them such that this tragic outcome could have been prevented.

Frankel (1995) contrasts two excerpts from medical consultations to illustrate problematic and effective ways of responding to patient's concerns. The first excerpt shows a physician's problematic response. In Excerpt 2 the doctor is asking a series of diagnostic questions about the patient's symptom of dizziness. While the patient answers the first two questions in a routine fashion, when the doctor asks, "What were you doing?" in line 7, the patient does not reply. The doctor repairs her absent response by repeating the question (line 8). When the patient answers (lines 9–11), her answer indicates significant emotional distress. However, instead of responding to the substance of her reply, the doctor merely acknowledges hearing it ("Okay."; line 12), and then immediately asks a question about another symptom ("Tell me a little more about the itching"; line 12). Instead of responding empathetically to the patient's report of emotional distress, the doctor ignored the emotional needs of the patient and kept the topic tightly focused on the diagnostic process.

> Excerpt 2: Frankel (1995, p. 244)
> 1   D: How long have you been having trouble feeling dizzy?
> 2   P: Around- I started back I would say about a week ago.
> 3   D: When do you notice that- that you feel dizzy?
> 4   (pause)
> 5   P: I think it was last Friday or Saturday (morning)//I forgot what day it
> 6   was.
> 7   D: What were you doing?
> 8   D: What were you doing at the time?
> 9   P: I (don't know) I just went to getting dizzy and I started crying, I told
> 10   Bobby I wanted to go to the hospital or somewhere so- I finally felt a
> 11   little better and I just got into bed and went to sleep.
> 12 D: Okay. Tell me a little more about the itching.

In Excerpt 3 Frankel (1995) shows a different doctor who takes a more empathetic approach to the emotional concerns raised by the patient. The doctor in Excerpt 3 follows the patient's lead and refocuses the topic onto the patient's emotional state instead of sticking rigidly to the structure of the diagnostic interview. As the excerpt begins, the doctor asks a question about when the patient had her last checkup (line 1). The patient first answers this question, but appends a concern to it (lines 2–3). The doctor responds with a minimal response (line 4) which indicates she is staying in the listening role rather than asking another question. This leaves the floor in the patient's hands, who is thus provided the space to continue speaking. The patient adds an explanation of the encounter with the other physician which suggests that she is concerned about her health (lines 5–14). The doctor's response is first to reassure the patient about her health ("You look fine."), and then to ask her about her feelings about her illness (lines 15–16). The patient responds to this question in lines 17–21, discussing her feelings about her medical issues. The doctor then develops the topic of the patient's emotional state ("You seem a little upset, you seem a little teary-eyed talking about it."; line 22). After the patient elaborates on her emotional state and the reasons for her concerns, the doctor acknowledges the validity of her fears (line 30).

Excerpt 3: Frankel (1995, pp. 245–6)
1   D: And you just had your six-month checkup//in December.
2   P: Yes, but I'm wondering about something because he (laugh)
3   instructed me to come back in four months, and that's unusual.
4   D: Hmmh.
5   P: But I think he might have noticed something, I don't know (he
6   didn't want to say) when I was there in December which was the first
7   week, cause they had to schedule me for the mammogram about a
8   week later. But anyway, about the first week…. Well, it was the
9   exact date fi- five years ago that I had the operation--four years ago.
10   I must have looked worried because he said, "Mrs. Fuller don't worry
11   about a thing, enjoy the holiday." These are things I have to do you
12   know to keep check on you so, uh- but when he was examining me it
13   was… sort of, you know, tender there. But, it was alright, I mean, I'm
14   okay. (laugh)
15 D: You look fine. Uh- how do you feel about… uh… the cancer and the
16   possibility of it coming back.
17 P: Well, it bothers me sometime, but I don't dwell on it, I don't (uh)…
18   here of late though, I don't know what it is, but I'm not as cheerful
19   about it as I was when I first had it. I just had, I don't know, look
20   like I just had a very good feelings that every-thing was going to be
21   alright, you know. I think it's because I dread another operation.
22 D: You seem a little upset, you seem a little teary-eyed talking about it.
23 P: Yeah, well, it gets to you. You know sometimes… you know uh its
24   the first time we've had a little session like this, see where you really
25   are talking to someone about it. But uh… I'm doing… I- I think I'm
26   blessed, I'm really- because so many people I've know had to have
27   the uh- because I had a very dear friend who passed… uh and she
28   had… but she waited too long and she had to have chemotherapy…
29   I guess that's why I'm crying… I don't know.
30 D: That's right, it's frightening//it's frightening.
         ((conversation continues))

The doctor in Excerpt 3 has thus allowed the patient an extended period of time to discuss her concerns and her emotional responses to her health problems. The doctor has used a variety of techniques to facilitate this communication, and to express empathy about her condition. By choosing to ask the patient about her feelings when she reports feeling anxious, a line of talk between the doctor and the patient about the patient's concerns is initiated. This discussion allows the doctor to express empathy and understanding of the patient's fears.

The contrast between the empathetic approach in Excerpt 3 and the less empathetic approach in Excerpt 2 serves to illustrate how the doctor's interactional style can affect the relationship between doctor and patient and the quality of care the patient receives. In order to provide the best possible medical care, it is important to train doctors not just in the scientific knowledge of the medical profession, but in the techniques for interacting with patients in the most effective ways possible.

Patient's role in diagnosis

Gill (1998) examined the patient's role in the diagnostic process during doctor/patient consultations with general medicine internists at an outpatient clinic. She notes that while individual patients may have theories about the causes of their medical symptoms, what they communicate to their doctor is dependent not only on these theories or beliefs but on how the interaction between the doctor and patient unfolds during the consultation. Gill (1998) argues that the relationship between the parties plays a role in how they collaboratively produce the diagnosis. The status and authority that comes with being a physician has an impact on how patients choose to formulate and place their concerns. While the doctor has both the status of their position as doctor and their superior knowledge of medical science, the patients have superior knowledge of their subjective experience (e.g., what pain are they feeling) and the types of symptoms they have had.

Gill found that when patients describe their symptoms they do so in a way that defers or otherwise displays an orientation to the doctor's professional role. For example, they may describe a symptom but leave it up to the doctor to articulate an explanation for it. Or, if the patient does venture to produce an explanation for their symptom or a theory as to what is causing it, they may do so in a way that leaves the doctor free to choose how to respond to the information.

Gill's (1998) collection of 15 videotaped doctor/patient consultations enabled her to use conversation analysis to study 80 instances of patients telling doctors their theories of the causes of their symptoms. She found that patients use a variety of techniques to downplay their certainty about the explanations for medical problems they provide. Some of these techniques are the use of uncertainty markers to indicate tentativeness, prefaces which allow for the possibility of alternative positions on the facts (e.g. "whether" or "whether or not"), and third party attributions. For example, in Excerpt 4 the patient states information about her medical condition that she has knowledge about (her migraine headaches; lines 1–2). However, when suggesting that there may be a link between her migraines and her allergies, she uses indirect language along with hedges and uncertainty markers ("I just have to really wonder…" line 5; "So that's s:ome possibilities" line 7).

Excerpt 4: Gill (1998, p. 345)

```
1   Ms. I:    I still ha::ve my: ordinary::: migraine
2             headaches, which I've ha:d for yea::rs?
3                      (1.3)
4   Ms. I:    °And ah:° (.) they come and go so badly I: just
5             have to really wonder what triggers that.
6             I know I do have some °allergies°.
7             So [that's    ] s:ome possibilities=
8   Dr. C:       [>M hm<]
9   Ms. I:    =an I know (.) .hh they do bother me
```

Gill (1998) also found that patients design their offers of explanations for their symptoms differently depending on where in the consultation the explanation occurs. Patients may avoid asking doctors about potential diagnoses during the early investigative phase of the consultation, in order to avoid distracting the doctor from their data-gathering process. And, when patients do make claims about possible causes of their symptoms (as in Excerpt 5 below), they do so in a parenthetical way which does not require (or even leave room for) a response from the physician, thus refraining from imposing on the doctor by requiring a response to their theory.

In Excerpt 5 the patient ("Ms. B") confidently and directly describes aches and pains in her chest (lines 52–3), and immediately provides an explanation for the pains ("but that's because there's not enough muscle over them…."; lines 54 and 56). Having had some muscle tissue removed from a prior surgery, the patient expresses her belief that the pain is caused by the lack of tissue. After completing this explanation in line 58, she immediately returns to the topic of the sick feeling ("But- (.) this is just is sick…."). With this construction of her turn, and with the statement about the chest pain inserted within the discussion of the sick feeling in her abdomen, she neither solicits nor leaves room for a response from the doctor about her explanation for the chest pain. She thus leaves it up to the doctor to choose whether to address the topic of her chest pain or to question her further about it, or not.

Excerpt 5: Gill (1998, p. 352)

```
47  Ms. B:    I've been getting- I jist- .hhhhhh
48            feel SICK hhhhh.
49            (1.2)
50  Ms. B:    A sort of glaagh (0.5) feeling right in here.
51            (1.0)
52  Ms. B:    And I- (.) I don' of cour- I'm always getting
53            aches and pains in the bones here, but
54            [that's because] there's not enough
55  Dr. A:    [M hm?         ]
56  Ms. B:    muscle over them. [Er    ] tissue I assume.
57  Dr. A:                      [M hm]
58  Ms. B:    .hhh From the surgical.
59            But- (.) this it just is sick. And whether I'm
```

```
60            not- (0.5) taking enough maybe I should take
61            the Gaviscon more regularly?
62            Or [maybe it's a]
63  Dr. A:       [Does it feel] like a nausea? to
64            yo[u:?
65  Ms. B :     [Y::::ah. It's [s::  ] more blea::h
66  Dr. A:                    [Kay]
```

The doctor does have some power and authority in the interaction, because of the social status of doctors and the medical knowledge they have. Gill (1998, p. 357) concludes that patients not only orient to the status and authority of the physician, but construct their contributions in such a way that they do not challenge the doctor's authority, thereby inter-actionally creating an unequal social relationship between doctor and patient:

> Structural features of doctor-patient interaction that are intertwined with asymmetries in knowledge, such as the relative authority of the patient and the doctor, can be viewed as social productions that come about through organized patterns of interaction. Through careful attention to the methods with which interactants display knowledge and respond to these displays, such as during explanation-response sequences in doctor-patient interaction, we can observe part of the social processes by which the distinctive social structural attributes of doctor-patient encounters are generated and sustained. (Gill, 1998, p. 357)

Patients orient to the doctor's rights and responsibilities, but at the same time may try to influence that decision. Gill (2005) conducts a single case analysis of a primary care visit to a general internal medicine outpatient clinic in order to show how patients can attempt to influence the doctor to prescribe a desired test. Her analysis shows that medical treatment, medical outcomes and ultimately the cost of medical care can all be affected by what happens in the interaction between the doctor and the patient. Thus doctors, who have multiple goals during the medical consultation, need to be interactionally skillful enough to manage patient's expectations while determining what is the best course of treatment or testing for the patient. They try to work in conjunction with the patient while still maintaining professional control and discretion in terms of what paths of action are appropriate and necessary for that particular patient. The doing of medicine is thus at least partly, the doing of talk.

One example of patient techniques for pressuring doctors to order diagnostic tests is citing the opinion of another physician or stating benefits to the patient of having the test done. Excerpt 6 shows the patient explaining that another doctor had given her a medical test which benefitted her by making her less nervous about her health.

```
        Excerpt 6: Gill (2005, p. 466)
29  Dr:    °An those kinds of things,°=
30  Pt:    =Mkay.
31  Dr:    [.hhh
32  Pt:    [(That- that-) >Cuz it-< it |n seemed tuh make me: (.)
33         An again. (.) cuz: (0.6) ah:m= (.) >I mus- I mean<
```

```
34       he was:: I have:- had very:- (.) good doctors as far as:
35       (2.5) explaining: to me what my pr(h)ob(h)l(h)ems are.=
36  Dr:  =[ln Mm hm?]
37  Pt:   [.hh         ]
38  Pt:  An:d=uh=h I had gotten:- (0.5) I always felt tht after
39       he did that if he said everything was fine it wa:s.
40  Pt:  .hh- (.) An I didn't get nervous about it. hh
41       (0.2)
42  Pt:  At least for another six months. HH
43  Dr:  Hih °ka(h)y.°
44 (Pt): .hhh
45  Pt:  It's: ah=h (0.6) >I don't know.<
46       (0.8)
47  Pt:  Our minds're th- (.) our biggest problems.
48       (7.4)
49  Dr:  So the ↑medicines that you're on no:w, are thee
50       amitriptyle:ne,
```

Some patients may be reluctant to make direct requests for tests because the request itself may be embarrassing or anxiety provoking. Gill et al. (2001) conduct a single case analysis of an interaction in which a patient was concerned that she might have been exposed to HIV, but did not want to directly articulate that fear or to ask for an HIV test. The patient instead used indirect means of communicating information which *suggested* to the doctor that such a test would be advisable. For example, she reported that her children were concerned about a blood transfusion that she had had in the past (lines 6–9 and 11–12). She also described some symptoms which could be consistent with an AIDs diagnosis (not shown). However, the patient never made a direct request for an HIV test. The physician did order the test, but he also did not directly discuss her need for such a test. The discussion about the possibility that the patient could have been exposed to HIV, and whether she needs a test for it or not, is therefore both delicately and indirectly accomplished, rather than being an explicit request which is explicitly granted. Gill et al. (2001) suggest that doctors need to be alert to patients who may make requests or formulate medical problems in indirect ways, so that they can be responsive both to patient's medical and psychological needs.

Excerpt 7: Gill et al. (2001, pp. 62–3)

```
1   Dr:  That's: [that' .s ah::      ]
2   Pt:          [Heh heh heh .hhh]
3   Dr:  one ah the changes: (.) we've a:ll had to adjust to I think.
4   Dr.  .hh Alright uh- hu- let's see- So:=uh >l:emme just look- <
5        (0.5)
6   Pt:  One uh [thuh things that's always worried] my kids-
7   Dr:         [look through some things here   ]
8   Pt:  .hh uh:: about that I (ws-) also had blood transfusions °when I had
9        (.) thee hysterec[tomy.°   ]
10  Dr:                   [mm hm?] Mm hm
```

```
11  Pt:   °>An they said<° did you ever get tested for AIDS
12        Didju ever get tested fe(h)r A(h)I(h)DS y(h)[kn(h)ow?] .hh
13  Dr:                                      [.hh      ]
14  Dr:   We[ll?   ]
15  Pt:      [No:?] I never got teste(h)d for AI::DS [y(h)a] kno:w,
16  Dr:                                              [ptch ]
```

Summary

The interaction between the doctor and patient displays many of the aspects of talk in institutional settings, such as the differentiated interactional roles of the participants (with doctors asking the majority of the questions, for example), and with patients displaying an orientation to the social status and professional role of the doctor through their reticence when communicating opinions about their condition or suggesting treatment or diagnostic options. While the consultation is therefore collaboratively produced, the doctor does have responsibility for the success of the interaction, not only because of his or her professional role but also because of the nature of the interaction between the two. How the doctor chooses to enact their role in the turn by turn exchange with the patient may have significant implications for the quality of patient care.

Student activity

Think about the last time you visited a physician. Did you raise all the concerns you had before you went to the appointment? Did the doctor carefully explain any instructions or advice? Did you follow the advice given? Do you think the nature of the interaction with your doctor affected how you answered any of these questions?

Recommended sources

Halkowski, Timothy. (2006), 'Realizing the illness: patients' narratives of symptom discovery', in Heritage, John and Douglas W. Maynard (eds). *Communication in Medical Care: Interaction between Primary Care Physicians and Patients*. Cambridge: Cambridge University Press, pp. 86–114.

Heath, Christian. (2002), 'Demonstrative suffering: the gestural (re)embodiment of symptoms', *Journal of Communication*, 52, (3), 597–617.

Kinnell, Ann Marie K. (2002), 'Soliciting client questions in HIV prevention and test counseling', *Research on Language and Social interaction*, 35, (3), 367–93.

Stivers, Tanya. (2006), 'Treatment decisions: negotiations between doctors and parents in acute care encounters', in Heritage, John and Douglas W. Maynard (eds). *Communication in Medical Care: Interaction between Primary Care Physicians and Patients*. Cambridge: Cambridge University Press, pp. 279–312.

Part V
Talk in Legal Settings

20 Trials and Other Public Legal Proceedings

Chapter contents

Introduction

As will now be clear from our study in previous chapters of talk in three different types of institutional settings (emergency service calls, medical interactions, and air traffic communications), such talk differs in several ways from ordinary conversation. In ordinary conversation, such things as the topic of talk, the distribution of turns and specific types of turns, the length of turns, and so on, are locally managed and free to vary. The turn-taking system of ordinary conversation provides the most flexibility and leaves the most control in the hands of the participants—what Sacks et al. (1974) called "local management." The speech exchange systems of talk in institutional settings involve variations on this fundamental turn taking system. One or more parameters of the interaction are constrained, thus creating interactions with different types of structures and roles.

For example, legal proceedings such as trials and hearings differ in several ways from ordinary conversation. There are explicit rules about how talk will be conducted during the procedure, and these rules are enforced by participants holding specific institutional roles—such as judge or attorney. In addition, legal proceedings tend to be more adversarial, especially when an attorney is interrogating an opposing witness. While in both emergency service calls and in doctor/patient interactions, the parties are filling complementary roles and working toward the same goal, in trials and other legal proceedings, parties are often on opposite sides. In this chapter we will examine the interactional organization of talk in legal proceedings and explore how the adversarial character of the interaction affects how the talk is organized. At the same time, this analysis shows how participants create the interactional occasion of a trial (or other legal proceeding) through their actions.

The overhearing audience and the legal record

While in ordinary conversation the primary audience for the interaction is the participants, in legal proceedings the primary audiences for interactions between attorneys and witnesses are the overhearing judge and jury (Heritage and Clayman, 2010). In addition, the talk is produced for the legal record—the transcript of the interaction which is created by the court recorder. Because the interaction in trials is focused on the problem at hand, there are rules and procedures governing not only what can be discussed during the hearing but also how the talk is organized. For example, attorneys interrogating witnesses are supposed to limit themselves to asking questions, and witnesses to answering them. There are also rules about when the opposing attorney can speak during an interrogation, as well as the types of reasons they are allowed to have for interrupting. The interaction during an interrogation in a trial therefore consists largely of a question/answer chain, with the attorney asking the questions and the witness answering them. One of the implications of this interactional structure is that the attorney controls the topic of talk that are addressed.

Heritage and Clayman (2010) note that both attorneys and witnesses typically withhold **minimal responses** and receipt markers which occur frequently in ordinary conversation. Minimal responses (also referred to as **continuers**) are brief utterances such as "yeah" or "um hm" produced by listeners in response to or within a speaker's turn (Schegloff, 1982). The absence of these listener responses both reflects and contributes to the construction of the adversarial nature of the interaction— with participants refraining from listener responses in order to avoid appearing to support the opposing side. The absence of these responses also enhances the impression that witness's answers are their own, rather than having been shaped or formed with the help of the attorney. Of course, there are a variety of ways in which witnesses' answers are shaped by the questions asked, and the attorneys' questions are designed to direct the nature of the witness's response. The order in which questions are asked is also consequential for the interpretation of the "facts" that emerge from the witness's answers.

In legal proceedings such as trials witnesses are supposed to answer the questions that are asked. If a witness violates this rule, they may be corrected and asked to change their response. Excerpt 1 is from the interrogation of a witness in the Timothy McVeigh Trial. Mr. McVeigh was accused of blowing up a federal building in Oklahoma City, resulting in great loss of life. The woman who is being interrogated in this excerpt was a witness to the crime, not a suspect. She was in the building when the explosion occurred.

> Excerpt 1: Transcript of Timothy McVeigh Trial, Oklahoma City (Testimony of Daina Bradley, May 23, 1997, Direct Examination, Attorney Ms. Ramsey).
>
> 1   Q: Ms. Bradley, how old are you?
> 2   A: I'm 2-- going to be 22.
> 3   Q: You're going to have to speak up.
> 4   A: 21.
> 5   Q: You're 21 now, soon to be 22? You need to answer yes or no.
> 6   A: Yes.
> 7   Q: Okay. And you do have an attorney representing you in this
> 8   case, don't you: Ms. Wallace?
> 9   A: Yes.
> 10 Q: And can you see her--
> 11 A: Yes.

While the excerpt shows the attorney and the witness confining their utterances to questions and answers respectively, the witness's answer in line 2 goes beyond what was asked. After first reminding her to speak more loudly (line 3), the attorney repeats the witness's answer and then reminds her to frame her responses as yes or no answers (line 5). The witness follows this instruction for the remainder of the excerpt (lines 6, 9 and 11). When the attorney asked the witness to speak up (line 3), it was for the benefit of the overhearing audience. As the attorney's turn in line 5 demonstrates, she was able to hear the witness's response in line 2, but works to ensure that the witness speaks loudly enough to be heard by the overhearing audience and the court recorder.

This example illustrates that the interactional organization of talk in trials and other legal proceedings differs in several key ways from that of ordinary conversation. Participants hold different social roles which are tied to their rights and obligations to speak during the procedure. In order to follow the conventions governing how trials are conducted, they must orient to expectations about the types of turns they produce, the topics they address, the order of speakership, and so on. These expectations differ from those in ordinary conversation.

Since utterances are interpreted in context, and the primary context for most utterances is the immediately prior utterance, how attorneys construct questions has an effect on the facts that can be established by the witness's testimony. Similarly, witnesses have a variety of techniques at their disposal to resist attorneys' construction of facts in their question design (Heritage and Clayman, 2010). We now turn to a consideration of how the adversarial relationship between the participants affects the unfolding structure of the interaction that they create during the hearing.

The prospective management of accusations

Atkinson and Drew (1979, p. 115) use the phrase "prospective management of accusations" to describe the dynamic process between attorneys and witnesses as they manage the adversarial question/answer exchange. While in everyday talk, accusations may be constructed as adjacency pair first pair parts, Atkinson and Drew (1979) found that accusations are often performed differently in courtroom talk. Accusations are led up to, even constructed, from the information obtained in a series of questions and answers. While not every question is an accusation per se, the series of questions produced by the attorney are typically structured to elicit information that will cumulatively lead up to an explicit or implicit accusation. These series of questions are designed to lead the witness to admit or display guilt.

Atkinson and Drew (1979) show how witnesses can often project the accusation that is being led up to from the nature of the questions, and work to deny or contest it before it has been produced. The attorney works to anticipate the types of denial-implicative moves the witness will make, and to construct their questions and to prospectively counter those denials. The interrogation therefore becomes a contest between the two participants.

These courtroom interrogations have some elements of what Schegloff (2007a) refers to as pre-expansion sequences. Because the attorney is constructing their line of questioning to support an eventual accusation, their actions could be considered "pre-accusations." Similarly, the witness is also oriented to the fact that an accusation is being led up to, and therefore may construct their answers as "pre-denials" or "anticipatory defenses" against eventual accusations. This could be thought of as an extreme version of the preferred response to an accusation— the denial, instead of being produced in the first possible place *after* the accusation has been produced, is instead produced *prior* to its production, thus attempting to pre-empt its effectiveness as an accusation (Garcia, 2010).

Resisting answer-categories

Witnesses in trials can not refuse to answer questions (without invoking the Fifth Amendment to the Constitution), but they can work to construct their answers so as to resist implications that are not in their favor. As noted above, when an attorney's question is formulated to project a specific type of answer (e.g. "yes" or "no" questions), the witness is supposed to produce an answer that fits into that category. However, they can resist these constraints by first answering the "yes/no" question and then appending an explanation to it which challenges the assumptions underlying the question. Or, they can construct an answer which avoids a yes or no answer while implicitly challenging the assumptions of the question. Heritage and Clayman (2010) refer to these types of responses as "implicit rejections." Excerpt 2, from the interrogation of a witness in a trial that occurred in Great Britain a number of years ago, is analyzed in Atkinson and Drew (1979). It shows a witness in a trial using several techniques in her answers to resist the Counselor's blame-implicative questions:

Excerpt 2: Atkinson and Drew (1979, pp. 70–1, 72)
```
 1   C:    And during that enti:re (.) evening (.) Miss
 2           Lebrette (.) its your testimony (2.3) that there was:
 3           (0.9) no indication as far as you could tell that the
 4           defendant had been drinking.
 5   W:    No.
 6   C:    Now Miss Lebrette (1.2) when you were intervie:wed by
 7           the poli::ce sometimes later- sometime later that
 8           evening (1.1) didn't you te:ll the police that the
 9           defendant had been drinking (.) [(did you tell them that)
10   W:                                        [No I told them that
11           there was a coo:ler in the ca:r and that I never opened it=
12   C:    =The answer er: may the (balance) be here stricken
13           your honour and the answer is *no*
14   J:    The answer is no
15           (5.1)
16   C:    We- wz *you:*r testimony (.) as far as you can conclude
17           (.) the defendant had not been drinking (.) [(right)
18   W:                                                     [Right
19   C:    n you never told the police that the defendant had
20           been drinking
21           (0.6)
22   W:    I told them about the cooler
23   C:    You never told the police the defendant had been
24           dri[nking ( )
25   W:        [No
```

While the Counselor's first question (lines 1–4) is a yes or no question (and is answered "no" by the witness), the second question (lines 6–9) reveals that the Counselor is working to "prospectively manage" an accusation. By first getting the witness to state that the defendant had *not* been drinking, and then immediately after that, getting her to admit that she had previously said that he *had* been drinking, the Counselor tries to portray the witness as inconsistent, if not dishonest, in her replies. However, apparently alert to the blame-implicative nature of the second question, the witness appends an implicit rejection to her response. First displaying an orientation to the requirement that she construct her response as an answer to the question by quickly saying "No" (line 10), she then appends an explanation which challenges the Counselor's construction of the facts (lines 10–11).

In response, the Counselor uses his prerogative as an attorney to enforce the rule restricting the types of answers witnesses can produce. He requests that her explanation be stricken from the record (lines 12–13), leaving only the "no" answer. After the judge concurs (line 14), the Counselor produces another question about whether the defendant had been drinking (lines 16–17). The witness agrees with this question ("Right"; line 18). After the Counselor's subsequent question in lines 19–20, the witness first delays her response (line 21) and then makes a statement instead of producing a yes or no answer to the question ("I told them about the cooler."). This time, instead of asking that her answer be stricken from the record, the Counselor merely repeats his question (lines 23–4). The witness answers the question with "No" in line 25.

This excerpt, taken as a whole, demonstrates how the question/answer chain in a trial interrogation involves a complex struggle between the two sides. By careful construction of questions an attorney can create an impression that is different from the impression that the witness wants to present, and by careful construction of responses the witness can attempt to resist giving those impressions.

Excerpt 3 is from the Scarman Tribunal of Inquiry held in 1969 to investigate a violent incident in Northern Ireland involving Protestant and Catholic residents. The transcript of this tribunal is analyzed by Atkinson and Drew (1979). This excerpt shows a Counselor asking a question which is blame-implicative and a witness using an implied rejection to counter the implicit accusation. The witness, a police officer, has been accused of excessive force against the Catholic crowd.

> Excerpt 3: Atkinson and Drew (1979, p. 73)
> 1   C: This is going back to the point which Mr Nicholson made
> 2   a moment or two ago but it is an important point. Did
> 3   you make any attempt to persuade the Catholic crowd to go
> 4   back before you baton-charged them?
> 5   W: I do not see how you could persuade them to go back.
> 6   C: Never mind that, just answer the question first and then
> 7   give your reason. Did you make any effort to persuade
> 8   the Catholic crowd to go back before you baton-charged
> 9   them?
> 10   W: No.
> 11   C: Why not?
> 12   W: I doubt if they could even hear me.

The excerpt begins with the Counselor asking a yes or no question (lines 1–4). However, the witness refrains from producing a yes or no answer, and instead argues that persuading the Catholic crowd to move back was not practical (line 5). This response displays an orientation to the implied accusation in the question. If the officer had answered no, he would be admitting that he failed to try verbal methods of controlling the crowd before escalating to the use of force. His response is therefore not an answer to the question asked, but an implied rejection of the attribution of blame that the question conveys (Heritage and Clayman, 2010).

The Counselor responds by instructing the witness on how to answer the question (lines 6–7), and then repeats the question. This time the witness produces the "no" answer the question was designed to produce (line 10). When asked to explain his failure to act (line 11), the witness's explanation works to justify his lack of action ("I doubt if they could even hear me."). This explanation attempts to deflect the blame that could be imputed from his "no" answer.

These examples have illustrated how participants manage institutional rules governing how questions are asked and answered to advance their preferred construction of the facts.

While attorneys clearly have more institutional power in these interactions, witnesses have interactional techniques at their disposal to contest that power and exert control over the impressions given by their answers.

Formulations and reformulations

Atkinson and Drew (1979) found that both attorneys and witnesses in court proceedings use formulations and **reformulations** to contest each other's construction of the facts. Formulations summarize an earlier utterance in a way that reframes what was meant (see Hutchby, 2005, pp. 309–10). Formulations enable the speaker to choose which aspects of prior utterances to emphasize. For example, Heritage and Clayman (2010, p. 182) analyze an excerpt from a sexual harassment case brought against former President Bill Clinton which was held during the time he was president. In this deposition President Clinton successfully used reformulations to deflect the negative implications of the attorney's questions. The issue under discussion was whether he had improperly gotten a federal job for a female employee. The attorney's question used the formulation "you appointed Kathleen Willey," thus claiming that President Clinton himself had been involved in the hiring. President Clinton's answer reformulated the hiring as "a White House appointee." This reformulation enabled him to remove himself from direct responsibility for the hiring, while at the same time not denying that Ms. Willey did get a federal job (Heritage and Clayman, 2010).

> Excerpt 4: Heritage and Clayman (2010, p. 182)
> 1 A: Now, you appointed Kathleen Willey to travel to
> 2   Copenhagen to serve on the official delegation of the
> 3   United States of America at a world summit for social
> 4   development, true?
> 5 W: She went as a White House appointee…

Excerpt 5 is from Atkinson and Drew's (1979) analysis of how accusations are managed in trials. It is from the transcript of the "Scarman Tribunal of Inquiry" held in 1969 in Northern Ireland about police response to a riot. This riot involved conflict between Catholic and Protestant residents of the city, which was segregated on the basis of religion. Atkinson and Drew (1979) describe how formulations and reformulations of place names and the religious identity of participants are consequential for the arguments and implied accusations that are being made in the tribunal. By getting witnesses (who were English army officers) to display that they knew which areas of the city were inhabited by Protestants and which by Catholics, they can then argue that their actions towards people in these different locations were based on discriminatory behavior toward Catholics.

In Excerpt 5 the Counselor's question in line 39 foregrounds that the houses on the streets they are talking about "would be Catholic houses." Since the purpose of the tribunal is to investigate charges that the police did not sufficiently protect Catholics and Catholic property during the riot, this specification that Catholics resided in the houses that were burning is accusation-implicative.

> Excerpt 5: Atkinson and Drew (1979, p. 108)
> 34 C: ... you have earlier an
> 35   intimation that a crowd are coming down Conway Street from
> 36   Shankill Road and then some minutes later houses are burning
> 37   in Conway Street.
> 38 W: Yes.
> 39 C: And those would be Catholic houses?
> 40 W: Yes.
> 41 C: Then at 02.00 hours 'Mothball--Cupar Street--fire
> 42   brigade needed at factory fire'.
> 43 W: Yes.

Excerpt 6 shows the Counselor then quoting the log of messages sent by the police during the riot (lines 44–5). With the formulation in this question the Counselor first establishes that the witness was the one who had sent the message, and then asks another accusation-implicative question in line 49: "Were those people you are referring to there Protestant people?" While on the face of it this is merely a factual question as to who the people were, in the context of this sequence of utterances (and the larger context of the tribunal), this question can be heard as leading up to a claim that there was something wrong with the message the witness had sent regarding the people on Percy Street. Note that the witness displays an orientation to these implications in his response in line 50. He avoids producing a yes or no response, and instead says "Presumably they were." This response suggests that at the time he had no knowledge of the religious affiliation of the people on Percy Street, but that now he now knows that they were "presumably" Protestant (Atkinson and Drew, 1979).

> Excerpt 6: Atkinson and Drew (1979, p. 108)
> 41 C: Then at 02.00 hours 'Mothball--Cupar Street--fire
> 42   brigade needed at factory fire'.
> 43 W: Yes.
> 44 C: Then a message from you, Deputy Commissioner, 'Ask people in
> 45   Percy Street to go home as they can't stand there'.
> 46 W: Yes.
> 47 C: Did you send that message?
> 48 W: Yes.
> 49 C: Were those people you are referring to there Protestant people?
> 50 W: Presumably they were.

Atkinson and Drew (1979) note that after establishing that the people on Percy Street were Protestants, the Counselor then reformulates his characterization of this group with his question in lines 51–2. This time he refers to them as a "Protestant mob."

Excerpt 7: Atkinson and Drew (1979, pp. 108–9)

50 W: Presumably they were.
51 C: Were they in fact a Protestant mob that was attempting to
52 burst into Divis Street?
53 W: Prior to sending this message I must have known that there was a
54 crowd of people there.
55 C: You know in fact now that quite a lot of devastation and
56 damage was done in Divis Street at that immediate junction?
57 W: Yes.
58 C: And that there was a petrol bomb attack on St. Comgall's
59 school?
60 W: Yes. Also fire was returned to St. Comgall's school.
61 C: From it or to it?
62 W: To it.
63 C: Yes, we are coming to that shortly. I want to ask you about
64 the phraseology there, 'Ask people in Percy Street to go home
65 as they can't stand there'. Was that your message?
66 W: Yes, that is my message.
67 C: That was a rather polite way of addressing a mob who had
68 burned and pillaged a Catholic area, was it not?
69 W: I did not know that. The object of that message, if I may
70 answer it this way, looking back, was that there was such
71 heavy firing in particular areas that it was in the interests
72 of saving life that this message of mine was sent.
73 C: What I am suggesting to you is that you had information
74 or means of information that this mob had burned and
75 petrol bombed Catholic property and Catholic people.

Note that in Excerpt 7 the participants use different terms to refer to the same group of people. In line 54 the witness refers to "a crowd of people," thus reformulating the Counselor's "Protestant mob." The transcript also shows the witness anticipating, by the nature of the counsel's questions, the accusation that the Counselor is leading up to (and eventually produces in lines 73–5). The witness produces a pre-emptive denial prior to its production (lines 69–72) (Atkinson and Drew, 1979, pp. 111–12).

Note also that the verb "standing" in the witness's log (quoted in line 45 in Excerpt 6 above) has now been reformulated as "attempting to burst into Divis Street" (lines 51–2). This reformulation portrays an out of control mob on the attack rather than a group of people merely standing in the street. This reformulation is a considerable upgrade of the severity of the situation. In the witness's response (lines 53–4) he counters this formulation with a reformulation which downgrades the severity of the situation, referring to "a crowd of people there" rather than a "mob bursting."

The terms used to refer to locations were used by the Counsel to prospectively manage the accusation, by a step-wise process of first getting the witness to identify specific streets and locations that crowds were on or moving along, then to identify the religious make-up of the crowd from their location, and eventually implying that the witness's actions must have been based on their knowledge of which group of residents were located on which streets (Atkinson and Drew, 1979). Both the attorneys and the witnesses use formulations and reformulations to support their interpretation of the facts.

Hostile witness's evasive actions

The Iran-Contra hearings were held in the mid-1980s to investigate a scandal that occurred during the Reagan Presidency. Briefly, the administration was accused of violating laws by trading arms for hostages and selling weapons to a nation that was categorized as terrorist, as well as violating U.S. laws prohibiting military assistance to the "Contra" rebels which were fighting against the Sandinista government in Nicaragua [see Lynch and Bogen (1996) for more details]. These televised public hearings were watched by a large audience. Lynch and Bogen's (1996) analysis of the videotapes of the Iran-Contra hearings reveals techniques used by witnesses to evade answers to questions.

In the excerpts from the hearings below, Lt. Colonel Oliver North is being interrogated by Mr. Nields. The goal of this interrogation is to reveal the culpability of Mr. North and others in the Iran-Contra affair. The excerpt shows Mr. Nields using a variety of techniques to get Mr. North to reveal information about the Iran-Contra affair and his role in it. As in the excerpts from the trials and tribunals analyzed above, the person being interrogated uses several techniques to resist the interrogation.

A major contentious issue in these hearings was whether, and if so to what extent, Mr. North shredded documents in an effort to hide the misconduct of himself and others. Excerpt 8 begins with Mr. Nields constructing a yes or no question about the shredding of documents, which is an implied accusation that North falsely claims not to remember specific documents (Lynch and Bogen, 1996, p. 41). In the transcript excerpts "NI" refers to Mr. Nields and "NO" refers to Mr. North.

Excerpt 8: Lynch and Bogen (1996, pp. 21–2)

1	NI:	Well that's the whole reason for shredding documents, isn't it,
2		Colonel North, so that you can later say you don't remember. (0.4)
3		whether you had 'em, and you don't remember what's in 'em.
4	NO:	No. Mister Nields, the reason for shredding documents, and the
5		reason the Government of the United States gave me a shredder, I
6		mean I didn't buy it myself, was to destroy documents that were no
7		longer relevant, that did not apply or that should not be divulged.
8		And again I want to go back to the whole intent of the covert
9		operation. Part of (in- eh) a covert operation is to offer plausible
10		deniability of the association of the government of the United States
11		with the activity, part of it is to deceive our adversaries. Part of it is
12		to insure that those people who are at great peril, carrying out those
13		activities are not further endangered. All of those are good and

14	sufficient reasons to destroy documents. And that's why the
15	government buys shredders by the tens and dozens. And gives them
16	to people running covert operations. Not so that they can have
17	convenient memories. I came here to tell you the truth. To tell you::
18	and this committee, and the American people the truth, and I'm
19	trying to do that Mister Nields, °hh and I don't like the insinuation
20	that I'm up here having a convenient memory lapse, like perhaps
21	some others have had.

Mr. North's response to Mr. Nields' question begins with "No." (line 4). While this sounds like a direct denial of the implied accusation, and is clearly "an answer to the question," Mr. North then appends an explanation to his answer (lines 4–7), which contradicts the assumptions in Mr. Nield's question as to the purpose of shredding documents. He then appends a second explanation to his answer (lines 8–17), in which he lists a number of "good and sufficient" reasons for shredding documents. Finally, Mr. North produces a counter-accusation in which he complains about Mr. Nield's "insinuation" that he was lying ("a convenient memory lapse"; lines 19–21).

This extended turn goes far beyond merely answering the question, and works successfully to evade the implied accusation in Mr. Nields' question. However, as Excerpt 9 illustrates, Mr. Nields immediately continues the interrogation by producing another question (lines 22–3), thus declining to respond to Mr. North's counter-accusation. In the continuation of the interrogation, Mr. Nields asks about the shredding of "these documents" (not just documents in general, but these specific documents). Excerpt 9 also shows Mr. North evading answering questions and evading the implied accusations underlying those questions.

Excerpt 9: Lynch and Bogen (1996, p. 22)

19		… trying to do that Mister Nields, °hh and I don't like the insinuation
20		that I'm up here having a convenient memory lapse, like perhaps
21		some others have had.
22	NI:	Colonel North, you shredded these documents on the Twenty-first
23		of November, Nineteen-eighty-six, isn't that true?
24		(1.2)
25	NO:	Try me again on the date.
26		(1.0)
27	NI:	Friday, the Twenty-first of November, Nineteen-eighty-six.
28		(1.8)
29	NO:	I started shredding documents as early as:: uh my return from Europe
30		in October
31		(0.4)
32	NO:	I have absolutely no recollection (0.2) when those documents were
33		des- were shredded. None whatsoever.=

Instead of answering the question, Mr. North first pauses and then initiates an other-repair of the date (line 25). Asking for a repeat of the question may work to highlight for the record (and the overhearing audience) that it is hard to remember what happened on a specific date. Mr. Nields then repeats the date (line 27). In Mr. North's response he first conveys that shredding happened over a period of time (lines 29–30), and then denies that he remembers when "those documents" were shredded (lines 32–3). He has thus evaded answering the question about whether specific documents were shredded on a particular date, while providing an account for why he does not remember when he shredded them.

Mr. North uses **extreme case formulations** (Pomerantz, 1986) to emphatically convey his position in lines 32 and 33. Extreme case formulations are one technique commonly used to persuade others in adversarial situations. They are words or phrases which present a situation as at the most extreme it could be portrayed at (Drew, 2003; Edwards, 2000; McCarthy and Carter, 2004; Pomerantz, 1986). Pomerantz (1986, p. 219) gives "forever," "everyone," "completely innocent," "brand new," and "he was driving perfectly," as examples of extreme case formulations. Extreme case formulations have been shown to be persuasive techniques in a range of institutional settings, including testimony at hearings (e.g. Sidnell, 2004), televised political debates (e.g. Iñigo-Mora, 2007), counseling sessions (e.g. Edwards, 2000), and small claims court hearings (e.g. Pomerantz,1986).

The examples in this section reveal that witnesses in Congressional hearings have more latitude to shape their answers than witnesses in a typical courtroom typically do. Mr. North was therefore able to marshal a wide range of techniques in his defense and in order to evade communicating information requested by the interrogators.

Interrogating the friendly witness

The excerpts above address the interrogation of "hostile" witnesses—when the interrogator and the witness are on opposing sides of the dispute. We will now review Lynch and Bogen's (1996) discussion of the interrogation of a "friendly" witness. In these excerpts, Mr. North is interrogated by Mr. Van Cleve, who is working to support Mr. North's construction of the facts and his justifications for his actions.

Lynch and Bogen (1996) note that in Excerpt 10 Mr. Van Cleve apologizes in advance for asking "painful" questions (lines 1 and 2). By repeatedly characterizing Mr. North's actions in a variety of contexts as "lying," and getting him to agree with those characterizations, Mr. Van Cleve constructs an argument that "lying" was a routine part of Mr. North's job and that he had to lie in variety of contexts in order to achieve the goals he was hired to achieve. This line of questioning thus has the effect of showing that Mr. North's lying was not indicative of a character flaw, but was rather a routine and normal part of his job (Lynch and Bogen, 1996). By asking this series of questions, Mr. Van Cleve works to dispel any notion that Mr. North is not trustworthy because he has admitted lying in the past, by showing that those were necessary lies. For example, when Mr. North says "I lied every time I met the Iranians." (line 5) he turns a negative action into a positive action, by representing his actions as being in support of United States interests, rather than self-serving.

Excerpt 10: Lynch and Bogen (1996, pp. 37–8)

1 VC: Colonel North, I have the- what I regard is the personal and painful
2   task of asking you the following questions: You've admitted before
3   this committee that you lied to representatives of the Iranians in
4   order to try and release the hostages. Is that correct?
5 NO: I lied every time I met the Iranians.
6 VC: And, you've admitted that you lied to General Secord with respect to
7   conversations that you supposedly had with the President? Is that
8   correct?
9 NO: In order to encourage him to stay with the project, yes.
10 VC: And, you've admitted that you lied to the Congress. Is that correct?
11 NO: I have.
12 VC: And, you admitted that you lied in creating false chronologies
13   these events. Is that correct?
14 NO: That is correct.

After the series of questions which enables Mr. North to admit several times that he lied about a number of things, in Excerpt 11 Mr. Van Cleve next asks if Mr. North is lying now "to protect your Commander in Chief" (lines 24–5). Lynch and Bogen (1996, p. 41) note that Mr. Van Cleve produced this question in a deferential manner, thus making clear that he did not intend it as an accusation. Mr. North's answer to this question is "I am not lying to protect anybody" (line 26). Notice that he does not actually say that he is not lying.

Excerpt 11: Lynch and Bogen (1996, pp. 37–8)

20 VC: I think I understand the reason for your hesitation. You certainly
21   have admitted that the documents themselves were completely false.
22   Is that correct?
23 NO: That is correct.
24 VC: Can you assure this committee that you are not here now lying to
25   protect your Commander in Chief?
26 NO: I am not lying to protect anybody, counsel. I came here to tell the
27   truth. I told you that I was going to tell it to you, the good, the bad,
28   and the ugly. Some of it has been ugly for me. I don't know how
29   many other witnesses have gone through the ordeal that I have before
30   arriving here and seeing their names smeared all over the
31   newspapers, and by some members of this committee, but I
32   committed when I raised my right hand and took an oath as a
33   midshipman that I would tell the truth, and I have done so, painful
34   though it may be for me and for others. I have told you the truth,
35   counsel, as best I can.
36 VC: I have no further questions for this witness, Mr. Chairman.

These examples have illustrated how the interrogation of a friendly witness differs from the interrogation of a hostile witness. Instead of projecting an accusation to come, Mr. Van Cleve's questions project an interpretation that will exonerate the witness from blame for lying. The witness, instead of taking steps to evade the implication of the questions, directly answers them and cooperates with the interrogator in his construction of the facts rather than resisting him.

Summary

This discussion has addressed how attorneys and witnesses use a range of techniques to produce accusations and contest or avoid implications of blame. While in the context of legal proceedings the attorney has the institutional power, the witness is by no means without means to exert control over the process. Witnesses in these excerpts were able to resist the court's power by routine interactional techniques such as the production of implicit rejections to pre-empt accusations, reformulations of attorneys' construction of the facts, and resistance of constraints on how answers should be formulated. In Chapter 20 we will examine how interrogations are conducted in behind the scene legal proceedings, such as the police interrogation of suspects and pre-trial interviews of victims of crimes.

Student activity

Watch a favorite television show or movie which depicts scenes from a trial. How many of the techniques for constructing and evading accusations that were reviewed in this chapter you can identify in that fictionalized portrayal of a trial?

Recommended sources

Atkinson, J. Maxwell and Drew, Paul. (1979), *Order in Court: The Organisation of Verbal Interaction in Judicial Settings.* London: MacMillan Press.

Sidnell, Jack. (2004), 'There's risks in everything: extreme case formulations and accountability in inquiry testimony. *Discourse & Society,* 15, (6), 745–66.

21 Behind the Scenes Interrogations in Institutional Context

Chapter contents

Introduction

As we saw in several earlier chapters, interviewing or interrogating may be done in a wide range of institutional contexts. The interrogative series in an emergency services call is a type of interrogation, in which the call taker asks a series of questions of the caller in order to obtain the information necessary to provide service. In medical consultations, doctors may conduct diagnostic interviews, in which they ask a series of questions in order to narrow down the possible causes of patients' symptoms. In Chapter 20 we considered how interrogations are done in public legal proceedings such as trials, hearings and tribunals. In this chapter we will contrast those types of public interrogations with legal proceedings which are conducted behind the scenes. We will examine police interrogation of suspects and pre-trial interviews of victims of crimes to show how the techniques and practices of interrogation differ depending on the institutional context, the social roles of the participants, and the purpose of the interaction. We will examine how the interactional techniques used to conduct the interrogation differ in these different contexts. We will examine the techniques interrogators use to elicit information, as well as the techniques suspects and victims use to resist or subvert these attempts.

Police interrogation of suspects

Before trials occur there are a number of types of legal proceedings that may take place behind the scenes. One such proceeding is the police interrogation of suspects in an effort to obtain a confession. While this type of interrogation is similar to that in trials and other legal proceedings in that it consists primarily of a question/answer chain, the goals of the interaction, the setting and social roles of the participants are different. The interrogation is typically done in a private setting with the interrogator and the suspect: a witness to the interrogation and/or a recording of it are also routine. While in the trial testimony discussed in Chapter 20, the attorney's goal is to elicit information from the witness to persuade the overhearing judge and jury, in the interrogation of suspects of a crime, the goal of the interrogating officer is to persuade the suspect that he or she should confess. Watson's (1990) analysis of the police interrogation of a murder suspect provides some vivid examples of the techniques police officers may use to try to persuade suspects to confess. It also reveals some of the techniques suspects can use to resist such efforts. Watson's (1990) data are recordings of the interrogation of murder suspects.

The interrogation of a suspect with the goal of getting them to confess to a crime is a paradoxical type of interaction. On the face of it, it would seem that the suspect has nothing to gain from confessing, and would be motivated to avoid confessing at all costs. Legal persuasions such as plea bargaining deals can be a practical incentive that may lead a suspect to confess to a crime in exchange for a lighter sentence. However, if no plea bargain is on the table there is little to motivate a suspect to confess. What Watson's (1990) analysis showed is that there are interactional techniques officers can use to convince or persuade the suspect to confess. If the officer is able to convince the suspect that they have nothing to gain from not confessing, they may then choose to give the confession. Read through this excerpt from the interview, and then the detailed explanation below which is based on Watson's (1990) analysis of the persuasive techniques used in the interrogation. In these excerpts "O" is the police officer and "R" is Mr. Riley, the suspect who is being interrogated.

Excerpt 1: Watson (1990, pp. 289–90)
```
1   O:  I don'know you seem like a pretty smart fella t'me.
2       (3.4)
3   O:  Are you smart enough tuh reali:ze thet the:: (2.0) police here in the
4       homicide bureau'v uh (.) build u(.)p uh:: (0.6) case against you tih
5       the point, (1.4) where we feel yu- we gotcha;:: (0.6) nailed t'the
6       wal,
7   R:  Couldn' say nothing about dat (boh),
8       (0.4)
9   O:  Pard'n,
10  R:  't Ah couldn' say noth'n about dat.
11      (0.3)
12  O:  Well,
```

```
13        (6.0)
14   O:   We work very hard et ar |v job, (0.9) mghhm. (3.4) We've taken
15        statements::,
16        (1.0)
17  (R):  °(hhm.)°
18        (1.8)
19   O:   A:nd un in these statements we have information, (3.0) whur you
20        ev to:ld, (0.9) people, (1.0) whatchu did. (3.5) There's no rea'sn::
21        (.) fer me tuh believe et this ti:me, (1.4) thet the people who gave
22        iss this information were lying, (3.9) A:nd there's nothing in these
23        statements thet- would,hh (0.2) indicate tuh me, (.) thet they are
24        not the truth.
25        (2.2)
26   O:   Based on ar ow:n? (0.3) independent, (0.5) investigation. before
27        the statements:. (2.2) we 'ad information. (2.4) thetchu ed done
28        this. (2.5) we 'ad a description::, (1.0) of the fella who ran away
29        fr'm: (0.5) Hank Stebbins' place. (1.6) witha red leather ja:cket,
30        (2.0) we know thetchu:d ↓ borrowed fr', a ↓ friend…
((four lines of transcript omitted))
35        (0.2) We know thetchu gave the gun to Jaine tuh put in'er purse et
36        one time, (0.4) u~durin that da:y, (4.2) We have recovered,h (3.5)
37        a stereo:: (.) unit, (1.2) an' a tape, (1.4) recorder, (0.4) tha'we
38        know:, (0.4) came fr'm the apartment, (0.3) of Charley Dawson.
39        (2.0)
40   O:   No:w,
41        (5.0) ((door squeaking))
42   O:   I'm not trying to: (1.2) con you? (1.0) I'm only telling you the truth
43        If you:, (1.3) fer one moment:, (2.0) thought, (.) or noo: fr'm what I
44        toldju (0.3) that I wz trying tuh bluff you, (3.2) then you noo:, (.)
45        ur: you would know, thet we didn't have (.) anyting ↓ ahn you.
46   R:   Right, °(Mh)°
47        (0.2)
48   O:   But fr'm what I've to:ldju: (1.0) I wantchu tuh think about it keep
49        en open mi:nd,
```

Creating interactional dilemmas

One technique used by the officer is to construct utterances which leave Mr. Riley no defensible position to take. For example, in Excerpt 1, the Officer says "I don'know you seem like a pretty smart fella t'me." (line 1). This utterance presents Riley with the option of denying that he is smart, or agreeing that he is smart, but only at the risk of aligning himself with the officer's statement. Since the officer is clearly "not on his side," anything that Mr. Riley does that can be seen as aligning with him is potentially risky. Thus Mr. Riley's silence in line 2 is a reasonable strategy. In addition, since the officer has not yet asked a question, withholding a response until a question is asked is an accountable move in an interrogation.

The officer's next move, in lines 3–6, ties Mr. Riley's being smart to Mr. Riley's realizing that the police case against him is strong.

Excerpt 2: From Watson (1990, p. 289)
```
1   O:  I don'know you seem like a pretty smart fella t'me.
2       (3.4)
3   O:  Are you smart enough tuh reali:ze thet the:: (2.0) police here in the
4       homicide bureau'v uh (.) build u(.)p uh:: (0.6) case against you tih
5       the point, (1.4) where we feel yu- we gotcha;:: (0.6) nailed t'the
6       wal,
```

This question puts Mr. Riley in an untenable position. The question is designed to prefer a yes answer (Sacks, 1987a), and answering yes would allow Mr. Riley to agree that he is smart. However, he would also be admitting that the police case against him is strong. If he answered no, then he would be saying that he is not smart.

Resisting persuasive techniques

Mr. Riley's response to the officer's lines 3–6 cleverly sidesteps the dilemma created by the question. He responds by saying "Couldn' say nothing about dat (boh)," (line 7).

Excerpt 3: From Watson (1990, p. 289)
```
3   O:  Are you smart enough tuh reali:ze thet the:: (2.0) police here in the
4       homicide bureau'v uh (.) build u(.)p uh:: (0.6) case against you tih
5       the point, (1.4) where we feel yu- we gotcha;:: (0.6) nailed t'the
6       wal,
7   R:  Couldn' say nothing about dat (boh),
```

Given the choices presented by the officer's statement, claiming to not be able to say anything about it is a viable way of resisting the unacceptable implications of the officer's statement. This utterance enables Mr. Riley to avoid aligning with the officer's representation of the case they have against him, while at the same time avoid agreeing that he is not smart. Most importantly, he avoids the implication that he is guilty, which would arise if he did not say anything. His comment provides an account for his failure to answer the question.

Resisting the resistance

In his line 9, "Pard'n," the Officer initiates a repair of Mr. Riley's line 7.

Excerpt 4: Watson (1990, p. 289)
```
7    R:  Couldn' say nothing about dat (boh),
8        (0.4)
9    O:  Pard'n,
10   R:  't Ah couldn' say noth'n about dat.
```

While this could be a straightforward other-initiation of repair (perhaps the officer had trouble hearing Riley's line 7), it could also be a challenge of Riley's claim in line 7. The "Pard'n," in line 9 could indicate skepticism of Riley's knowledge claim (his claim that he "couldn't say"). It could also be an attempt to solicit a different type of response, rather than simply a repeat of the original response. However, Mr. Riley repeats his original answer more or less verbatim (line 10), thus declining an opportunity to elaborate on or change his answer.

In Excerpt 5, the officer's "Well," in line 12 is a disagreement-implicative response to Mr. Riley's claim, expressing skepticism of Riley's claim that he cannot say anything about it.

Excerpt 5: Watson (1990, p. 289)
```
10  R:    't Ah couldn' say noth'n about dat.
11        (0.3)
12  O:    Well,
13        (6.0)
```

By foreshadowing his disagreement with Riley's line 10, the officer displays his commitment to his claim that the police have a strong case against him, which he proceeds to demonstrate in this continued turn in lines 14–15 and 19–24.

Excerpt 6: Watson (1990, p. 289)
```
12  O:    Well,
13        (6.0)
14  O:    We work very hard et ar ↓ job, (0.9) mghhm. (3.4) We've taken
15        statements::,
16        (1.0)
17 (R):   °(hhm.)°
18        (1.8)
19  O:    A:nd un in these statements we have information, (3.0) whur you
20        ev to:ld, (0.9) people, (1.0) whatchu did. (3.5) There's no rea'sn::
21        (.) fer me tuh believe et this ti:me, (1.4) thet the people who gave
22        iss this information were lying, (3.9) A:nd there's nothing in these
23        statements thet- would,hh (0.2) indicate tuh me, (.) thet they are
24        not the truth.
```

"We work very hard et ar ↓ job," is a rebuttal of Mr. Riley's implied rejection of the claim that the case is strong. The officer claims that the information was obtained through hard work. When the officer says "we've taken statements" (lines 14–15) he is using a police jargon term to refer to the practice of talking to witnesses and writing down what they have said. Using the police term "taking statements" makes this process seem more objective than if the information were obtained through an informal conversation. The officer is making a case for his case by displaying the nature of the evidence and how it was obtained in order to strengthen its credibility. The officer characterizes the informants' statements as "information" (line 19); the word information has a higher claim to truth than merely repeating gossip or hearsay. The officer's characterization of the methods used to obtain the information as professional procedures rather than informal interactions buttresses his claim to knowledge of the facts.

The officer's turn anticipates and answers in advance several defenses that Riley might make. For example, the officer pre-empts a potential counter-claim that the officer's sources of information were unreliable by stating that the people they took statements from were telling the truth (lines 20–4).

In addition, note that the officer does not produce a direct accusation of Mr. Riley at this point. At this point in the exchange, the accusation is implied by the statements they have collected from the informants. Because the accusation is indirect, Mr. Riley does not have to respond to it immediately. A direct accusation is an adjacency pair first pair part, which would have an immediate denial as its second pair part. The officer does not want Mr. Riley to deny the accusation at this point in the interrogation. Once some one has committed themself to a position, it is typically harder for them to back down or reverse that position (Clayman, 1985).

Excerpt 7: Watson (1990, p. 290)

```
26  O:   Based on ar ow:n? (0.3) independent, (0.5) investigation. before
27       the statements:. (2.2) we 'ad information. (2.4) thetchu ed done
28       this. (2.5) we 'ad a description::, (1.0) of the fella who ran away
29       fr'm: (0.5) Hank Stebbins' place. (1.6) witha red leather ja:cket,
30       (2.0) we know thetchu:d ↓ borrowed fr', a ↓ friend….
((four lines of transcript omitted))
35       We know thetchu gave the gun to Jaine tuh put in'er purse et
36       one time, (0.4) u~durin that da:y, (4.2) We have recovered,h (3.5)
37       a stereo:: (.) unit, (1.2) an' a tape, (1.4) recorder, (0.4) tha'we
38     ʸ know:, (0.4) came fr'm the apartment, (0.3) of Charley Dawson.
```

Buttressing a position

In his extended turn the officer uses several techniques to present his case in the strongest possible light. In lines 26–8 the officer makes a distinction between the police's "own independent investigation" (line 26) and the "statements" they have collected from others. He makes clear that these are two separate sources of information which support and reinforce each other's findings. He notes that they did the independent investigation first (to show that their investigation was not biased by the statements made by others). Note that the officer uses specific terms to characterize what the police have learned from their investigation as facts rather than beliefs or guesses. For example, he uses the terms "information" and "description" rather than "claims."

In lines 28–9, the officer says "the fella who ran away fr'm:… with a red leather jacket." Note that he does not say "you ran away", he says "the fella who ran away." If the officer had said "you ran away" it would constitute a direct accusation. Since the preferred response to an accusation is a denial, Mr. Riley would have been under pressure to produce a denial at that point. As explained above, the officer does not want Mr. Riley to deny the accusation now, because that position, once taken, would be hard to back down from. The officer does not want to put Mr. Riley in a position of confirming or denying any accusations until he thinks Mr. Riley is ready to confess. The evidence about the jacket, the gun and the stolen goods are presented as independently arrived at facts, which are supported by the witnesses' statements. The independent nature of the source of information for these facts reinforces their strength.

In Excerpt 8 (line 42), the officer says "I'm not trying to: (1.2) con you? (1.0) I'm only telling you the truth." By making these truth claims, the officer works to pre-empt an accusation that he is lying.

Excerpt 8: Watson (1990, p. 290)

```
40  O:   No:w,
41       (5.0) ((door squeaking))
42  O:   I'm not trying to: (1.2) con you? (1.0) I'm only telling you the truth
43       If you:, (1.3) fer one moment:, (2.0) thought, (.) or noo: fr'm what I
44       toldju (0.3) that I wz trying tuh bluff you, (3.2) then you noo:, (.)
45       ur: you would know, thet we didn't have (.) anyting ⊡ ahn you.
46  R:   Right, °(Mh)°
47       (0.2)
48  O:   But fr'm what I've to:ldju: (1.0) I wantchu tuh think about it keep
49       en open mi:nd,
```

Knowledge claims

The participants in an interrogation are engaged in a contest over what the facts are. Each side may use different interactional techniques to make and support "knowledge claims;" their reasons for knowing and believing a fact. Watson (1990) outlines several procedures police use to construct knowledge claims in the interrogation of suspects. For example, in line 30 from Excerpt 7, the officer prefaces a statement with "we know" rather than saying something like "we believe." With "we know" the officer conveys an impression of certainty about the information he is conveying: "the policeman's presentation of his claims as *knowledge* rather than supposition work to "establish" the facticity of his version or reconstruction" (Watson, 1990, p. 266). In addition, by providing contrasting characterizations for his account (for example, "the truth" vs. "a con"; line 42 in Excerpt 8), the officer both claims facticity for his version of the facts and preemptively buttresses it against a potential future accusation by the suspect that he is lying (Watson, 1990, p. 269). The police officer's statements are thus constructed to forestall both denials and counter-arguments on the part of the suspect (Watson, 1990, p. 267).

Listener responses

Watson (1990) notes that suspects typically refrain from producing minimal responses during interrogations. Like the interviewees in televised news interviews, and the witnesses interrogated by attorneys in trials, producing listener responses might create the impression of aligning or agreeing with the questioner. In Excerpt 8 above, Mr. Riley avoids the risk of appearing to align with the interrogating officer by withholding listener responses. The question therefore becomes why, after withholding responses to the officer's utterances throughout the excerpt, does Mr. Riley produce a listener response at line 46 ["Right, °(Mh) °"]?. He has refrained from any response during the officer's extended turn which might be seen as affirming or aligning with the evidence the officer is portraying. In lines 42 to 45 the officer started out saying he was not trying to "con" Mr. Riley, and he ended up with "you would k<u>n</u>ow, thet we didn't <u>h</u>ave (.) anyting ↓ ahn you." Sacks' (1992a) observed that there is a preference for contiguity. If a speaker produces two different actions in their turn, the next speaker tends to respond to the most recent action first—the one that is contiguous with it. So when Mr. Riley responds at the point he does, he may be displaying alignment with the last part of the officer's utterance "you would k<u>n</u>ow, thet we didn't <u>h</u>ave (.) anyting ↓ ahn you."

Watson (1990, p. 272) also points out that the murder suspect's confession, when it is eventually produced, is not just a simple statement of responsibility (e.g., "I just did it"), but a story explaining the details of how, when and why it was done. Because of this, the officer takes care not to elicit a simple admittance of guilt, but to get the suspect to tell a story in which he provides an explanation of the crime. As the "inviter" of this story, the police officer can shape the story in several ways, for example by the type of solicit used and by questions produced during the story to request clarifications or elaborations. Watson (1990) argues that because these stories are invited rather than volunteered, the recipient of the story (the police officer) has more control over its production than when a suspect offers to tell their story.

This discussion of Watson's (1990) analysis of police interrogations has shown that interrogating someone who is not motivated to cooperate with you is a different interactional process than interrogating someone who is cooperating (such as the "friendly" witnesses discussed in Chapter 20, the doctors' questioning of their patients discussed in Chapters 18 and 19, or the callers to emergency services discussed in Chapter 14). In the police interrogation of a suspect, the officer cannot just ask questions and expect them to be answered. They have to work to create an interactional context in which the suspect can be persuaded that there is nothing to be gained from not answering them.

Pre-trial interrogation of victims

As the analysis of excerpts from legal proceedings in Chapter 20 has shown, the interrogation of "friendly" witnesses is actually quite different from the interrogation of "hostile" witnesses. Both of these types of interrogations may have the same superficial structure—a question/answer chain. However, the purpose of the exchange and the techniques used to construct the questions are actually quite different.

When victims of crimes are interviewed prior to trial in order to get information that may help attorneys in the preparation of their cases, the relationship between the interviewer and the interviewee is quite different from the relationship between the officers and the suspects they interrogate. When the victims (or potential victims) are children, the nature of the interaction is even more sensitive.

Lloyd (1992) conducted research on a case that occurred a number of years ago. Staff members at a private preschool were accused of sexually abusing children during the school day. Because of the sensitivity of interviewing young children about these topics, therapists were hired to conduct the interrogations and were instructed to take care to protect the emotional state of the children during the interviews. The therapists used anatomically correct dolls to assist the children in reporting events that had happened, and worked hard to conduct the interviews in a friendly and nonthreatening way. The therapists used euphemisms the children had used to talk about the different types of abuse "games" that the staff members are alleged to have played with the children. The adult therapist interrogators also complimented the children when they gave a positive answer—an answer that indicated that abuse had occurred. On other occasions, when the child denied abuse occurred, the child was not complimented on their response, and instead was often asked the question again until they produced a positive answer.

The value of these interviews as evidence became controversial because the same techniques used to be sensitive to the childrens' emotions also detracted from their value in eliciting the facts of the case. Ultimately, their value as evidence was challenged. For example, in order to avoid requiring the children to make potentially embarrassing statements, the therapists deliberately asked "leading questions." In addition, at times they appeared to pressure the children to agree to claims of abuse. These actions were justified on the basis that the children would be too embarrassed to admit the truth unless the adult they were talking to showed that they really wanted to hear it. The therapists believed that the children needed the reassurance that others believed the events had happened in order for them to be able to admit it. The therapists would thus at times tell them that other children had said that certain things had happened. The therapist thus engaged in the production of the information to a much greater extent than in is typically allowable in legal proceedings.

We will now examine one of the excerpts from these interviews to see what interactional techniques were used to obtain information from the children while at the same time protecting them from embarrassment or anxiety. These interviews took place several years after the children were attending the school, so the children were between five and ten years old at the time of the interviews (Lloyd, 1992, p. 111).

In Excerpt 9 the therapist asks the child about problematic behavior in lines 1–2. The child produces a negative response in line 3. Instead of accepting the child's response, the therapist initiates an other-repair (line 4). The child again produces a negative response (line 5). The therapist responds by producing a third repair initiator ("No?" in line 6), followed by a question which specifies one adult in particular. The child's answer to this question is ambiguous ("Umm." in line 7). As the interaction continues, the most definite response the therapist receives is the "I think sometimes.", the child produces in line 13.

Excerpt 9: Lloyd (1992, pp. 115–16)
((Nathan and an adult discuss adults who may have touched kids, including Dave. Adult treats Nathan as animating the Houndy puppet.))

1 A: How about any of the other adults, did any of them
2   touch the kids?
3 C: No.
4 A: No? Not even sometimes?
5 C: No.
6 A: No? How about when Dave played with you.
7 C: Umm.
8 A: I went and got a doll.
9 C: When Dave played with me, no.
10 A: Yeah. No? Dave never touched the kids, Houndy?
11 C: Well
12 A: Just sometimes?
13 C: I think sometimes.

In the child abuse interviews Lloyd analyzes, the child witnesses were interviewed in a manner appropriate to their ages, by being allowed to use toys to communicate, to be imprecise and vague in their answers, and to have the burden of articulating painful information put on the therapist rather than the children. In addition, the typical legal procedures of collecting evidence were adjusted, to allow leading questions, compliments of the witnesses, and pursuit of answers to enable the children to produce the problematic information. However, Lloyd (1992) argues that each of these techniques could also be seen to contaminate the evidence, by not making clear what information was produced by the therapist and what by the children, and by the therapist appearing to lead the children to produce positive rather than negative answers to the questions.

Summary

The interactional organization of interrogations differ greatly depending on the interactional context they occur within, because participants make different choices about how to formulate and position their actions. What an interrogation is, and what form it takes, depends on who is being interrogated, and why.

Student activity

Other than legal proceedings, in what other types of interactions are persuasive and evasive techniques such as the ones described above likely to be used? Can you find an example of one of them being used in an ordinary conversation?

Recommended sources

Manzo, John F. (1996), 'Taking turns and taking sides: opening scenes from two jury deliberations', *Social Psychology Quarterly*, 59, (2), 107–25.

Maynard, Douglas W. (1984), *Inside Plea Bargaining: The Language of Negotiation*. New York and London: Plenum Press.

Maynard, Douglas W. and Manzo, John F. (1993), 'On the sociology of justice: theoretical notes from an actual jury deliberation', *Sociological Theory*, 11, (2), 171–93.

Talk in Mediation Sessions

22

Introduction

Mediation is an alternative dispute resolution procedure in which a neutral third party acts as a facilitator to help disputing parties resolve their disagreement and come up with a solution that is acceptable to both. The goals of mediation include avoiding the adversarial relationship that can be fostered between disputants in legal procedures, and facilitating autonomy and self-determination as the disputants work to resolve their dispute. Mediation is used to resolve a wide range of disputes, including divorce and family, small claims, landlord/tenant, and neighborhood and community issues. Because the participants, goals and institutional context of mediation are different from those in the legal proceedings discussed in Chapters 20 and 21, the interactional organization of mediation sessions is consequently different as well.

In this chapter we will first examine how arguing is done in ordinary conversation, in order to be able to understand why mediation is a useful method of dispute resolution for people who have not been able to resolve their disagreement. We will show how the interactional organization of mediation sessions facilitates dispute resolution while minimizing non-productive arguing. One of the main challenges for mediators is how to do the work of facilitating the session while maintaining neutrality and impartiality in how they treat the disputants and the issues under dispute. We will examine how this work is done, and look at some examples where mediators failed to achieve a neutral stance in the session.

Arguing in ordinary conversation

In order to understand how mediation minimizes arguing, we will begin by examining how arguing is done in ordinary conversation. Arguing consists of adjacently placed oppositional utterances which tend not to be mitigated. While in ordinary conversation, disagreements are typically mitigated by the use of dispreferred turn formats (as described in Chapter 6), when arguing occurs disagreements may be placed immediately rather than delayed, formulated directly, and produced without (or at least before) any accounts or explanations which might mitigate their face-threatening impact.

Excerpt 1 shows an argument between a parent and her child. This excerpt is from an informal interaction videotaped for a British reality television program about parenting children with behavioral difficulties (McIlvenny, 2009). McIlvenny (2009) reports that before the excerpt began, Isabel (the mother) had been having difficulty getting her son Joshua dressed. When Isabel directs her son Joshua to "stop being nasty… and aggressive with people" (lines 52 and 56), Joshua responds with a threat (line 58). This is an example of an argumentative response. Isabel responds to Joshua's threat with an oppositional utterance using format tying (Goodwin and Goodwin, 1987); repeating aspects of his utterance (line 59). The mother and her child continue to exchange oppositional turns for the rest of the excerpt.

> Excerpt 1: McIlvenny (2009, p. 2023)
> 52 I: STO:p bei:ng NA:sty:
> 53 J: NGHHHH
> 54   (camera switches shot)
> 55   Joshua leans back slightly
> 56 I: and aggre:ssive with people.
> 57   (camera switches shot)
> 58 J: i'll punch yer
> 59 I: YOU WILL NO:T PU:NCH ME:
> 60 J: i will?
> 61 I: YOU WILL NO:T
> 62 J: i WILL ((Joshua turns away))

While we might expect this type of argument when a child is involved, arguments between adults can have a very similar structure when there is a high level of conflict between the participants and the argument has escalated. Excerpt 2 shows two adults using similar techniques to construct their argument.

> Excerpt 2: Garcia (1991, p. 820)
> 1   Dan: I want to talk to you (   )=

```
2   Mary:                              =I DI:DN'T: (0.3) HAVE ANY
3                THING.=
4   Dan:    YOU HAD (RIGHT) TO DO WITH=IT!
5   Dan:    [(YOU ARE ALWAYS)]
6   Mary:   [YOU KNOW THAT IS] BULL I DIDN'T
7   Dan:    [YOU ALLOWED IT]
8   Mary:   [(  see it          )] I DIDN'T EVEN DO THAT CRAP I
9                DIDN'T SEE THAT.
```

While arguments and disagreements between adults are typically much less heated than the one excerpted above, this example serves to illustrate how disagreements can escalate into heated arguments. This type of interaction does not facilitate cooperation and understanding between the parties. The advantage of mediation for disputing parties is that they can rely on the mediators to facilitate the session in such a way that escalated arguments do not emerge. We turn now to a discussion of how that is accomplished.

The interactional organization of mediation sessions

Mediation is an alternative dispute resolution procedure in which a third party (or often a pair of co-mediators) facilitate an interaction between disputing parties to help them come to a mutually acceptable agreement. The interaction in mediation has some of the elements of the speech exchange system of ordinary conversation, but also some key differences. It is these differences which enable mediators to create an interactional context in which disputing parties can talk without escalating into argument. We will first examine the speech exchange system of mediation, and then explain how it minimizes arguing between disputing parties.

Recall from Chapter 5 that in ordinary conversation, turn taking is locally managed and all participants have equal rights to produce turns at talk, ask questions, introduce new topics, and so on. The interaction in mediation sessions at times approaches the structure of ordinary conversation, and differs markedly from the question/answer chains of which interactions in trials are constructed. However, the speech exchange system of mediation differs from ordinary conversation in several respects (Garcia, 1991). First, the turn taking system in mediation sessions is partly pre-allocated. Mediators open the session, explain the mediation process, introduce the participants, and then typically begin by soliciting one disputant to speak first. That disputant will either state their complaint or describe the problem they are having with the opposing disputant. This opening statement often has the structure of an extended story (Garcia, 2010).

Second, disputants typically wait until selected to speak by a mediator. In some mediation programs a more conversational format may emerge and will be tolerated by mediators unless arguing ensues. Mediators often ask disputants a series of questions after they have told their story. Mediators then give the opposing disputant a chance to respond. Disputants are typically not allowed to interrupt during another disputant's story. In some mediation programs disputants are expected to avoid addressing the opposing disputant directly, and may be sanctioned by mediators for doing so (Garcia, 1991). In other programs disputants are allowed to speak directly to each other, and a reasonable amount of arguing between the participants is allowed to occur without mediator intervention (Greatbatch and Dingwall, 1997).

Excerpt 3 is from a family mediation session in which two mediators (Mediator A and Mediator B) are facilitating a session between two fathers. "Ted" is married to "Dan's" ex-wife. The two men are in mediation to resolve problems around care and visitation arrangements for Dan's three children. As the excerpt begins, Dan is telling a story about Ted's behavior with his children. At the end of line 4, Dan's story reaches a possible turn completion. After a brief pause, Ted makes a comment ("°That's [not true at all°]"; line 6). Dan overlaps this turn to continue his story (lines 7 and 8). In line 9, Mediator A intervenes and sanctions Ted for his interruption (Mediator A's gaze direction as he produces this sanction indicates that it is Ted's utterance in line 6 which he found problematic).

However, note that Ted has not interrupted Dan. If this exchange had occurred in an ordinary conversation, the end of Dan's turn at line 4 would be a clear transition relevance place. However, in the speech exchange system of mediation, mediators can give the disputants the floor for longer than a single turn at talk. The opposing disputant may therefore be sanctioned for interrupting if they select themself to speak when they do not have the floor. This is one of the mechanisms by which mediation minimizes arguing between disputants (by eliminating opportunities for adjacently placed oppositional utterances).

Excerpt 3: Garcia (1991, p. 824)

1	Dan:	… the CHILDren coming ho::me and <u>him</u> (0.4) <u>ta:</u>king them into
2		the BA::throom, (0.4) and <u>looking</u> in their EYE:S!, because their:
3		<u>pupils</u> might be di=l=lated 'cause they've <u>had</u>=too=many- (0.1) <u>too</u>
4		much sugar from <u>milk</u>shakes that they <u>drink</u> in at my HOU:SE!
5		(0.2)
6	Ted:	°That's [not true at all°]
7	Dan:	[And=MY- M]Y KI:DS: (0.2) my <u>kids</u> have cry: (0.1)
8		cried over [that.]
9	MA:	[Excuse] me for inter<u>rupt</u> for <u>just</u>=a=minute.=I forgot to,
10		(0.1) mention, <u>one</u> of the GROU:ND ru:les!, (0.2) and that i:s
11		wehn- (0.2) <u>you're</u> telling your story, (0.7) you say <u>nothing</u>.

When accusations or complaints are produced in the context of an ordinary conversation, they are typically addressed directly to the target of the complaint. Denials of accusations are typically presented immediately and directly, using the format of a preferred second pair part. Note that this creates an adjacency pair with the components of arguing—adjacently placed oppositional utterances. This is how accusations and denials can be the source of an arguing segment in ordinary conversation.

But in mediation sessions accusations are typically formulated indirectly and produced in utterances directed at the mediators rather than at the opposing disputant. If the opposing disputant has to wait until solicited by the mediators to respond, the denial of the accusation is delayed. Accusations and denials therefore do not constitute adjacency pairs in mediation, and hence do not create an interactional environment for arguing.

In addition to having restricted rights as to when they can select themselves to speak, disputants in mediation sessions are often expected to address their remarks to the mediators rather than to the opposing disputant (see Greatbatch and Dingwall, [1997] for an example of a mediation program where direct interaction between disputants was routine). By addressing complaints and accusations to the mediators rather than directly to the opposing disputant, these interactional moves can be made in a way that does not provoke an immediate defensive or antagonistic response from the opposing disputant.

For example, in Excerpt 4 from a dispute between two neighbors over noise complaints and other issues, the disputant "Nancy" makes an accusation. Nancy describes an attack on her car and accuses the opposing disputant of responsibility for the vandalism. Note that she does this in an utterance directed to the mediators and that she refers to the opposing disputant with a third person pronoun or by her name ("she," "herself," and "Jane" in lines 10 and 11). The accusation is thus not a first pair part and does not create an expectation that the next thing in the interaction will be a denial of the accusation. In fact, Jane did not respond to this accusation until about 30 minutes later on in the mediation session. Because of the non-adjacency of her eventual denial, the denial was not an adjacently placed oppositional utterance, and hence did not initiate an arguing sequence.

Excerpt 4: Garcia (1991, p. 828)

```
1   N:    My car was vandali:zed!, hh (0.3) early in the mo::rning, (0.1) I
2         came ba:ck I was away (0.2) for the night (.) I came back, and
3         there was paint:, (0.6) on the interior?, (0.7) uh latex paint, (1.5)
4         garbag:e. (0.8) powdered milk. (0.4) I've got pictures of that=if-
5         (0.3) you'd like to see it.
6         (0.4)
7   MA:   °um=hmh.°
8         (0.2)
9   N:    °What looked like.° (2.1) A:::nd: the only conceivable person:
10        (0.3) that=it=could=do (0.4) that would be responsible whether she
11        did=it=or not herse:lf?, (0.1) would be Jane!,...
```

When disputants engage in arguing in mediation sessions, mediators will often take steps to stop the arguing. One method of doing so is a direct sanction. Another method mediators may use is to redirect the talk in another direction, as we see in Excerpt 5 from Greatbatch and Dingwall's (1997) analysis of divorce mediation sessions in Great

Britain. The disputants in this excerpt produce adjacently placed oppositional utterances. The arguing techniques they use include curses, accusations, format tying, and interruptions. In line 10 the mediator intervenes in the arguing sequence in by redirecting the conversation after a series of oppositional utterances which show signs of escalating levels of conflict.

Excerpt 5: Greatbatch and Dingwall (1997, p. 156)
```
 1  W:  =But there's lots of things you can do.=You don't have to
 2      just (0.6) sit i:n (0.5) in the flat or take them to the pub.=
 3      loads of things you can do:.
 4  H:  I take them to the pa::rk?
 5  W:  [(              )-
 6  H:  [I take them to the park a darn sight more than what you
 7      do.=
 8  W:  Yeah as long as there's pub you're [up there.
 9  H:                                     [O:h no:.
10  M1: What d'you think (.) what is it you fear is going to hap[pen.
```

Constructing mediator neutrality

Impartiality and self-determination are two of the key values of mediation that underlie the procedures used in most mediation programs (American Arbitration Association et al., 2005; see also Heisterkamp, 2006; Jacobs, 2002). Mediators are instructed to avoid siding with either of the disputants, to treat all disputants as equally as possible, and to avoid both actual bias and the appearance of bias. In this section we examine how mediators can create a neutral stance and also discuss some instances in which they failed to do so.

Treating Disputants Equally. Greatbatch and Dingwall (1999) found that if mediators direct advice or suggestions to one disputant, the other disputant may feel that they are being treated unfairly. The importance of treating both disputants equally is demonstrated in Excerpt 6. In this excerpt, which comes at the end of a long segment of mediator advice, the mediator recommends that the divorcing parents establish consistent times for the father's visits with the children. The father then repairs the mediator's suggestion, reminding her that the principle should apply to the children's mother as well (line 57, "Or mum.").

Excerpt 6: Greatbatch and Dingwall (1999, p. 281)
```
50  M1:  Well it's important that's what you need to work out between
51       yourselves. A new structure and new routine. And avoi:ding if
52       you ca[n
53  H:         [Mm
54       (1.1)
55  M1:  dad popping up at (.) unexpected moments. I think that's very
56       important.
```

```
57  H:      Or mum.
58  M1:     .hh Or mu[m
59  ?:                  [(      [      )
60  M1:     Or mum.
61  (M1):   hhuh
62          (.)
63  M1:     The same applies.
```

Representing Disputants' Positions. A major mediator technique for facilitating communication and understanding in the session is restating or rephrasing disputants' positions. This
can be done in a neutral way by simply paraphrasing the disputant's stated position. For
example, in Excerpt 7, from a mediation session between a divorced couple over care and
visitation arrangements for their three children, the mediator restates Dan's offer (not shown)
to give up two Thursdays a month of visitation with his children. The mediator paraphrases
Dan's offer (line 1) and also briefly summarizes Dan's justifications for the offer (lines 3 and
4). The mediator is able to maintain her stance of neutrality while restating this offer because
she makes it clear that it is Dan's position she is articulating. Note her use of the pronoun "he"
in line 1, and her reference to having gotten the information from him ("I heard") in line 3.

```
Excerpt 7: Garcia (1995, p. 32)
1   M:   And he is willing to give up two of those Thursdays.
2   J:   I know.
3   M:   Number one I heard it to make it consistent for the children, and
4        that that would please you!
5   R:   I'll just I'll do it, just to meet him half way,…
```

In Excerpt 8, from a mediation session in which two neighbors were in disagreement over
who should pay for some drainage work between the two properties, the mediator is not as
successful at maintaining a neutral stance while articulating a disputant's position. In this
instance, the mediator restates Chris' position, but does it in such a way that he goes beyond
animating Chris' stated position, and in effect replaces Chris in the subsequent negotiation
with the opposing disputant ("Rick"). The mediator does not just paraphrase Chris' position,
but creates new arguments in support of his position. This degree of engagement with one
disputant's position may create the impression that the mediator is biased in favor of that
disputant's position (Garcia, 1995).

```
Excerpt 8: Garcia (1995, p. 36)
1   Rick:  Damned for my troubles that I went through, and the money that I
2          paid the county to improve his property and getting the base rock
3          fill, and everything else, that he should compensate me for part of
4          my expenses.
5   MB:    Let's try to understand one thing, Mister Smith, the work and the
6          money that you expended in putting in this culvert, and actually
7          rescuing your property from destruction, you did it, for your sake.
```

8   Rick: I went with a compromise with the county,

9   MA: Yes.

10 MB: Yes.

11 Rick: That I would take my fences and they would accept the

12 MA: You went with the compromise with the county, not these folks.

13   You went there. You did it.

14 Rick: They wouldn't have done it,

15 MA: You decided it was worth it to you to do it, otherwise you wouldn't

16   [have   ]

17 Rick: [It's not] only to my advantage, though I'm protecting my

18   neighbor's advantage also.

19 MA: THAT is something you were giving your neighbors unwittingly.

20   You were between a rock and a hard place. I will agree! But you

21   can not, you could not have committed them to something they

22   didn't agree to. Now, if you feel that equity is on your side. Then

23   you can after the fact sue them for their share. If you feel that you

24   want to do arbitration on that you can do that. But we're talking

25   about something else here. Remember we defined the area. You

26   put five thousand dollars in there but that wasn't his statement of

27   the problem.

The following excerpt from Jacobs (2002) also shows a mediator crossing the bounds between neutrally representing a disputant's expressed position and articulating their own position regarding the issues under dispute. Jacobs (2002) analyzed a divorce mediation session in which one disputant felt the mediator was biased against him and decided to end the mediation (by walking out). The mediator in this instance started the mediation process with lengthy individual caucuses with both disputants, then brought them together and began the session. Shortly after that, they began discussing the problem of where the couple's son Jason was going to sleep when spending overnights at his father's house. The father states that the child will sleep in bed with him. The mediator's responses to the father's plan to have his young son sleep in his bed with him are initially ambiguous. Her initiation of other-repair in line 14 could be heard either as an attempt to verify that she has heard him correctly, and/or as a skeptical response to his plan which is disagreement-implicative. When the father justifies his plan to have his son sleep with him by claiming he does not have enough money to buy a crib, the mediator rejects that claim as an inadequate reason (lines 17–18). The mediator then goes on to restate the father's position (lines 20–1), but again, the end of her utterance is ambiguous as to whether she is beginning a challenge of his position. In lines 27 and 29 the mediator then challenges the father's claim that the child would not get out of bed in the morning until he was awake. Here the mediator is animating the mother's positions (e.g., "she says you're a heavy sleeper."). Up until this point, although the mediator has challenged the father on several points, her challenges have either been ambiguous (potentially neutral responses) or clearly marked as animations of the mother's position. However, this changes in the next segment when the mediator discovers that the father plans to have his son sleep in the bed with him and his girlfriend ("Kathy") when she stays over night as well. The mediator's response to this plan is to express disagreement directly (lines 43–5). She formulates this utterance as her own opinion, rather than restating the perspective of the mother. The father responds to the mediator's position by rejecting it and claiming that it is his right to decide where his son sleeps (lines 46–9). The argument between the mediator and the father continues, and after several more exchanges of turns the father walks out, thus ending the mediation session.

Excerpt 9: Jacobs (2002, pp. 1408–9)

```
11  M:  To give her some idea you know like where would Jason sleep
12      when you stay overnight?
13  H:  Probably sleep in my bed
14  M:  Probably sleep in your bed?
15  H:  Mhm with me (.) I don't I don't have the money to, go out and buy
16      him (  ) a crib. (.) Will you let me have yours?
17  M:  That's not really the point you know, because if you felt Jason
18      really needed a crib you'd find the money and you'd get the crib
19  H:  Mhm
20  M:  But you feel he doesn't need a crib and he does just as well
21      sleeping with me uh you know th[at's
22  H:                                 [Well she's afraid that in- in the
23      morning he'll get up and I won't get up with him (.) Jason wouldn't
24      get up and leave the room you know he wouldn't get up without me
25      knowing
26      ((pause))
27  M:  Why wouldn't he
28  H:  Cause I'd, wake up when he got up. [I must-
29  M:                                     [She says you're a heavy
30      sleeper
31  H:  I'm usually uh, I get up at six every day during the week, and I'm
32      usually up, just as early on the weekends (.) if I'm not- don't go out
33      partying with friends the night before, and when I have Jason I
34      don't party, I'm very (.) and when I pick up Kathy I don't go out
35      partying (  ) either
36      ((pause))
37  M:  Well if your girlfriend sleeps overnight then where is Jason going
38      to sleep
39  H:  Hmm
40  M:  What if your girlfriend sleeps overnight then where is Jason going
41      to sleep
42  H:  Uh they'll still sleep with me I guess
43  M:  I don't think it's a good idea having him sleep between you and
44      your girlfriend (.) that wouldn't be, that wouldn't be
45      [a good plan you ought to have another ] room for [him ]
46  H:  [Well I plan I'm gonna (          )]          [Now] listen,
47      Jason is my son. What I do with my son I think is my business, not
```

48   yours of course or anybody else's as long as he is taken care of,
49   he's, well who [does] but as long as, he's my son too

How Proposals are Formulated. While in many mediation programs, a mediator producing a suggestion for resolution of the dispute would be seen as contrary to the goal of disputant self-determination, in some programs mediators do occasionally make proposals. There is a variety of ways that mediators can contribute ideas to the dispute resolution process while working to maintain a neutral stance. For example, Garcia (1997) found that while disputant's suggestions for resolution of the dispute are constructed as "position reports," (they were seen to be committed to the solution they suggested), mediator's suggestions were typically formulated as "proposals," without expressing a commitment to the value of the proposed suggestion. In Excerpt 10, from a dispute from a divorced couple over visitation arrangements for their children, the mediator constructs her proposal as a suggestion rather than as a position report. She constructs her proposal as a question and explicitly requests a response from the disputant. There is some hesitation in her utterance as well as tentativeness in her tone of voice, both of which work to convey the mediator's lack of commitment to her proposal. These techniques enable the mediator to contribute to the idea-generation process in a constructive way without imposing her ideas on the disputants or pressuring them to accept her ideas. Notice that when Dan explains why he does not think the proposal would work (lines 8 to 23), the mediator readily accepts his explanation (line 24).

Excerpt 10: Garcia (1997, p. 227)
1   MB: Is it PO:Ssible then that- that tu:h, (0.2) if you:: A:Lternate
2   responsibility for com<u>plete</u> transportation, (0.3) for vi:sits? (0.1) In
3   o:ther wo:rds, if you're going to- (0.1) blun- (0.3) <u>one</u>=visit you:
4   (0.4) PICK them up, bring them ba::ck, (0.3) The next time you
5   pick them up, (0.2) and bring them back, (0.1) In other words (that
6   u:h) (1.0) O:NE (0.7) <u>one</u> parent, ih- in <u>each</u> visit will take assume
7   full responsibility for- (0.3) <u>go:</u>ing and <u>co:</u>ming? (0.4)
8   Dan: tch .h I: (0.2) I <u>think</u> tha:t, (0.3) that SOU:NDS good to ME:: bu:t
9   bu:t (0.1) loGI:Stically I don't think that can ha:ppen. (0.1) <u>Due</u>
10   to the fact, the <u>twi:ns</u> go to school in Arden. DURing the
11   SU:Mers, it has worked out fi:ne. (0.1)
12 MB: Um hmh=
13 Dan: =Because there's no:: (0.1) you [know]
14 MB: [Yeah.]
15   (0.1)
16 Dan: SCHE:dules and the twins will spend a couple weeks with <u>me::</u>,
17   and <u>like</u>wise Sharon. .hh (0.1) But during the schoo::l year, (0.2)
18   .h it is: it- just VE:ry difficult=and .hh it's- you know, it <u>is</u>
19   HARDship O:N me::, (0.4) and Helen to (0.4) go pick them up
20   after schoo:l, (0.3) You know? They spend the night=then drive
21   them all the way to ARden agai:n, (0.2) to drop them off to

22   schoo::l, .hh and then la:ter that afternoon to go
23   [pick them up again]
24 MB: [go back again   ] ye:ah.

In contrast, disputants' suggestions for resolution of the dispute are formulated as position reports, and display the disputant's commitment to the suggestion they are making. In Excerpt 11 Mary explains what she is willing to do (line 2) and what she'd like (lines 3 and 5).

Excerpt 11: Garcia (1997, pp. 225–6)
1   Mary: I just <u>see</u> a (0.1) <u>real</u> disharmony in (0.6) in them <u>be</u>ing there (0.3)
2   ha:lf ti:me. (1.4) And (1.5) I:'M (1.2) fully (0.2) uh- <u>willing</u> to
3   give him <u>any</u> time after school, till fi:ve thirty, I'd like them home
4   at <u>dinner</u> a::nd uhm tch FRIday to SATurday, <u>over</u> night is fi:ne.
5   But I'd like them home by Saturday e:vening.

These findings about how proposals are made in mediation sessions show how mediators can create a neutral stance toward the issues under dispute by formulating their ideas for resolution as proposals rather than position statements. Mediators thus display an orientation to the value of disputant self determination.

Summary

The interactional organization of mediation differs in several key ways from both ordinary conversation and from talk in other types of legal procedures. Instead of relying almost exclusively on question/answer chains, as we saw being done in trials and hearings in Chapter 19, the interaction in mediation session incorporates a variety of different formats and structures. Thus we may find parts of the session that are very conversational in nature, parts that consist primarily of question/answer sequences, and parts that consist of extended stories by disputants or monologues by mediators. These differences in interactional organization work to facilitate the process of helping disputants discuss and resolve their differences.

Student activity

1. Think of a time when you engaged in an argument with someone or observed two people arguing. List at least three things the participants could have done differently to de-escalate the argument and discuss the issues in a non-argumentative way.
2. Take a look at an argument scene in a fictional movie or play (for example Edward Albee's "Who's Afraid of Virginia Wolf?"). What are some techniques the participants used to engage in arguing? How did the arguing segments differ from parts of the show where they were not arguing?

Recommended sources

Burns, Stacy. (2001), ' "Think you blackest thoughts and darken them": judicial mediation of large money damage disputes', *Human Studies*, 24, (3), 227–49.

Edstrom, Anne. (2004), 'Expressions of disagreement by Venezuelans in conversation: Reconsidering the influence of culture', *Journal of Pragmatics*, 36, pp. 1499–518.

Greatbatch, David and Robert Dingwall. 1997, Argumentative talk in divorce mediation sessions. *American Sociological Review* 62: 151–70.

Heisterkamp, Brian L. 2006, "Taking the Footing of a Neutral Mediator," *Conflict Resolution Quarterly* 23(3): 301–15.

Jacobs, Scott. 2002, "Maintaining Neutrality in Dispute Mediation: Managing Disagreement while Managing not to Disagree." *Journal of Pragmatics* 34: 1403–26.

Stokoe, Elizabeth and Derek Edwards. (2007), ' "Black this, black that": racial insults and reported speech in neighbour complaints and police interrogations', *Discourse & Society*, 18, 337–72.

Williams, Ashley. (2005), 'Fighting words and challenging expectations: Language alternation and social roles in a family dispute', *Journal of Pragmatics*, 37, 317–28.

Part VI
Talk in Broadcast Media

23

Television News Interviews

Chapter contents

Introduction

In this chapter we will first examine the speech exchange system of television news interviews, and then explore how the work of interviewing is done. Since the purpose of television news interviews (to inform and entertain the viewing public and to explore important and often controversial news issues with invited guests) differs from that of ordinary conversations, the structure of the interaction and the procedures used to organize it will also differ.

The interactional organization of television news interviews

Opening television news interviews

The opening segment of television news interviews achieves multiple goals. It introduces the show, the participants and the topic of the interview (Clayman, 1991; Heritage et al., 1988). The opening segment can also convey to the audience whether the purpose of the interview is primarily informational, or whether it is to debate contrasting positions on the issue. What typically follows the opening is a story segment providing background information to set up the subject of the interview (Clayman, 1991). After the story segment the interviewer ("IR") introduces the interviewee(s) ("IE"), typically explaining who they are and what they have to contribute to the discussion of the topic (Clayman, 1991). The IR then opens the interview proper and begins the questioning of the IE. The IR also closes the interview at the end of the show (Greatbatch, 1988).

Turn taking in television news interviews

Heritage et al., (1988) and others note several ways in which the turn taking system of television news interviews differs from that of ordinary conversation. These seemingly small differences have significant implications for the nature of the talk that is produced in this setting (Clayman and Whalen, 1988/89; Heritage et al., 1988; Greatbatch, 1988). For example, while participants in ordinary conversation are not constrained in advance as to the types of turns they can produce or when they can speak, in television news interviews the IR produces the questions, and the IE typically restricts themself to providing answers to those questions (Heritage, et al., 1988; Greatbatch, 1986; 1988).

When IRs convey information in an utterance that is not a question, they typically format it as background information in support of a question rather than as a free-standing comment (Clayman and Whalen, 1988/89). In addition, "IRs avoid stating their opinions or evaluations of IEs' actions or responses and only support or challenge IE positions indirectly through the types of questions they ask" (Heritage et al., 1988, pp. 86–7). Similarly, when IE's turns stray beyond simply answering a question, they typically work to fit that information into a component of the answering turn.

Because IRs ask the questions, they control the topical agenda of the interview (Greatbatch, 1986, p. 441). However, as Greatbatch (1986) demonstrates, IEs can resist the IR's prerogative to set the topical agenda by making topic shifts either prior to or after answering a question. Turns in television news interviews are typically longer than in ordinary conversation because IRs often include background information in their questions, and IEs generally produce extended answers which include explanations and evidence (Heritage et al., 1988).

Another difference between ordinary conversation and television news interviews is that when one participant is talking the listener does not typically provide minimal responses (Greatbatch, 1988; Heritage et al., 1988; Heritage, 1985; Clayman and Whalen, 1988/89). The minimal responses or continuers and news receipts which occur commonly in ordinary conversation are regularly withheld by IEs. Change of state tokens such as "oh," (Heritage, 1998) and listener responses such as "I see," and "really" are also commonly withheld (Heritage et al., 1988; see also Heritage, 1985; Clayman and Whalen, 1988/89).

In Excerpt 1 the IR withholds listener responses to the IE's answer-in-progress. When the answer is complete, the IR uses probing questions to elicit further information from the IE.

In this excerpt from Heritage (1985) the interviewee, a British official, is being interviewed about a commission's report on tea prices.

Excerpt 1: (Heritage, 1985, pp. 108–9)

```
1   C:    What in fact happened was that in the course of last year,
2         .hh the price went up really very sharply, .hhh and-uh the blenders
3         did take advantage of this:-uh to obviously to raise their price to
4         retailers. (0.7) .hhh They haven't been so quick in reducing prices
5         when the world market prices come down. (0.3) .hh And so this
6         means that price in the sh- the prices in the shops have stayed up .hh
7         really rather higher than we'd like to see them.
8   Int:  So you-you're really accusing them of profiteering.
9   C:    .hhh No they're in business to make money that's perfectly
10        sensible.=We'r' also saying that-uh: .hh it's not a trade which is
11        competitive as we would like it.=Th're four (0.2) blenders which
12        have together eighty-five percent of the market .hhh and-uh we're not
13        saying they (.) move in concert or anything like that but we'd like the
14        trade to be a bit more competitive.=
15  Int:  =But you're giving them: a heavy instruction (.) as it were to (.)
16        reduce their prices.
17  C:    .hh What we're saying is we think that prices could come without the
18        blenders losing their profit margins that they had .hhh before the big
19        rise in prices last year.
```

In Excerpt 1 the IR is acting on behalf of the viewing audience, attempting to elicit information and perspectives that the IE may not be eager to articulate. Instead of providing a listener response during their turn, the IR will typically respond to the IE's answer in a neutral fashion while focusing on a newsworthy or dramatic aspect of their response in order to convey the upshot of the answer to the listening audience (Heritage, 1985).

As in the legal proceedings and interrogations discussed in Chapters 20 and 21, the relationship between the participants in televised news interviews is often an adversarial one. The IE is often in a position of defending their position and actions, and the IR, on behalf of

Table 23.1 Comparison of turn taking systems for tv news interviews and ordinary conversation

Ordinary Conversation	Televised News Interviews
1. Order of speakership free to vary	1. IR speaks first
2. Turn type free to vary	2. IRs ask questions, IEs produce answers
3. Topic free to vary	3. IRs determine topic of interview
4. Length of interaction free to vary	4. Specific length of show limits length of interaction
5. Turn exchange occurs at transition relevance places	5. Turn exchange occurs when question or answer is complete
6. Listeners may produce acknowledgment tokens or other listener responses	6. Listener responses typically withheld
7. Either party free to begin or end conversation	7. IR opens and closes the interview

the viewing audience, often challenges the IE to make statements that they may prefer not to make. This "information game" (Goffman, 1969) is often conducted through the details of how questions and answers are designed. In this section we will examine a variety of techniques that participants use in this information game. We will begin with a consideration of how IRs construct questions then then examine IEs techniques for answering questions.

Taking a neutral stance in television news interviews

Clayman (1988; 1992) explores how participants in television news interviews create an interaction in which the IR can present him or herself as taking a "neutral stance" regarding the IE and the IE's stated positions. Clayman (1992, p. 163) notes that journalists are supposed to be objective and "not allow their personal opinions to enter into the interviewing process; to the best of their ability, they are supposed to remain neutral as they interact with public figures." As in other ethnomethodological studies of work done in professional settings (e.g., Zimmerman's 1969 study of welfare workers), the issue is not whether the IE is actually neutral and unbiased in their beliefs or attitudes, but rather whether she or he takes a neutral "stance" in the interview. Regardless of what the IR's beliefs are, they can maintain a stance of neutrality if they and the other participants in the interview use the appropriate procedures to create that stance. Note that the IRs' neutral stance can only be maintained with the cooperation of the IE. IRs are motivated to maintain a neutral stance because it is one of the requirements of the job of journalists. IEs, on the other hand, may be motivated at times to challenge the neutral stance of the IR. The success of IRs in portraying a professionally appropriate neutral stance is therefore a product of the actions of both participants, not just their own actions.

Neutrality as an interactional achievement

While IRs display their neutrality constructing their utterances as questions, and restricting their use of statements and position-taking to the service of questioning, IEs assist the IR in their display of neutrality by refraining from responding to their statements until the question has been completed (Clayman, 1988; Greatbatch,1988). IEs also refrain from listener responses during the production of the statement, thus treating the IRs' turn as incomplete at that point. The statement is treated as a preliminary to a question rather than something that requires a response. Clayman (1988) describes how the withholding of responses to IR's preliminary statement helps construct the IR's stance of neutrality:

> The absence of talk by IEs is thus not a mere chance occurrence, and it has important implications for the collaborative nature of this form of neutrality. As a purely physical matter, IEs enable IRs to produce turns of this type by withholding speech. But in addition, they are in effect ratifying the

neutrality proposed by this turn structure. By declining to talk at relevant junctures, IEs exhibit an analysis of each successive statement as indeed the preliminary component of a not-yet-completed action. This has the effect of ratifying, if only in an implicit and provisional sense, their character as neutral question components. The questioning character of the resulting turn must therefore be regarded as the interactional achievement of both IRs and IEs, who collaborate to produce turns that are structured in this way. (Clayman, 1988, p. 480)

In Excerpt 2 the IE refrains from responding to a series of statements that the IR presents as preliminary to his question. Note that even though the IR's talk reaches what would be considered transition relevance places in an ordinary conversation at several points in the interaction (e.g., at the end of lines 2, 3, 6, and 10), the IE does not respond until the question has been completed in line 11 (Clayman, 1988; see also Greatbatch, 1988).

Excerpt 2: (Clayman, 1988, pp. 479–80) [Nightline 7/22/85: 4–5]
```
 1  IR:   As Peter Sharp said in that piece it is a lot easier to impose a state of
 2         emergency than it is to lift it.
 3         .hhh You still have the root cause when you lift it.
 4         And black leaders in that country have made it very clear that this kind of
 5         situation there's no way of stopping this kind of situation unless there is an
 6         end to apartheid.
 7         It seems to me that by doing this by eh imposing I guess this kind of
 8         repression you really set up uh system where you can do nothing it seems
 9         to me when you lift it except to change the system that exists there
10         (.) thuh basic system.
11         .hhhh Is that unfair?
12  IE:   I would think it's unfair what is being said...
```

Displaying a perspective

Clayman (1988) notes that IRs can display a stance of neutrality when displaying a perspective by following it with a question about that perspective, thus showing that it was produced in service of the question rather than being an attempt to take a position.

Excerpt 3: Clayman (1988, p. 478) [MacNeil/Lehrer 7/22/85a:2]
```
 1  IR:   Reports today are of course that the violence has continued
 2         What have you heard whether or not the state of emergency is in fact
 3         working
```

"Footing" shifts

Clayman (1988) notes that presenting questions as neutral becomes more problematic when questions are perceived as "hostile," e.g., by being accusatory, leading, or argumentative. When IEs make these types of complaints, IRs have a number of ways to defend themselves against them, including the claim that they were just asking a question. One way to avoid such accusations is to use a footing shift to produce a statement while distancing oneself from that statement:

Goffman observes that the terms "speaker" and "hearer" are too gross to capture the variety of ways that coparticipants may be engaged in an interaction over its course: these engagements amount to distinct interactional footings. Speakers, for example, may adopt a variety of footings in relation to their remarks. They do so through various "production formats" (1981: 45) that distinguish between the "animator," "author," and "principal" of what is said. The "animator" is the person who presently utters a sequence of words. The one who originated the position or point of view and perhaps also composed the specific words in which it is encoded is the "author." Finally, the "principal" is the person whose viewpoint is now being expressed in and through the spoken words. (Clayman, 1988, p. 482)

Excerpt 4 shows an IR using footing shifts to avoid taking responsibility for a potentially inflammatory statement. In line 4, he attributes the statement to "the critics" rather than claiming to be animating his own position. Controversial information and positions can by these means be presented to IEs without threatening the IR's neutral stance.

Excerpt 4: Clayman (1988, p. 482) [MacNeil/Lehrer 7/22/85a:5]
((The IE is the South African ambassador to the United States, and is explaining why the South African government recently imposed a state of emergency.))

```
1   IE:    … And we would just want to avoid any possible situation that might
2          lead to more violence.
3   IR:    Finally Mister Ambassador as you know
4          the critics say
5          that the purpose of the state of emergency the real
6          purpose of the state of emergency is to suppress political dissent.
           those who
7          are opposed to the apartheid government of South Africa. Is that so
8   IE:    I would have to take issue with the premise because…
```

However, just because IRs use a technique such as footing shifts to present their statements as neutral, does not mean these statements will be unchallenged by IEs. While IEs typically cooperate in the IR's construction of a neutral stance by treating the author of the statement as the same that the IR has presented, they can also challenge the IR's neutral stance. Treating the IR as the author of the statement is one technique for doing so (Clayman, 1988, pp. 484–5).

Clayman notes that footing shifts tend to be used when the interviewer is producing controversial opinion statements. Excerpt 5 below shows the IR first producing apparently innocuous "factual" information (lines 1–3) and then shifting his footing to attribute two statements to others ("It is s::aid…" in line 4 and "It is said by some people at thuh White House…" in line 7). The later two points contain criticisms.

Excerpt 5: Clayman (1992, p. 169) [Meet the Press 12/8/85: 18] (The IE here is Robert Dole, then Senate majority leader for the Republican party.)

```
1   IR    Senator, (0.5) uh: President Reagan's elected
2         thirteen months ago: an enormous landslide.
3         (0.8)
4         It is s::aid that his programs are in trouble,
5         though he seems to be terribly popular with
```

```
6          the American people. (0.6)
7          It is said by some people at thuh White House
8          we could get those programs through if only we
9          ha:d perhaps more: .hh effective leadership
10         on on thuh hill an' I [suppose] indirectly=
11  RD:              [hhhheh ]
12  IR:    =that might (0.5) relate t'you as well:. (0.6)
13         Uh whad d'you think thuh problem is really.
14         is=it (0.2) thuh leadership as it might be
15         claimed up on thuh hill, er is it thuh
16         programs themselves.
```

Interviewee's strategies for evading answering

Clayman (2001) found several ways that IEs avoid answering IR questions and IRs pursue answers in light of these evasions. Simply ignoring a question that an IE does not want to answer will not be an effective strategy, since it makes the IE's failure to respond visible. Clayman (2001) has described a variety of techniques IEs use to frame their responses as answering the question which we will review below.

Answering then elaborating

One technique for evading answering an IR's question is for the IE to begin their turn with a direct but brief answer to the question, and then elaborate the answer. The elaboration can be heard as relevant to an answer to the question because of its positioning and formulation as an explanation of that answer. IEs can use elaboration to distract attention from the nature of their answer or to shift the topic in a different direction. In Excerpt 6 the IE first briefly answers the question (line 4), and then begins an extended elaboration of their answer in which they put their own "spin" on the information.

```
Excerpt 6: Clayman (2001, p. 409) [US, 22 Feb. 1985, Nightline: South African State of Emergency]
1   IR:   tch .hh Are you willing (.) personally to renounce
2         the violence (.) in that country.
3         (0.6)
4   AB:   .hh Yes I will.
5         I mean I have said so on Saturday I was on a platform…
```

Reformulating the question

IEs can "reformulate" an IR's question in order to avoid having to answer problematic parts of the question while still framing their utterance as an "answer" (Clayman, 1993b). This procedure may enable the IE to avoid appearing evasive while obscuring the fact that the original question was not answered. The reformulation works to create a revised "frame" for the IE's answer by separating it from prior talk and paraphrasing or restating the question. The reformulated question thus becomes the context for the IE's answer, rather than the IR's version of the question. Of course, IRs can respond to IEs' attempts to evade answering and can use such techniques as reissuing the original question to get the IE to answer the original question (Clayman, 1993b). In Excerpt 7 from a debate between two candidates (Mr. Bensen and Mr. Quayle), Dan Quayle reformulates the IR's question in lines 18–22. He then answers the reformulated version of the question in line 21, and appends an elaboration to it (lines 21–32).

Excerpt 7: Clayman (1993b, pp. 162–3) [Lloyd Bentsen-Quayle Debate 10/5/88 0:30:28]

```
1   JRN:  Senator Quayle (.) in recent years thuh Reagan administration has
2         scaled back thee activities: of thee Occupational Safety and Health
3         Administration .hhh prompted in part by Vice President Bush's task
4         force on regulatory relief. .hhhh Thee uh budget for thee agency has
5         been cut by twenty percent, (0.2) and thuh number of inspections at
6         manufacturing plants .hhh has been reduced by thirty three percent.
7         .hhhh This's had a special effect in this area where many people work
8         in tuh meat packing industry, .hh which (.) has a far: higher rate of
9         serious injuries than almost any other injury, .hh a rate which appears
10        to've been rising: although we're not really su:re .hh bec=some- some
11        o'thuh lar:gest companies have allegedly been falsifying thuh reports.
12        .hhhh Would you:: uh (0.5) acknowledge to thuh hundreds of injured
13        and maimed people, (.) in Nebraska (.) Iowa: and elsewhere in thuh
14        midwest .hhh that in this case deregulation may have gone too far:,
15        and thuh government should reassert itself in protecting workers
16        rights
17        (0.8)
18  DQ:   .hhh Thuh premise of your question John: .hh is that somehow this
19        administration has been la::x. .hh in enforcement. .h of thee OSHA
20        regulations. .hh
21        And I disagree with that. (0.3) And
22        I'll tell ya why:. .hh If you wanna:
23        ask some business people. (1.2) that I talk to
24        periodically (0.8) they complain:. (1.2) about
25        th' tough enforcement (0.7) of this administration,
26        .hhh and furthermore, (0.6) lemme tellya this
27        for thuh record. (1.1) When we: have foun:d
28        violations in this administration. (1.0) there has not only been (0.5)
29        tough enforcement. (1.2) but there have been: thuh most severe:
30        penalties .hh thuh lar::gest penalties in thuh history. .hh (0.9) of thuh
31        Department of Labor (0.2) have been le::vied (0.2) when we- these
32        eh violations have been found…
```

Using "because" to introduce an answer

If an IR produces a "why" question, a IE can frame their response as an answer to the IR's question by beginning with "because." This frames what follows as the explanation that was requested by the question (Clayman, 2001, p. 411). In Excerpt 8 below from a television news interview with Ross Perot, who in 1992 became a candidate for president, the IE uses "because" as a device to present his turn as an answer to the question. He then goes on to do something other than answering it.

> Excerpt 8: Clayman (2001, p. 411) [US, 18 Sept. 1992, MacNeil/Lehrer: Perot]
> 1 IR: So why don't you go ahead and (.) say:
> 2   I'm (.) a candidate for pr[esident?
> 3 RP: [Because that's not (.)
> 4   where the organization is now.
> 5   Our organization (.) is to:tally focused on try:ing
> 6   to get both parties to do the job. (0.7) That's why.

Providing incomplete or hyper-complete responses

Clayman (2001) found that IEs can resist answering IRs' questions by both positive and negative approaches. A "negative" approach is constructed by providing less than a complete answer, and a "positive" approach is constructed by providing more information than was asked for. In Excerpt 9 from a television news interview, the Attorney General evades answering the IR's question by giving one word responses to the IR's questions (lines 10 and 15).

> Excerpt 9: Clayman (2001, p. 413) [US, Meet the Press, 24 Oct. 1993]
> 1 IR: … .hh Madam Attorney General you've testified this
> 2   week- u- in front of Congress abou:t .h violence
> 3   and television. .hhh And said that if the TV
> 4   industry didn't in effect clean itself up,
> 5   clean its act up, .hhh there may be government
> 6   intervention. Government regulation. (0.4)
> 7   Thuh New York Ti:mes in an editorial said that
> 8   (.) you embarked on a quote <dangerous embrace
> 9   of censorship.> (0.3) Didju?
> 10 IE: No.
> 11   (0.2)
> 12 IR: .hhhh Wha:t kind of government intervention
> 13   are you thinking about? Would you <u>ban</u>: programs
> 14   like NYPD: Law and Order, would you [uh:
> 15 IE: [No.
> 16   (.)
> 17 IR: W- Wh:at are we talking about.
> 18 IE: We're talkin about (.) <u>asking</u> the media
> 19   to <u>stop</u> talking (.) about what it promises
> 20   to do, and do it.

Excerpt 10 below illustrates what Clayman (2001) calls "positive resistance." The IE shifts topic in order to avoid a direct answer to IR's question. The question was about nuclear power waste disposal, but the IE's answer is about nuclear accidents.

Excerpt 10: Clayman (2001, p. 414) [US, 6 June 1985, Nightline: Nuclear Waste]
1 IR: Continuing our conversation now with Doctor Rosalyn Yalow.
2   Doctor Yalow uh- ehh lemme put it in very simple terms.
3   If it's doable, if it is: easily disposible, why don't we.
4   (1.0)
5 RY: Well frankly I cannot- (.) ANswer all these scientific
6   questions in one minute given to me. On the other
7   hand there was one horrible thing that happened tonight
8   that you have- .h in addition extended. .hh And that is
9   thuh NOtion that there is an increased incidence of
10   cancer associated with the Three Mile Island accident.

IR's counters to IE's evasive answers

Clayman (2001) found that regardless of the techniques IEs use to evade answers, there are always IR techniques that can be used to counter them. Romaniuk (2013) found that even when an IE produces a response that is recognizable as an answer, it is not always an answer to the question. She found that IRs use a variety of techniques to pursue an answer, including verbatim repeats of the question, repeats with variations (including emphasis or stress on key words) or even explicit sanctions for not answering the question that was asked.

Clayman (2001) notes that the IE in Excerpt 11 uses several techniques to avoid answering the IR's questions. The IR counters these evasive techniques by reissuing and revising his initial question in an attempt to elicit an answer from the IE. While the IR is not successful in these efforts, the fact that he has made them and the IE has repeatedly evaded them, is available to the viewing audience who can then form their own opinion of how forthcoming the IE is.

Excerpt 11: Clayman (2001, p. 415) [US, 12 March 1995 60 Minutes: Gulf War Syndrome]
1 JD: hh Our most th:orough (0.2) and careful efforts to
2   determine (.) whether chemical agents were us:ed in
3   the Gulf, (.) .hh lead us to conclu:de that there was
4   no: (.) w:idespread use of chemicals against U.S. troops.=
5 IR: =Was there any use.=Forget w[idespread. Was there any use.]
6 JD: [I- I do not belie:ve]
7   I do not believe there was any: o:ffensive use of chemical
8   agents by: .hh uh- Iraqi: (0.2) military: (.) troops.
9   Ther[e was not-
10 IR: [Was there any- any accidental use. Were our troops
11   exposed in any way:.
12   (0.4)
13 JD: .hhh Uh- I do not believe that our troops were:
14   expo:sed in any widespread way to: u[h: chemical
15 IR: [In any narrow
16   way.=In any way.

```
17  JD:   hh .hh The defense science board did an independent
18        study of this matter: .hh [and fou:nd in their judgement=
19  IR:                            [(        )
20  JD:   =that there was no:: confirmation .hh of chemical:
21        (0.2) weapon (0.2) widespread use: in the Gulf.
```

The techniques described in this chapter to construct IR neutrality and to construct and contest evasive answers are part of the routine work of participating in televised news interviews. However, these interactions do not always flow smoothly and unproblematically. We now turn to an examination of a televised news interview in which the participants departed from these routine methods of constructing their talk.

Problematic tv interviews: Conflict between IRs and IEs

Television news interviewers tread a fine line between adversarialness and neutrality (Clayman, 2002). The IR has a responsibility to challenge the IE, but there is a line that should not be crossed, and if it is crossed a perception of bias may be created (Emmertsen, 2007). During a television news interview from the 1980s, an IR was perceived by the public and the media to fail in his responsibility to maintain a stance of neutrality. This event occurred during a television news interview between the journalist Dan Rather and George Bush, who was then Vice President and was running for president. This nine-minute interview started out in a routine fashion, but gradually degenerated into an argument. Public opinion was strongly against Mr. Rather, with many feeling that his behavior during the interview was unprofessional (Clayman and Whalen, 1988/89). Vice President George Bush, on the other hand, probably benefitted politically from the event. He was able to counter his reputation as a relatively mild mannered personality by behaving in a way that made him seem strong and assertive. In Clayman and Whalen's (1988/89) analysis of this interview, they demonstrate how both parties contributed toward the nature of the interaction and showed how it transitioned from the structure of a televised news interview to that of an argument.

The interview began with a taped news segment in which Vice President Bush is criticized because Mr. Donald Gregg had continued to work in the White House even though he had been accused of involvement in the Iran-Contra affair. The opening phase of the interview directly follows this taped background report.

At first glance, the opening of this interview (Excerpt 12) closely follows the typical format of a television news interview. Mr. Rather opens the interview and asks the first question (lines 1–9). Vice President Bush waits for Mr. Rather to complete his question before speaking. When he does begin, he marks his response as an answer to the question by beginning with the word "because" (line 10). However, there are a number of ways in which

Vice President Bush's response goes far beyond just answering the question, and is in several ways a departure from the speech exchange system of television news interviews.

Clayman and Whalen (1988/89, p. 250) note that, "To the extent that Bush does not confine himself to simply answering the question, he has departed from the strict provisions of the interview turn taking system." Vice President Bush's opening turn goes far beyond just answering the question. Within this extended turn are several complaints and accusations (in lines 15–16, 19–23, 28–33), which are generally considered first pair parts of adjacency pairs.

Excerpt 12: Clayman and Whalen (1988/89, pp. 249) [Rather-Bush: 1–41]

```
 1   DR:   Mister Vice President, thank you for being with us
 2           tonigh:t, .hh Donald Gregg still serves as your
 3           trusted advisor, he was deeply involved in running
 4           arms to the Contras, 'n 'e didn't inform you. .hhh
 5           Now when President Reagan's (  ) trusted advisor:
 6           Admiral Poindexter: (  ) failed to inform HIM::,
 7           (  ) thuh President (  ) fired 'im. (  ) Why is
 8           Mister Gregg still:: (  ) inside thuh White House
 9           'n still a trusted advisor.
10   GB:   Because I have confidence in him, (  ) 'n because
11           this matter Dan:, as you well know:, 'n your editors
12           know:, has been looked at by .hh thee ten million
13           dollar study by thee: (.) Senate 'n thuh Hou:se, .hh
14           it's been looked at by thuh Tower Commission, .hh thuh
15           Rodriguez testimony thet you put on here, I jus' think
16           it's outrageous, because he was totally vindicated,
17           .hh swore under oath thet 'e never talked to me about
18           .hh thuh Contras, 'n yet this: (.) report you're
19           making which you told me:: er your people did, you
20           have a Mister Cohen thet works for you, .hh was gonna
21           be a political profile. .hh now if this is a political
22           profile fer an election, .hh uh: I have a very
23           different opinion ez to what one should be:. (d-)
24           Don Gregg w- worked for me:, .hh because I don't
25           think he's done anything wro:ng. .h an' I think if
26           'e ha:d, this exHAUStive examination, .hh that went
27           into: thet'd gone into by thuh Senate, (  ) 'n by thuh
28           House, (  ) would've showed it. (  ) And you've impugned
29           the: .hh eh my integrity by suggesting with one o'
30           your little boards here, .hh that I didn't tell thuh
31           truth w- bout what- what uh Felix Rodriguez. .h ya
32           didn't accuse me of it, (  ) but you made that
33           suggestion. and OTHer people in thuh media,=including
34           Mister Nick Brady, (  ) and HE 'as said thet- (.) my
35           (.) version is corre:ct, .hh and so I find this tuh
36           be ay rehash .hh and a li:ttle bit (.) if you'll excuse
```

37   me ay misrepresentated- tation on thuh part of
38   CBS who said yer doin' political profiles .hh
39   on all thuh candidates, .h and then you- (0.2) come
40   up with something thet 'as been exhaustively looked
41   into.

If Mr. Rather had responded to these first pair parts, he also would have stepped out of interview format. However, when Vice President Bush is done speaking, Mr. Rather briefly acknowledges his last complaint (lines 43–5 in Excerpt 13) then reinstates the interview format by shifting the topic away from Vice President Bush's complaints to set up another question (lines 46–7). However, instead of waiting until Mr. Rather has completed his question, as he did with the first question in the interview, Vice President Bush violates the interview turn taking system. He not only speaks before a question has been completed, but also places his utterance interruptively with Mr. Rather's question-in-progress. Clayman and Whalen (1988–89) describe this move as both a "turn type" and a "turn space" departure. Through these actions he challenges Mr. Rather's agenda for the interview.

Excerpt 13: Clayman and Whalen (1988/89, p. 251)[Rather-Bush: 43–8]
42   ( )
43 DR: Mister Vice President what (.) we agreed to or didn't
44   agree to I think- you will- agree fer thuh moment,
45   .hh can be dealt with >in another way.<
46   Let's talk about thuh record. You say that
47   we'[ve misrepresented your record]
48 GB: [Let's talk about thuh whole rec]ord.

Vice President Bush's response is not only interruptively placed, it is an oppositional utterance which has several of the characteristics of arguing. Argumentative sequences are constructed from adjacently placed oppositional utterances. As Goodwin and Goodwin (1987) describe, format tying (repeating words or phrases from a prior speaker's utterance) is often used in arguing sequences. In this interview, Vice President Bush challenges Mr. Rather's representation of "the record," repairing it to "the whole record." (line 48). Note that by failing to cooperate with the turn taking system of interviews, Vice President Bush has problematized Mr. Rather's prior utterance and challenged its status as a preliminary to a question (Clayman and Whalen, 1988/89, p. 254). Vice President Bush thus fails to cooperate in Mr. Rather's attempts to take a neutral stance in the interaction by producing his controversial statements as preliminaries to questions.

As the interaction continues, departures from the turn taking system of interviews become more prevalent and more egregious. Initially, it is Vice President Bush who departs from the framework, while Mr. Rather makes repeated efforts to restore interview format. However, Clayman and Whalen (1988–89) observe that by the end of the encounter, both participants have largely abandoned the speech exchange system of interviews and are now engaging in an argument. Excerpt 14, from the later portion of the interview, serves to illustrate the extent to which the interaction was transformed into an argument.

Excerpt 14: Clayman and Whalen (1988/89, p. 261)
```
205   DR:   President himself 'ez said he wants
206         all thuh facts out. .hhh He gave up
207         such things ez even 'is own diary. every principal
208         including [:: Secretary s- Schulz        ]
209   GB:            [He did not give up his own] diary,
210         's [diary (was briefs    )] (   )
211   DR:     [He gave up some of it.]
212         (.)
213   GB:   Well, [Dan, let's be careful he[re because .hh=
214   DR:         [(   )              [(   )
215   GB:   =[yer   (creating)    a    political    profile,]
216   DR:   =[Yes sir I want you to be careful Mist' Vice President]
217         be[cause thuh problem here]
218   GB:     [I   will   be   careful]l, .hh but
219         [I wanta get my side o' this out      ]
220   DR:   [(But) thuh PROBlem HERE: IS: that you] repeatedly sat in
221         thuh meetings, .hhh you sat in thuh meeting: in which
222         Secretary Schultz .hh in thuh most forceful way: .hhh
223         rai- registeh his objections.
224         ['n then you said you NEVER HEARD ANYBODY REGister
              object-
225   GB:   [I never ('s there) is it was thuh most forceful way.-
226         if it was thuh most forceful way…
```

In this excerpt, Vice President Bush speaks at places where Mr. Rather has not completed a question (e.g., line 209), speaks out of turn without being selected to speak by the IR (e.g., line 213), and fails to format his utterances as answers to the IR's questions (throughout the excerpt). At this point in the exchange Mr. Rather has also largely departed from the interview format. For example, he responds in line 211 to Vice President Bush's challenge in lines 209–10 instead of attempting to restore the question/answer format, as he had done earlier in the interaction. If an interviewee interrupts and challenges a statement before a question is produced, they are treating the statement as a position rather than as background to a question.

This excerpt has several characteristics of an argument in a conversational speech exchange system. There are adjacently placed oppositional utterances (as in lines 206–7 and 209; 209 and 211), direct disagreements which are unmitigated and immediate rather than delayed (for example, lines 209 and 211 are placed interruptively). There is also considerable use of format tying (e.g. "he did not give up his own diary" (line 209) and "he gave up some of it (line 211); "let's be careful…" (line 213) and "I want you to be careful" (line 216). In addition, there are times where voices are raised (e.g., lines 220 and 224).

Clayman and Whalen (1988/89) conclude from their analysis that it was Vice President Bush who initiated the change from the interview framework to a conversational mode. While the public and the media were largely of the opinion that Mr. Rather was to blame for the events that took place, Clayman and Whalen's (1988/89) analysis shows that he stuck steadfastly to the interview format far longer than Vice President Bush did, and only joined him in arguing towards the end of the interview. This line of research thus illustrates why it is essential to understand the turn taking system of talk in institutional settings. Whether an interaction is a news interview or not, depends not just on whether it is conducted in a television studio between those holding the roles of interviewer and interviewee, but on the actions of these participants. The choices the participants make about whether to stay within the structure of the speech exchange system, in this case a television news interview, determine whether the interaction will proceed as expected, and whether the participants can be seen to be competent performers of their social roles. The same actions that make it a news interview also make the IR "neutral." The interviewee must cooperate in the neutralistic stance taken by the interviewer in order for them to be successful in the role.

Summary

This chapter has shown how critical the turn taking system and interactional organization of participants' activities more generally are for the accomplishment of various types of work done through talk in institutional settings. While the common-sense perspective is to view one's job performance (whether as an interviewer or an interviewee, for example) as something accomplished by an individual, and dependent on their skill and ability, the analysis of television news interviews by conversation analysts clearly reveals the interactional nature of the accomplishment of these social roles and tasks. The level of skill one is able to project, and the ability to portray oneself as a competent professional, are dependent on the actions of all participants in the interaction, never on one's own self alone. While the interviewer may desire to portray a neutral stance and may take actions to create that stance, whether these efforts are successful or not depends on the actions of the interviewee as well.

Student activity

Listen to your favorite televised news interview show.

1. How many of the aspects of the turn taking system for televised news interview can you identify in the show? Use Table 23.1 as a guide.
2. How many techniques for evading answers can you identify in the IEs' responses?
3. Can you observe IRs using any of the techniques for pursuing IE responses when evasive answers occurred?

Recommended sources

Clayman, Steven and Heritage, John. (2002), *The News Interview: Journalists and Public Figures on the Air*. Cambridge: Cambridge University Press.

Ekstrom, Mats. (2009), 'Announced refusal to answer: a study of norms and accountability in broadcast political interviews', *Discourse Studies*, 11, 6, 681–702.

Guillot, Marie-Noëlle. (2008), 'Freedoms and constraints in semi-institutional television discussions: The case of mixed format panel discussions', *Journal of Pragmatics*, 40, pp. 179–204.

Heritage, John. (2002), 'The limits of questioning: negative interrogatives and hostile question content', *Journal of Pragmatics*, 34, 1427–46.

Heritage, John C. and Roth, Andrew L. (1995), 'Grammar and institution: questions and questioning in the broadcast news interview', *Research on Language and Social Interaction*, 28(1), 1–60.

Ikeda, Keiko. (2009), 'Third party involvement in Japanese political television interviews', in Hanh thi Nguyen and Gabriele Kasper (eds) *Talk-in-interaction: Multilingual perspectives*. Honolulu, Hawaii: National Foreign Language Resource Center; University of Hawaii, pp. 157–80.

Rautajoki, Hanna. (2012), "Membership categorization as a tool for moral casting in TV discussion: The dramaturgical consequentiality of guest introductions', *Discourse Studies*, 14(20), pp. 243–60.

Schegloff, Emanuel A. (1988/89), 'From interview to confrontation: observations of the Bush/Rather encounter', *Research on Language and Social Interaction*, 22, 215–40.

24 Call-in Talk Shows on Radio and Television

Chapter contents

Introduction

While the television news interviews discussed in Chapter 23 are designed for an overhearing audience, that audience does not get to participate directly in the interaction. However, the genre of "call-in" radio talk shows provides for such direct audience participation. The radio call-in talk show therefore combines two types of mediated interaction—the broadcast interaction between the host and on air interviewees, and the telephone interaction between audience members and the host and any on air guests. In this chapter we analyze the interactions in these telephone calls to radio talk shows. We will discuss how these calls are opened, how the interaction in the body of the call is managed, and how interaction in the call varies depending on the identities of the callers.

Routine telephone call openings to radio talk shows

In this section of the chapter we will discuss routine openings of interactions between radio talk show hosts and audience members who call in to ask questions. We will analyze how their contributions are initiated and incorporated into the ongoing activities in the show. Telephone call openings to radio talk shows differ in several ways from the ordinary telephone call openings we examined in Chapter 8. Thornborrow (2001) notes that callers are typically pre-screened by off air staff, so an extensive opening sequence does not need to be repeated once the caller gets put on the air. Hutchby (1999, p. 46) notes that "on talk radio, calls are opened with a systematically compacted variant of that kind of opening." Like the emergency telephone calls we analyzed in Chapters 14 and 15, the opening sequences are truncated in order to accomplish the business of the opening in as little time as possible.

> Here, two turns are sufficient to place the parties on a footing of mutually ratified participation and to get the first topical business introduced. In the first turn the host announces the caller by name, and additionally identifies them in terms of an urban locality from which the call is being placed. To this announcement he appends a first greeting. In the second turn, the caller reciprocates by greeting the host by name, and then pretty much straight away launches into their chosen topic. (Hutchby, 1999, p. 46)

Hutchby (1999) notes that by opening the call with the caller's name and city, the host alerts any on-air guests and the viewing audience that he is taking a call. At the same time, he alerts the caller (who has been on hold) that it is their turn to speak. The caller can thus be ready not just to respond to the host's greeting but to begin his question or comment without delay. While the first part of the host's opening (the name and city) can be heard as addressed both to the caller and the listening audience (who might be interested in where the caller is from), the greeting which follows is unambiguously addressed to the caller. The greeting, as the first pair part of an adjacency pair, makes a return greeting relevant. It therefore alerts the caller that it is now time for them to begin speaking. The caller does not have to think about how to begin their utterance, because they will begin with a return greeting, and then follow that with their comment or question. Hutchby provides several examples of "conventional" openings in radio talk show calls which illustrate how participants align their identities and prepare for topical talk:

Excerpt 1: Hutchby (1999, p. 46)
1   Host: Pete is calling from Ilford. Good morning.
2   Caller: .h Good morning Brian. (0.4) .hh What I'm phoning up is
3   about the cricket... ((continues))

Excerpt 2: Hutchby (1999, p. 46)
1   Host: Brian from Uxbridge now. Good morning.

> 2 Caller: .h Er, g'morning Brian. .hh Emm:, I have some advi:ce
> 3   that might be, a little bit more practical… ((continues))

However, Hutchby (1999) notes that callers do not always immediately begin their topical talk after their return greeting. They typically precede their substantive turn with a space filler (such as "Erm") and/or an audible inhalation (see also Thornborrow, 2001). Hutchby argues that this "filler" utterance, which he calls a "buffer" device, is similar to the use of fillers observed in responses to topic initial elicitors (Button and Casey, 1984). By means of this device, the responder displays that the topic they are producing is in response to the previous utterance—the topic initial elicitor: "In other words, speakers thereby display that they are comprehending the prior turn as one that is specifically requiring them to search for a topic on which to talk" (Hutchby, 1999, p. 55). However, Hutchby also notes that in talk radio the caller does not have to search for a topic, because the caller has presumably called the station because they have a point they want to share or a question they want to ask about the topic being discussed on the show.

Another interpretation of the role of the buffer device in this location in talk show calls is that it is analogous to the "Yes" or "um" that typically precedes caller's first turns in emergency phone calls (Zimmerman, 1984; Whalen and Zimmerman, 1990). The "buffer device" in caller's first turns in emergency service calls is heard as acknowledging the call taker's institutional identification in the first line of the call. It works to display that the caller understands that they have dialed emergency services. The filler particles in the buffer position in emergency service calls could be seen to acknowledge that the opening sequence of the emergency telephone call is truncated. The "yes" or "um" serves to mark the place where, in an ordinary conversation, an exchange of greetings and perhaps initial inquiries would have occurred. In the context of talk show calls, the item in the buffer position could serve to allow the host one last time to speak before the caller launches into the substance of their call.

Misalignments in call openings in radio talk shows

Not all calls to radio talk shows open in the routine manner described above. When openings are atypical, the work that routine openings do to align the identities and activities of the callers (what Hutchby (1999, p. 56) refers to as "frame attunement") becomes visible. There is a variety of misalignments that can occur in radio talk show call openings.

Some callers stop speaking after their return greeting instead of moving forward with a buffer device followed by their question or comment. This may result in an unwanted silence. Excerpt 3 shows a host repairing such a gap. In this case, the problem in alignment between the participants may have occurred because the host neglected to provide a greeting in line 1. The caller's greeting in line 3 is therefore a first pair part, and as such creates an expectation that a return greeting will be forthcoming (from the host). However, a one-second pause occurs instead (line 4). The host then solicits the caller's turn ("Ye̲s̲." in line 5). This excerpt exhibits "frame misattunement" in that the caller and the host are orienting to different interactional frames. The caller is orienting to the interactional convention that a greeting should be followed by a return greeting, while the host is orienting to the radio talk show frame in which his introduction of the caller constitutes an invitation to speak.

> Excerpt 3: Hutchby (1999, p. 56)
> 1   Host: .hh It's B̲arry next in Woodford Gre̲en.
> 2   (.)
> 3   Caller: Good m̲orning Brian.
> 4   (1.0)
> 5   Host: Ye̲s̲.
> 6   Caller: Er I'm c̲alling about thee rep̲ort… ((continues))

Callers are typically first answered by an off-air staff member and then put on hold. Some misalignments may therefore occur when callers do not realize that they are on the air when the host takes them off hold and addresses them. Other misalignments may occur when callers (perhaps more often first time callers) do not understand the conventional way openings are handled in radio talk shows.

Bilmes (2005) analyzes calls to a television call-in talk show. The host of this show is informed of the city and state the caller is calling from, and he uses this information to address the caller as he takes them off hold. Bilmes (2005) argues that the location of the caller serves as a summons; since they have been on hold the host uses this summons to verify that they are still on the line and still available to speak. In Excerpt 4 the host ("D") takes the caller ("C") off hold and announces the location of the caller ("Boca Raton Florida"). This works as a summons to the caller and identifies them to the overhearing audience. The host of this show typically follows the location address term with either an explicit query as to the caller's availability (as in line 1 in Excerpt 4) or with a greeting which serves as a solicit of the caller's response. In Excerpt 4 the caller responds to the summons, inquiry, and greeting with an answer to the inquiry in line 2, but does not go on to produce a question or comment. Therefore, in line 3 the host initiates a repair of their absent utterance by soliciting it ("You wanted to say"). The caller then begins speaking (line 4).

> Excerpt 4: Bilmes (2005, p. 158)
> 1   D: Boca Raton Florida. Are you there. Hi.
> 2   C: Yes I'm here.
> 3   D: You wanted to say
> 4   C: …..

At times it is to the host's advantage when the caller does not immediately begin their turn. For example, in Excerpt 5 the host ("D") is able to get the caller ("C") on the air but asks them to hold their question until after a commercial break. This task is smoothly accomplished because the caller in line 2 restricts themselves to answering the summons.

> Excerpt 5: Bilmes (2005, p. 157)
> 1 D: Los Angeles, you're there aren't you?
> 2 C: Yes, I am.
> 3 D: All right, you're first when we come back ((from a commercial
> 4   break)). Hang on a minute. We want you on.

Excerpt 6 from a radio show analyzed by Reed (2009) shows the host of the show working to get the caller to acknowledge the summons and produce their question or comment. When the first summons in line 1 is not responded to, the host ("Alan") produces another summons (line 3). This second summons is also followed by silence (line 4), but the caller ("Daniel") does begin speaking in line 5. However, when they speak they provide a return greeting and an initial inquiry ("how are YOU mate."). While greetings and return greetings are common in radio talk show call openings, the exchange of initial inquiries are relatively rare. The host then produces a solicit (line 7) in order to get the caller to produce their question.

> Excerpt 6: Reed (2009, p. 1223)
> 1 -> Alan: let's move on to DANiel in BEDfordshire.
> 2 ->   (1.32)
> 3 ->   <<h>> HEllo DANiel,>
> 4 ->   (1.12)
> 5 -> D: heLLO there;
> 6   how are YOU mate.
> 7   Alan: what's on YOUR mind tonight.
> 8   D: uhm I just want to talk about macLARen;

Integration of the call with the ongoing interaction

Bilmes (2005) found that hosts in the television call-in show he analyzed used their discretion in deciding when to take calls. Hosts often took calls when an on air guest was wrapping up a theme or topic. A call would then be connected and a caller invited to participate. Thus calls were often places where topic changes occurred, because the caller's turn would direct where the topic would go next.

In Excerpt 7 below the host ("D") provides a brief transition segment between the guest's ("B") utterance (lines 5–6) and the opening of the next telephone phone call (line 7). He does this by providing the guest an opportunity to clarify or extend their remarks on the topic. In this excerpt the host summarizes the guest's point and then asks the guest whether he has understood it correctly. The guest takes advantage of this opening to add a qualification (lines 5–6). After the guest has indicated they are done (note the transition relevance place at the end of line 6 which is followed by a 0.5 second pause), the host then connects a caller and invites them to speak (line 7).

> Excerpt 7: Bilmes (2005, p. 154)
> 1 D: … a one time only incident is not enough to get you before the
> 2   supreme a du- b- before a court of law and entitle you to redress
> 3   from our judicial system. Do I understand you- b- what you're
> 4   [saying.
> 5 B: [Yeah I'd like ta- I like to qualify that…. What the court said is that
> 6   a single epithet or single racist or sexist joke is not enough. (0.5)
> 7 D: (°All right°) .hh Ah Kalamazoo are you there?

While most hosts allow the caller to decide the topic of their question, at times hosts initiate the interaction with the caller by asking them a question. This mode of opening the call provides the host with control over the subject of the call in addition to its positioning. Fitzgerald and Housley (2002) note that these direct questions present a problem for the caller. The host's question puts the caller in the position of "answerer." The caller is expected to use their turn to answer the question that has been posed. If they want to do something else with their turn, they then must work to transition from the role of answerer to another interactional role. In Excerpt 8 the caller follows the host's lead and frames their utterance as an answer to the question.

> Excerpt 8: Fitzgerald and Housley (2002, p. 586)
> 1 Host: Frances Smith from from Birmingham what do you think
> 2 Caller: urhh… I.. feel that the age of consent should stay at…

In Excerpt 9, on the other hand, the caller hesitates, then uses a "yes, but" format to move the topic in a different direction.

> Excerpt 9: Fitzgerald and Housley (2002, p. 586)
> 1 Host: John Smith from Staffordshire do you agree with that
> 2 Caller: (0.3) ur ( ) well huh.. huh ( ) in a way yes but I've got my

The interaction between host, callers, and on air guests

Recall that in the routine televised news interviews we examined in Chapter 23, participants typically restricted themselves to a question/answer format, with the interviewer asking questions and the interviewee answering them. While some radio call-in shows use a similar format, there are variations in the type and number of participants as well as in the interactional organization of the shows. A British radio call-in show analyzed by Thornborrow (2001) followed a traditional format. A host moderated callers' questions for in-studio guests who were high ranking political figures. Other radio talk shows are more conversational in structure.

A Swedish radio talk show about society and fashion has a format which is very close to ordinary conversation (Korolija, 1998).

> From a targeted listener's point of view, the episodes involving entertainment, puns, jokes, interruptions, and the like give the impression that the participants forget that they are on the air. The participants also use various intonational and rhythmic cues to dramatize moods in the course of telling their investigations. The same cues are effective as devices for reactions from the coparticipants (Müller, 1992). Speech at a very high volume, increased or decreased pace, and falsetto are a few characteristics of the conversational mode; the quality of voice is an important means in the playing of small narrative dramas sometimes triggered by the investigations. Simultaneous talk as well as competitive, dramatic, and sometimes even apparently provocative strategies for floor taking and floor holding occur. Laughter and onomatopoetic outbursts of personally held attitudes toward a debated issue or a current speaker are other features. Flooding out (Goffman, 1974), "breaking up" or "cracking up," happens frequently. The participants' individual conversational styles can be argued to support or legitimize their distinct roles and behaviors. In a broader perspective, variety and avoidance of monotony are also important devices for getting and maintaining attention when speaking on the radio to a broad public (Oliver & Cortright, 1970). (Korolija, 1998, pp. 104–5)

Excerpt 10 shows a brief excerpt from this show which illustrates the conversational structure of the interaction as well as the informality of its topic. This show, which is produced for entertainment, is very different from the television news interviews analyzed in Chapter 23. This excerpt is translated from Swedish (Korolija, 1998). Korolija (1998) uses some transcribing conventions which differ from the Jeffersonian system conversation analysts typically use. For example, she uses italics to indicate stress, and underlining to indicate simultaneous talk or other activities which occur simultaneously (Korolija, 1998). The show consists of interactions between a host ("H") and three guests (guests "A" and "G" speak in the excerpt below).

Excerpt 10: Korolija (1998, pp. 111–12)

1 H: in family life one often finds these situations when only *one*
2   macaroon remains… and then one has *two* sons and *one* father (.)
3   and both the sons want the macaroon? so what happens is that-
4 A: =the *mother* then? isn't she-?
5 G: and *you* have two sons right?
6 H: ye:s
7 A: ye:s
8 H: then-
9 G: you usually accuse me from getting your- *my* lousy examples from
10   my own life
11 H: ha ha this was just one *example*
12 G: =and here you pull your own
13 H: yes but I mean we never get *out* of your apartment

```
14  G:  ="two sons" (.) "a family has two sons and a daddy" {A laughs}
15  H:  how many times (.) ha- have we ro- roved roved about in your
16      apartment and among your- among your euphoric-
17  G:  >it is you yourself< you might as well admit it that YOU WANT
18      THIS macaroon YOU WANT THIS MACAROON you don't want
19      YOU BEGRUDGE YOUR own CHILDREN a macaroon well
20      DAMN!!!! that's what I say #my god what is this!#
        ((episode continues))
```

A television talk show from the United States analyzed by Bilmes (2005) is also closer to a conversational exchange than an interview. In Excerpt 11, the interaction between the co-hosts (Donahue and Posner) and their on air guest (Debbie Brake) involves more than just asking and answering questions (see, for example, the story Posner tells starting in lines 1–4). The participants also interrupt each other and overlap each other's utterances rather than waiting to be solicited to speak. The guest, Ms. Brake ("B"), self selects herself to speak in lines 15 and 17 rather waiting for a question from one of the hosts. In addition, there are listener responses in lines 5 and 16.

```
Excerpt 11: Bilmes (2005, p. 151–2)
1   P:  [Well I'll tell you what (.) I (was in) (.) I was in a bu:s in New
2       York City=I got up to give my seat to a woman (.) who told me: (.)
3       I was a male sexist (.) because I (.) I was taught by my mother that
4       when a woman comes in an' she's got no place to sit down=
5   D:                                                    =Yeah
6   P:  you: get up as a sign of respect.=
7   D:                      =She thought
8   D:  [you were being patronizing?=
9   P:  [(So you know)          =and she thought I was
10  P:  [hitting on her or something. I don' know
11  D:  [(you were * izing her)=
12  P:                  =something. I don' know=
13  D:                              =No no no she was
14  D:  sa[ying don't' treat me
15  B:    [Let me just bring us back t' r:ealty [here.
16  D:                              [Yeah
17  B:  There's a very big difference between T .hh calling someone a
18      sexist for giving up their sea:t and actually bringing a sexual
19      harassment claim.
```

Conveying identities through talk radio

In Chapter 13 we introduced membership categorization analysis ("MCA"), which grew out of the early work of Harvey Sacks (1974). MCA is an approach to the study of how participants use and orient to categories of individuals, objects, or collectivities. Several aspects of membership categorization analysis are relevant for our consideration of how and when callers to talk radio shows convey aspects of their identity and group membership.

While callers are likely to have heard the host by listening to the show on previous occasions, the host does not know the callers or anything about them except their first name and usually their location. The problem for the caller then becomes how to frame their talk for a recipient who does not know very much about them. In order to frame their question or comment in a comprehensible way, they often must decide how to identify themselves and what relevant background information to convey about themselves. While some questions can clearly be addressed without knowing much or anything about the caller, other topics require some background information. Even when background information is not necessary, callers often frame their contributions to the show to convey some information about who they are. In this section we explore the issues about identification in terms of caller status (e.g., first time versus returning callers), as well as a range of other identities that can be made relevant for a particular topic.

Types of callers

Dori-Hacohen (2012) found that callers to political radio talk shows in the U.S. and Israel constructed identities through interactional practices vis a vis their relationship to the show they were calling. The four categories of callers she found were regular listeners, returning callers, anonymous callers, and first time callers. Callers who did not frame their identity with one of these four categories were "unmarked standard callers" (Dori-Hacohen, 2012).

The anonymous caller is not usually found in American talk radio shows, which routinely pre-screen callers (although many shows use first names only on the air). Dori-Hacohen (2012) found that in the talk shows in Israel she studied, some callers were allowed to refrain from giving a name. For example, in Excerpt 12 when the host ("H") asked the caller ("C") their name, the caller explicitly asked to remain anonymous (line 5). They later give a reason to justify their request (their occupation; line 8). The English translations follow each line of transcript.

Excerpt 12: Dori-Hacohen (2012, p. 284)

```
1  H:   shalom.
        Hi.
2  C:   (0.4 shalom uvraxa.
        Hi and greeting.
3  H:   (0.5)  im mi yesh li ha' oneg?
        With whom do I have the pleasure?
4  C:   (0.8) eh: texef tavin la::ma,
        Eh:: soon you'll understand wh::y,
5        a::ni mevakeshet lehisha' er be' ilum shem.
         I:: ask to remain anonymous.
6  H:   ani mexabed et pratiyutex, beva [kasha.
        I respect your privacy, plea   [se].
7  C:                                  [toda raba.
                                       [Thanks very much.
```

8   (0.3) me' axar ve' ani morat derex beyisrael.
        since i am a tourist guide in Israel.
9   H: ah::a, vakasha.
        O::h, please.

Regular callers often identify themselves as such. Revealing their previous "relationship" with the host changes the opening sequence of the call. Dori-Hacohen (2012) found an instance in which the host ("H") recognized a regular caller ("C") by voice:

Excerpt 13: Dori-Hacohen (2012, p. 288)
1   C: shalom lexa mar yaakov axime'ir.
        Hi to you mister Yaakov Aximeir.
2   H: shalom lexa sasi.
        Hi there Sasi.
3   C: (0.3) shalom. ma shlomxa?
        Hi. How are you?
4   H: besder, ata sasi miramat gan?=
        Fine, are you Sasi from Ramat Ga:n?=
5   C: =ken.
        =Yes.

First time callers also sometimes identified themselves as first time callers. Dori-Hacohen (2012) notes that in Excerpt 14, while the caller admits to being a first time caller, they temper the potentially lower status implications of that identity by also identifying themself as a "long time listener" (line 5).

Excerpt 14: Dori-Hacohen (2012, p. 295)
1   H: Ah Jeff in Fresno kay em jay:. Jeff, hey, how
2   are you, welcome to the program.
3   C: (0.5) How are you doing Sean.
4   H: (0.4) What's up sir.
5   C: .h wll long time listener first time calle:r.
6   H: Yes sir. [Welcome aboard sir.

Callers' choices for self-identifications

Rendle-Short (2005) explores how callers to radio call-in shows either explicitly identify their sexual orientation, or more often, imply it by references to relationships or circumstances in their life which communicate their orientation. For example, a caller may refer to their marriage. In the time and place in which Rendle-Short was conducting her study, marriage was only legal between people of "opposite" sex. Callers may also refer to their husband or wife, thus implicitly conveying to the host and the listening audience that they are heterosexual. Partners could also be referred to with gendered pronouns ("he" or "she"). Of the 249 callers in her data set, Rendle-Short (2005) found only two callers who specifically identified themselves as homosexual. She therefore concludes that the "default" identify is heterosexual. Callers do not have to explicitly identify themselves as such, and instead can use commonplace referents (such as husband and wife or gendered pronouns) to identify their partner as of the opposite sex without marking it as newsworthy, delicate, or problematic.

Claiming a normal identity while having an eating disorder

Brooks (2009) studied a collection of British radio talk shows about the topic of eating disorders such as anorexia and bulimia. She found that people with eating disorders who called in to the show used a variety of interactional techniques to convey their relationship to their behavior. They worked to present the best possible face to the host and viewing audience. For many of these callers, utilizing the contemporary medical perspective that an eating disorder is an illness enabled them to both acknowledge having the condition and to claim moral blamelessness for the behaviors associated it. By claiming an identity as someone with an illness, they are implicitly rejecting an identity of someone who is merely weak, vain, or lacking in willpower.

The callers used specific interactional techniques to convey their relationship to the disorder in an "accountable" way. In Excerpt 15, the caller Lindsay uses psychological jargon (e.g., "anxious" in line 1 and "phobia" in line 6) which is consistent with her claim to the "illness" identity. Brooks (2009) notes that by saying "instantly" (line 4) Lindsay presents her response as an automatic, instinctual response rather than as a choice. This implication leaves her blameless for her rejection of food.

Excerpt 15: Brooks (2009, p. 364)

```
1  Lin:   I'm very anxious around food. .hhh u:m I: er I find it er
2         particularly difficult if I'm going out (.) to eat (.) um
3         you know I receive a plate that's you know covered in
4         mountains of food .hh that just instantly makes me lose
5         my appetite (.) .hh u:m and er I I feel that u:m that
6         I've got lots of rituals around food I have a phobia
7         that's also around fo:od
```

Excerpt 16 shows another caller, "Grace," characterizing her anorexia as an addiction to dieting and losing weight. She also characterizes the condition in a way that diminishes her individual responsibility for the problem. In contemporary society, addiction is also considered a medical problem.

Excerpt 16: Brooks (2009, p. 366)

```
1  Host:  I mean you were very very thin [indeed
2  G:                                    [absolutely
3  Host:  but you didn't notice that [or did you?
4  G:                                [.hh I think I did notice
```

5	that yes but by that point I'd lost (.) all self este:em and (.) the diet
6	had actually made me feel terrible about myself ↑where I looked in
7	the mirror, I just covered it up, I didn't think it looked nice at a:ll
8	.hhhh but what happens is you get in a cycle of addiction, an
9	addiction to um .hhh starving yourself, an addiction to watching
10	the numbers fall on the sca:le

In short, Brook's (2009) analysis shows how callers to radio talk shows took care to present their contributions to the show in a way that would promote the most positive identity for themselves they possibly can, given their "disordered eating" behaviors. Brooks (2009, p. 371) notes that "pathologising behaviour may be a way of managing accountability and avoiding blame; if behaviour is occurring for a *medical* reason, one cannot be held personally responsible for the behaviour…"

Cultural differences in radio talk shows

While some of the examples discussed in this chapter so far have reflected variations due to style of show, identity of participants, and topics of discussion, there are also specific ways in which cultural differences can affect the interaction between callers and hosts. Zhang (2005) analyzes radio talk shows in a city in China. The standard dialect "Putonghua" differs substantially from the regional dialect (Cantonese) in the area the shows she studied are broadcast. Hosts of local community radio talk shows therefore sometimes switch from one dialect to the other in order to accommodate callers' preferences. Zhang (2005) notes that the caller's level of facility with a dialect may be one of the reasons for switching dialects, but at times the switch has to do with the social status of a dialect.

Zhang's (2005) data are from a community radio talk show which is about social issues. The host of the show is able to speak both dialects fluently. While Zhang (2005) found that about a third of the conversations were conducted solely in Cantonese (the regional dialect), in roughly two thirds of the calls there was a switch from Cantonese to Putonghua. These transitions were initiated by the callers. Some callers explicitly stated a preference for speaking in Putonghua, while others simply began using the other language. The host typically followed their lead by also switching to Putonghua, as illustrated in Excerpt 17 below. In this excerpt the regular font is the Cantonese transcription and the italicized font is Putonghua. The English translation is in parentheses below the Chinese versions of each turn.

Excerpt 17: Zhang (2005, p. 364)

1	Host:	Si4gaan3 hai6 sap6jat1dim2 ge3 sap6ng5fan1. Ni1dou6hai6 Can4
2		Gin6 wai6 nei5zyu2ci4 ge3 sam1zan3si6daai6gaa1ji5ge3. Haa6
3		jat1 wai2 hai6 lau4sin1saang1.
		(Now the time is eleven fifteen. This is Chen Jin hosting the
		Forum. Our next caller is Mr. Lau.)

4   Lau4 sin1saang1 nei5 hou2.
           (Hello Mr Lau.)

5   Call: *Ai:: ni3 hao3.*
           (Yeah:: hello.)

6   Host: *Ai, ni hao.*
           (Yeah, Hello.)

7   Call: *Uhn:: wo3 xizng3 tan2 na4 ge4 hao2hua2 che1dui4 a.*
           (Uhn:: I'd like to talk about that luxurious limo parade.)

Summary

While the interactions between hosts and on air guests often share some of the characteristics of television news interviews that we studied in Chapter 23, there are a variety of formats for radio talk shows, with some being much more conversational in nature. When callers are invited to participate, the hosts can use a number of techniques to manage how and when their talk is integrated into the ongoing interaction. From the caller's point of view, they must not only negotiate the opening sequence but also work to control how they present their contribution to be understandable. Revealing aspects of one's identity, as relevant, is one of the ways of making their talk understandable. While both television interviews and radio talk shows are often informative and educational, they also serve as entertainment for the listening audience. In the next chapter we turn to interactions which are not produced for the purpose of entertainment—workplace interactions in businesses and related organizational settings.

Student activity

Listen to your favorite radio call-in show and observe how the calls are conducted.

1. How many differences can you find between these telephone call openings and those of ordinary call openings between friends?
2. How are the different roles of the host and the callers displayed in the talk that occurs and how it is organized?

Recommended sources

Hutchby, Ian. (2006), *Media Talk: Conversation Analysis and the Study of Broadcasting*. New York: Open University Press.

Reed, Beatrice Szczepek. (2009), 'Prosodic orientation: a practice for sequential organization in broadcast telephone openings', *Journal of Pragmatics*, 41, 1223–47.

Rendle-Short, Johanna. (2005), '"I've got a paper-shuffler for a husband": indexing sexuality on talk-back radio', *Discourse & Society*, 16, (4), 561–78.

Part VII
Talk in Business Settings

25 Talk in Business Contexts: Doing Customer Service

Chapter contents

Introduction

In this chapter and the next we address talk in business contexts. We begin by analyzing how customer service work is done in face to face and telephone interactions.

Face to face customer service encounters

Conversation analytic research can be useful in discovering how face to face customer service encounters work and how their effectiveness can be optimized. Vinkhuyzen (2011) studied interactions between customers and production staff at a copy shop. He observes that very subtle aspects of the interaction between staff and customers can be critical for understanding the customer's perspective. The ability to understand these interactional cues can therefore make the difference between filling an order correctly or incorrectly.

Vinkhuyzen (2011) gives an example of a customer who was unhappy with the copies she had ordered because they looked smaller than she had thought they would. When Vinkhuyzen analyzed the videotape of the ordering process, he found several aspects of the interaction that were problematic. This interaction is shown in Excerpt 1. In this excerpt "EMP" is the employee and "CUS" is the customer. First, Vinkhuyzen (2011) noted that when the customer requested the copies she spoke in a way that indicated tentativeness and uncertainty. In lines 5–6 the customer says "and then (.) this (.) these these I'd like ehm (.) ((looks at EMP)) half this size?". The customer exhibited uncertainty through hesitations, repetitions, error avoidance and repair. These aspects of her turn delayed the production of her actual request until the end of her utterance. When the customer finally makes the request, she uses questioning intonation (which again indicates uncertainty ("half this size?"; line 6). The customer has thus indicated her uncertainty about what she wants in several ways.

However, instead of responding to the uncertainty she expressed and showing the customer how much smaller a "half size" copy would look compared to the original, the employee simply says "mkay" (line 7). The employee then checks the box on the order form indicating that the copies should be made with a 50 percent reduction in size.

Excerpt 1: Vinkhuyzen (2011, p. 210)
01 EMP: Hi, can I help you
02 CUS: Hi… I'd like ten of these please
03 EMP: In color?
04 CUS: Yes please
05 CUS: and then (.) this (.) these these I'd like ehm (.) ((looks at EMP))
06   half this size?
07 EMP: mkay
08 CUS And I just want a copy of each
09 CUS: I'm not sure how many there are (.) do you want me to
10   count them?
11 EMP: In color also? No
12 CUS: eh yeah (.) same color
13 EMP: And your name is?
         ((conversation continues))

When the customer picked up the copies a few hours later, she was unhappy with how small they were. Vinkhuyzen (2011) explains that it is not easy to visualize how much smaller a 50 percent reduction will make a copy. A 50 percent reduction actually results in a picture that is only 25 percent of the *area* of the original, since both length and width of the image are reduced by 50 percent. This customer's dissatisfaction with her order could have been avoided if the employee had picked up on the implications of the interactional techniques she used in her initial request. Vinkhuyzen's (2011) analysis of this customer service encounter has illustrated that the knowledge the employee needed to do their job well is not just technical knowledge about how to make copies. Interactional competence—an understanding of how talk is organized—is also critical for the successful performance of customer service work.

Customer service calls

In today's business world only a portion of contacts between the organization and the customer or client are face-to-face interactions. A large portion of these contacts are technologically mediated, with an increasing proportion being performed over the internet. However, telephone calls between customers and representatives of businesses or other organizations are still prevalent and continue to serve a wide range of purposes. Common reasons for customer calls are to make purchases or to obtain information or services. These calls are referred to generically as "customer service calls." We begin with a discussion of how these calls are opened, and how the nature of the opening of the call impacts how the business of the call is managed.

Customer service call openings

Recall from our discussion of opening sequences in routine emergency service calls (in Chapter 14) that they differ in several ways from opening sequences in ordinary telephone calls. Zimmerman (1984) found that emergency service call openings are systematically condensed in order to display an orientation to the institutional roles and tasks being accomplished through the call, including the need to complete the call in a timely manner. Briefly, Zimmerman noted that in emergency service calls the answer to the summons was combined in the same turn as the institutional identification and solicitation of the caller's first turn, the calls did not have an exchange of greetings and initial inquiries, and the callers used their first turn to produce an explicit or implicit request for help. Zimmerman also found that the interrogative series was a major component of emergency service calls, with the call taker asking a series of questions to get the information necessary to help the caller.

Wakin and Zimmerman (1999) found that many of these characteristics also apply to service calls in other types of organizations. Excerpt 2 is a customer call to a bus information number.

Excerpt 2: Zimmerman and Wakin (1995, p. 5)
```
1  A:  Good morning bus information
2  C:  Is there uh: thirty-four that leaves from thuh University at around
3      seven thirty?
4      (1.0)
5  A:  Are you speaking AM or PM
6  C:  Uh:m AM
7  A:  There's a bus that leaves at seven thirty five.
8  C:  Thank you=
9  A:           =Your welcome.
```

Research by Reiter (2006) reveals some cross cultural variations in the organization of service calls. Reiter (2006) studied openings in service calls to a Uruguayan company which coordinates care for patients in hospitals. She found that openings in these calls (which were conducted in Montevidean Spanish, the language of the Uruguayan middle class), differed in several ways from the English language openings studied by Wakin and Zimmerman (1995). Recall from the English language data we reviewed in Chapter 8 that ordinary telephone call openings between acquainted persons typically have an exchange of greetings, while in emergency phone calls to the police, greetings are absent. However, in the Uruguayan context Reiter (2006) studies, this pattern is reversed. She found that ordinary conversation openings typically do not have greetings, while the service calls she studied typically do. In addition, the Uruguayan service calls often had individual self identification by the call taker, in addition to the institutional identification. Each line of the Spanish language transcript (in Italics) is followed first by a literal English translation and then by an idiomatic English translation on the line below.

Excerpt 3: Reiter (2006, p. 20)

1 CT: *CSC Coordinación de Servicios buenas tardes (.) habla Claudia*
CSC Coordination of Services good afternoons (.) speaking Claudia
CSC Service coordination good afternoon (.) Claudia speaking

2 C: *Ho:la sí buenas tardes↑ (.2) mirá para para::: m::: (.) para que vayan por un*
Hello yes good afternoon (.2) look$^{T/V}$ for for:::em:: (.) for to go to for a
Hello yes good afternoon (.2) look for for:::em:: (.) for someone to go and look after a

3 C: *paciente para cuidarlo mañana de noche::↑*
patient to look after him tomorrow night
patient tomorrow night

Impact of opening sequences on the business of the call

The study of opening sequences is important because the nature of the opening sequence has implications for the trajectory of the call, and hence for how the business of the call is conducted. In an analysis of customer service calls to a major software firm, Baker et al. (2001) found a flexible but highly structured process in the opening sequences of the calls. The call takers displayed an orientation to time constraints and other organizational concerns by answering calls with an extended turn. This complex opening turn accomplished several tasks before the caller got a chance to produce a single turn. Excerpt 4 shows the call taker accomplishing three tasks in their opening turn. They first produce an institutional identification, then identify themself by first name, and lastly ask for the caller's customer number. This method of initiating the opening sequence leaves no place for an exchange of greetings or initial inquiries.

Excerpt 4: Baker et al. (2001, pp. 43–4)

1 CT: welcome to Microsoft technical support, this is Leena,
2   can I start with your customer number please
3 C: yes that's three five oh (.) six four four
4   (1.8)

```
 5  CT:  it's Benny is it?
 6  C:   yeah that's right
 7  CT:  how can I help you?
 8  C:   I've recently installed Microsoft office pro:
 9       (0.4)
10  CT:  yeah
11  C:   and in the access part of the thing I've- I wanna use
12       the membership (.) but I've got those Americanized
13       dates an' phone numbers an' erm there's some form of
14       ma:sking on them?
15  CT:  yes there's an input mask on them?
16  C:   yeah I wanna- how do I get that bin to an Australian
17       sta:ndard?
18  CT:  you need to edit the mask
((conversation continues))
```

In line 3 of the call, the customer provides their customer number, which allows the call taker to access the customer's information on their computer screen. Notice that there is a pause in line 4 after the customer provides the number. Neither party treats this pause as problematic, thus displaying their mutual understanding that the call taker is engaged in typing the number and waiting for the computer to display the relevant information. By asking to confirm the name of the caller in line 5 the call taker displays that they now have the customer's information visible on their computer screen, so that the call can proceed. This action also fills an organizational goal by verifying that they are talking to the person who has paid for the technical support service that will be provided. The caller uses their next turn to answer this question (line 6), and the call taker then follows up with the question "how can I help you?" in line 7. The caller replies with their description of the problem. Baker et al. (2001) note that the wording of the call taker's question in line 7 is precise and deliberate. The call taker does not ask "can I help you?", which might add another sequence of utterances prior to getting to the business at hand. It might also be noted that by saying "how can I help you" the call taker displays some confidence that they can provide the help and directs the caller to provide a specific problem that needs to be addressed.

Baker et al. (2001, p. 46) found that once the caller has begun their description of the problem, they typically construct it to contain three components: naming the software or product, identifying where the problem is, and identifying the concern. Call takers typically waited until all three components were expressed before responding, although minimal responses were sometimes produced in support of the caller's production of their story. In Excerpt 4 (above), we see the caller conveying this information in lines 8, 11–14 and 16–17. The call taker provides a minimal response in line 10.

When organizations have specific goals they want to accomplish, there is a temptation to try to control employees' actions, even to the extent of "micro managing." When the type of work being done is answering customer service calls, Martin and O'Neill (2011) found that some employers attempt to script the calls. Call takers are trained in exactly what they should be saying and how they should be saying it. When these scripted calls go smoothly, they can be effective ways of achieving organizational goals by improving customer service to maintain good relations with customers and handle calls quickly and efficiently. However, even with scripted calls, call takers must adjust their actions to "local contingencies." One such local contingency is how the caller responds. These responses are not always accurately predicted by the script. In addition, call takers typically have to use their computer during the call, so the coordination of the work of using the computer with the work of interacting with the customer is another potential source of problems.

Martin and O'Neill's (2011) analysis of Excerpt 5 illustrates some of these contingencies. The "<k->" and "<-k>" symbols in the transcript show where the call taker began and stopped keyboarding, respectively, and the asterisks show where the customer's security numbers have been deleted for confidentiality. Note that even though the call opening is scripted, the operator uses ordinary conversational procedures when necessary to handle local contingencies. For example, in line 5 the operator misspeaks and then self-initiates a repair of her mistake ("have your secur eh sorry have your account number?"). In this excerpt the call taker starts typing the numbers the customer gives her as soon as the customer begins producing them (line 6). The act of typing provides an account for the call taker's silence after the caller finishes communicating her customer number. The keyboarding is presumably audible to the caller as well, thus providing justification for her silence.

In line 19 the operator repeats the amount the customer wants transferred ("A hundred"), thus displaying her understanding of the amount and allowing the caller an opportunity to correct her if that is not the correct figure. She is then silent for 2.5 seconds as she completes keyboarding the customer request.

Excerpt 5: Martin and O'Neill (2011, pp. 113–4)

1 O: Good morning customer services Stella speaking (0.2) may I help
2   you?
3 C: Hello I'd like to make a payment please for my Visa Card.
4   (1.2)
5 O: Right can I have your secur eh sorry have your account number?
6 C: Yes oh * *<K-> * ****** * Romford oh ***** (2.0) <-k>
7 O: And your name please?
8 C: Mrs Smith.
9 O: Could I have the second character in your security number please
10   Mrs Smith?
11 C: Four.
12 O: (<k>) (0.2) And the first character please?
13 C: One <k> NO two sorry.
14   (0.3)
15 O: Right your Gold Card number ending * ** * *
16 C: That's it.
17 O: Okay and how much you wishing to pay?
18 C: A hundred pounds please <k->

```
19 O:   A hundred (2.5) <-k>
20 O:   Okay that's been actioned it'll be about two days before it hits your
21      Gold Card Account.
22 C:   Lovely thanks a lot.
23 O:   You're welcome.
24 C:   Bye=
25 O:       =Bye.
```

Martin and O'Neill (2011) also demonstrate how interactional analysis of customer service calls can reveal information that is important to achieving organizational objectives. Excerpt 6 is from a customer service call in which the call taker (the "operator") is required to attempt to sell an additional service to every customer who calls. In this excerpt, the operator makes this attempt at the point in the call when closing is relevant. First, the operator grants the caller's request in lines 13–14. As we know from our discussion of closings in emergency phone calls in Chapter 14, once the request has been granted the closing of the call becomes relevant. The closing sequence is typically quite brief and compact in business calls when compared to ordinary phone calls between acquainted persons, which can go on for several exchanges of turns. The operator must therefore work quickly to introduce the new topic once the request has been granted to get it on the table before the caller has hung up the phone. Note that the operator responds to the caller's receipt of the granting of the request with "okay," (line 16). After the very briefest of pauses the caller starts to say "Thank you...", which is closing implicative (line 17). The operator immediately interrupts and talks over the caller in a loud voice, using an and-preface to indicate "something else" is coming (Heritage and Sorjonen, 1994). The caller thereby interrupts the closing sequence of the call and creates the space to introduce a new topic.

Excerpt 6: Martin and O'Neill (2011, pp. 120–1)

```
1   O:   That's fine no problem (.hhh) and how can I help you [u:h] today?
2   C:                                                        [w- ]
3   C:   It's just that I re- I really need some more paying in slips.
4        (0.5)
5   O:   Right.
6   C:   And em' envelopes (0.2) paying in envelopes as well.
7        (0.4)
8   O:   So you need some eh paying in envelopes as well?
9   C:   Yes.
10  O:   Is it the post office envelopes?
11  C:   Yes the post office ones (0.3) please.
12       (0.6)
13  O:   Right oh (0.5) so let me just get you a paying in book (7.5) there
14       we are there's a paying in book on its way as well.
15  C:   That's lovely.
16  O:   Okay (.)
17  C:   T[hank you very much       ]
```

18 O: [AND JUST BEFORE YOU GO] Mrs Lee.
19 C: Yes.
20 O: Em (0.3) have you heard of our moneyplus account?
21   (0.5)
22 C: Moneyplus?
23 O: Yeah basic- you know your current account no longer pays any
24   interest on your account (0.5) well this account does would you
25   like me to send you some information about on that.
26 C: Eh::m (1.0) (.hh) (.hh) no I don't think so no=
27 O: =not at the moment.
28 C: No I- I use my current account
29   (0.6)
30 C: [to (   )]
31 O: [okay then that's] fine no [problem] with that.
32 C: [okay   ]
33 C: Right lovely [thank you]
34 O: [thank you]
35 C: Bye

Notice also the technique the operator uses to transform the caller's rejection of the proposed new account into an open-ended response. When the caller declines the offer of information on the new type of account (line 26) the operator immediately produces an extension of her utterance ("=not at the moment."; line 27). This latched utterance works to transform the customer's clear declination of the offer into a potential interest at some point in the future. Martin and O'Neill (2011, p. 121) explain both the operator's motivations and potential organizational concerns based on this analysis of how the call unfolded. In line 26,

> the customer begins a mediated refusal 'no I don't think so…' to which the operator latches on '=Not at the moment'. This places the refusal in one of the system categories for classifying selling outcomes. Interestingly, the call centre management wondered why so few of the 'not at the moment' customers took up second selling attempts by post a month later, little realising that 'not at the moment' can often simply mean no. (Martin and O'Neill, 2011, p. 121)

Martin and O'Neill's (2011) research has illustrated how well-intentioned policies and employee training can have unintended consequences that may not be in the best interests of the company. While employers may believe that they have more control over the interaction when the call is scripted, local contingencies always arise which must be dealt with spontaneously by the call taker, and at the same time do not ensure that company goals will always be achieved in the way they were intended. Close examination of these interactions using the techniques of conversation analysis reveals information that can lead to potential solutions for these problems.

Whalen and Whalen (2011) present an example of how the organizational structure of a business can filter down to the level of person-to-person interaction in customer service calls. They studied a large copier machine and supplies firm that wanted to improve their delivery of customer service. The company (and its related customer service call centers) was divided into three separate areas: technical service, supplies and account administration. Callers were directed to separate phone lines for each of these areas. The organizational separation of these functions meant that call takers were experienced only in their area's functions, and were inadequately equipped to deal with any cross-functional concerns the customer might have. Whalen and Whalen (2011) illustrate some of these potential problems in Excerpt 7. After a brief and efficient opening sequence (lines 1–5) the caller begins describing a problem she is having with her copier. The call taker, Nan, listens to the customer's story. However, when the customer gets to their request in line 14, it is apparent that she is making a request for a technician to come out and fix the machine. The call taker now knows that the customer was directed to the wrong phone number. While she only handles billing issues, the caller clearly needs to talk to the customer service representative. Both the call taker and the customer have thus lost considerable time discussing something that should have been discussed with another employee.

Excerpt 7: Whalen and Whalen (2011, pp. 181–2)

1 Nan: Thank you for calling INK, this is Nan.
2 Cust: Yes. This is Stephanie Dales from M.A. Wilkin's office in
3   Louisville, Kentucky.
4   ((Nan writes "Stephanie" on a piece of paper))
5 Nan: Huh hum.
6 Cust: And, uhm, last week we had a problem with our copier, uhm
7   copying really dark
8 Nan: Uhum
9 Cust: and not gettin' all the- not copying everything. 'n some man came
10   out here and supposedly fixed it. But it's getting worse. Now
11   there's like black lines across the page. 'n we can't even send
12   anything out to the clients because it looks so bad.
13 Nan: Hm…
14 Cust: Is there any way he could come as soon as possible today?
15 Nan: Uhm. I think you got customer billing instead of customer service.
16 Cust: Oh I did? (laughing)
17 Nan: Yeah. (return laughter) Let me transfer you back over to- do you
18   have your serial number? I can go and give 'em
19 Cust: Yeah. It's sixty two H,
20 Nan: Uhhum. (writing on paper).
21 Cust: four nine three, two four three.
22 Nan: Okay. Let me transfer you back over there.
23 Cust: Okay. Thanks.
24 Nan: Huhum. (Dialing sounds)
25 Deb: I.N.K. services. This is Deb Smart. How can I help you?
26 Nan: Hi Deb. This is Nan with the Customer Account Center
27 Deb: Huhum. (very softly)
28 Nan: I have Stephanie who needs to place a- um- a service call but she
29   got us instead

30 Deb: Okay
31 Nan: You want 'er s- You want her serial number?
32 Deb: Sure.
33 Nan: It's sixty two H, four nine three, two four three.
34 Deb: Mary Wilkins?
35 Nan: Uh… Stephanie's her name.
36 Deb: Uh oh! Give me the serial number again.
37 Nan: Sixty-two H, four nine three, two four three.
38 Deb: I'm gettin' Mary Wilkins C.P.A.
39 Nan: Oh, for the- customer?
40 Deb: Uh huh. Let me uh- talk let me talk to 'em.=
41 Nan: Okay
42 Deb: Thanks
43 Nan: Uhhuh (transfers the call)

When the call taker has to transfer the customer to another line, the information she has given Nan about the problems she is having with her copier is not transferred with the call. The customer will therefore have to repeat this information to the technical service call taker after she is transferred. This repetition creates frustration for callers as they have to repeat their story, and also wastes time for both the caller and the call takers. If Nan had been trained to handle technical questions as well as accounting questions, the transfer would not have been necessary. A lot of time, repetition of information, and frustration for the customer could have been prevented. Note that the customer is on hold from line 25 to line 43 as Nan and Deb work out the transfer of the call.

The company instituted a pilot study of a program in which call takers were trained to respond to calls regarding all three areas (technical service, supplies and accounts). For example, if a customer calls to place an order for paper, the call taker is also able to help her with a technical problem requiring a service call rather than having to transfer her to someone else. They found that once employees were trained, call takers in the pilot program were able to handle all of the customers' needs in one phone call. These cross-trained employees provided better service and were able to take advantage of more opportunities for sales of supplies than had been possible in the old system. Whalen and Whalen (2011) were able to use conversation analysis, in conjunction with an ethnographic study of the organization and its transition to a new way of organizing customer service work, in a way that could to improve both employee performance and customer satisfaction.

Summary

The research reviewed in this chapter serves to illustrate several ways that conversation analytic research can be of use to businesses and other organizations. Such studies can reveal how work is being done in a variety of organizational contexts. The conversation analytic method can be used as a diagnostic technique to solve problems or to discover problems that the firm might not even be know existed. Conversation analytic research findings can also be used to determine which interactional strategies are most effective, and to assist in instructing employees in best practices for conducting various types of interactions.

Student activity

The next time you make a call to a business or institution, note how the call taker answers the phone. Do different types of businesses use different types of openings? Are the openings they use well suited to the type of business and the purpose of the call? What changes, if any, would you recommend in these call taker's practices?

Recommended sources

Baker, Carolyn, Emmison, Michael, and Firth, Alan. (2001), 'Discovering order in opening sequences: calls to a software helpline', in A. McHoul and M. Rapley (eds), *How to Analyse Talk in Institutional Settings: A Casebook of Methods*. London and New York: Continuum, pp. 41–56.

Boden, Deborah. (1994), *The Business of Talk: Organisations in Action*. Cambridge: Polity Press.

Hougaard, Gitte Rasmussen. (2008), 'Membership categorization in international business phone calls: The importance of "being international"', *Journal of Pragmatics*, 40, pp. 307–32.

Martin, David, and O'Neill, Jacki. (2011), 'Talk: talking the organisation into being', in Mark Rouncefield and Peter Tolmie (eds), *Ethnomethodology at Work*. Farnham: Ashgate, pp. 109–29.

Talk in Business Contexts: Meetings, Interviews, and Performance Appraisals 26

Chapter contents

Meetings in businesses and other organizational contexts

Barnes (2007) notes that the speech exchange system of meetings differs from that of ordinary conversation in several ways. Meetings are typically chaired or facilitated, and there is usually an explicit or implicit agenda of topics that needs to be discussed and often decided on. The interactional organization of talk in meetings differs depending on their purpose and size, as well as on the preferences of participants:

> Depending on the level of formality, talk structures can be pre-planned and speaker roles pre-allocated. Consider for example, the role of the chair in controlling talk, and scheduling the topic or items of discussion into recordable episodes to reflect business. The existence of counter-conversations, asides or side engagements helps to distinguish this 'official' meeting talk, i.e., that which has a common focus of attention and talk. (Barnes, 2007, p. 275)

Vinkhuyzen and Ikeya (2011) studied Project Assessment (PA) meetings held in a manufacturing company. The purpose of these meetings was for Project Managers ("PM") to communicate the actual status of projects to Senior Managers ("SM") so that any problems that existed could be solved. The authors describe the interactional organization of typical meetings as follows:

Like any meeting, the PA meeting begins after the people have arrived and taken a seat and the premeeting chitchat ends. Documents are distributed by the project team. Then, the PM begins by listing the documents that all participants have received to ensure that everybody has a complete set. The meeting officially starts when the PM goes through these documents in detail. The senior managers (SMs) listen and whenever they have questions or concerns, they interrupt the PM's reporting.

The PA meeting has a modified turn taking system, characteristic of institutional talk (Heritage and Drew, 1992). When the project team does its reporting, turn taking (Schegloff and Jefferson [sic—Sacks, Schegloff and Jefferson], 1974) is suspended. However, whenever the reporting is interrupted by a question or comment and a discussion ensues, ordinary turn-taking resumes. The reporting can only recommence after the discussion is closed, which is usually achieved by one of the SMs saying "okay." (Vinkhuyzen and Ikeya, 2011, p. 314)

Excerpt 1 shows a Senior Manager questioning a Project Manager about his concern about cost estimates for ongoing work. The Senior Manager constructs his/er professional role in this context by constructing a series of questions which ask the Project Manager to justify and explain his/er actions. The goal of this series of questions is to make sure the project is proceeding properly and according to schedule.

```
Excerpt 1: Vinkhuyzen and Ikeya (2011, p. 317)
01  SM:   So, have you presented it ((the cost estimate))
02        yet?
03  PM:   Well, regarding the items we have not presented
04        cost estimates which are probably not included in
05        the list I mentioned earlier are, well, the
06        linkage with Ultimate, sorry, I am going to bring
07        this (to the customer) as well, as they seem to
08        want to start it from July next year, so, in fact,
09        the linkage with Package Antilope is yet
10        to be determined
11  SM1:  How much were the estimates you have presented so
12        far?
13  PM:   Well, about 60 to 70 million ((yen))
14        ((pause))
15        ((other talk))…
16  SM1:  In a nutshell, regardless of the money
17        negotiations, is the work already going forward?
18        Or will you start the work after you get the
19        (contract)?
```

Note that the Senior Managers ("SM" and "SM1") use several techniques to convey their role and authority through talk. In addition to asking questions (e.g. lines 1, 11, and 16–17), they request more information from the Project Manager (line 11) and ask for clarification (lines 18–19). SM1 controls the direction of the topic by returning to the issue of the contract (line 16).

On the surface the interaction described above appears effective and well organized for an interaction between superiors and their subordinates. However, Vinkhuyzen and Ikeya (2011) found that these meetings were not effective for achieving the goals they were supposed to achieve: identifying problems with work-in-progress so that Senior Managers could help solve them. Based on an ethnographic study of the organization in combination with their conversation analytic study of the videotaped meetings, they concluded that a few simple changes in meeting procedures could transform the dynamics of the process and make them more effective. They recommended that the meetings have an official agenda with detailed plans for what would be discussed and outcomes that would be produced. A new activity would be added to the agenda, in which Project Managers would ask Senior Managers for advice. In addition, written status reports would be circulated in advance for each project to facilitate understanding and discussion. They also suggested that a neutral facilitator run the meetings instead of one of the Senior Managers.

Barnes (2007) studied meetings between staff and faculty members at a medical school. About 12 staff and faculty members met repeatedly to design curriculum for a new medical program. Barnes (2007) studied the interactional techniques used by the chair of these meetings to facilitate the goals of the group. For example, she found that the chair worked to bring discussion of issues to a close in a way that facilitated the creation of agreement among the participants. In Excerpt 2 below, "Mic" is chair of the meeting. In line 5 he produces a transitional turn that sums up the implications of prior talk and opens up space for a new topic to be discussed.

```
Excerpt 2: Barnes (2007, p. 283)
1   Tom:  An use a telematic lecture theatre to y'know in
2          [ in ] locality week y'know to do that [kind] of induction
3   Lau:  [Yeh]                                    [Yeh ]
4          (2.7)
5   Mic:  ->So we'll put that down as a as a plenary slot
6          (4.2)
7   Lau:  Whe:re are they going to learn about y'know the the sort'ov
8          new timetable and the new sort'ov methods of delivery
```

In general, the chair produced closing-implicative summaries of prior talk that proposed a "gloss" of the discussion. These summaries served to close down the current topic and initiate a movement to the next topic that needed to be dealt with in the meeting. The formulations used the transition marker "so" at the beginning of the turn to provide a pivot (as in line 5 in Excerpt 2). This pivot connected the formulation to prior talk and oriented participants to what was to come next. In addition, the chair used "pro-terms" in their summaries (such as "this" or "that") to provide a link to prior talk. The formulation itself could perform one of two interactional functions: "summarizing the *gist* of a stretch of talk, or drawing out its relevant implication or *upshot*." (Barnes, 2007, p. 278). The chairs in the meetings she observed typically used formulations to sum up the aspects of previous discussion that could be taken as agreed upon, and at the same time open up the floor for additional issues or a new topic.

Barske (2009) also studied the interactional construction of role of meeting chair. He found that one way in which the person in a leadership position constructs their role as facilitator is through the use of the freestanding "okay" as a response to other's turns. Barske (2009) found that chairpersons in German business meetings used different patterns of gaze direction with the production of "okay." These patterns of gaze direction accomplished different goals in their facilitation of the meeting. First, he noted that in every meeting the employer (who also facilitated the meetings) produced more instances of the freestanding "okay" than any other participant. The use of this type of response to a prior utterance is therefore part of what Barske (2009, p. 126) calls "doing-being-facilitator." When the employer produced the freestanding "okay" while moving his gaze away from the prior speaker, he indicated that a topic transition was relevant. He often followed this move with the solicitation of a new speaker or another means of initiating a new topic. When the employer produced the freestanding "okay" while maintaining his gaze toward the prior speaker, that speaker typically continued with on topic talk. In Excerpt 3, the first line is Barske's (2009) original German transcription, the second and third lines (in italics) are his literal and idiomatic English translations of the excerpt, respectively. This excerpt shows a previous speaker continuing with on topic talk after the chair produces a free standing "okay." (line 16) while maintaining his gaze at the prior speaker.

Excerpt 3: Barske (2009, p. 137)

```
10 L:    was den abverkauf (0.8) ä:hm (0.2) dieser (.) einheiten
         what the sale     (0.8) u:hm (0.2) of these (.) units
         regarding the sale (0.8) u:hm (0.2) of these (.) units.

11       angeht. =weil es    i[s'    n]icht so als ob nichts verkauft
         regards.=because it i[s     n]ot so as if nothing sold
                  =because it's[          ] like nothing is being

12 SCH:                        [mhm.   ]
                               [uh huh.]

13 L:    [wird.     ]
         [becomes.]
         [sold.     ]
14 SCH: [mhm?    ]  m[hm.  ]
         [uh huh? ] uh [ huh.]
15 L:                  [ das ] kann man nicht sagen.
                       [ that] can one not say.
                       [ one ] can't say that.
16 SCH: ok. ((SCH keeps looking at L))
         ok.
```

17   (0.5)
18   L: ja. (0.2) das läuft halt auch noch so nebenher und geht dann-
          yes (0.2) that runs just also still so next to and goes then-
          yes (0.2) that's going on on the side and happens-

Vöge (2010) studied how social status and position in the organizational hierarchy affected the interaction in business meetings in a large German corporation. The focus of her study was situations in which one person in the meeting was complaining about another member of the organization, who was not present at the meeting. These types of utterances are called "indirect complaints." Vöge (2010) found that these situations were interactionally awkward, and hence often accompanied by laughter. In the business meeting context, laughter can be used instead of an explicit formulation of the complaint, in order to avoid saying things that may be awkward.

> Complaints in a business setting can be a difficult undertaking. The epistemics of complaining— who complains about what to whom in which manner—and the possible consequences of this activity bear different risks than the same activity does in an everyday setting. The institutional setting imposes certain restrictions to the interaction (see Vöge, 2008; Heinemann, 2009; Ruusuvuori, 2009): an open complaint about a superior's misconduct could result in drawbacks for the employee. In contrast to everyday settings, organizational roles and organizational hierarchy can play a decisive part in the interactional trajectories in an institutional business setting. This constraint may be one reason why most complaints produced by a person lower in the hierarchy than the complainee involve laughter, and why direct complaints, that is complaints that are made against a person present during the interaction, are realized in a very implicit way. The data reveals that all team members do complain occasionally, and that there is no tendency towards only team leaders or particular team members complaining 'all of the time'. (Vöge, 2010, p. 1558)

By using conversation analytic techniques, Vöge was able to discover how laughter was used by people at different levels of the status hierarchy to achieve specific goals in the meeting. When participants in the meeting were at the same level of the hierarchy, the indirect complaints were formulated more explicitly than when the participants were at different levels of the hierarchy. When a subordinate made an indirect complaint about a nonpresent employee to a superior, they did not formulate the complaint explicitly. The recipient of the complaint responded with laughter to indicate that they understood the issue about the person referred to. Neither party had to put the sensitive material into words, thus avoiding gossiping or badmouthing other employees, while still getting the problematic information communicated so that the reasons for the problems can be understood by all.

Excerpt 4 shows Vöge's (2010) transcript. The first line is the original German, the second line (in italics) is the English translation. Embodied action is indicated by asterisks in the transcript, with a description of the action following the asterisk(s). Vöge (2010, p. 1568) sums up her analysis of this excerpt thusly: "Laura employs laughter in order to actually express the complaint; in labeling Mr. Eckler as "our friend", she invites Corinna and others to laugh. Neither an actual complaint nor explicit formulations are articulated."

Excerpt 4: Vöge (2010, p. 1567)

01 Laura: und es war sehr kompliziert die ganze sache?, weil: ich
            and it was very complicated the whole thing?, be: cause
                    *mimics a list   **gaze to Corinna
            ***gestures to Corinna

02   ha*tte schon eine schöne liste** und dann ** kam
            *I h*ad already a   nice   list** and then ** came*
                            *Laura lifts hands and gaze upwards,
                              swings head moanfully

03   [unser freund (.)* her[r eckler?   ]
            *[our friend   (.) *mis[ter eckler,   ]*

04 Corinna: [hmff

05 Corinna: [herr eckler,   ] hhhehehe .hhm
                                 [mister eckler?] hhhehehe .hhm

06   (0.2)

07 Laura: und uh er hat gesagt (.) das is alles nich gut. HHEHHEheh
            *and uh he said (.) that all is not good. HHE*HHEheh*

Status differences are also relevant in an excerpt from a meeting analyzed by Fairhurst (1993; 2007). In Excerpt 5 a team leader ("L") is working to educate a team member ("TM") about the "Total Quality Assessment" approach the team is being asked to implement.

Excerpt 5: Fairhurst (2007, pp. 58–9)

1 TM: If this- if we're getting the savings now with the system we got,
2   why even look at the damn (TQA) thing? (.9) I'm- I'm struggling
3   with that
4 L: We::ll (1.0: maybe [(Indistinguishable)
5 TM: [(Indistinguishable) in the quality method. In
6   TQA, lookin' at it though in TQA. I'm struggling with that=
7 L: =Okay
8 TM: for- for savings, pure out and outright savings. Yes. We may be
9   able to get something out of there, but is it- (.6) is it- is it
10   contributing to the quality of (.6) product, whatever product we're
11   puttin' out here (1.0) [okay
12 L: [Well (.8) think about (.8) think about (hhh)
13   though, what is the product we're providing? We're not making
14   soap. You're not. I'm not, okay?
15   (1.1)
16 TM: The plant is.

17		(.9)
18	L:	Yeah the plant is and- but- but you and I:: indirectly are. (2.2) You
19		know, one of the things is this- this thing and I- I believe you
20		have- have a copy of that=
21	TM:	=I have a copy
22	L:	the seven fundamental questions, you know. (1.0) Who are my customers? What do they need? What's my- my product or service, not the plant's? (.6) your product or service. (1.6) What are our expectations? (1.7) What's the process for providing my product or service? What action is required to improve? So it deals with your specific- don't worry if I turn it around, my (1.1) specific product. (1.6) And right now that's a service, and the service is project engineering, project management, project development. (1.8) So in this specific piece okay, (3.5) what do your customers need? If you think about it, who are your customers if you think about it that way….

As the excerpt begins, the Team Member is expressing their concerns about the new "TQA" system. Note that although he is of lower status than the Leader, the Team Member speaks very informally (lines 1–3). The Leader also responds in a conversational way. Instead of producing a direct disagreement with the Team Member's position, he begins his utterance with the disagreement-implicative "We::ll" (line 4), thus constructing his disagreement as a dispreferred second pair part. This formulation both avoids the direct assertion of authority and avoids arguing or conflict. As the Leader continues his argument in lines 12–14 he ends his utterance with a solicitation of a response ("okay?"; line 14), thus inviting the Team Member's feedback. After receiving this response (line 16), the Team Leader structures his turn in lines 18–20 with a "yes, but" format, thus packaging it as an agreement. He goes on in the remainder of the excerpt to explain the idea behind the TQA system and illustrating how it could be helpful. The work of the organization is therefore accomplished through a meeting which has many of the elements of an ordinary conversational exchange, which avoids the direct imposition of authority or "pulling rank," but which yet reflects the different actions that the participants take depending on their role in the interaction—team member versus leader.

Variations in interviews: Job interviews and job appraisal meetings

In this section we examine several types of interviews in business and other organizational contexts.

Job interviews

Our first impression of what a job interview is like might be an interviewer grilling the interviewee with a series of questions designed to figure out whether they would be a good person

Very shy interview

to hire. When we look at actual examples of job interviews, however, we find that they contain a much wider range of patterns of interactional structures. Part of the interview may be devoted to the interviewer giving information to the applicant about the firm, job responsibilities, salary and benefits, and so on. This part of the interaction may also be structured as a series of questions and answers, but with the interviewee asking the questions instead of the interviewer. Glenn's (2010) research illustrates some of the varied ways of organizing interaction in job interviews.

While they may often have the structure of a question/answer chair, with the interviewer asking the questions and the interviewee answering them, researchers studying videotaped job interviews found a range of interactional structures occurring in the interviews. Job interviews differ greatly in their degree of formality, and it is typically the interviewer who sets the tone for the interview. For example, Glenn (2010) analyzes a job interview in which the interviewer ("Jill") begins by expressing a desire for a more "conversational" style of interview:

Excerpt 6: Glenn (2010, pp. 1485–6)
((Recording begins as they are entering the room))
1   JILL: … I wanted to do is to have more of a conversation
2   than anything else,
3   BET: ↑O[kay]
4   JILL: [.hh][u:m t]o get ta understand what you're looking for,
5   JILL: [(((sits))]

Regardless of the degree of formality or informality of the interaction, there are nevertheless differences in the power and authority of the participants in job interviews. Asymmetries in power and authority in institutional talk can be played out in the details of the interaction. Glenn (2010) found that invitations to laugh and their responses were performed asymmetrically in the job interviews he studied. For example, in Excerpt 7 the interviewer ("Jill") produces an invitation to laugh in line 8 by inserting laugh particles into her ongoing talk (Jefferson, 1979). The interviewee ("Betty") responds by accepting that invitation to laugh in line 9. She produces laughter particles at the end of the word "Yeahhahah," and then produces what Glenn (2010) calls "silent laughter" (displaying the act of laughing with facial expressions and/or body movements, but without producing sound) at the end of line 9. The laughter invitations may have been functional for the interviewer Jill as she tried to construct a more informal, conversational tone for her job interviews, but they also display the power imbalance between the two participants, as the interviewee responds to the laughter invitation, but then lets the interviewer guide the conversation back to the topic at hand or decide to initiate a new topic after the laughter interlude.

Excerpt 7: Glenn (2010, pp. 1485–98)
1   BET: How 'bout Carson Education in other countries.
2   JILL: Mm hm=
3   BET: =Does that=

```
 4   JILL:                      =Y[eah they're all over I mean] every (.) you
 5          know Spain, France .hh um Africa: Australia=
 6   BET:                                      =O[h wow]
 7   JILL:                                        [you kn]ow so
 8          e[hhihehe that's my [goal.     ↑I'd l]ike to go to
 9   BET:    [Yeahhahah        [(Yeah I wanna)] ((silent laugh))
10   JILL:  Australia please?
11   BET:   I(hh) know(hh)
12   JILL:  Um and pay for it all?
13   BET:   Ehuh yeah .hhh
14   JILL:  So what other things do you need to know from me I mean
```

Performance appraisal interviews

Performance appraisal interviews, or "annual reviews," are a key way organizations communicate with employees about and document the strengths and weaknesses of employees and the areas they need to improve. Asmuß (2008) analyzes how supervisors can formulate negative feedback in these interviews, and explores the interactional implications of several methods of doing so. She first notes that giving negative feedback is a socially awkward, potentially face-threatening action, and is thus often performed with some delicacy in order to avoid offending or embarrassing the person being criticized. However, since honest communication about employee performance is the purpose of the appraisal interview, it is important to find effective ways to communicate this feedback. The interview is intended to benefit both the organization and the employee.

Asmuß (2008) found three main ways the feedback was given. The most complex way turned out to be attempting to mitigate the impact of the negative feedback. We reviewed a variety of mitigation techniques in our discussion of dispreferred responses in Chapter 6. Recall that Pomerantz (1984), in her study of responses to assessments, found that dispreferred responses were often characterized by delay and indirectness. Asmuß (2008) found that not only the responses, but also the feedback itself, could be formulated to present the negative feedback as a dispreferred action.

Asmuß's (2008) data are from a large Danish firm. In her excerpts, the English gloss is placed *above* the Danish original, and is typed in bold face italics. In Excerpt 8 the supervisor pre-emptively mitigates the social awkwardness of his negative criticism by a preface that minimizes its import (line 1). He then produces a delaying move in line 3, which presents the feedback as not a serious criticism because it is something the supervisor has done as well. This is followed by an explanation which further delays the criticism and uses a humorous frame to package the feedback in a non-threatening way (lines 4 and 5). When the supervisor finally produces the criticism in lines 9–19 it has been considerably delayed and mitigated. Asmuß (2008) notes that while this formulation may be an attempt to save face for the employee, it may be dysfunctional for the organization because it delays the input of the employee and minimizes the importance of their perspective on the problem.

Excerpt 8: Asmuß (2008, p. 419)
[S = supervisor, E = employee]

1 S: ***I   I   I have alike a few things that***
      [job- job- job h<u>ar</u> da: e- e:- <u>e</u>t par t<u>i</u>ng s<u>o</u>m:

2 E: [( )

3 S: ***that I have experienced myself uh hrhr***
      som jog solv har oplevet (.) æ:: hr <u>hr</u>:

4 S: ***I have I actually believe this is a term I have invented myself***
      jog har jo- je- jeg tr<u>or</u> nok det=er et begr<u>e</u>b <u>je</u>g har <u>o</u>pfundet:

5 S: ***.hh (I call   it situation sensitive presentation technique.***
      .hh <j[eg kalder det situat<u>io</u>nsbestemt præsentat<u>io</u>nst<u>e</u>knik.>

6 E: **[.hf::**

7   (.)

8 E: ***uhu [hu***
      a<u>ha</u> [ha

9 S: ***[uhu he he uh this is perhaps a   l[ittle long isn't it?***
      [a<u>ha</u> h<u>e</u> he .h æ det er måsk<u>e</u> l[idt <u>langt</u> <u>i</u>kk?=

10 E: **[ahgh**

11 S: ***but=uh   [but it   it has much to do with [these there uh***
      =m<u>e</u>n=æ: (.) [men det- det har <u>me</u>get o' g<u>ø</u>re med [d<u>e</u> de:r ↓æ:

12 E: [ha   [((nods))

13   (.)

14 S: ***where there [perhaps is] prepared for a twenty-minute***
          presentation
      .hh hvor der s<u>å</u> (0.5) [måske er] <u>fo</u>rberedt t<u>y</u>ve minutters <u>i</u>ndlæg

15 E: [(   )]

16 S: ***[and there is just three and a half minutes left, [right?***
      [og der er k<u>un</u> tr<u>ee</u>halvt minut trib<u>ag</u>   [ikk<u>o</u>s?

17 E: [hhr   [((smiles))

18 S: ***and the people sit and shuffle their feet because they'd***
         o:g (.) folk de sidder og tripper fordi de vil egentlig

19 S: ***rather end the   [mee[ting.***
         gerne ↓æ: videre (.) [(med do(n)

20 E: ***[yes yes y[es***
                               [jo- (.) jo j[o

         ((S continues for 38 more lines accounting for his criticism))

61 S: ***so   you know it it   it is my impression that there***
         sån-   (0.4) altså det-jo- det- det=er <mit indtryk> (.) at der

62 S: ***perhaps can be done a little bit more there right?   Uhm***
         måske kan gøres en lille smule mere der ikkos? .hhh æh [m:

In contrast, consider the trajectory of the discussion when a supervisor uses a more direct mode of communicating the negative feedback. In the appraisal interview in Excerpt 9, the supervisor is also communicating negative criticism. The supervisor directly communicates the criticism in lines 1–7, with few delays or mitigation techniques. The employee responds (after a pause in line 8) with a straightforward response to the supervisor's criticism in which she both acknowledges the criticism and explains it. Through this more direct method of communicating negative feedback, a discussion has been opened up between the two that can lead to a solution. The conclusion of Asmuß's (2008) analysis is that the more straightforward method of communicating negative feedback may well be more functional for the organization.

Excerpt 9: Asmuß (2008, p. 422)

1   S: ***and then I have written it=it   it uh it was this***
          og så har jeg skrevet >det=det< det æ: det var det

2   S: ***there about initiative >I have written< you may very***
          der me:d initiativ >jeg har skrevet< du må godt

3   S: ***well be a little more visible:***
          være lidt mere synlig:

4   (0.4)

5   S: ***I am sure   you can***
          Jet er sikker på du ka:::

6   S: ***.hh you can contribute with with more also on the***
          .hh du kan bidrage me::d me mere (.) også på det

7 S: ***strategic level.***
strategiske nive<u>au</u>.

8 (2.1)

9 E: ***.mth I have actually uh some times   been***
.mth jeg har <u>fak</u>tisk æ:: >noget gange< (0.2) været

10 E: ***a little afraid,   I asked Peter when we have come***
lidt bange, >jeg spurgte< peter når vi er kommet

11 E: ***home from the=department meeting whether I appeared***
hj<u>e</u>m fra: <u>a</u>fdelingsmødet .hh om jeg <u>v</u>irkede

12 E: ***too critical   [when   asking   questions***
for <u>kri</u>tisk såd[an: ved at st- st<u>i</u>lle spørgsmålstgn:

13 S: ***[.H YES***
[.H Y<u>A</u>,

14 E: ***[about something and***
[til <u>no</u>get og:

15 S: ***[yes***
[ya

Summary

The research reviewed in this chapter illustrates how the work of businesses and other organizations is done through talk. Whether that talk occurs while doing the work itself, or in meetings or interviews of various kinds, participants display and construct their institutional roles through their use of routine interactional procedures and task or institution-specific procedures. The use of conversation analysis is an effective way of identifying and solving problems in interaction in a wide range of communication genres in business settings.

Student activities

1. The research cited above by Asmuß (2008) suggested that employee appraisal meetings might be more effective in improving employee performance if the manager communicated the criticism directly. Do you think the perspective display series that Maynard found used in medical settings for delivering bad news would be effective in this institutional context? Why or why not?

2. With another student, conduct two role plays of an employee appraisal meeting in which the person playing the manager role has to tell the employee that their chronic lateness has caused problems for the organization. For the first role play, use a roundabout method as in Asmuß (2008), and for the second role play use a direct method. Then discuss the experience. Which approach felt more comfortable? Which approach was more informative? Which approach did a better job of providing an opening for a discussion of the problematic issues?

Recommended sources

Boden, Deborah. (1994), *The Business of Talk: Organisations in Action*. Cambridge: Polity Press.

Ford, Cecilia E. (2008), *Women Speaking Up: Getting and Using Turns in Meetings*. New York: Palgrave Macmillan.

Glenn, Phillip. (2010), 'Interviewer laughs: shared laughter and asymmetries in employment interviews', *Journal of Pragmatics*, 42, 1485–98.

Martin, David, and O'Neill, Jacki. (2011), 'Talk: talking the organisation into being', in Mark Rouncefield and Peter Tolmie (eds), *Ethnomethodology at Work*. Farnham: Ashgate, pp. 109–29.

Maynard, Douglas W., Schaeffer, Nora Cate, and Freese, Jeremy. (2011), 'Improving response rates in telephone interviews', in Charles Antaki (ed.), *Applied Conversation Analysis: Interventions and Change in Institutional Talk*. London: Palgrave-MacMillan, pp. 54–74.

27 Conclusions

Chapter contents

Understanding talk

Recall that in Chapter 1 of this text book we introduced the subject of conversation analysis by asking you to examine two simplified transcripts. These short excerpts were both from mediation sessions. Now that we have learned how to read conversation analytic transcripts and apply the basic findings of conversation analysis to analyzing talk in interaction, take a few minutes to review these detailed transcripts of the same excerpts and compare them to the simplified transcripts in Chapter 1. What types of information do the transcription symbols give you that are missing from the simplified transcripts? Now that you understand how to do conversation analysis, what do you know about this interaction that you didn't know at the beginning of the course? How does this knowledge help you understand the nature of the communication between these participants, and the ways they were successful or unsuccessful in conducting the mediation session and working toward achieving its goals? How did the participants work to create what is clearly a "mediation session" and not an ordinary conversation? How do the mediators do the work of mediation by their actions during the session? Can you think of any different actions the participants could have taken which would have made these interactions more successful? After the two excerpts you will find a brief discussion and analysis of each excerpt. Compare these with your own observations.

Excerpt 1 is from a mediation session between a divorcing couple (Ken and Cindy). They have a four-year-old daughter, Tina.

Excerpt 1: Garcia Midwest Data Site A Tape 8, page 19

1   Ken: [i nor]mally pick='er <u>up</u>?, (1.5) >i=guess=at< (0.3) after i get off

2		work. (0.2) juss'=anywhere=between <u>five</u> thirty en six. (0.4) en i
3		usually keep='er un<u>til</u>?, (1.8) ni:ne? (0.4) ten uh clock.
4		(1.3)
5	MB:	°um=hm°
6		(1.1)
7	MA:	mm<u>kay</u>. (3.6) so what is it that you would like (0.2) ken.
8		(1.0)
9	Ken:	that <u>i</u>'d like?
10		(0.3)
11	MA:	yes. (0.4) in terms of (0.7) uhm parenting time with Tina.
12		(3.1)
13	Ken:	<u>i</u> would like tuh see 'er every day.
14		(1.4)
15	MA:	tch (1.1) that's what most parents tell us. (0.2) thet=that's (0.4)
16		thuh <u>hard</u>est thing. (0.3) about divorce. (0.8) 's=not seeing yer
17		child every day. (3.0) tch yuh think that's possible tuh see='er
18		every day?
19		(0.7)
20	Ken:	i don'=<u>know</u>.
21		(3.1)
22	MB:	tch do you live? (0.4) pretty near one another? how's your:
23		[resident]ial (0.3) set [up.]
24	Ken:	[live about five] ['t'<u>s=in</u>] about five minutes of each other.
25		(1.3)
26	MB:	and what is <u>tina</u>'s? schedule look like. d'is she in child care? or
27		(0.4)
28	Ken:	u:h
29		(0.5)
30	Cindy:	no: i work at home.=
31	Ken:	=nyeah [she lives]
32	Cindy:	[she <u>lives</u>] with me.
33		(0.4)
34	MB:	°okay so she's home with you all day.°
35		(0.5)
36	Cindy:	°mm hmm°
37		(1.3)
38	Ken:	tch she'll start school i think (0.4) well?, (0.4) she='as tuh start
39		<u>school</u> next year. (1.1) °u:h° (0.5) kindergarten.

Excerpt 2 is from a mediation session between two neighbors in an apartment complex who are trying to resolve conflicts over noise and other issues.

Excerpt 2: Garcia (1991, p. 826)

1	Liz:	=The SA:ME woman that organized that parked: °eh°=so that I
2		could not get out=of my co:-h-mplex.=
3	MB:	=hm::?,
4	Nancy:	You were parked=

```
 5  Liz:                         =one morning.
 6        (0.2)
 7  Nancy: She was parked, in h[er space and she            ]
 8  MB:                          [yeah, chum! yeah but=I=WAS]=JUST
 9  MB:    [SAYING I- I REME:MBER y]ou you SA:Ying, you=know?
10  Nancy: [(parked next) to you:     ]
11  MB:    [that you felt you       ] were o:::ver, whe::lmed with
12  Liz:   [There was nowhere else to park.]
13  MB:    [peop   ]le.
14  Nancy: [You still]
15        (0.2)
16  Nancy: can not park in some one el[se's parking place.]
17  MB:                              [um so I thought   ]
18  Liz:                             [(sorry) it        ]ha:ppens a:ll thuh
19        time Na[:ncy,] why doesn't she do it with other people, an' that's
20  MB:          [yes ]
21  Nancy: [(not                                )]
22  MA:    [I DON'T WANT ANY CROSS TALK, thank you.]
```

How the detailed transcripts differ from the simplified transcripts

You have undoubtedly noticed many ways that the two sets of transcripts differ from each other. For example, in Excerpt 1 there are many pauses in Ken's utterance in lines 1–3. Some of these indicate error avoidance or error repair. The pauses at the end of possibly complete turn constructional units reflect the turn taking system of mediation sessions. In this type of mediation session the disputants have the floor for extended turns, and are not typically interrupted by the opposing disputant, who is supposed to wait until solicited by a mediator to respond. Both mediators let fairly lengthy pauses elapse (in lines 4 and 6) before producing minimal responses; these listener responses display attentiveness to Ken's utterance. Their delayed placement ensures that he is done before a mediator takes control of the floor again by asking a question in line 7.

Ken's utterance in line 9 is an other-initiation of repair. He is trying to make sure he understands the mediator's question before he answers it. Even after the mediator repairs her question (line 11), specifying that she's asking him how much parenting time he wants with his daughter Tina, a very long pause elapses before Ken answers the question in line 13 ("i would like tuh see 'er every day."). The pause conveys the thoughtfulness of his response.

There is an instance of overlapped talk in the excerpt (line 24). When Ken did not answer Mediator B's question in line 22 immediately ("tch do you live? (0.4) pretty near one another?"), she initiated a self-repair of her question (her continuation of the utterance in lines 22–3). Ken overlaps this continuation in order to reply to her initial question.

In Chapter 1 we characterized Excerpt 1 as the more successful interaction, and it still appears more successful than Excerpt 2 when the detailed transcripts are examined. The mediators allow Ken lots of space to formulate his thoughts. Other than some minor overlaps due to brief misunderstandings (which the participants successfully repair (e.g. lines 30–2), the talk is clear and understandable. The topics of discussion are relevant to the issues the disputants need to resolve in the mediation session. The spouses participate in the discussion without arguing or conveying hostility. The mediators maintain control of the interaction by asking questions and directing the topic, while simultaneously allowing the spouses plenty of time and space to communicate their thoughts and ideas. This excerpt is consistent with what is expected for routine interactions in this type of mediation session.

Excerpt 2, on the other hand, although also from a mediation session, has quite a different feel and a different interactional structure. This excerpt is from a dispute between two neighbors in an apartment complex who are in mediation to resolve problems with noise and other issues. Just from looking at the transcript you can see that the pace and tone of this interaction was quite different from that in Excerpt 1. In Excerpt 2 there are overlaps or latches between almost every exchange of turns at talk. There are only two brief pauses in the entire excerpt, both only 0.2 seconds long. This is a fast paced exchange. Everyone is beginning to speak as soon as possible, often not waiting for a transition relevance place to begin a new turn. Very few pauses are allowed for people to think before responding. Another difference you will see is that at times voices are raised. Mediator B's utterance in lines 8–9 and Mediator A's utterance in line 22 are both partially transcribed in capital letters, which indicates that they were speaking markedly louder than surrounding talk. Both mediators needed to raise their voices at these points in order to be heard over the disputants, who were engaged in arguing with each other and were not listening to Mediator B's more subtle attempts to stop the argument in lines 11, 13, 17 and 20.

This excerpt illustrates why mediators are needed to facilitate the interaction between the disputing parties. If Liz and Nancy had been allowed to continue arguing indefinitely, they probably would not have reached a resolution of their dispute, and may well have ended up even angrier at each other than they were before the mediation session started.

Note also how the success of the mediator at doing the job of facilitating the session depends on the cooperation of the disputants. As we learned with regard to the job of television news interviewer, which we explored in Chapter 23, a person in a leadership role (whether a TV interviewer, a mediator or the chair of a business meeting) can only do a good job in their professional role if the other participants in the interaction cooperate with the rules and procedures for that type of interaction.

The techniques of arguing are also evident in this exchange. For example, in line 1 Liz makes a complaint about another tenant in the apartment complex blocking her into a parking space. In line 4 Nancy violates the turn taking system of these mediation sessions (in which she is supposed to wait until solicited by a mediator to respond to Liz), to produce an oppositional utterance (lines 4 and 7). The mediator tries to intervene in lines 8 and 9, but Nancy continues talking to Liz, producing her utterance simultaneously with the mediator. Liz responds to Nancy in line 12, defending her actions ("There was nowhere else to park.") and also interrupting the mediator. Nancy also ignores the mediator's attempted intervention and responds to Liz's defense of her position (lines 14 and 16). The exchange of argumentative, oppositional utterances between the two disputants continues until Mediator

A sanctions them in line 22. Note that Mediator A has to speak quite loudly in order to be heard.

The mediators in Excerpt 2 thus enacted their roles in very different ways than did the mediators in Excerpt 1. The interaction unfolded quite differently in the two exchanges, largely because of the failure of the disputants in Excerpt 2 to abide by the rules of the process (such as not interrupting and waiting until they are solicited by a mediator to respond to the opposing disputant).

It should be clear that the detailed transcripts add an enormous amount of information that is not in the simplified excerpts we saw in Chapter 1. In addition, you now have sufficient knowledge of the conversation analytic method to analyze utterances in their sequential context and observe how each utterance displays its understanding of prior talk. You can apply the basic findings of conversation analytic research (e.g. how turns of talk are routinely exchanged, how arguing sequences are constructed and avoided, how errors are repaired and overlaps resolved, and how topic shifts are successfully accomplished) to enrich your understanding of these two excerpts. You can now fully appreciate the extent to which the work of the mediators involves the successful use of routine interactional procedures and the cooperation of the disputants with the turn taking system of mediation. The comparison of these two excerpts also illustrates the observation made by Boden (1994), Gronn (1983), Fairhurst (2007) and others about how the work of organizations is done through talk. In this example the mediation session itself is created by how participants organize their talk. The use of the conversation analytic method enables us to understand and study the procedures people use to conduct the interactions through which they do their work and live their lives.

Using conversation analysis in daily life and in the workplace

After completing this text book you should be thoroughly grounded in the conversation analytic perspective. Your ear should be finely tuned, so for example, when someone hesitates or says "um hm" you will notice that behavior and understand the work that is being done by that action. This should lead to greater understanding of the people you interact with and a more accurate understanding of what they are communicating. It is to be hoped that if you find yourself in the midst of an argument you would like to avoid, you can keep the argument from escalating by avoiding responding immediately with unmitigated oppositional utterances, and instead can pause briefly, mitigate your response with qualifiers and hesitation markers and other techniques, and otherwise work to deescalate the confrontation. On the other hand, if you are in a debate which you would like to win, it is to be hoped that you can call upon some of the techniques for constructing strong answers and avoiding negative implications of other's questions or attacks.

The analytic perspective conversation analysis provides may also be useful to you in interactions in the workplace. Fairhurst (2007; 2011) argues that we can improve our ability to communicate effectively in the workplace in part through increasing our knowledge of how successful communications work. If your work involves telephone interactions, for example either doing telephone sales work or supervising those who do, how can you increase the chance that the person you are calling will talk to you and be convinced by your arguments? If you're doing customer service work, how do you find out what the customer wants, get enough information from them to understand their problem, and successfully resolve it for them? If you're working in any type of position where people come to you with problems, how will you work to understand their problem and propose an effective solution? If you are in a position where you have to convey bad news to someone, how will you do so in a sensitive way that will increase the chances of the recipient understanding and accepting the news? For those of you engaged in research on talk and interaction, the conversation analytic perspective will provide a powerful means of discovery in a wide range of interactional settings.

References

American Arbitration Association, American Bar Association, and the Association for Conflict Resolution. (2005), *The Model Standard for Conduct of Mediators*. Washington, DC: American Bar Association. http://www.americanbar.org/content/dam/aba/migrated/dispute/documents/model_standards_conduct_april2007.authcheckdam.pdf

Arminen, Ilkka. (2005), 'Sequential order and sequence structure: the case of incommensurable studies on mobile phone calls', *Discourse Studies*, 7, (6), 649–62.

—(2006), 'Social functions of location in mobile telephony', *Personal Ubiquitous Computing*, 10, 319–23.

Arminen, Ilkka, Auvinen, Petra and Palukka, Hannele. (2010), 'Repairs as the last orderly provided defense of safety in aviation', *Journal of Pragmatics*, 42, 443–65.

Arminen, Ilkka and Leinonen, Minna. (2006), 'Mobile phone call openings: tailoring answers to personalized summonses', *Discourse Studies*, 8, (3), 339–68.

Arminen, Ilkka and Weilenmann, Alexandra. (2009), 'Mobile presence and intimacy—reshaping social actions in mobile contextual configuration', *Journal of Pragmatics*, 41, 1905–23.

Asch, Solomon E. (1946), 'Forming impressions of personality', *The Journal of Abnormal and Social Psychology*, 41, 258–90.

—(1951), 'The effects of group pressure on the modification and distortion of judgments', in H. Guetzkow (ed.), *Groups, Leadership, and Men*. Pittsburgh: Carnegie Press, pp. 45–53.

Asmuß, Birte. (2008), 'Performance appraisal interviews: preference organization in assessment sequences', *Journal of Business Communication*, 45, (4), 408–29.

Atkinson, J. Maxwell. (1982), 'Understanding formality: notes on the categorisation and production of "formal" interaction', *British Journal of Sociology*, 33, 86–117.

—(1984), 'Public speaking and audience responses: some techniques for inviting applause', in J. M. Atkinson and John Heritage (eds), *Structures of Social Action: Studies in Conversation Analysis*. Cambridge: Cambridge University Press, pp. 370–409.

Atkinson, J. Maxwell and Drew, Paul. (1979), *Order in Court: The Organization of Verbal Interaction in Judicial Settings*. London: MacMillan Press.

Atkinson, J. Maxwell and Heritage, John (eds), (1984), *Structures of Social Action: Studies in Conversation Analysis*. Cambridge: Cambridge University Press.

Baker, Carolyn, Emmison, Michael and Firth, Alan. (2001), 'Discovering order in opening sequences: calls to a software helpline', in A. McHoul and M. Rapley (eds), *How to Analyse Talk in Institutional Settings: A Casebook of Methods*. London and New York: Continuum, pp. 41–56.

Baker, Carolyn D., Emmison, Michael, and Firth, Alan (eds). (2005), *Calling for Help: Language and Social Interaction in Telephone Helplines*. Amsterdam and Philadelphia: John Benjamins.

Barnes, Rebecca. (2007), 'Formulations and the facilitation of common agreement in meetings talk', *Text & Talk*, 27, (3), 273–96.

Barske, Tobias. (2009), 'Same token, different actions: a conversation analytic study of social roles, embodied actions, and ok in German business meetings', *Journal of Business Communication*, 46, (1), 120–49.

Beckman, H. B. and Frankel, Richard M. (1984), 'The effect of physician behavior on the collection of data', *Annals of Internal Medicine*, 101, 692–6.

—(1985), 'Soliciting the patient's complete agenda: a relationship to the distribution of concerns', *Clinical Research*, 33, 714A.

Berg, Sara, Taylor, Alex S. and Harper, Richard. (2005), 'Gift of the gab', in Richard Harper, Leysia Palen and Alex Taylor (eds), *The Inside Text: Social, Cultural and Design Perspectives on SMS*. The Netherlands: Springer, pp. 271–85.

Bilmes, Jack. (2005), 'The call-on-hold as conversational resource', *Text*, 25, (2), 149–70.

Boden, Deborah. (1994), *The Business of Talk: Organisations in Action*. Cambridge: Polity Press.

Bogen, David and Lynch, Michael. (1989), 'Taking account of the hostile native: plausible deniability and the production of conventional history in the Iran-Contra hearings', *Social Problems*, 36, (3), 197–224.

Brooks, Samantha. (2009), 'Radio food disorder: the conversational constitution of eating disorders in radio phone-ins', *Journal of Community & Applied Social Psychology*, 19, 360–73.

Bruner, Jerome. (1961), 'The cognitive consequences of early sensory deprivation', in P. Solomon, P. E. Kubzansky, P. H. Leiderman, J. H. Mendelson, R. Trumball, and D. Wextler (eds), *Sensory Deprivation: A Symposium Held at Harvard Medical School*. Cambridge, MA: Harvard University Press, pp. 195–207.

Bruner, Jerome and Postman, L. (1949), 'The perception of incongruity', *Journal of Personality*, 18, 1–20.

Burns, Stacy. (2001), '"Think your blackest thoughts and darken them": judicial mediation of large money damage disputes', *Human Studies*, 24, (3), 227–49.

Button, Graham. (1987), 'Moving out of closings', in G. Button and J. R. E. Lee (eds), *Talk and Social Organization*. Clevedon: Multilingual Matters, pp. 101–51.

—(1991), 'Conversation-in-a-series', in Deirdre Boden and Don H. Zimmerman (eds), *Talk and Social Structure*. Berkeley, CA: University of California Press, pp. 251–77.

Button, Graham and Casey, Neil. (1984), 'Generating topic: the use of topic initial elicitors', in J. Maxwell Atkinson and John Heritage (eds), *Structures of Social Action: Studies in Conversation Analysis*. Cambridge: Cambridge University Press, pp. 167–90.

—(1985), 'Topic nomination and topic pursuit', *Human Studies*, 8, 3–55.

—(1988/89), 'Topic initiation: business-at-hand', *Research on Language and Social Interaction*, 22, 61–92.

Carlin, Andrew P. (2010), 'Reading "A tutorial on membership categorization" by Emanuel Schegloff', *Journal of Pragmatics*, 42, 257–61.

Chong, Eun. (2006), Ph.D. Dissertation. Department of English. University of Cincinnati.

Clark, William. (1995), 'Effective interviewing and intervention for alcohol problems', in Lipkin, Mack Jr, Samuel Putnam, Aaron Lazare (eds), *The Medical Interview: Clinical Care, Education, and Research*. Springer-Verlag, pp. 284–93.

Clayman, Steven E. (1985), 'Managing Disjunctures in Conversation: Their Avoidance and Repair', M.A. Thesis, Department of Sociology. University of California, Santa Barbara.

—(1988), 'Displaying neutrality in television news interviews', *Social Problems*, 35, (4), 474–92.

—(1991), 'News interview openings: aspects of sequential organization', in Paddy Scannell (ed.), *Broadcast Talk*. London: Sage, pp. 47–76.

—(1992), 'Footing in the achievement of neutrality: the case of news-interview discourse', in Drew, Paul and John Heritage (eds), *Talk at Work: Interaction in Institutional Settings*. Cambridge: Cambridge University Press, pp. 163–98.

—(1993a), 'Booing: the anatomy of a disaffiliative response', *American Sociological Review*, 58, 110–30.

—(1993b), 'Reformulating the question: a device for answering/not answering questions in news interviews and press conferences', *Text*, 13, (2), 159–88.

—(2001), 'Answers and evasions', *Language in Society*, 30, 403–22.

—(2002), 'Disagreements and third parties: dilemmas of neutralism in panel news interviews', *Journal of Pragmatics*, 34, 1385–401.

Clayman, Steven E. and Heritage, John. (2002), *The News Interview: Journalists and Public Figures on the Air*. Cambridge: Cambridge University Press.

Clayman, Steven and Whalen, Jack. (1988/89), 'When the medium becomes the message: the case of the Rather-Bush encounter', *Research on Language and Social Interaction*, 22, 241–72.

Clifton, J. (2006), 'A conversation analytic approach to business communication: the case of leadership', *Journal of Business Communication*, 43, (3), 202–19.

Cuff, E. C. and Francis, D. W. (1978), 'Some features of "invited" stories about marriage breakdown', *International Journal of the Sociology of Language*, 18, 111–33.

Cunningham, C. C., Morgan, P. A., and McGucken, R. B. (1984), 'Down's syndrome: is dissatisfaction with disclosure of diagnosis inevitable?', *Developmental Medicine & Child Neurology*, 26, 33–9.

Cushing, S. (1994), *Fatal Words: Communication Clashes and Airplane Crashes*. Chicago: University of Chicago Press.

Darline, James. (1967), 'On headmastering', In B. W. Hone and P. J. McKeown (eds), *The Independent School: Papers Presented to the Headmasters Conference*, Melbourne: Oxford University Press, pp. 61–71.

Davis, Fred. (1972), *Illness, Interaction and the Self*. Belmont: Wadsworth.

DeVault, Marjorie. (1990), 'Talking and listening from women's standpoint: feminist strategies for interviewing and analysis', *Social Problems*, 37, (1), 96–116.

Di Mateo, M. R. and Di Nicola, D. D. (1984), *Achieving Patient Compliance: The Psychology of the Practitioner's Role*. New York: Pergamon.

Dori-Hacohen, Gonen. (2012), 'With whom do I have the pleasure?: callers' categories in political talk radio programs', *Journal of Pragmatics*, 44, 280–97.

Drew, Paul. (1984), 'Speakers' reportings in invitation sequences', in J. Maxwell Atkinson and John Heritage (eds), *Structures of Social Action: Studies in Conversation Analysis*. Cambridge: Cambridge University Press, pp. 129–51.

—(2003), 'Precision and exaggeration', *American Sociological Review*, 68, (6), 917–38.

Drew, Paul and Heritage, John. (1992), *Talk at Work: Interaction in Institutional Settings*. Cambridge: Cambridge University Press.

Edstrom, Anne. (2004), 'Expressions of disagreement by Venezuelans in conversation: Reconsidering the influence of culture', *Journal of Pragmatics*, 36, 1499–518.

Edwards, Derek. (2000), 'Extreme case formulations: softeners, investment, and doing nonliteral', *Research on Language and Social Interaction*, 33, (4), 347–73.

Eglin, Peter, and Hester, Stephen. (2003), *The Montreal Massacre: A Story of Membership Categorization Analysis*. Waterloo, Ontario: Wilfried Laurier Press.

Ekstrom, Mats. (2009), 'Announced refusal to answer: a study of norms and accountability in broadcast political interviews', *Discourse Studies*,11, 6, 681–702.

Emmertsen, Sofie. (2007), 'Interviewers' challenging questions in British debate interviews', *Journal of Pragmatics*, 39, 570–91.

Esbjörnsson, Mattias, Juhlin, Oskar, Weilenmann, Alexandra. (2007), 'Drivers using mobile phones in traffic: an ethnographic study of interactional adaptation', *International Journal of Human Computer Interaction*, 22, (1), 39–60.

Fairhurst, Gail. (1993), 'Echoes of the vision: When the rest of the organization talks Total Quality', *Management Communication Quarterly*, 6, 331–71.

—(2007), *Discursive Leadership: In Conversation with Leadership Psychology*. Thousand Oaks, CA: Sage.

—(2009), 'Considering context in discursive leadership research', *Human Relations*, 62(11), 1607–33.

—(2011), 'Leadership and the power of framing', *Executive Forum*, 61, 43–7.

Fallowfield, Lesley J. and Lipkin, Mack Jr. (1995), 'Delivering sad or bad news', in Lipkin, Mack, Samuel Putnam, Aaron Lazare (eds), *The Medical Interview: Clinical Care, Education, and Research*. New York: Springer-Verlag, pp. 316–23.

Finlay, I. and Dallimore, D. (1991), 'Your child is dead', *British Medical Journal*, 302, 1524–5.

Fitzgerald, Richard. (2012), 'Membership categorization analysis: wild and promiscuous or simply the joy of Sacks?', *Discourse Studies*, 14(3), 305–11.

Fitzgerald, Richard and Housley, William. (2002), 'Identity, categorization, and sequential organization: the sequential and categorical flow of identity in a radio phone-in', *Discourse & Society*, 13, (5), 579–602.

Ford, Cecilia E. (2008), *Women Speaking Up: Getting and Using Turns in Meetings*. New York: Palgrave Macmillan.

Forrester, Michael A. (2008), 'The emergence of self-repair: a case study of one child during the early preschool years', *Research on Language and Social Interaction*, 41(1), 99–128.

Frankel, Richard M. (2000), '"Captain, I was trying earlier to tell you that you made a mistake": Deference and demeanor at 30,000 feet', in J. K. Peyton, P. Griffin, W. Wolfram, and R. Fasold (eds). *Language in Action: New Studies of Language in Society: Essays in honor of Roger W. Shuy*, Cresskill, NJ: Hampton, pp. 289–301.

—(1989), '"I wz wondering—uhm could *Raid* uhm effect the brain permanently d'y know?": some observations on the intersection of speaking and writing in calls to a poison control center', *Western Journal of Speech Communication*, 53, 195–226.

—(1990), 'Talking in interviews: a dispreference for patient-initiated questions in physician-initiated questions in physician-patient encounters', in George Psathas (ed.) *Interaction Competence*. Washington, DC: International Institute for Ethnomethodology and Conversation Analysis and University Press of America, pp. 231–62.

—(1995), 'Some answers about questions in clinical interviews', in G. H. Morris and Ronald J. Chenail (eds), *The Talk of the Clinic: Explorations in the Analysis of Medical and Therapeutic Discourse*. Hillsdale, NJ: Lawrence Erlbaum, pp. 233–57.

—(2001), 'Clinical care and conversational contingencies: the role of patients' self-diagnosis in medical encounters', *Text*, 21, (1/2), 83–11.

Frankel, Richard M. and Beckman, Howard B. (1989), 'Conversation and compliance with treatment recommendations: an application of micro-interactional analysis in medicine', in Brenda Dervin, Lawrence Grossberg, Barbara J. O'Keefe, and Ellen Wartella (eds), *Rethinking Communication: Volume 2: Paradigm Exemplars*, Newbury Park, CA: Sage, pp. 60–74.

Garcia, Angela Cora. (1989), *The Creation of Agreement in Mediation Hearings*, Ph.D. Dissertation, Department of Sociology, University of California, Santa Cruz.

—(1991), 'Dispute resolution without disputing: how the interactional organization of mediation hearings minimizes argument', *American Sociological Review*, 56, 818–35.

—(1994), 'Presenting a united front: team work, alignment, and collaboration in community mediation hearings', Paper presented at the International Sociological Association, XIII World Congress of Sociology in Bielefeld, Germany. July 18–25, 1994.

—(1995), 'The problematics of representation in community mediation hearings: implications for mediation practice', *Journal of Sociology and Social Welfare*, XXII, (4), 23–46.

—(1997), 'Interactional constraints on proposal generation in mediation hearings: a preliminary investigation.' *Discourse & Society*, 8, (2), 219–47.

—(2010), 'The role of interactional competence in mediation', *Conflict Resolution Quarterly*, 28, (2), 205–28.

Garcia, Angela Cora, Dawes, Mark, Kohne, Mary Lou, Miller, Felicia, and Groschwitz, Stephan. (2006), 'Workplace studies and technological change', *Annual Review of Information Science & Technology*, 40, 393–437.

Garcia, Angela Cora and Fisher, Lisa M. (2011), 'Being there for the children: the collaborative construction of gender inequality in divorce mediation', in Susan A. Speer and Elizabeth Stokoe (eds), *Conversation and Gender*. Cambridge: Cambridge University Press, pp. 272–93.

Garcia, Angela Cora and Parmer, Penelope. (1999), 'Misplaced mistrust: the collaborative construction of doubt in 911 emergency calls', *Symbolic Interaction*, 22, (4), 297–324.

Garcia, Angela Cora, Vise, Kristi and Whitaker, Stephen. (2002), 'Disputing neutrality: a case study of a bias complaint during mediation', *Conflict Resolution Quarterly*, 20, (2), 205–30.

Gardner, Rod. (2012), 'Enriching CA through MCA? Stokoe's MCA keys', *Discourse Studies*, 14(3), 313–19.

Garfinkel, Harold. (1963), 'A conception of, and experiments with 'trust' as a condition of stable concerted actions', in O. J. Harvey (ed.), *Motivation and Social Interaction*. New York: Ronald Press, pp. 187–238.

—(1967), *Studies in Ethnomethodology*. Cambridge: Polity Press.

Garfinkel, Harold, Lynch, Michael, Livingston, Eric. (1981), 'The work of a discovering science construed with materials from the optically discovered pulsar', *Philosophy of the Social Sciences*, 11, (2), 131–58.

Gill, Virginia Teas. (1998), 'Doing attributions in medical interaction: patients' explanations for illness and doctors' responses', *Social Psychology Quarterly*, 61, (4), 342–60.

—(2005), 'Patient "demand" for medical interventions: exerting pressure for an offer in a primary care clinic visit', *Research on Language and Social Interaction*, 38, (4), 451–79.

Gill, Virginia Teas, Halkowski, Timothy, and Roberts, Felicia. (2001), 'Accomplishing a request without making one: a single case analysis of a primary care visit', *Text*, 21, (1/2), 55–81.

Gill, Virginia Teas and Maynard, Douglas W. (1995), 'On "labelling" in actual interaction: delivering and receiving diagnoses of developmental disabilities', *Social Problems*, 42, (1), 11–37.

—(2006), 'Explaining illness: patients' proposals and physicians' responses', in John Heritage and Douglas W. Maynard (eds), *Communication in Medical Care: Interaction between Primary Care Physicians and Patients*. Cambridge: Cambridge University Press, pp. 115–50.

Glaser, Barney and Strauss, Anselm L. (1965), *Awareness of Dying*. Chicago: Aldine.

Glenn, Phillip. (2010), 'Interviewer laughs: shared laughter and asymmetries in employment interviews', *Journal of Pragmatics*, 42, 1485–98.

Goffman, Erving. (1959), *Presentation of Self in Everyday Life*. New York: Anchor Books.

—(1967), *Interaction Ritual: Essays on Face-to-Face Behavior*. Garden City, New York: Anchor Books.

—(1969), *Strategic Interaction*. New York: Ballantine Books.

—(1974), *Frame Analysis: An Essay on the Organization of Experience*. Cambridge, MA: Harvard University Press.

—(1981), *Forms of Talk*. Philadelphia: University of Pennsylvania Press.

Goodwin, Charles. (1984), 'Notes on story structure and the organization of participation', in J. Maxwell Atkinson and John Heritage (eds), *Structures of Social Action: Studies in Conversation Analysis*. Cambridge: Cambridge University Press, pp. 225–46.

—(1987), 'Forgetfulness as an interactive resource', *Social Psychology Quarterly*, 50, (2), 115–30.

—(1989), 'Turn construction and conversational organization', in Brenda Dervin, Lawrence Grossberg, Barbara J. O'Keefe, and Ellen Wartella (eds), *Rethinking Communication, Volume 2: Paradigm Exemplars*. Newbury Park, CA: Sage, pp. 88–102.

—(1995), 'The negotiation of coherence within conversation', in Morton Ann Gernsbacher and T. Givón (eds), *Coherence in Spontaneous Text*. Amsterdam/Philadelphia: John Benjamins Publishing Company, pp. 117–37.

—(2000), 'Gesture, aphasia, and interaction', in David McNeill (ed.), *Language and Gesture*. Cambridge: Cambridge University Press.

Goodwin, Marjorie Harness. (1983), Aggravated correction and disagreement in children's conversations', *Journal of Pragmatics*, 7, 657–77.

—(2007), 'Participation and embodied action in preadolescent girls' assessment activity', *Research on Language and Social Interaction*, 40, (4), 353–75.

Goodwin, Marjorie Harness and Goodwin, Charles. (1987), 'Children's arguing', in S. Philips, S. Steele, and C. Tanz (eds), *Language, Gender and Sex in Comparative Perspective*. Cambridge: Cambridge University Press, pp. 200–48.

Greatbatch, David. (1986), 'Aspects of topical organization in news interviews: the use of agenda-shifting procedures by interviewees', *Media, Culture and Society*, 8, 441–55.

—(1988), 'A turn-taking system for British news interviews', *Language in Society*, 17, 401–30.

Greatbatch, David and Dingwall, Robert. (1997), 'Argumentative talk in divorce mediation sessions', *American Sociological Review*, 62, 151–70.

—(1999), 'Professional neutralism in family mediation', in Srikant Sarangi and Celia Roberts (eds), *Talk, Work and Institutional Order: Discourse in Medical, Mediation and Management Settings*. Berlin/NY: Mouton de Gruyter, pp. 271–92.

Gronn, Peter C. (1983), 'Talk as the work: the accomplishment of school administration', *Administrative Science Quarterly*, 28, 1–21.

Guillot, Marie-Noëlle. (2008), 'Freedoms and constraints in semi-institutional television discussions: the case of mixed format panel discussions', *Journal of Pragmatics*, 40, 179–204.

Haddington, Pentti and Keisanen, Tiina. (2009), 'Location, mobility and the body as resources in selecting a route', *Journal of Pragmatics*, 41, (10), 1938–61.

Halkowski, Timothy. (1990), '"Role" as an interactional device', *Social Problems*, 37, (4), 564–77.

—(2006), 'Realizing the illness: patients' narratives of symptom discovery', in Heritage, John and Douglas W. Maynard (eds), *Communication in Medical Care: Interaction between Primary Care Physicians and Patients*. Cambridge: Cambridge University Press, pp. 86–114.

Harper, Richard. (2010), *Texture: Human Expression in the Age of Communications Overload*. Cambridge, MA: MIT Press.

Harper, Richard and Taylor, Stuart. (2009), 'Glancephone: an exploration of human expression', *MobileHCI'09*, September 15–18, Bonn, Germany. ACM 978-1-60558-281-8.

Have, Paul ten. (1999), *Doing Conversation Analysis: A Practical Guide*. London: Sage.

—(2007), *Doing Conversation Analysis: A Practical Guide, Second Edition*. London: Sage.

Heath, Christian. (1986), *Body Movement and Speech in Medical Interaction*. Cambridge: Cambridge University Press.

—(1992), 'The delivery and reception of diagnosis in the general-practice consultation', in Paul Drew and John Heritage (eds), *Talk at Work: Interaction in Institutional Settings*. Cambridge: Cambridge University Press, pp. 235–67.

—(2002), 'Demonstrative suffering: the gestural (re)embodiment of symptoms', *Journal of Communication*, 52, (3), 597–617.

Heath, Christian and Luff, Paul. (2000), *Technology in Action*. Cambridge: Cambridge University Press.

Heinemann, Trine. (2009), 'Participation and exclusion in third party complaints', *Journal of Pragmatics*, 41, (12), 2435–51.

Heisterkamp, Brian L. (2006), 'Taking the footing of a neutral mediator', *Conflict Resolution Quarterly*, 23, (3), 301–15.

Heritage, John. (1984), *Garfinkel and Ethnomethodology*. Cambridge: Cambridge University Press.

—(1985), 'Analysing news interviews: aspects of the production of talk for an overhearing audience', in T. A. van Dijk (ed.), *Handbook of Discourse Analysis, Volume 3: Discourse and Dialogue*. London: Academic Press, pp. 95–119.

—(1987), 'Ethnomethodology', in Anthony Giddens and Jonathan Turner (eds), *Social Theory Today*. Cambridge: Polity Press.

—(1997), 'Conversation analysis and institutional talk', in D. Silverman (ed.), *Qualitative Research: Theory, Method and Practice*. London: Sage, pp. 161–82.

—(1998), 'Oh-prefaced responses to inquiry', *Language in Society*, 27, 291–334.

—(2002), 'The limits of questioning: negative interrogatives and hostile question content', *Journal of Pragmatics*, 34, 1427–46.

Heritage, John and Clayman, Steven E. (2010), *Talk in Action: Interactions, Identities, and Institutions*. Boston, MA: Wiley Blackwell.

Heritage, John C., Clayman, Steven E., and Zimmerman, Don H. (1988), 'Discourse and message analysis: the micro-structure of mass media messages', in Robert Hawkins et al. (eds), *Advancing Communication Science: Merging Mass and Interpersonal Processes. Sage Annual Review of Communication Research Vol. 16*. Newbury Park, CA: Sage, pp. 77–109.

Heritage, John and Maynard, Douglas W. (eds). (2006a), *Communication in Medical Care: Interaction between Primary Care Physicians and Patients*. Cambridge: Cambridge University Press.

—(2006b), 'Problems and prospects in the study of physician-patient interaction: 30 years of research', *Annual Review of Sociology*, 32, 351–74.

Heritage, John and Robinson, Jeffrey D. (2006), 'Accounting for the visit: giving reasons for seeking medical care', in J. Heritage and D. Maynard (eds), *Communication in Medical Care: Interactions between Primary Care Physicians and Patients*. Cambridge: Cambridge University Press, pp. 48–85.

Heritage, John, Robinson, Jeffrey D, Elliott, Marc N., Beckett, Megan, and Wilkes, Michael. (2007), 'Reducing patients' unmet concerns in primary care: the difference one word can make', *Society of General Internal Medicine*, 22, (10), 1429–33.

Heritage, John and Roth, Andrew L. (1995), 'Grammar and institution: questions and questioning in the broadcast news interview', *Research on Language and Social Interaction*, 28, (1), 1–60.

Heritage, John and Sue Sefi. (1992), 'Dilemmas of advice: aspects of the delivery and reception of advice in interactions between health visitors and first-time mothers', in Paul Drew and John Heritage (eds), *Talk at Work: Interaction in Institutional Settings*. Cambridge: Cambridge University Press, pp. 359–417.

Heritage, John, and Sorjonen, Marja-Leena. (1994), 'Constituting and maintaining activities across sequences: *and*-prefacing as a feature of question design', *Language in Society*, 23, 1–29.

Hester, Sally and Stephen Hester. (2012), 'Categorial occasionality and transformation: Analyzing culture in action', *Human Studies*, 35, 563–81.

Hester, Stephen and Eglin, Peter (eds). (1997), *Culture in Action: Studies in Membership Categorization Analysis*. Washington, DC: International Institute for Ethnomethodology and Conversation Analysis and University Press of America.

Hester, Stephen, and Francis, David. (2000), *Local Educational Order: Ethnomethodological Studies of Knowledge in Action*. Amsterdam: John Benjamins.

Hopper, R. and LeBaron, C. (1998), 'How gender creeps into talk', *Research on Language and Social Interaction*, 31, (1), 59–74.

Hougaard, Gitte Rasmussen. (2008), 'Membership categorization in international business phone calls: the importance of "being international"', *Journal of Pragmatics*, 40, 307–32.

Houtkoop-Steenstra, Hanneke. (1991), 'Opening sequences in Dutch telephone conversations', in Deborah Boden and Don H. Zimmerman (eds), *Talk and Social Structure: Studies in Ethnomethodology and Conversation Analysis*. Cambridge: Polity Press, pp. 232–50.

—(2000), *Interaction and the Standardized Survey Interview: The Living Questionnaire*. Cambridge: Cambridge University Press.

Hutchby, Ian. (1999), 'Frame attunement and footing in the organisation of talk radio openings', *Journal of Sociolinguistics*, 3, (1), 41–63.

—(2001), *Conversation and Technology: From the Telephone to the Internet*. Cambridge: Polity Press.

—(2005), '"Active listening": formulations and the elicitation of feelings-talk in child counseling', *Research on Language and Social Interaction*, 38, (3), 303–29.

—(2006), *Media Talk: Conversation Analysis and the Study of Broadcasting*. New York: Open University Press.

Ikeda, Keiko. (2009), 'Third party involvement in Japanese political television interviews', in Hanh thi Nguyen and Gabriele Kasper (eds), *Talk-in-Interaction: Multilingual Perspectives*. Honolulu, Hawaii: National Foreign Language Resource Center; University of Hawaii, pp. 157–80.

Iñigo-Mora, I. (2007), 'Extreme case formulations in Spanish pre-electoral debates and English panel interviews', *Discourse Studies*, 9, (3), 341–63.

Jacobs, Scott. (2002), 'Maintaining neutrality in dispute mediation: managing disagreement while managing not to disagree', *Journal of Pragmatics*, 34, 1403–26.

Jayyusi, Lena. (1984), *Categorization and the Moral Order*. Boston: Routledge & Kegan Paul.

Jefferson, Gail. (1972), 'Side sequences', in David Sudnow (ed.), *Studies in Social Interaction*. New York: Free Press, pp. 294–338.

—(1973), 'A case of precision timing in ordinary conversation: overlapped tag-positioned address terms in closing sequences', *Semiotica*, 9, 47–96.

—(1974), 'Error correction as an interactional resource', *Language in Society*, 13, (2), 181–99.

—(1977), 'Some sequential negotiations in conversation: unexpanded and expanded versions of projected action sequences', *Sociology*, 11, (1), 87–103.

—(1978), 'Sequential aspects of storytelling in conversation', in Jim Schenkein (ed.), *Studies in the Organization of Conversational Interaction*. New York and London: Academic Press, pp. 219–48.

—(1979), 'A technique for inviting laughter and its subsequent acceptance declination', in George Psathas (ed.), *Everyday Language: Studies in Ethnomethodology*. New York: Irvington Press, pp. 79–96.

—(1984a), 'Transcript notation', in J. Maxwell Atkinson, and John Heritage (eds), *Structures of Social Action: Studies in Conversation Analysis*. Cambridge: Cambridge University Press, pp. ix–xvi.

—(1984b), 'On stepwise transition from talk about a trouble to inappropriately next-positioned matters', in Atkinson and Heritage (eds), *Structures of Social Action: Studies in Conversation Analysis*. Cambridge: Cambridge University Press, pp. 191–222.

—(1985), 'An exercise in the transcription and analysis of laughter', in T. Van Dijk (ed.), *Handbook of Discourse Analysis, Vol. 3: Discourse and Dialogue*. London: Academic Press, pp. 25–34.

—(1987), 'On exposed and embedded correction in conversation', in Graham Button and John R. E. Lee (eds), *Talk and Social Organization*. Clevedon and Philadelphia, PA: Multilingual Matters, pp. 86–100.

—(1989), 'Preliminary notes on a possible metric which provides for a "standard maximum" silence of approximately one second in conversation', in Derek Roger and Peter Bull (eds), *Conversation: An Interdisciplinary Perspective*. Clevedon: Multilingual Matters, pp. 166–96.

—(1993), 'Caveat speaker: preliminary notes on recipient topic-shift implicature', *Research on Language and Social Interaction*, 26, (1), 1–30.

—(2002), 'Is "no" an acknowledgment token?: Comparing American and British use of (+)(-) tokens', *Journal of Pragmatics*, 34, 1345–83.

—(2004a), 'Glossary of transcript symbols with an introduction', in Gene H. Lerner (ed.), *Conversation Analysis: Studies from the First Generation*. Amsterdam and Philadelphia: John Benjamins, pp. 13–31.

—(2004b), 'A note on laughter in 'male-female' interaction', *Discourse Studies*, 6, (1), 117–33.

—(2004c), 'A sketch of some orderly aspects of overlap in natural conversation', in Gene H. Lerner (ed.), *Conversation Analysis: Studies from the First Generation*. Amsterdam/Philadelphia: John Benjamins, pp. 43–59.

—(2010), 'Sometimes a frog in your throat is just a frog in your throat: gutturals as (sometimes) laughter-implicative', *Journal of Pragmatics*, 42, 1476–84.

Kinnell, Ann Marie K. (2002), 'Soliciting client questions in HIV prevention and test counseling', *Research on Language and Social interaction*, 35, (3), 367–93.

Kinnell, Ann Marie K., and Maynard, Douglas W. (1996), 'The delivery and receipt of safer sex advice in pretest counseling sessions for HIV and AIDS', *Journal of Contemporary Ethnography*, 24, (4), 405–37.

Koester, Almut. (2004), 'Relational sequences in workplace genres', *Journal of Pragmatics*, 36, 1405–28.

Korolija, Natascha. (1998), 'Recycling context: the impact of prior conversation on the emergence of episodes in a multiparty radio talk show', *Discourse Processes*, 25, (1), 99–125.

Lavin, Danielle and Maynard, Douglas W. (2001), 'Standardization vs. rapport: respondent laughter and interviewer reaction during telephone surveys', *American Sociological Review*, 66, 3, 453–79.

Lazare, Aaron, Putnam, Samuel M., and Lipkin, Mack Jr. (1995), 'Three functions of the medical interview', in Lipkin, Mack, Samuel Putnam, Aaron Lazare (eds), *The Medical Interview: Clinical Care, Education, and Research*. Springer-Verlag, pp. 3–19.

Lepper, Georgia. (2000), *Categories in Text and Talk: A Practical Introduction to Categorization Analysis*. London: Sage.

Lerner, Gene H. (1992), 'Assisted storytelling: deploying shared knowledge as a practical matter', *Qualitative Sociology*, 15, (3), 247–71.

Lerner, Gene. (1993), 'Collectivities in action: establishing the relevance of conjoined participation in conversation', *Text*, 13, (2), 213–45.

Lewis, Catherine and Pantell, Robert. (1995), 'Interviewing pediatric patients', in Lipkin, Mack Jr, Samuel Putnam, and Aaron Lazare (eds), *The Medical Interview: Clinical Care, Education, and Research*. Springer-Verlag, pp. 209–20.

Lindström, Anna. (1994), 'Identification and recognition in Swedish telephone conversation openings', *Language in Society*, 34, 231–52.

Lloyd, Robin M. (1992), 'Negotiating child sexual abuse: the interactional character of investigative practices', *Social Problems*, 39, (2), 109–24.

Luff, Paul, Hindmarsh, Jon, and Heath, Christian (eds). (2000), *Workplace Studies: Recovering Work Practice and Informing System Design*. Cambridge: Cambridge University Press.

Lutfey, Karen. (2004), 'Assessment, objectivity, and interaction: the case of patient compliance with medical treatment regimens', *Social Psychology Quarterly*, 67, (4), 343–68.

Lutfey, Karen and Maynard, Douglas W. (1998), 'Bad news in oncology: how physician and patient talk about death and dying without using those words', *Social Psychology Quarterly*, 6, (4), 321–41.

Lynch, Michael. (1991), 'Laboratory space and the technological complex: an investigation of topical contextures', *Science in Context*, 4, 51–78.

Lynch, Michael and Bogen, David. (1996), *The Spectacle of History: Speech, Text, and Memory at the Iran-Contra Hearings*. Durham, NC: Duke University Press.

Manzo, John F. (1996), 'Taking turns and taking sides: opening scenes from two jury deliberations', *Social Psychology Quarterly*, 59, (2), 107–25.

Markaki, Vassiliki and Mondada, Lorenza. (2012), 'Embodied orientations towards co-participants in multinational meetings', *Discourse Studies*, 14, (1), 31–52.

Martin, David, and O'Neill, Jacki. (2011), 'Talk: talking the organization into being', in Mark Rouncefield and Peter Tolmie (eds), *Ethnomethodology at Work*. Farnham: Ashgate, pp. 109–29.

Maynard, Douglas W. (1980), 'Placement of topic changes in conversation', *Semiotica*, 30, (3/4), 263–90.

—(1984), *Inside Plea Bargaining: The Language of Negotiation*. New York and London: Plenum Press.

—(1985), 'How children start arguments', *Language in Society*, 14, 1–29.

—(1989), 'Perspective-display sequences in conversation', *Western Journal of Speech Communication*, 53, 91–113.

—(1992), 'On clinicians co-implicating recipients' perspective in the delivery of diagnostic news', in Paul Drew and John Heritage (eds), *Talk at Work: Interaction in Institutional Settings*. Cambridge: Cambridge University Press, pp. 331–58.

—(2003), *Bad News, Good News: Conversational Order in Everyday Talk and Clinical Settings*. Chicago and London: Chicago University Press.

Maynard, Douglas W. and Clayman, Steven E. (2003), 'Ethnomethodology and conversation analysis', in L. T. Reynolds and N. J. Herman-Kinney (eds), *Handbook of Symbolic Interaction*. Lanham, Maryland: Rowman & Littlefield, pp. 173–202.

Maynard, Douglas W., Freese, Jeremy, and Schaeffer, Nora Cate. (2010), 'Calling for participation: requests, blocking moves, and rational (inter)action in survey introductions', *American Sociological Review*, 75, 5, 791–814.

Maynard, Douglas W. and Manzo, John F. (1993), 'On the sociology of justice: theoretical notes from an actual jury deliberation', *Sociological Theory*, 11, (2), 171–93.

Maynard, Douglas W. and Marlaire, Courtney L. (1992), 'Good reasons for bad testing performance: the interactional substrate of educational exams', *Qualitative Sociology*, 15, 177–22.

Maynard, Douglas W., Schaeffer, Nora Cate, and Freese, Jeremy. (2011), 'Improving response rates in telephone interviews', Charles Antaki (ed.), *Applied Conversation Analysis: Interventions and Change in Institutional Talk*. London: Palgrave-MacMillan.

Maynard, Douglas W. and Zimmerman, Don H. (1984), 'Topical talk, ritual, and the social organization of relationships', *Social Psychology Quarterly*, 47, (4), 301–16.

Mazeland, Harrie and Jan Berenst. (2008), 'Sorting pupils in a report-card meeting: Categorization in a situated activity system', *Text & Talk*, 28, (1), 55–78.

McCarthy, M. and Carter, R. (2004), '"There's millions of them": hyperbole in everyday conversation', *Journal of Pragmatics*, 36, 149–84.

McFadden, Robert D. (2009), 'Pilot is hailed after jetliner's icy plunge', *New York Times*, January 16, 2009, p. A1. http://www.nytimes.com/2009/01/16/nyregion/16crash.html?pagewanted=all

McHoul, Alec. (2007), '"Killers" and "friendlies": names can hurt me', *Social Identities*, 13, (4), 459–69.

McHoul, Alec and Rapley, Mark. (2001), *How to Analyze Talk in Institutional Settings: A Casebook of Methods*. London and New York: Continuum Press.

McIlvenny, Paul. (2009), 'Communicating a 'time-out' in parent-child conflict: embodied interaction, domestic space and discipline in a reality tv parenting programme', *Journal of Pragmatics*, 41, 2017–32.

Meehan, Albert J. (1986), 'Record-keeping practices in the policing of juveniles', *Urban Life*, 15, (1), 70–102.

Meldrum, Helen. (2010), *Characteristics of Compassion: Portraits of Exemplary Physicians*. Sudbury, MA: Jones and Bartlett Publishers.

Miller, E. A. (2002), 'Telemedicine and doctor-patient communication: an analytical survey of the literature', *Journal of Telemedicine and Telecare*, 8, 311–18.

Mirivel, Julien C. and Tracy, Karen. (2005), 'Premeeting talk: an organizationally crucial form of talk', *Research on Language and Social Interaction*, 38, (1), 1–34.

Mondada, Lorenza. (2009), 'Emergent focused interactions in public places: a systematic analysis of the multi-modal achievement of a common interactional space', *Journal of Pragmatics*, 41, 1977–97.

Müller, K. (1992), 'Theatrical moments: on contextualizing funny and dramatic moods in the course of telling a story in conversation', in P. Auer and A. di Luzio (eds), *The Contextualization of Language*. Amsterdam: Benjamins, pp. 205–21.

Nevile, Maurice. (2001), 'Understanding who's who in the airline cockpit: pilots' pronominal choices and cockpit roles', in A. McHoul and Mark Rapley (eds), *How to Analyse Talk in Institutional Settings*. New York: Continuum Press, pp. 57–71.

—(2004a), 'Integrity in the airline cockpit: embodying claims about progress for the conduct of an approach briefing', *Research on Language and Social Interaction*, 37, (4), 447–80.

—(2004b), *Beyond the Black Box: Talk-in-Interaction in the Airline Cockpit*. Aldershot: Ashgate.

—(2006), 'Making sequentiality salient: and-prefacing in the talk of airline pilots', *Discourse Studies*, 8, 279–302.

—(2007), 'Action in time: ensuring timeliness for collaborative work in the airline cockpit', *Language in Society*, 36, 233–57.

Nofsinger, Robert E. (1991), *Everyday Conversation*. Newbury Park, CA: Sage.

Novak, Dennis H. (1995), 'Therapeutic aspects of the clinical encounter', in Lipkin, Mack Jr, Samuel Putnam and Aaron Lazare (eds), *The Medical Interview: Clinical Care, Education, and Research*. New York: Springer-Verlag, pp. 32–49.

Oak, Arlene. (2009), 'Performing architecture: talking "architect" and "client" into being', *CoDesign*, 5, (1), 51–63.

Oliver, R. T. and Cortright, R. I. (1970), *Effective Speech*. New York: Holt, Rinehart & Winston.

Pappas, Yannis and Seale, Clive. (2009), 'The opening phase of telemedicine consultations: an analysis of interaction', *Social Science & Medicine*, 68, 1229–37.

Pillet-Shore, Danielle. (2011), 'Doing introductions: the work involved in meeting someone new', *Communication Monographs*, 78, (1), 73–95.

Polly, Matthew. (2007), *American Shaolin: Flying Kicks, Buddhist Monks, and the Legend of the Iron Crotch: An Odyssey in the New China*. New York: Gotham Books.

Pomerantz, Anita. (1978a), 'Compliment responses: notes on the co-operation of multiple constraints', in J. Schenkein (ed.), *Studies in the Organization of Conversational Interaction*. New York: Academic Press, pp. 79–112.

—(1978b), 'Attributions of responsibility: blamings', *Sociology*, 12, 115–21.

—(1984), 'Agreeing and disagreeing with assessments: some features of preferred-dispreferred turn shapes', in J. M. Atkinson and John Heritage (eds), *Structures of Social Action: Studies in Conversation Analysis*. Cambridge: Cambridge University Press, pp. 57–101.

—(1986), 'Extreme case formulations: a way of legitimizing claims', *Human Studies*, 9, (2–3), 219–30.

—(1988), 'Offering a candidate answer: an information seeking strategy', *Communication Monographs*, 55, 360–73.

Potter, Jonathan. (1996), 'Ethnomethodology and conversation analysis', *Representing Reality: Discourse, Rhetoric, and Social Construction*, London: Sage, pp. 42–67.

Potter, Jonathan and Hepburn, Alexa. (2010), 'Putting aspiration into words: 'laugh particles', managing descriptive trouble and modulating action', *Journal of Pragmatics*, 42, 1543–55.

Rautajoki, Hanna. (2012), 'Membership categorization as a tool for moral casting in TV discussion: the dramaturgical consequentiality of guest introductions', *Discourse Studies*, 14(20), 243–60.

Raymond, Geoffrey and Don H. Zimmerman. (2007), 'Rights and responsibilities in calls for help: the case of the Mountain Glade fire', *Research on Language and Social Interaction*, 40, (1), 33–61.

Reed, Beatrice Szczepek. (2009), 'Prosodic orientation: a practice for sequential organization in broadcast telephone openings', *Journal of Pragmatics*, 41, 1223–47.

Reiter, Rosina Márquez. (2006), 'Interactional closeness in service calls to a Montevidean carer service company', *Research on Language and Social Interaction*, 39, (1), 7–39.

Rendle-Short, Johanna. (2005), '"I've got a paper-shuffler for a husband": indexing sexuality on talk-back radio', *Discourse & Society*, 16, (4), 561–78.

Riessman, Catherine Kohler. (1987), 'When gender is not enough: women interviewing women', *Gender and Society*, 1, 172–207.

Romaniuk, Tanya. (2013), 'Pursuing answers to questions in broadcast journalism', *Research on Language and Social Interaction* 46(2), 144–164.

Roter, Debra and Hall, Judith A. (1993), *Doctors Talking with Patients/Patients Talking with Doctors*. Westport, CT and London: Auburn House.

Rouncefield, Mark and Tolmie, Peter (eds). (2011), *Ethnomethodology at Work*. Farnham: Ashgate.

Ruusuvuori, Johanna. (2009), 'Complaining about previous treatment in health care settings', *Journal of Pragmatics*, 41, (12), 2415–34.

Sackett, D. L. and Snow, J. C. (1979), 'The magnitude of compliance and non-compliance', in R. B. Haynes, D. W. Taylor, and D. L. Sackett (eds), *Compliance in Health Care*. Baltimore: Johns Hopkins University Press, pp. 11–12.

Sacks, Harvey. (1972), 'On the analyzability of stories told by children', in John Gumperz and Dell Hymes (eds), *Directions in Sociolinguistics*. New York: Holt, Rinehart and Winston.

— (1974), 'On the analysability of stories by children', in R. Turner (ed.), *Ethnomethodology*. Harmondsworth, England: Penguin.

—(1984a), 'On doing being ordinary', in J. Maxwell Atkinson and John Heritage (eds), *Structures of Social Action: Studies in Conversation Analysis*. Cambridge: Cambridge University Press, pp. 413–29.

—(1984b), 'Notes on methodology', in J. Mawell Atkinson and John Heritage (eds), *Structures of Social Action: Studies in Conversation Analysis*. Cambridge: Cambridge University Press, pp. 21–7.

—(1985), 'The inference-making machine: notes on observability', in Teun A. van Dijk (ed.), *Handbook of Discourse Analysis, Volume 3, Discourse and Dialogue*. New York: Academic Press, pp. 13–23.

—(1987a), 'On the preferences for agreement and contiguity in sequences in conversation', in Graham Button and John R. E. Lee (eds), *Talk and Social Organisation*. Clevedon: Multilingual Matters, pp. 54–69.

—(1987b), 'You want to find out if anybody really does care', in Graham Button and John R. E. Lee (eds), *Talk and Social Organisation*. Clevedon: Multilingual Matters, pp. 219–25.

—(1989), 'Lecture eleven: on exchanging glances', in Gail Jefferson (ed.), *Special Issue Lectures 1964–1965, Human Studies*,12, (3/4), 333–48.

—(1992a), *Lectures on Conversation, Volume 1*, Gail Jefferson (ed.), Oxford and Cambridge: Blackwell.

—(1992b), *Lectures on Conversation, Volume II*, Gail Jefferson (ed.), Oxford and Cambridge: Blackwell.

Sacks, Harvey and Schegloff, Emanuel A. (1979), 'Two preferences in the organization of reference to persons and their interaction', in George Psathas (ed.), *Everyday Language: Studies in Ethnomethodology*. New York: Irvington Publishers, pp. 15–21.

Sacks, Harvey, Schegloff, Emanuel A. and Jefferson, Gail. (1974), 'A simplest systematics for the organization of turn-taking for conversation', *Language*, 50, (4), 696–735.

Schaeffer, Nora Cate and Maynad, Douglas W. (1996), 'From paradigm to prototype and back again: interactive aspects of "cognitive processing" in standardized survey interviews', in N. Schwarz and S. Sudman (eds),

Answering Questions: Methodology for Determining Cognitive and Communicating Processes in Survey Research. San Francisco, CA: Jossey-Bass, pp. 75–88.

Schegloff, Emanuel A. (1968), 'Sequencing in conversational openings', *American Anthropologist*, 70, 346–80.

—(1979), 'Identification and recognition in telephone conversation openings', in George Psathas (ed.), *Everyday Language: Studies in Ethnomethodology*. New York: Irvington, pp. 23–78.

—(1980), 'Preliminaries to preliminaries, "can I ask you a question?"', *Sociological Inquiry*, 50, 104–52.

—(1982), 'Discourse as an interactional achievement: some uses of "uh huh" and other things that come between sentences', in D. Tannen (ed.), *Georgetown University Round Table on Languages and Linguistics 1981: Analyzing Discourse: Text and Talk*. Washington, DC: Georgetown University Press, pp. 71–93.

—(1986), 'The Routine as Achievement', *Human Studies*, 9, 111–51.

—(1987), 'Analyzing single episodes of interaction: an exercise in conversation analysis', *Social Psychology Quarterly*, 50, (2), 101–14.

—(1988/89), 'From interview to confrontation: observations of the Bush/Rather encounter', *Research on Language and Social Interaction*, 22, 215–40.

—(1990), 'On the organization of sequences as a source of "coherence" in talk-in-interaction', in Bruce Dorval (ed.), *Conversational Organization and its Development, Vol. XXXVIII in the series Advances in Discourse Processes*. Norwood, NJ: Ablex, pp. 51–77.

—(1992), 'Repair after next turn: the last structurally provided defense of intersubjectivity in conversation', *American Journal of Sociology*, 97, (5), 1295–345.

—(1996), 'Confirming allusions: toward an empirical account of action', *American Journal of Sociology*, 102, (1), 161–216.

—(2000), 'When "others" initiate repair', *Applied Linguistics*, 21, (2), 205–43.

—(2002a), 'Beginnings on the telephone', in J. Katz and M. Aakhus (eds), *Perpetual Contact: Mobile Communication, Private Talk, Public Performance*. Cambridge: Cambridge University Press, pp. 284–300.

—(2002b), 'Opening sequencing,' in J. Katz and M. Aakhus (eds), *Perpetual Contact: Mobile Communication, Private Talk, Public Performance*. Cambridge: Cambridge University Press, pp. 326–85.

—(2005), 'On integrity in inquiry… of the investigated, not the investigator', *Discourse Studies*, 7, (4–5), 455–80.

—(2007a), *Sequence Organization in Interaction: A Primer in Conversation Analysis, Volume 1*, Cambridge: Cambridge University Press.

—(2007b), 'A tutorial on membership categorization', *Journal of Pragmatics*, 39, 462–82.

Schegloff, Emanuel A., Jefferson, Gail and Sacks, Harvey. (1977), 'The preference for self-correction in the organization of repair in conversation', *Language*, 53, 361–82.

Schegloff, Emanuel A. and Sacks, Harvey. (1973), 'Opening up closings', *Semiotica*, 8, 289–327.

Shorter, Edward. (1985), *Bedside Manners*. New York: Simon & Schuster.

Sidnell, Jack. (2004), 'There's risks in everything: extreme case formulations and accountability in inquiry testimony', *Discourse & Society*, 15, (6), 745–66.

Sidnell, Jack (2010), *Conversation Analysis: An Introduction*. Oxford: Wiley-Blackwell.

Silverman, David, (1987), *Communication and Medical Practice: Social Relations in the Clinic*. London: Sage.

—(1997), *Discourses of Counseling: HIV Counseling as Social Interaction*. London: Sage.

—(1998), *Harvey Sacks: Social Science and Conversation Analysis*. Oxford: Oxford University Press.

Smith, Allen C. III and Kleinman, Sherryl. (1989), 'Managing emotions in medical school: students' contacts with the living and the dead', *Social Psychology Quarterly*, 52, (1), 56–69.

Stivers, Tanya. (2005), 'Parent resistance to physicians' treatment recommendations: one resource for initiating a negotiation of the treatment decision', *Health Communication*, 18, (1), 41–74.

—(2006), 'Treatment decisions: negotiations between doctors and parents in acute care encounters', in John Heritage and Douglas W. Maynard (eds), *Communication in Medical Care: Interaction between Primary Care Physicians and Patients*. Cambridge: Cambridge University Press, pp. 279–312.

—(2008), 'Stance, alignment, and affiliation during storytelling: when nodding is a token of affiliation', *Research on Language and Social Interaction*, 41, (1), 31–57.

Stokoe, Elizabeth. (2009), 'Doing actions with identity categories: complaints and denials in neighbor disputes', *Text & Talk*, 29, (1), 75–97.

—(2010), '"I'm not gonna hit a lady": conversation analysis, membership categorization and men's denials of violence towards women', *Discourse & Society*, 21, (1), 59–82.

—(2012), 'Moving forward with membership categorization analysis: methods for systematic analysis', *Discourse Studies*, 14, (3), 277–303.

Stokoe, Elizabeth and Edwards, Derek. (2007), '"Black this, black that": racial insults and reported speech in neighbour complaints and police interrogations', *Discourse & Society*, 18, 337–72.

Sun, Hao. (2004), 'Opening moves in informal Chinese telephone conversations', *Journal of Pragmatics*, 36, 1429–65.

Svenson, Ola and Patten, J. D. (2005), 'Mobile phones and driving: a review of contemporary research', *Cognition, Technology & Work*, 7, (3), 182–97.

Tannen, Deborah. (1994), *Talking from 9 to 5: Women and Men in the Workplace*. New York: Avon.

Taylor, Alex S. and Harper, Richard. (2003), 'The gift of the gab?: a design oriented sociology of young people's use of mobiles', *Computer Supported Cooperative Work*, 12, 267–96.

Terasaki, Alene Kiku. (2004), 'Pre-announcement sequences in conversation', in Gene H. Lerner (ed.), *Conversation Analysis: Studies from the First Generation*. Amsterdam and Philadelphia: John Benjamins, pp. 171–224.

Thornborrow, Joanna. (2001), 'Questions, control and the organization of talk in calls to a radio phone-in', *Discourse Studies*, 3, (1), 119–43.

Tuckett, D., Boulton, M., Olson, C. and Williams, A. (1986), *Meetings Between Experts: An Approach to Sharing Ideas in Medical Consultations*. London and New York: Tavistock Publications.

Vinkhuyzen, Erik. (2011), 'Interactions at a reprographics store', in Margaret H. Szymanski and Jack Whalen (eds), *Making Work Visible*. Cambridge: Cambridge University Press, pp. 205–24.

Vinkhuyzen, Erik and Ikeya, Nozomi. (2011), 'Rethinking how projects are managed: meeting communication across the organizational hierarchy', in Margaret H. Szmanski and Jack Whalen (eds), *Making Work Visible*. Cambridge: Cambridge University Press, pp. 312–23.

Vise, Kristi. (1999), Master's Thesis. Department of Sociology, University of Cincinnati.

Vöge, Monika. (2008), *All You Need is Laugh—Interactional Implications of Laughter in Business Meetings*. Unpublished Doctoral Dissertation. University of Southern Denmark.

—(2010), 'Local identity processes in business meetings displayed through laughter in complaint sequences', *Journal of Pragmatics*, 42, 1556–76.

Waitzkin, H. (1984), 'Doctor-patient communication: clinical implications of social scientific research', *JAMA*, 252, 2441–46.

Waitzkin, H. and Stoeckle, J. D. (1972), 'The communication of information about illness: clinical, sociological, and methodological considerations', *Advances in Psychosomatic Medicine*, 8, 180–215.

Wakin, Michele A. and Psathas, George. (1994), 'What is information?: calls to directory assistance', Paper presented at the *International Conference of Semiotics and Linguistics*, Urbino, Italy.

Wakin, Michele A. and Zimmerman, Don H. (1999), 'Reduction and specialization in emergency and directory assistance calls', *Research on Language and Social Interaction*, 32, (4), 409–37.

Wald, Matthew L. and Baker, Al. (2009), '1549 to tower: "we're gonna end up in the Hudson"', *New York Times*. (Appeared in print on January 18, 2009, on page A29 of the New York edition) http://www.nytimes.com/2009/01/18/nyregion/18plane.html?_r=1

Watson, D. Rodney. (1990), 'Some features of the elicitation of confessions in murder interrogations', in George Psathas (ed.), *Interaction Competence*. Washington, DC: University Press of America, pp. 263–96.

Watson, Rod. (1997), 'Some general reflections on 'categorization' and 'sequence' in the analysis of conversation', in S. Hester and P. Eglin (eds), *Culture in Action: Studies in Membership Categorization Analysis*. Washington, DC: University Press of America, pp. 49–75.

Weilenmann, Alexandra. (2003), '"I can't talk now, I'm in a fitting room": formulating availability and location in mobile-phone conversations', *Environment and Planning*, 35, 1589–605.

Weilenmann, Alexandra and Catrine Larsson. (2002), 'Local use and sharing of mobile phones', in B. Brown, N. Green and R. Harper (eds), *Wireless World: Social and Interactional Aspects of the Mobile Age*. London: Springer, pp. 92–107.

West, Candace. (2006), 'Coordinating closings in primary care visits: producing continuity of care', in John Heritage and Douglas W. Maynard (eds), *Communication in Medical Care: Interactions between Primary Care Physicians and Patients*. Cambridge: Cambridge University Press, pp. 379–415.

West, Candace and Garcia, Angela Cora. (1988), 'Conversational shift work: a study of topical transitions between women and men', *Social Problems*, 35, (5), 551–75.

West, Candace and Zimmerman, Don H. (1983), 'Small insults: a study of interruptions in cross-sex conversations between unacquainted persons', in Barrie Thorne, Cheris Kramarae and Nancy Henley (eds), *Language, Gender and Society*. Rowley, MA: Newbury House Publishers, pp. 102–17.

—(1987), 'Doing gender', *Gender and Society*, 1, (2), 125–51.

Whalen, Jack and Whalen, Marilyn R. (2011), 'Integrated customer service reinventing a workscape', in Margaret H. Szymanski and Jack Whalen (eds), *Making Work Visible*. Cambridge: Cambridge University Press, pp. 181–204.

Whalen, Jack and Zimmerman, Don H. (1987), 'Sequential and institutional contexts in calls for help', *Social Psychology Quarterly*, 50, (2), 172–85.

—(1990), 'Describing trouble: practical epistemology in citizen calls to the police', *Language in Society*, 19, 465–92.

—(1998), 'Observations on the display and management of emotion in naturally occurring activities: the case of 'hysteria in calls to 9-1-1', *Social Psychology Quarterly*, 61, (2), 141–59.

—(2005), 'Working a call: multiparty management and interactional infrastructure in calls for help', in Carolyn D. Baker, Michael Emmison, and Alan Firth (eds), *Calling for Help: Language and Social Interaction in Telephone Helplines*. Amsterdam: John Benjamins, pp. 309–45.

Whalen, Jack, Zimmerman, Don H. and Whalen, Marilyn. (1988), 'When words fail: a single case analysis', *Social Problems*, 35, (4), 35–362.

Wieder, Lawrence D. (1974), *Language and Social Reality*. The Netherlands: Mouton.

Williams, Ashley. (2005), 'Fighting words and challenging expectations: language alternation and social roles in a family dispute', *Journal of Pragmatics*, 37, 317–28.

Winiecki, Don. (2008), 'The expert witnesses and courtroom discourse: applying micro and macro forms of discourse analysis to study process and the "doings of doings" for individuals and for society', *Discourse & Society*, 19, (6), 765–81.

Woods, N. (1988), 'Talking shop: sex and status as determinants of floor apportionment in a work setting', in J. Coates and D. Cameron (eds), *Women in their Speech Communities*. London: Longman, pp. 141–57.

Young, Linda Wai Ling. (1982), 'Inscrutability revisited', in John Gumperz (ed.), *Language and Social Identity*. Cambridge: Cambridge University Press, pp. 72–84.

Zhang, Wei. (2005), 'Code-choice in bidialectal interaction: the choice between Putonghua and Cantonese in a radio phone-in program in Shenzhen', *Journal of Pragmatics*, 37, 355–74.

Zimmerman, Don H. (1969), 'Record-keeping and the intake process in a public welfare agency', in S. Wheeler (ed.), *On Record: Files and Dossiers in American Life*. Beverly Hills, CA: Sage.

—(1984), 'Talk and its occasion: the case of calling the police', in Deborah Schiffrin (ed.), *Meaning, Form, and Use in Context: Linguistic Applications*. Washington, DC: Georgetown University Press, pp. 210–28.

—(1992a), 'The interactional organization of calls for emergency assistance', in Paul Drew and John Heritage (eds), *Talk at Work: Interaction in Institutional Settings*. Cambridge: Cambridge University Press, pp. 418–69.

—(1992b), 'Achieving context: openings in emergency calls', in Graham Watson and Robert M. Seiler (eds), *Text in Context: Contributions to Ethnomethodology*. Newbury Park, CA: Sage, pp. 35–51.

Zimmerman, Don H. and Wakin, Michele. (1995), '"Thank you's" and the management of closings in emergency calls', *Paper presented at the annual meetings of the American Sociological Association*, Washington, DC.

Zimmerman, Don H. and West, Candace. (1975), 'Sex roles, interruptions and silences in convesation', in B. Thorne and Nancy Henley (eds), *Language and Sex: Difference and Dominance*. Rowley, MA: Newbury House, pp. 105–29.

Index

References in italic denote a figure; references in bold denote a table

Major concepts are shown in bold in the text where they are defined and explained. For each major concept that is shown in bold, the concept and the page number on which the definition occurs will be boldfaced in the index.